A Lexicon of Three U.S. Constitutional Provisions

A Lexicon of Three U.S. Constitutional Provisions

Richard H.W. Maloy

Vandeplas Publishing, LLC

United States of America

Lexicon of three U.S. constitutional provisions

Maloy, Richard H.W.

Published by:

Vandeplas Publishing - February 2012

801 International Parkway, 5th Floor
Lake Mary, FL. 32746
USA

www.vandeplaspublishing.com

ISBN 978-1-60042-151-8

Acknowledgements

I wish to acknowledge and thank St. Thomas Law School Professor Mary Munson, Legal Director, Center for Earth Jurisprudence, for reading the manuscript of this book, and offering helpful suggestions

I also acknowledge Fort Lauderdale attorney Mengjun Qiu, St. Thomas Law School and U. of Miami graduate, and genius (member of Mensa, International) for her review and helpful suggestions.

I also acknowledge and thank James Hill. One of my most sagacious friends, Jim, a gentleman of African descent checked over my description of the *Dred Scott* case, to make sure that it contains no offensive language to either its primary author, nor the subjects of his writing.

Richard H.W. Maloy

Dedication

I dedicate this book to U.S. Supreme Court Justice Stephen Breyer. I do not always agree with him in his Opinions, but in his recent book "Making Our Democracy Work," an autographed copy of which, was given to me by my Law School, as a gift, upon my ascendancy to the status of Professor Emeritus, Justice Breyer explained why Chief Justice Roger B. Taney, a brilliant jurist, wrote such a bad Opinion in the *Dred Scot* case. I have always been bewildered why Taney, a brilliant jurist, opined that people of African descent could never be citizens of the United States. His reason was not that he was a racist, because Taney indeed was not. Justice Breyer said that he was an "originalist" – a jurist who believes that every word in our Constitution must be interpreted in the same manner as the framers would have interpreted it when they drafted that document. This is an error which can, and in the *Scott* case did, have serious consequences. We must interpret such numerals as "two," referring to the number of Senators to which each state is entitled, as the framers intended. Such words as "citizen" like "commerce" and others, however, did not have the same meaning in 1787, when the Constitution was drafted, as in 1857, when the *Scott* case was decided, or in 2011, when this book was written.

Richard H.W. Maloy

TABLE OF CONTENTS

Chapter I
Full Faith and Credit

A. Introduction

If a court in one state renders a written decision and a court in another state concludes that that the facts of that case are similar to the facts of a case it is considering, the second court is at liberty to accept or reject the decision as non-binding precedent. If the facts of the two cases were identical to each other, rather than being just similar, and the parties, or their privities in both cases are identical the first decision will be binding precedent, rather than non-binding precedent. Reason: Article IV, § 1 of the federal Constitution – the Full Faith and Credit Clause. This constitutional provision which, in effect, converts the decisions of one state into binding precedents of another state, and requires states to honor functions of other states, is what this lexicon is about

1. About The Subject Matter

Virtually everyone is aware of Article IV, § 1 of the Federal Constitution. It provides that all states must respect the final judgments and other muniments of the authority of other states[1] by the following words:

> Full Faith and Credit shall be given in each State to the public Acts, Records, and judicial Proceedings of every other State. And the Congress may by general Laws prescribe the Manner in which such Acts, Records and Proceedings shall be proved, and the Effect thereof.

The then Justice Harlan F. Stone of the U.S. Supreme Court described the Full Faith and Credit Clause in the following words:

> The very purpose of the full-faith and credit clause was to alter the status of the several states as independent foreign sovereignties, each free to

[1] *See* Davis v. Davis, 305 U.S. 32, 40 (1939). .*See infra* text accompanying notes 6. 15, 46, 725-727 for further reference to that case. *See also* OIAC Cml. Assets, LLC v. Stonegate Village, LP, 2009 W.L.2182601 at * 3 (D. Ariz. 2009).

> ignore obligations created under the laws or by the judicial proceedings of the others, and to make them integral parts of a single nation throughout which a remedy upon a just obligation might be demanded as of right, irrespective of the state of its origin.[2]

Not long after the Constitution was signed by the delegates,[3] and ratified by the states,[4] Congress on May 26, 1790 enacted a statute extending the Constitutional directive to the federal courts in their review of state court judgments. [5] When the federal statutes were codified in 1926 the statute was codified as 28 U.S.C § 687. In 1948, with the revision of the Judicial Code, the wording of the first "implementing" statute was amended to include state statutes within its command.[6] At present the statute is codified as 28 U.S.C. § 1738, and provides:

---

[2] Milwaukee County v. M.E. White Co. 296 U.S. 268, 276, 277 (1935). For a similar statement *see* Justice John Paul Stevens' Concurring Opinion in Allstate Ins. Co. v. Hague, 449 U.S. 302, 323 (1981). *See infra* text accompanying notes 436-439, 517, 518, 519 and 1080 for further reference to the Hague case.

[3] On September 17, 1787.

[4] On June 21, 1788, by New Hampshire, the ninth state to ratify.

[5] 1 Stat. 122. This statute provided that: "the acts of the legislatures of the several states shall be authenticated by having the seal of their respective states affixed thereto: That the records and judicial proceedings of the courts of any state, shall be proved or admitted in any other court within the United States, by the attestation of the clerk, and the seal of the court annexed, if there be a seal, together with a certificate of the judge, chief justice, or presiding magistrate, as the case may be, that the said attestation is in due form. And the said records and judicial proceedings authenticated as aforesaid, shall have such faith and credit given to them in every court within the United States, as they have by law or usage in the courts of the state from whence [sic] the said records are or shall be taken."

[6] The statute then provided as follows: "The acts of the legislature of any State or Territory, or of any country subject to the jurisdiction of the United States, shall be authenticated by having the seals of such State, Territory, or country affixed thereto. The records and judicial proceedings of the courts of any State or Territory, or of any such country, shall be proved or admitted in any other court within the United States, by the attestation of the clerk, and the seal of the court annexed, if there be a seal, together with a certificate of the judge, chief justice, or presiding magistrate, that the said attestation is in due form. And the said records and judicial proceedings, so authenticated, shall have such faith and credit given to them in every court within the United States as they have by law or

> The Acts of the legislature of any State, Territory, or Possession of the United States, or copies thereof, shall be authenticated by affixing the seal of such State, Territory or Possession thereto.
>
> The records and judicial proceedings of any court of any such State, Territory or Possession, or copies thereof, shall be proved or admitted in other courts within the United States and its Territories and Possessions by the attestation of the clerk and seal of the court annexed, if a seal exists, together with a certificate of a judge of the court that the said attestation is in proper form.
>
> Such Acts, records and judicial proceedings or copies thereof, so authenticated, shall have the same full faith and credit in every court within the United States and its Territories and Possessions as they have by law or usage in the courts of such State, Territory or Possession from which they are taken.[7]

In *Stoll v. Gottlieb*,[8] the United States Supreme Court acknowledged that the statute of May 26, 1790 also requires that full faith and credit be given to judgments of federal courts in their review of state court judgments.[9] *Mills v. Duryee*[10] established that by the statute, Congress provided that its terms apply to the records and courts of the territories of the United States and countries subject to

---

usage in the courts of the State from which they are taken." *See* Davis v. Davis 305 U.S. 32 (1938).

[7] The statute was initially codified (in 1940), as 28 U.S.C. § 687, and is presently codified as 28 U.S.C. § 1738. Chief Justice John Marshall in Church v. Hubbart, 6 U.S. (2 Cranch) 187, 237 (1804) said that the authentication of the reports was highly important to the full faith and credit concept.

[8] 305 U.S. 165 (1938).

[9] *Id.* at 170.

[10] 11 U.S. (7 Cranch) 481 (1813). See infra text accompanying notes 12, 13, 14, 15, 75, 76, 481, 483, 493 for additional reference to this case.

the jurisdiction of the United States[11] as to the records and courts of the several states.[12]

U.S. Supreme Court Justice Joseph Story, in *Mills v. Duryee*[13] said about the statute that:

> The act declares that the record duly authenticated shall have such faith and credit as it has in the state Court from whence it is taken. If in such Court it has the faith and credit of evidence of the highest nature, viz. *record evidence*, it must have the same faith and credit in every other Court. Congress has therefore declared the *effect* of the record by declaring what faith and credit shall be given to it.[14]

He added that the 1790 Act extended the Constitutional provision to all courts, federal as well as state.[15] That means that the concept must be applied where the first court is a state court and the second court is a federal court,[16] or where the first court is a federal court and the second court is a state court.[17] The constitutional and statutory principle of full faith and credit does not apply to situations in which the first court is a federal court and the second court is also a federal court. One might suppose that the words "every court within the United States and its Territories and Possessions" of the statute would mean that federal courts are also supposed to give other federal courts full faith and credit, but the U.S. Supreme Court has proclaimed that the judicial proceedings of one federal

---

[11] Puerto Rico is the functional equivalent of a state for full faith and credit purposes. *See* Cruz v. Malecio, 204 F 3d 14 (1st Cir. 2000); Garcia-Managas v. W Holding Co., Inc., 2009 W.L. 483146 at *7 (D. P.R. 2009).

[12] *Mills* at 483.

[13] *See supra* note 10.

[14] *Mills.* at 484.

[15] *Id.* at 485. *See also* Davis v. Davis, 305 U.S. 32, 40 (1938) to the same effect.

[16] *See* Johnson v. McClure, 2009 W.L. 2356147 at * 20 (N.D. N.Y. 2009).

[17] *See* Higgason v. Stogdill, 818 N.E.2d 486, 491 (Ind. App. 2009); Crevelling v. Treser, 2009 W.L. 4678929 (Wash. App. 2009).

court are not required to be given full faith and credit by another federal court pursuant to the Full Faith and Credit Clause or its implementing statute.[18]

In *Baldwin v. Iowa State Traveling Men's Ass'n*[19] the author of the Opinion of the Court, Justice Owen J. Roberts, realizing that there must be an end to litigation, did not base the Court's holding on full faith and credit, but on "public policy." He said:

> Public policy dictates that there be an end of litigation; that those who have contested an issue shall be bound by the result of the contest; and that matters once tried shall be considered forever settled as between the parties. We see no reason why this doctrine should not apply in every . . . case where one voluntarily appears, presents his case and is fully heard, and why he should not, in the absence of fraud, be thereafter concluded by the judgment of the tribunal to which he has submitted his cause.[20]

In *Thompson v. Whitman*[21] U.S. Supreme Court Justice Joseph P. Bradley said about the statute and the Constitutional Clause that:

> It has been supposed that this act, in connection with the constitutional provision which it was intended to carry out, had the effect of rendering the judgments of each State equivalent to domestic judgments in every other State, or at least of giving to them in every other State the same

---

[18] *See* Baldwin v. Iowa State Traveling Men's Ass'n, 283 U.S. 522, 524 (1931). In Allen v. McCurry, 449 U.S. 90, 96 (1980), however, Justice Potter Stewart made it clear that the federal courts give each other preclusive effect under the common law concepts of *res judicata* and collateral estoppel. *See infra* text accompanying notes 147-196 for further discussion of this point.

[19] 283 U.S. 522 (1931). *See supra* text accompanying note 18, and *infra* text accompanying notes 20, 25, 155, 427.

[20] *Id.* at 525, 526. In the Baldwin case the plaintiff (Baldwin) obtained a default judgment in a U.S. District Court in Missouri. When he wanted to enforce the judgment in a U.S. District Court in Iowa that court recognized the first judgment, but the Eighth Circuit overruled. The U.S. Supreme Court reversed the Eighth Circuit.

[21] 85 U.S. 457 (1873).

> effect, in all respects, which they have in the State where they are rendered.[22]

In *State of Minnesota v. Northern Securities Co.*[23] U.S. Supreme Court Justice John Marshall Harlan, I, described the Constitution and the statute in the following words:

> [A]rticle 4 must be so construed as to make the constitutional enactments of Minnesota effective throughout the United States, so far as they apply to and affect property rights within the state. Otherwise the policy and laws of any state may be easily evaded. . . . [T]he clause of the Constitution . . . only prescribes a rule by which courts, Federal and state, are to be guided when a question arises in the progress of a pending suit as to the faith and credit to be given by the court to the public acts, records, and judicial proceedings of a state other than that in which the court is sitting. Even if it be assumed that the word 'acts' includes 'statutes,' the clause has nothing to do [sic] with the conduct of individuals or corporations; and to invoke the rule which it prescribes does not make a case arising under the Constitution or laws of the United States.[24]

In summary, we see that the Full Faith and Credit Clause extended the full faith and credit principle to judicial decisions in which the relationship is between two courts of different states. The implementing statute extended the full faith and credit principle to judicial decisions in which the relationship is between state and federal courts. The full faith and credit principle was not, and has not been by constitutional amendment or Congressional statute, extended to situations in which the relationship is between different federal courts. Federal courts, however, do have judicially authorized powers of observation as to other federal courts in obligations as to matters of preclusion.[25]

---

[22] *Id.* at 462.

[23] 194 U.S. 48 (1904).

[24] *Id.* at 72.

[25] *See supra* note 18.

Perhaps few people are aware of Congress' December 28, 1980,[26] November 12, 1998,[27] and October. 28, 2000[28] amendments of § 1738, referred to as the Parental Kidnapping Prevention Act (PKPA), codified as 28 U.S.C. § 1738 A, and which provide:

> **§ 1738 A. Full faith and credit given to child custody determinations.**[29]
>
> (a) The appropriate authorities of every State shall enforce according to its terms, and shall not modify except as provided in subsections (f), (g), and (h) of this section, any custody determination or visitation determination made consistently with the provisions of this section by a court of another State.
>
> (b) As used in this section, the term—
>
> (1) "child" means a person under the age of eighteen;
>
> (2) "contestant" means a person, including a parent or grandparent, who claims a right to custody or visitation of a child;
>
> (3) "custody determination" means a judgment, decree, or other order of a court providing for the custody of a child, and includes permanent and temporary orders, and initial orders and modifications;
>
> (4) "home State" means the State in which, immediately preceding the time involved, the child lived with his parents, a parent, or a person acting as parent, for at least six consecutive months, and in the case of a child less than six months old, the State in which the child lived from birth with any of such persons. Periods of temporary absence of any of such persons are counted as part of the six-month or other period;
>
> (5) "modification" and "modify" refer to a custody or visitation determination which modifies, replaces, supersedes, or otherwise is made subsequent to, a prior custody or visitation determination concerning the same child, whether made by the same court or not;

---

[26] Pub. L. 96-611, § 8(a), 94 Stat. 3566. Pub.L.106-386, Div. B, Title III, § 1303(d), 114 Stat. 1464.

[27] Pub .L. 105-374, § 1, 112 Stat. 3383.

[28] Pub. L. 106-386, Div. B, Title III, § 1303(d), 114 Stat. 1464.

[29] It has been said that by enacting these amendments to § 1738 "Congress has extended full faith and credit requirements to child custody orders." *See* Yaw v. State of New York, 2009 W.L. 3817674 at * 2 (W.D. N.Y 2009).

(6) "person acting as a parent" means a person, other than a parent, who has physical custody of a child and who has either been awarded custody by a court or claims a right to custody;

(7) "physical custody" means actual possession and control of a child;

(8) "State" means a State of the United States, the District of Columbia, the Commonwealth of Puerto Rico, or a territory or possession of the United States; and

(9) "visitation determination" means a judgment, decree, or other order of a court providing for the visitation of a child and includes permanent and temporary orders and initial orders and modifications.

(c) A child custody or visitation determination made by a court of a State is consistent with the provisions of this section only if—

(1) such court has jurisdiction under the law of such State; and

(2) one of the following conditions is met:

(A) such State (i) is the home State of the child on the date of the commencement of the proceeding, or (ii) had been the child's home State within six months before the date of the commencement of the proceeding and the child is absent from such State because of his removal or retention by a contestant or for other reasons, and a contestant continues to live in such State;

(B) (i) it appears that no other State would have jurisdiction under subparagraph (A), and (ii) it is in the best interest of the child that a court of such State assume jurisdiction because (I) the child and his parents, or the child and at least one contestant, have a significant connection with such State other than mere physical presence in such State, and (II) there is available in such State substantial evidence concerning the child's present or future care, protection, training, and personal relationships;

(C) the child is physically present in such State and (i) the child has been abandoned, or (ii) it is necessary in an emergency to protect the child because the child, a sibling, or parent of the child has been subjected to or threatened with mistreatment or abuse;

(D) (i) it appears that no other State would have jurisdiction under subparagraph (A), (B), (C), or (E), or another State has declined to exercise jurisdiction on the ground that the State whose jurisdiction is in issue is the more appropriate forum to determine the custody or visitation of the child, and (ii) it is in the best interest of the child that such court assume jurisdiction; or

(E) the court has continuing jurisdiction pursuant to subsection (d) of this section.

(d) The jurisdiction of a court of a State which has made a child custody or visitation determination consistently with the provisions of this section continues as long as the requirement of subsection (c) (1) of this section continues to be met and such State remains the residence of the child or of any contestant.

(e) Before a child custody or visitation determination is made, reasonable notice and opportunity to be heard shall be given to the contestants, any parent whose parental rights have not been previously terminated and any person who has physical custody of a child.

(f) A court of a State may modify a determination of the custody of the same child made by a court of another State, if—

(1) it has jurisdiction to make such a child custody determination; and

(2) the court of the other State no longer has jurisdiction, or it has declined to exercise such jurisdiction to modify such determination.

(g) A court of a State shall not exercise jurisdiction in any proceeding for a custody or visitation determination commenced during the pendency of a proceeding in a court of another State where such court of that other State is exercising jurisdiction consistently with the pro-visions of this section to make a custody or visitation determination.[30]

(h) A court of a State may not modify a visitation determination made by a court of another State unless the court of the other State no longer has jurisdiction to modify such determination or has declined to exercise jurisdiction to modify such determination.

In *Thompson v. Thompson*[31] Justice Thurgood Marshall informed us of the purpose of PKPA in these words:

---

[30] This specific provision has been referred to as an "incarnation" of the full faith and credit requirement of our government. *See* Yaw v. State of New York, 2009 W.L. 3817674 at * 2 (W.D. N.Y 2009).

[31] 484 U.S. 174 (1988). *See infra* text accompanying notes 32, 819, 820 for additional cases referring to this case.

> The significance of Congress' full faith and credit approach to the problem of child snatching is that the Full Faith and Credit Clause, in either its constitutional or statutory incarnations, does not give rise to an implied federal cause of action. (Citations omitted). Rather, the Clause "only prescribes a rule by which courts, Federal and state, are to be guided when a question arises in the . . . progress of a pending suit as to the faith and credit to be given by the court to the public acts, records, and judicial proceedings of a State other than that in which the court is sitting." (Citation omitted). Because Congress' chief aim in enacting the PKPA was to extend the requirements of the Full Faith and Credit Clause to custody determinations, the Act is most naturally construed to furnish a rule of decision for courts to use in adjudicating custody disputes and not to create an entirely new cause of action. It thus is not compatible with the purpose and context of the legislative scheme to infer a private cause of action.[32]

Perhaps few people are aware of Congress' October 22, 1994,[33] August 22, 1996,[34] and August 5, 1997[35] amendments of § 1738 (sometimes referred to as the Congressional "Full Faith and Credit for Child Support Orders Act" or the sobriquet "FFCCSOA."[36] They provide:

> **§ 1738 B. Full faith and credit for child support orders.**
>
> (a) General rule. —The appropriate authorities of each State—
>
> (1) shall enforce according to its terms a child support order made consistently with this section by a court of another State; and

---

[32] *Id.* at 182,183. Virginia Court of Appeals Judge Powell has written that: "the chief purpose of 28 U.S.C. § 1738 A was to 'avoid jurisdictional competition and conflict between State courts.'" Prashad v. Copeland 685 S.E.2d 199 ,204 (Va. App. 2009). *See infra* text accompanying notes 38, 800, 831, 803, 809, 840, 841, 1123 for further consideration of this case.

[33] Pub. L. 103-383, § 3(a), 108 Stat. 4064.

[34] Pub. L. 104-193, Title III, § 322, 110 Stat. 2105.

[35] Pub. L. 105-33, Title V, § 5554, 111 Stat. 251.

[36] *See* Heckman v. Heckman, 2009 W.L. 2872714 at *2 (Conn. Super. 2009). The statute's "short" title is so long, that those who must work with it at times simply refer to it as "PKPA," which it certainly is not. *See* Stewart v. Lastaiti, 2010 W.L. 1993884 at *2 (S.D. Fla. 2010).

(2) shall not seek or make a modification of such an order except in accordance with subsections (e), (f), and (i).

(b) Definitions. —In this section:

"child" means—

(A) a person under 18 years of age; and

(B) a person 18 or more years of age with respect to whom a child support order has been issued pursuant to the laws of a State.

"child's State" means the State in which a child resides.

"child's home State" means the State in which a child lived with a parent or a person acting as parent for at least 6 consecutive months immediately preceding the time of filing of a petition or comparable pleading for support and, if a child is less than 6 months old, the State in which the child lived from birth with any of them. A period of temporary absence of any of them is counted as part of the 6-month period.

"child support" means a payment of money, continuing support, or arrearages or the provision of a benefit (including payment of health insurance, child care, and educational expenses) for the support of a child.

"child support order"-

(A) means a judgment, decree, or order of a court requiring the payment of child support in periodic amounts or in a lump sum; and

(B) includes—

(i) a permanent or temporary order; and

(ii) an initial order or a modification of an order.

"contestant" means—

(A) a person (including a parent) who—

(i) claims a right to receive child support;

(ii) is a party to a proceeding that may result in the issuance of a child support order; or

(iii) is under a child support order; and

(B) a State or political subdivision of a State to which the right to obtain child support has been assigned.

"court" means a court or administrative agency of a State that is authorized by State law to establish the amount of child support payable by a contestant or make a modification of a child support order.

"modification" means a change in a child support order that affects the amount, scope, or duration of the order and modifies, replaces, supersedes, or otherwise is made subsequent to the child support order.

"State" means a State of the United States, the District of Columbia, the Commonwealth of Puerto Rico, the territories and possessions of the United States, and Indian country (as defined in section 1151 of title 18).

(c) Requirements of child support orders. —A child support order made by a court of a State is made consistently with this section if—

(1) a court that makes the order, pursuant to the laws of the State in which the court is located and subsections (e), (f), and (g)—

(A) has subject matter jurisdiction to hear the matter and enter such an order; and

(B) has personal jurisdiction over the contestants; and

(2) reasonable notice and opportunity to be heard is given to the contestants.

(d) Continuing jurisdiction. —A court of a State that has made a child support order consistently with this section has continuing, exclusive jurisdiction over the order if the State is the child's State or the residence of any individual contestant unless the court of another State, acting in accordance with subsections (e) and (f), has made a modification of the order.

(e) Authority to modify orders. —A court of a State may modify a child support order issued by a court of another State if—

(1) the court has jurisdiction to make such a child support order pursuant to subsection (i); and

(2)

(A) the court of the other State no longer has continuing, exclusive jurisdiction of the child support order because that State no longer is the child's State or the residence of any individual contestant; or

(B) each individual contestant has filed written consent with the State of continuing, exclusive jurisdiction for a court of another State to modify the order and assume continuing, exclusive jurisdiction over the order.

(f) Recognition of child support orders. —If 1 or more child support orders have been issued with regard to an obligor and a child, a court shall apply the following rules in determining which order to recognize for purposes of continuing, exclusive jurisdiction and enforcement:

(1) If only 1 court has issued a child support order, the order of that court must be recognized.

(2) If 2 or more courts have issued child support orders for the same obligor and child, and only 1 of the courts would have

continuing, exclusive jurisdiction under this section, the order of that court must be recognized.

(3) If 2 or more courts have issued child support orders for the same obligor and child, and more than 1 of the courts would have continuing, exclusive jurisdiction under this section, an order issued by a court in the current home State of the child must be recognized, but if an order has not been issued in the current home State of the child, the order most recently issued must be recognized.

(4) If 2 or more courts have issued child support orders for the same obligor and child, and none of the courts would have continuing, exclusive jurisdiction under this section, a court having jurisdiction over the parties shall issue a child support order, which must be recognized.

(5) The court that has issued an order recognized under this subsection is the court having continuing, exclusive jurisdiction under subsection (d).

(g) Enforcement of modified orders. —A court of a State that no longer has continuing, exclusive jurisdiction of a child support order may enforce the order with respect to nonmodifiable obligations and unsatisfied obligations that accrued before the date on which a modification of the order is made under subsections (e) and (f).

(h) Choice of law. —

(1) In general. —In a proceeding to establish, modify, or enforce a child support order, the forum State's law shall apply except as provided in paragraphs (2) and (3).

(2) Law of State of issuance of order. —In interpreting a child support order including the duration of current payments and other obligations of support, a court shall apply the law of the State of the court that issued the order.

(3) Period of limitation. —In an action to enforce arrears under a child support order, a court shall apply the statute of limitation of the forum State or the State of the court that issued the order, whichever statute provides the longer period of limitation.

(i) Registration for modification. —If there is no individual contestant or child residing in the issuing State, the party or support enforcement agency seeking to modify, or to modify and enforce, a child support order issued in another State shall register that order in a State with jurisdiction over the nonmovant for the purpose of modification.

Perhaps few people are aware of Congress' September 26, 1996 amendment[37] of the statute. Known as the Defense of Marriage Act (DOMA) it provides as follows:

> **§ 1738 C. Certain acts, records, and proceedings and the effect thereof.**
>
> No State, territory, or possession of the United States, or Indian tribe, shall be required to give effect to any public act, record, or judicial proceeding of any other State, territory, possession, or tribe respecting a relationship between persons of the same sex that is treated as a marriage under the laws of such other State, territory, possession, or tribe, or a right or claim arising from such relationship.

Virginia Court of Appeals Judge Powell has written that:

> DOMA allows a state to refuse to give full faith and credit to another state's determination that 'a relationship between persons of the same sex . . . is treated as marriage.' . . . Similarly, DOMA allows a state to deny recognition of 'a right or claim arising from such relationship.' . . . Thus, DOMA is permissive in nature, meaning that it allows each state to decide for itself what effect, if any, that state will give to same sex relationships that are treated as a marriage under the laws of another state and the rights or claims arising therefrom.[38]

The words "full faith and credit" appear in both the Constitution, the Federal statute, its three amendments, and in many uniform Acts which, along with the Congressional statutes have expanded the reach of full faith and credit. U. S. Supreme Court Justice Antonin Scalia in *Crowe v. Emison*[39] has opined that the Full Faith and Credit Clause and statute have embodied the principles of

---

[37] Pub. L. 104-199, § 2(a), 110 Stat. 2419.

[38] Prashad v. Copeland 685 S.E.2d 199, 206 (Va. App. 2009). The constitutionality of 1 U.S.C. § 7 defining some terms of 28 U.S.C. § 1738C has been called into question by Gill v. Office of Personnel Management, 2010 W.L. 2695652 at *16 (D. Mass. 2010).

[39] 507 U.S. 25 (1993).

federalism and comity.[40] Neither the Clause nor the statute, however, expand the reach of those principles to require that all courts must follow the first court to rule on a matter. There are permissibly varying legal determinations in our jurisprudence. The only time that the second jurisdiction must follow the ruling of a prior jurisdiction is when the same parties or their privies are parties in both actions.[41] Otherwise this country would be ruled by the first court to speak upon a subject. That proposition is not made clear in the Constitution or in the statute as amended. All of those varying nuances will be explored in this lexicon.

What do those words "full faith and credit" and the judicial descriptions of them mean? Without judicial explanation it is virtually impossible to provide a definitive disquisition. Even with judicial explanation there are so many variations that they must be considered individually, so that they may collectively form a pattern of application. The general explanation of the jurists, made without the connection of the facts involved are helpful, but they do not render a completely understandable explanation. It is to remedy that deficit that this lexicon has been written.

At times an author's hesitancy in offering a cogent description of the meaning of a word or phrase under consideration might be interpreted as a real lack of importance of the subject under examination. Such is not the case with the present phrase. Oh, "full faith and credit" is vitally important. U.S. Supreme Chief Justice John Marshall described the Constitutional provision, as implemented by the statute, in the following words:

> judgment of a state court should have the same credit, validity and effect, in every other court of the United States, which it had in the state where it was pronounced, and that whatever pleas would be good to a suit thereon in such state, and none others, could be pleaded in any other court in the United States.[42]

---

[40] *Id.* at 35.

[41] At times the identity of the principal and/or its privy can be almost stifling. *See* Ice Stores, Inc. v. Holmes, 2008 W.L. 4981007 at *6 (Tenn Ct. App. 2008), in which a corporation's business name and its incorporated name presented confusion. *See infra* text accompanying notes 258, 265, 311, 962, and 963 for further considerations of this case.

[42] Hampton v. M'Connel 16 U.S. 234, 235 (1818).

Justice Thurgood Marshall referred to the Constitution in the following words:

> The concept of full faith and credit is central to our system of jurisprudence. Ours is a union of States, each having its . . . own judicial system capable of adjudicating the rights and responsibilities of the parties brought before it. Given this structure, there is always a risk that two or more States will exercise their power over the same case or controversy, with the uncertainty, confusion, and delay that necessarily accompany relitigation of the same issue. . . . Recognizing that this risk of relitigation inheres in our federal system, the Framers provided that "Full Faith and Credit shall be given in each State to the public Acts, Records, and judicial Proceedings of every other State." U.S. Const., Art. IV, § 1. This Court has consistently recognized that, in order to fulfill this constitutional mandate, 'the judgment of a state court should have the same credit, validity, and effect, in every other court of the United States, which it had in the state where it was pronounced.'[43]

Thurgood Marshall referred to the Act of 1790 (presently 28 U.S.C. § 1738) in the *Underwriters Nat. Assur. Co* case with the following words:

> This construction is also compelled by 28 U.S.C. § 1738, the statutory codification of this constitutional guarantee. This provision requires that 'Acts, records and judicial proceedings . . . shall have the same full faith and credit in every court within the United States ... as they have by law or usage in the courts of such State . . . from which they are taken.'[44]

Those words of explanation, are very illuminating, but what do they actually tell us about what "full faith and credit" really means?[45] Let's take a simple situation. A court, be it a state court or a federal court sitting in a state; let's call it F-1, enters a money judgment. For some reason the prevailing plaintiff wants to

---

[43] Underwriters Nat. Assur. Co. v. North Carolina Life and Acc. and Health Ins. Guaranty Ass'n 455 U.S. 691, 703-704 (1982). *See infra* text accompanying notes 44, 539, and 540 for further consideration of the Underwriters Nat. Assur. Co case.

[44] *Id.* at 704 n. 9.

[45] Justice William O. Douglas recognized the "generality" of those words. *See* Williams v. North Carolina, 317 U.S. 287, 301 (1942). *See* text accompanying other notes 47, 50, 51, 312, 724, and 728-737 for further discussion of Williams, I.

take that judgment to another place, some other state, usually because the defendant has insufficient assets in the state in which F-1 was located to satisfy that judgment. Suppose, further, that the court, be it a state or federal court in that other state, (let's call that court F-2), believes that the F-1 court did not have either subject-matter jurisdiction, or personal jurisdiction over the defendant at the time the judgment was entered. What recognition and/or enforcement must F-2 give to that F-1 judgment in order to comply with constitutional and/or statutory requirements that recognition and/or enforcement be "full" and not just "some faith and credit" as Justice Pierce Butler informed us[46] and Justice William O. Douglas, reminded us,[47] as did Justice Stanley F. Reed?[48] We might ask the same question if F-1, instead of entering a money judgment, entered an injunction, or specific performance of a contract, or a declaratory decree, or a decree to quiet title, invoke a statutory remedy, or grant a divorce, or alimony, or child support, or render a custody order, or an order of adoption, or convict a criminal. We might also ask the same questions if F-1 was a Bankruptcy Court, an Indian tribal court, or a court of some foreign country. Can any of us, without hesitation, give a specific answer? There being "substantially no legislative history" concerning the Clause or the 1790 statute,[49] the most authoritative source of what those words mean are the analyses of the jurists who have worked with them. Hence this lexicon.

Before we begin our quest we should consider some basics about full faith and credit that the courts have established. The Constitutional provision, Art. IV, § 1 refers only to states. That is the reason for the 1790 statute (now 28 U.S.C. § 1738) – Congress thought that full faith and credit should apply to federal courts and not just state courts. Since we are talking about the states' judicial system and the federal judicial system, and they are to be considered the same as far as full faith and credit are concerned, the courts of both judicial systems should be referred to as "jurisdictions." Full faith and credit is applicable only if there are different jurisdictions, e. g. (1) the first court is a state court in state A, and the second court is a federal court in state A; or (2) the first court is a federal court in state A and

---

46 *See* Davis v. Davis, 305 U.S. 32, 40 (1938).

47 *See* Williams, 317 U.S. at 294. *See* text accompanying notes 45, 50, 312, 724, 729, and 728-737 for further discussion of Williams, I.

48 When in Johnson v. Muelberger, 340 U.S. 581, 584 (1951), Justice Reed said that the guarantee must be "not niggardly but generous, full." *See* text accompanying notes 49, 51, 202, 592, 744, 745, and 761-764 for further consideration of this case.

49 *Id.*

the second court is a state court in state A; or (3) the first court is a state court in state A, and the second court is a state court in state B; or (4) the first court is a state court in state A and the second court is a federal court in state B; or (5) the first court is a federal court in state A and second court is a state court in state B. In other words there is complete diversity between the two jurisdictions. The first jurisdiction must be followed by the second jurisdiction for full faith and credit to be honored where the parties are identical or in privity with each other in the different jurisdictions. If the parties are not the same or in privity with each other full faith and credit does not apply. If Mr. W. prevails in state A in his case against Mr. X. the fact that Mr. Y. does not prevail against Mr. Z. on virtually the same facts and cause of action in state B is not a violation of full faith and credit. One of Mr. Y.'s assignments of error in a state B appellate court might be that the state A rendering is better law, but none of his Assignments of Error would be that he was denied full faith and credit because the parties were not the same, nor in privity with each other. If Mr. W. looses his claim against Mr. X. in state A the fact that Mr. W. looses a second attempt against Mr. X. in state A does not involve full faith and credit because the jurisdiction in the two cases is the same; the reason for his second loss is claim preclusion. If Mr. W. prevails in state A in his case against Mr. X. but Mr. Y. fails to prevail in state A against Mr. Z. on the same facts and cause of action, Mr. Y.'s Assignment of error to a state A appellate court might be inconsistent judgments, but none of Mr. Y.'s Assignments of Error to a state A appellate court would be denial of full faith and credit because the jurisdiction in both cases was the same. A simple rule is that for full faith to apply if the jurisdictions are different the parties must be the same, or in privity with each other; but full faith will not apply if the jurisdiction in both cases is the same.

Justice William O. Douglas said in *Williams v. North Carolina*[50] that when it comes to questions about what are the limits of full faith and credit the Supreme Court is the final arbiter.[51] Judge Ozalis in *Shore Winds, L.L.C. v. Timeus*[52] has written that the interpretation of the Full Faith and Credit Clause is a matter of federal law, and that state courts must look to decisions of the U.S. Supreme Court

---

[50] 317 U.S. 287 (1942). *See* text accompanying notes 45, 47, 312, 724, 729, and 728-737 for further discussion of Williams, I

[51] *Id.* at 302. That same analysis was confirmed by Justice James Reed in Johnson v, Muelberger, 340 U.S. 581, 585 (1951). *See* text accompanying notes 49, 50, 202, 592, 744 and 761 for further consideration of this case.

[52] 2010 W.L. 1224319 (Conn. Super. 2010).

for guidance in its application.[53] It is for that reason that this lexicon concentrates on Supreme Court decisions. Lower court decisions are helpful to fill in the interstices, but the Supreme has the final word.

Hopefully the above words justify a study of full faith and credit, but lest there be any doubt about it, Justice Robert H. Jackson's words in his Columbia Law School's Law Review– "Full Faith and Credit – The Lawyer's Clause of the Constitution," will be the ultimate proof. Justice Jackson said at page 5 of his treatise that there was little contemporary material defining what the "forefathers" had in mind to accomplish by the Full Faith and Credit Clause, but his concluding remark, on page 34, was a message to the lawyers. for whom the clause was intended – "you must not suffer this lawyer's clause to become the orphan clause of the Constitution." [54]

In 1887 U.S. Supreme Court Chief Justice Morrison R. Waite referred to the Full Faith and Credit Clause as the "Due Faith and Credit Clause" in his Opinion of the Court in *Plumb v. Crane*.[55] Westlaw reports that for some, never definitively reported, reason[56] a total of 134 cases have used the irregular wording.[57] None of those decisions alter the meaning of the concept, and it appears to have departed into the past as an unexplained aberration.[58]

---

[53] *Id.* at *6.

[54] *See* ROBERT H. JACKSON, FULL FAITH AND CREDIT – THE LAWYER'S CLAUSE OF THE CONSTITUTION, 45 Columbia Law Review 1 (Vol XLV, January 1945).

[55] 123 U.S. 560, 562 (1887).

[56] Law student James Y. Stern in 94 Va. L. Rev. 1509, 1527, Choice of Law, the Constitution and Lochner (Oct. 2008) opines that it was possibly the result of confusing the similarity between the Due Process Clause and the Full Faith and Credit Clause.

[57] U.S. Supreme Court Chief Justices Fuller, Hughes, Vinson and White in addition to Waite have used it; as well as Justices Brown, Day, Gray, Holmes, McKenna, Sanford and Van Dervanter. The U.S. Court of Appeals for the Fifth Circuit used it several times, and the Court for the Seventh used it once. One U.S. District Judge used it, and several state courts have used it.

[58] Chief Justice Fred Vinson in Sherrer v. Sherrer, 334 U.S. 343, 355 (1948) was the last federal judge to use the wording. The last state court to use it was the Idaho Supreme Cot in Andre v. Morrow, 680 P. 2d 1355, 1376 (Idaho 1984). *See infra* text accompanying notes 141, 142, 658, 755-758 for further consideration of Sherrer. v. Sherrer.

2. About The Writing of This Chapter

In this book there are certain terms that will be used. "The rendering court" means the court which rendered the judgment sought to be enforced. If we are referring to a judgment of one jurisdiction being submitted to another jurisdiction to be recognized and enforced by a second jurisdiction, it makes the explanation clearer if the first court is referred to as "F-1" and the second court is referred to as "F-2." If three courts are involved the third court will be referred to as "F-3." Similar terms will also be used where statutes of different states conflict. "S-1" will refer to the state which has a statute which conflicts with a statute of the forum – "F-2." The "enforcing court" refers to one or more courts in which the "F-1" judgment is sought to be enforced. That, or those, courts will sometimes be referred to as "F-2." The "judgment creditor" refers to a creditor who prevailed in the "F-1" suit; the "judgment debtor" refers to a debtor who did not prevail in "F-1," i.e. a party against whom a judgment was entered. The words "full faith and credit" are initially capitalized when used in connection with the constitutional provision (Art IV, § 1), or the statute (28 U.S.C. § 1738). They are referred to in lower case, however, when the reference is merely to the concept of full faith and credit, except when that term is used in a Section, heading. The term "foreign court" means a court which is from a different jurisdiction than that of the forum. When courts from places outside the United States are referred to they will be identified by the term "foreign-country court." The word "judgment" refers to any final order of a court, whether the rendering court refers to its final orders as "judgments," or "degrees," which are often used in connection with matters in equity, or as probate courts often do, or any such designation of the final order in a court of law.

The more one learns about full faith and credit she or he will appreciate the importance of the Uniform Acts, especially in certain areas of the law. The courts rely on the Uniform Acts in recognizing and enforcing judgments. That is why the Uniform Foreign Money Judgments Recognition Act (UFMJRA) and the Uniform Enforcement of Foreign Judgments Act (UEFJA) appear in verbatim in this book. The Uniform Acts are also used extensively in connection with child custody and child support. That is why the Uniform Child Custody Jurisdiction and Enforcement Act (UCCJEA) and the Uniform Interstate Family Support Act (UIFSA) also appear verbatim in the book. The judgments of foreign countries are not required to be recognized and enforced, but their recognition and enforcement are not forbidden under the Full Faith and Credit Clause or its implementing statutes, as amended. Such judgments are becoming more prevalent in today's intensive international climate. It is for that reason that the Uniform Foreign Country Money Judgment Recognition Act (UFCMJRA) appears verbatim in the book. States are not obligated to adopt a Uniform Act verbatim when it enacts one. Therefore there may be varying versions of an Act to which one's study takes one. Having the original within the covers of this book, however, will be authoritative and helpful, because state legislatures do not vary from the basic tenets of the proposed legislation that they use as their guide.

B. The Do's and Dont's of the F-2 Court

At times the learning process is enhanced by considering over-implications, such as the following examples before delving into the fine points.

1. What Must Be Done

Later in this Chapter we discuss what full faith and Credit does not demand. Let us first explore what the term does demand.

a. Give Full Faith and Credit in Each State to public Acts, Records and judicial Proceedings of Every Other State

Unless something is a public Act, Record and judicial Proceeding of a State the Full Faith and Credit Clause has no application to it.[59]

---

[59] In Watson v. Employer's Liability Assurance Corp., 348 U.S. 66, 71 (1954), the U.S. Supreme Court held that Louisiana was not obligated to apply either a Massachusetts or illinois statute requiring that before a direct action may be brought against an insurance company there must have been a final determination made against the insured, even though the policy was issued in Massachusetts and the negligent insured was an Illinois corporation, where suit was brought in Louisiana which had substantial contacts with the case and had a statute which conflicted with the Massachusetts and Illinois statutes.. In Clay v. Sun Ins. Office, Ltd., 377 U.S. 179, 182 (1964) the Supreme Court permitted, despite full faith and credit objections, a state (Florida), to enact a statute giving an insured a longer period within which to sue on a policy than the limitations period contained in the policy, where that state had substantial contacts with the insurance transaction. The policy was issued in Illinois, and would have been enforceable by the Illinois statute, had the insured not moved to Florida, and brought his action within the time specified by a Florida

i. Public Acts

U.S. Supreme Court Justices Stone[60] and Brandeis[61] have said that a public Act is a statute. It is, however, more than that. It is, according to Justices Byron White[62] and John Paul Stevens[63] a *jure imperii*.[64] Chief Justice Burger cautioned that Public Acts do not include a state's "strictly commercial acts."[65] Justice Condon of the Rhode Island Supreme Court in *McGrath v. Tobin*[66] using U.S. Supreme Court Justice Stephen J. Field's Opinion in *Maynard v. Hill*[67] has written that:

---

statute. The ambulatory Illinois statute, under the facts of the case, was completely inapplicable.

60 *See* Alaska Packer Ass'n v. Industrial Acc. Co., 294 U.S. 532, 546 n.3 (1935). *See infra* text accompanying notes 72, 213, 423, and 622-624, for further reference to this case..

61 *See* Bradford Elect. Light Co. v. Clapper, 286 U.S. 145, 156 (1932) (n which he also referred to them as "the legislative function of the enacting statute"); and Broderick v. Rosner, 294 U.S. 629, 644 (1935). *See* State of Ohio ex rel Squire v. Porter, 129 P.2d 691, 697 (Cal. 1942) and Bowles v. Barde Steel Co., 164 P. 2d 692, 699 (Ore. 1945) to the same effect.

62 *See* Alfred Dunhill of London, Inc. v. Republic of Cuba, 425 U.S. 682, 711 (1976).

63 *See* Republic of Austria v. Altmann, 541 U.S. 677, 690, 700 (2004) (emphasizing that the Act was promulgated within the sovereign's "own territory;" *id.* at 699).

64 Black's Law Dictionary. 8th Edition (2004) defines a *jure imperii* in the following words: "[Latin "by right of"] The public acts that a nation undertakes as a sovereign state, for which the sovereign is usu. immune from suit or liability in a foreign country; commercial-activity exception. *See* restrictive principle of sovereign immunity.". . . as distinguished from a *jure gestionis* which is defined as: [Latin "by way of doing business"] A nation's acts that are essentially commercial or private, in contrast to its public or governmental acts. Under the Foreign Sovereign Immunities Act, a foreign country's immunity is limited to claims involving its public acts. The statutory immunity does not extend to claims arising from the private or commercial acts of a foreign state. 28 USCA § 1605. Cf. *jure imperii* . *See* commercial-activity exception; restrictive principle of sovereign immunity. In Chisholm v. Georgia, 2 U.S. 419, 472 (1793) U.S. Supreme Court Chief Justice John Jay defined "sovereignty" as the right to govern. *See infra* text accompanying notes 463, 464 for further consideration of Chisholm v. Georgia.

65 *See* Verlinden B.V. v. Central Bank of Nigeria, 461 U.S. 480, 487 (1983).

66 103 A.2d 795 (R.I. 1954).

67 125 U.S. 190 (1888).

> It is by no means certain that the framers intended that all legislative acts should be given credit along with 'records, and judicial proceedings.' On the contrary it is reasonably inferable that they intended to include only acts that were akin to judgments. It is a matter of historical record that at the time of the adoption of the federal constitution some if not all of the state legislatures possessed judicial power and that in registering their decisions in the exercise of such power they did so by act or resolution rather than by entering judgment as a court would do. Such acts were recognized as judgments.[68]

Justice Oliver Wendell Holmes in *Bi-Metallic Inv. Co. v. State Bd. of Equalization* [69] wrote:

> The Constitution does not require all public acts to be done in town meeting or an assembly of the whole. General statutes within the state power are passed that affect the person or property of individuals, sometimes to the point of ruin, without giving them a chance to be heard. Their rights are protected in the only way that they can be in a complex society, by their power, immediate or remote, over those who make the rule.[70]

In *Bradford Electric Light & Power Co. v. Clapper*,[71] U.S. Supreme Court Justice Lewis Brandeis wrote that full faith and credit is enjoined by the

---

[68] *McGrath*, 103 A.2d at 798.

[69] 239 U.S. 441 (1915).

[70] *Id.* at 445. Justice William O. Douglas recognized the quotation with approval in Bowles v. Willingham, 321 U.S. 503, 519 (1944). Justice Harry A. Blackmon recognized the quotation with approval in O'Bannion v. Town Court Nursing Center, 447 U.S. 773, 799 (1980). Justice Sandra Day O'Connor recognized the quotation with approval in Minnesota State Board v. Knight, 465 U.S. 271, 284 (1984). Jrstice John Paul Stevens recognized the quotation with approval in Atkins v. Parker, 472 U.S. 115, 130 n.33 (1985).

[71] 286 U.S. 145 (1932). *See supra* in connection with note 61 quotation in an Opinion which mentions this case and *infra* text accompanying notes 72, 647, 621, and 640 for further reference to this case.

Constitution only in respect to those public Acts which are within the legislative jurisdiction of the enacting state.[72]

Examples of public Acts are revealing.[73]

ii. Records

The "records" referred to in the Full Faith and Credit Clause and implementing statutes do not appear to have been definitively defined by the courts or scholarly writings, or Black's Law Dictionary. It is submitted that common sense would

---

[72] *Id.* at 156. What the Justice must have been referring to was that in that case Vermont's statute establishing an exclusive workers' compensation remedy, which rejected a common law damages remedy was not to be enjoined by an exception to the Full Faith and Credit clause, merely because another state (New Hampshire), which had an interest in the case, allowed common law damages. The Justice's pronouncement is probably still accurate, but not under the facts of the case in which he made it because the court in Alaska Packers Ass'n v. Industrial Acc. Comm, (*see infra* text accompanying notes 213, 423, 439, 622-624, 634); Pacific Employers Ins. Co v. Industrial Acc. Comm., 306 U.S. 493 (1989) (*see infra* text accompanying notes 213, 407, 423, 463, 629, 630, 634, 1116), and Crider v. Zurich Ins. Ins. Co., 380 U.S. 39 (1965), (*see infra* text accompanying notes 614, 645, 646, 648-650) modified the holding of the Clapper case in which he made the statement.

[73] They are a state's Wrongful Death Statute – Hughes v. Fetter, 341 U.S. 609, 611 (1951); Acts which- prohibit the dumping of garbage in public waters – Lake Carriers Ass'n v. MacMullan, 406 U.S. 498, 515 (1972); regulate desegregation of public schools — Milliken v. Bradley, 418 U.S. 717, 791 (1974); impose criminal sanctions – Clinton v. Jones, 520 U.S. 681, 719 (1997); govern the taking of the census – New Jersey v. New York, 523 U.S. 767, 818 (1998); authorize the filing of federal tax lien notices with county Registers of Deeds – United States v. Estate of Donnelly, 397 U.S. 286, 289 n.2 (1970); apportion members of a state's General Assembly among the state's counties - Baker v. Carr, 369 U.S. 186, 187 n.1 (1962); levy a tax on common stock of national banks owned by the public – Michigan Nat. Bank v. State of Michigan, 365 U.S. 467, 470 n.1 (1961); require bridge builders to furnish bond to protect the sovereign and assure payment of their creditors – Int'l Steel & Iron Co. v. Nat'l Sur. Co., 297 U.S. 657, 658 n.1(1936): authorize a state highway commissioner to require that when a roadway crosses a railway there be a difference in road levels – Nashville, C. & St. Louis Ry. v. Walters, 294 U.S. 405, 410 NS. 1,2 (1935); designate boundaries of a state – Vermont v. New Hampshire, 289 U.S. 593, 613 (1933); specify the location of building a fire station in a national park – Reichelderfer v. Quinn, 287 U.S.315, 315 in passim (1982); define a national fraternal benefit society's restrictions on beneficiaries' payments - Order of Commercial Travelers of America v. Wolfe, 331 U.S. 586, 590 (1940).

approve of a description that the archives and cartulary designations that governments make in fulfillment of their governing procedures and proceedings would qualify.[74]

We know from *Mills v. Duryee*[75] that the first Congress in the Act of 1790 provided for the authenticating of records of evidence taken in trials. Justice Joseph Story, in that case, wrote:

> The act declares that the record duly authenticated shall have such faith and credit as it has in the state Court from whence [sic] it is taken. If in such Court it has the faith and credit of evidence of the highest nature, viz. *record evidence*, it must have the same faith and credit in every other Court. Congress have therefore declared the *effect* of the record by declaring what faith and credit shall be given to it.[76]

Justice Nathan Clifford in *Christmas v. Russell*[77] referred to records as "instruments of evidence."

In *Hood v. McGehee*[78] it was held that a state's documentation of adoption proceedings constitute a "record."[79] The court made it clear, however, that such were records within the meaning of full faith and credit "in the sense of compelling recognition by other states of the adoptive filial relation created by them. It does

---

[74] Black's Law Dictionary, 8th Edition (2004) defines "public-records doctrine." as "[the principle, applicable in many states, that a third person acquiring or interested in real or immovable property may rely on the face of relevant public records and need not investigate further for unrecorded interests." In other words the government makes recording of certain events and happenings so that no one need rely on memory to establish the vital statistics concerning it.

[75] 11 U.S. (7 Cranch.) 481 (1813).

[76] Id. at 484.

[77] 72 U.S. 290, 295 (1866). *See infra* text accompanying notes 94, 95, 490, 492, 494 regarding additional reference to this case.

[78] 189 F. 205 (Cir. Ct. N.D. Ala. 1911). *See infra* text accompanying notes 79, 80, 394, 399, 579, 580, 908-910 for further reference to this case.

[79] *Id.* at 206.

not follow that the right of inheritance to real property follows such status when recognized."[80]

In *Milwaukee County v. M.E. White Co.*[81] U.S. Supreme Court Chief Justice Harlan F. Stone said that a court's findings are "records."[82]

In *In re Estate of Gardiner*[83] a full faith and credit case, it was held that a birth certificate is a "record."[84]

In *Adam v. Saenger*[85] it was established that a judgment can be considered a record. Justice Stone wrote that if a judgment appears to be a "record of a court of genera jurisdiction, such jurisdiction over the cause and the parties is to be presumed, unless disproved by extrinsic evidence, or by the record itself."[86]

iii. Judicial Proceedings

In *Tilt v. Kelsey*[87] U.S. Supreme Court Justice William H. Moody said that "the states of the Union are sovereign and may give to their judicial proceedings . . . conclusive effect, subject to the requirements of due process of law and to any other constitutional limitation which may be applicable."[88] What are the "judicial proceedings" which must be given full faith and credit, according to the

---

[80] *Id.*

[81] 296 U.S. 268 (1935). *See supra* text accompanying note 2 considering this case, and *infra* notes 81, 82, 347,362, 440, 452, 453, 627, 680, 681, 940, and 1085.

[82] *Id.* at 279, 280.

[83] 42 P.2d 120 (Kan. 2002). *See infra* text accompanying notes 84, 287, 288 for further reference to this case.

[84] *Id.* at 126.

[85] 303 U.S. 59 (1962). *See infra* text accompanying notes 86, 514-516 for other reference to this case.

[86] *Id.* at 62.

[87] 207 U.S. 43 (1907). *See infra* text accompanying notes 88, 90, 110, 111 for further comment about this case.

[88] *Id*, at 56.

Constitution and its implementing statutes? That is a question which defies the pronouncement of an easy answer. Black's Law Dictionary defines a "judicial proceeding" as "[a]ny court proceeding; any proceeding initiated to procure an order or decree, whether in law or in equity."[89] The Dictionary defines "proceeding" as:

> **1.** The regular and orderly progression of a lawsuit, including all acts and events between the time of commencement and the entry of judgment. **2.** Any procedural means for seeking redress from a tribunal or agency. **3.** An act or step that is part of a larger action. **4.** The business conducted by a court or other official body; a hearing. **5.** *Bankruptcy.* A particular dispute or matter arising within a pending case — as opposed to the case as a whole. [Cases: Bankruptcy 2156. C.J.S. *Bankruptcy* § 26.]
>
> 'Proceeding' is a word much used to express the business done in courts. A proceeding in court is an act done by the authority or direction of the court, express or implied. It is more comprehensive than the word 'action,' but it may include in its general sense all the steps taken or measures adopted in the prosecution or defense of an action, including the pleadings and judgment. As applied to actions, the term 'proceeding' may include — (1) the institution of the action; (2) the appearance of the defendant; (3) all ancillary or provisional steps, such as arrest, attachment of property, garnishment, injunction, writ of *ne exeat*; (4) the pleadings; (5) the taking of testimony before trial; (6) all motions made in the action; (7) the trial; (8) the judgment; (9) the execution; (10) proceedings supplementary to execution, in code practice; (11) the taking of the appeal or writ of error; (12) the *remittitur*, or sending back of the record to the lower court from the appellate or reviewing court; (13) the enforcement of the judgment, or a new trial, as may be directed by the court of last resort.. — Edwin E. Bryant, *The Law of Pleading Under the Codes of Civil Procedure* 3–4 (2d ed. 1899).[90]

Is that what the framers of the Constitution had in mind? The law Dictionary definition is not terribly unlike the usual dictionary definition of those terms. But did the framers have other thoughts in mind when they were constructing Article

---

[89] Black's Law Dictionary, 8th Edition (2004).

[90] *Id.*

IV, § 1 of the Constitution? Did they intend to provide that full faith and credit would be given to all those events and actions that take place during a proceeding? Or did they have in mind what is usually the end result of those judicial proceedings, i.e. a judgment? Apparently the first Congress thought they meant something tangible, rather than an on-going event, for when they drafted the Act of 1790, which implements the constitutional clause, they wrote on May 26, 1790, in the First Congress, Session II, Ch.11, the following words:

> Be it enacted by the Senate and the House of Representatives of the United States of America in Congress assembled, That the acts of the legislatures of the several States shall be authenticated by having the seal of their respective states affixed thereto: That the records and judicial proceedings of the courts of any state, shall be proved or omitted in any other court within the United States, by the attestation of the clerk, and the seal of the court annexed, if there be a seal, together with a certificate of the judge, chief judge, or presiding magistrate, as the case may be, that the said attestation is in due form. And the said records and judicial proceedings authenticated as aforesaid, shall have such faith and credit given to them in every court within the United States, as they have by law or usage in the courts of the state from whence, [sic] the said records are or shall be taken.
> Approved May 26, 1790.[91]

One authenticates a symbol, or representation of an event; one does not authenticate an event. In *Converce v. Hamilton*[92] U.S. Supreme Court Justice Willis Van Devanter referred to a court's consideration of whether to enforce another court's judgment as a "judicial proceeding.[93] In *Christmas v. Russell*[94] U.S. Supreme Court Justice Nathan Clifford referred to "judicial proceedings, together with records," as "instruments of evidence."[95] An "instrument of evidence" sounds more like a tangible "thing" than a proceeding. In *In re Adoption of Sebastian*[96]

---

[91] 1 Stat. 122.

[92] 224 U.S. 243 (1912). *See infra* text accompanying notes 93, 610, 611 concerning reference to this case.

[93] *Id.* at 253.

[94] 72 U.S. 290 (1866).

[95] *Id.* at 290.

[96] 879 N.Y.S. 2d 677 (N.Y. Surr. 2009). *See infra* text accompanying notes 97, 108, 109 915-921, for addional decisions dealing with this case.

New York Surrogate Judge Kristin Booth Glen described an adoption as a "judicial proceeding."[97] Under the Law Dictionary's definition of a "judicial proceeding," the conference which the highest court of a jurisdiction at times holds to formulate rules of civil procedure is a "judicial proceeding." One would not suppose, however, that the framers in 1787 had such judicial proceedings in mind when they wrote that the judicial proceedings of one state must be given full faith and credit by other states. Congress, moreover, did not have such judicial proceedings in mind when it constructed the implementing statute of 1790.

The fact that in neither the Clause of the Constitution nor the words of the implementing statute or its amendments use the word "judgment"[98] might indicate that neither the framers of the Constitution nor the members of Congress intended that the term "judicial proceedings" meant to encompass only judgments. The fact that the vast majority of cases dealing with full faith and credit, however, involve judgments, as the subject of the dispute, indicates that the courts are interpreting the term "judicial proceeding" as consisting of judgments predominantly.[99] An intriguing question remains – what, if any, other proceedings of the courts are included in the term. There are a few, but there are not many. U.S. Supreme Court Justice Henry B. Brown in his dissent in *Johnson v. Powers*[100] envisioned that a court[101] might, on its own authority, appoint commissioners in an estate proceeding, whose function it would be to receive, examine and adjust all claims and demands of each person who had a claim against a deceased. Even though the commissioners would not enter a judgment Justice Brown, plausibly, thought their functions to be "judicial proceedings."[102] Alabama Supreme Court Justice Bouldin said in his *City of Greenville v. Goodwyn*[103] dissenting Opinion that estate

---

[97] *Id.* at 681.

[98] *See* Barber v. Barber, 323 U.S. 77, 87 (1944). *See infra* text accompanying notes 528, 529, 788, and 789 for further reference to this case.

[99] In Clarke v. Clarke, 178 U.S. 186, 188 (1900) Justice Edward White, in his statement of the case, uses the disjunctive "judicial proceedings and judgments" of South Carolina, which would indicate that he thought of the two as being separate components of a case.

[100] 139 U.S. 156 (1891).

[101] A Michigan court in that case.

[102] *Johnson*, 139 U.S. at 164.

[103] 169 So. 699 (Ala.1936).

administrations are "judicial proceedings.[104] He also suggested that guardianships, trust administrations and receiverships are "judicial proceedings."[105] U.S. District Judge Neville in *Fireman's Fund Ins. Co. v. St. Paul Fire & Marine Ins. Co.*[106] considered a receivership to be a "judicial proceeding."[107] New York Surrogate Kristin Booth Glen in *In re Adoption of Sebastian*[108] said that an adoption was a "judicial proceeding."[109]Although there appears to be no recorded authority to that effect, it would seem that the functions of Masters in Chancery, appraisers, and accountants are "judicial proceedings." In *Tilt v. Kelsey*[110] the Court held that a New York state tax assessment denied a New Jersey estate administration full faith and credit. Of course we recognize that this case involved a decree entered by the New Jersey Surrogate's Court, and not the estate administration, which denied the full faith and credit.[111] In *Daniels v. Arapahoe County Dist. Court*[112] the Tenth Circuit held that a sex offender's in-prison classifications proceeding was not a "judicial proceeding."[113]

In the first U.S. Supreme Court decision involving full faith and credit, the 1839 case of *McElmoyle, for the Use of Bailey v. Cohen*[114] which concerned a judgment of South Carolina not being enforced by Georgia due to the Georgia

---

[104] *Id.* at 703.

[105] *Id.* Would not garnishment and/or attachments proceedings (*see* American Surety Co. v. Baldwin, 287 U.S. 156, 166 (1932)), insolvency proceedings (*see* Clark v. Willard, 292 U.S. 112 (1934)), or even a perfunctory Municipal Court hearing (*see* Wells Fargo & Co. v. Ford, 238 U.S. 503 (1915)), governmental agency functions (*see* Kremer v. Chemical Const Corp., 456 U.S. 461 (1983) all be considered "judicial proceedings"?

[106] 357 F. Supp. 464 (D.C. Minn. 1973).

[107] *Id*, at 464.

[108] 879 N.Y.S.2d 677 (N.Y. Surr. 2009).

[109] *Id.* at 681. To the same effect *see* Russell v. Bridgens, 647 N.W.2d 56, 59, 60 (Neb.2002).

[110] 207 U.S. 43 (1907).

[111] *Id.* at 54.

[112] 2010 W.L. 1645978 (10th Cir. 2010).

[113] *Id.* at *2.

[114] 38 U.S. (13 Pet.) 312 (1839). *See infra* text accompanying notes 115-117, 217, 247, 486, 488 for further considerations of this case.

statute of limitations having expired, Justice James M. Wayne gave a lengthy dissertation on judgments. He said that a judgment is a "record;"[115] and that foreign judgments are "prima facie evidence of the right and matter they purport to decide."[116] He added that a judgment of F-1 does not automatically become a judgment of F-2; it must be reduced to being a judgment by an independent procedure of F-2.[117] The Court's holding was to the effect that matters concerning the enforcement of a judgment (i.e. a statute of limitations) do not travel with it, but reside with, and are employed by, the enforcing court. In 1872 Supreme Court Justice Nathan Clifford in *Crapo v. Kelley*[118] was the second member of the Court to use the word "judgment" in one of his Opinions. He was followed in 1873 by Justice Joseph P. Bradley in *Thompson v. Whitman.*[119] By 1900 Chief Justices Morrison R. Waite,[120] and Melville W. Fuller[121] as well as Justices Horace Gray,[122] David J. Brewer,[123] and Harlan F. Stone[124] had used the word in their Opinions, all without any particular emphasis. Since that time it has appeared taken for granted that judgments are "judicial proceedings" to which the constitutional provision applies.

From an academic point of view it would seem that "judicial proceedings" include a myriad of functions presided over by courts. From a functional standpoint, however, it appears that judgments, or decrees, of the courts are the almost, but not quite, solitary components of "judicial proceedings" with which this lexicon will be concerned in its exploration of the meaning of "full faith and credit."

---

115 *Id.* at 325. *See supra* text accompanying notes 74-86 dealing with records.

116 *Id.*

117 *Id.*

118 83 U.S. 610, 637 (1872).

119 85 U.S. 457, 463 (1873).

120 In Chicago & A.R. Co. v. Wiggins Ferry Co., 119 U.S. 615, 616 (1887).

121 In Cole v. Cunningham, 133 U.S. 107, 111 (1890), Blount v. Walker, 134 U.S. 607, 612 (1890), and Lloyd v. Matthews, 155 U.S. 222, 226 (1894).

122 In Henley v. Donoghue, 116 U.S. 1, 4 (1885).

123 In Reynolds v. Stockton, 140 U.S. 250, 255 (1891).

124 In Huntington v. Attrill, 146 U.S. 657, 683 (Dissenting Opinion) (1892). *See infra* text accompanying notes 441, 941, 943, and 945 for further reference to this case.

b. Follow F-1 Judgment if it Meets Certain Requirements, Even if it is Wrong on the Law[125]

Perhaps one of the most difficult concepts to accept is the edict that F-2 must give full credit to F-1's judgments even if they are wrong, i.e. based on a misconception of law. Such holding was made by the Case of *Fauntleroy v. Lum.*[126] There parties in Mississippi entered into a gambling debt involving cotton futures, which were illegal in Mississippi. Despite that obstruction to the creditor prevailing, an arbitration panel rendered an award in his favor. The prevailing party followed his adversary to Missouri and secured a Missouri judgment against him, based on the incorrect arbitration award. When the creditor attempted to have Mississippi recognize the Missouri judgment its court refused, on the basis that the Missouri judgment was based on an error as to the law of Mississippi. The U.S. Supreme Court, in a 5-4 split decision, required Mississippi to honor the Missouri judgment even though it was based on a mistake of Mississippi law, which the five member majority acknowledged.[127] The only balm Justice Oliver Wendell Holmes, the author of the majority Opinion, gave to the losing defendant was that "[m]istakes will be rare."[128] Justice Holmes offered no epistemological reason for the slim majority decision. Instead the last 77 words of his Opinion blamed it on the Constitution in words not of the usual caliber emanating from the great jurist:

> In this case the Missouri court no doubt supposed that the award was binding by the law of Mississippi. If it was mistaken, it made a natural mistake. The validity of its judgment, even in Mississippi is, as we believe, the result of the Constitution as it always has been understood, and is not a matter to arouse the susceptibilities . . . of the states, all of which are equally concerned in the question and equally on both sides.[129]

---

[125] The requirements for having a judgment recognized and enforced are covered in Chapter I, Section C., text accompanying notes 217-258..

[126] 210 U.S. 230 (1908). *See infra* text accompanying notes 127, 128, 129, 505, 506, 508, 512, 1122 for further reference to this case.

[127] *Id.* at 237.

[128] *Id.* at 237, 238.

[129] *Id.* at 238.

If *Fauntelroy v. Lum* were not enough to raise concerns over the authoritativeness of the full faith and credit concept, the case of *Treinies v. Sunshine Mining Co.*[130] might be worth looking at. In that case a Washington state probate court (F-1), found that it had jurisdiction to determine the ownership of certain corporate stock. Later an Idaho state court (F-2) found that the Washington court was mistaken about its determination of jurisdiction. Still later, in an interpleader, case a federal court, sitting in Idaho (F-3), held that under full faith and credit it was bound by F-2's ruling – that the Washington probate court lacked jurisdiction to render its decision. The Ninth Circuit affirmed, and the U.S. Supreme court affirmed the Ninth Circuit. Justice Stanley F. Reed, writing for the 8-0 majority referred to the fact that the Washington (F-1) court might just be in a better position to determine whether or not it had jurisdiction than the Idaho (F-2) court, but none the less it was the Idaho (F-2) court which must be followed because of full faith and credit. Justice Reed wrote:

> The power of the Idaho court to examine into the jurisdiction of the Washington court is beyond question. . . . Even where the decision against validity of the original judgment is erroneous, it is a valid exercise of judicial power by the second court.[131]

It would seem that the Court gave the Idaho (F-2) court too much power. It has been held that F-2 may not delve into the merits of a case;[132] but this pronouncement gives F-2 the power to delve into whether F-1 (in this case the Washington probate court) correctly examined whether or not it had jurisdiction. The reason may be that jurisdiction is of greater importance than who wins the case; but a classic chance to elucidate was lost by the Court and Justice Reed ignoring the issue, and not expounding upon it. Justice Reed's reason was curious, to say the least: "[o]ne trial of an issue is enough."[133] The record reveals that the issue went to a court for resolution, not one, but three times. Two courts reached opposite decisions as to the jurisdiction of the first court, and the third court considered it was bound by the second, which was a secondary observer, compared

130 308 U.S. 66 (1939). *See infra* text accompanying notes 131, 134, 135, 137, and 574. for additional reference to this case.

131 *Id.* at 78.

132 *See infra* text accompanying notes 214. and 405.

133 *Treines*, 308 U.S. at 78.

with the first (Washington) court, which was primarily concerned with its own power to make the determination requested of it.

Perhaps the Supreme Court lost another opportunity to clarify an apparent conflict, when it decided *Durfee v. Duke*.[134] In that case a Nebraska appellate court found that its trial court (F-1), had jurisdiction to try title to land bordering a shifting river. When a Missouri court (F-2) was called upon to try title to the same land the U.S. Supreme Court held that it could not do so because it was bound by full faith and credit to abide by the finding of trial court jurisdiction made by the Nebraska (F-1) court, a decision, which appears to conflict with *Treines v. Sunshine Mining Co.*.[135]

Another case which seems to conflict with *Treines* is *In re L.S.*[136] where the Colorado appellate court said that all that a party seeking enforcement of a foreign judgment need do is provide "a colorable basis" for finding F-1 jurisdiction.[137]

In 1925 the U.S. Supreme Court in *North Carolina R.R. v. Story*[138] made the statement that no matter how erroneous a state court judgment is, if not appealed to its own appellate courts, it is authority for preclusive purposes.[139] Admittedly it has not been cited recently for that proposition,[140] but it is still the law of the land.

---

[134] 375 U.S. 106 (1963). *See infra* text accompanying notes 198. 392, 427, 581-585, and 587 for further reference to this case.

[135] 308 U.S. 66 (1939).

[136] 226 P.3d 1227 (Colo. App. 2009).

[137] *Id.* at 1234.

[138] 268 U.S. 288 (1925).

[139] *Id.* at 293.

[140] There is a series of North Carolina decisions approving the doctrine to which the Story case refers: Smathers v. Northwestern Mut. Life Ins. Co., 190 S.E.229, 229 (N.C. 1937); Cameron v. McDonald, 6 S.E.2d 497, 499 (N.C. 1940); Ex Parte Young, 24 S.E.2d 539, 540 (N.C. 1943), Hampton v. North Carolina Pulp Co., 27 S. E.2d 538, 541 (N.C. 1943); King v. Grinstaff, 200 S.E.2d 799, 808 (N.C. 1973).

U.S. Supreme Court Chief Justice Fred Vinson, in *Sherrer v. Sherrer*[141] offered a plausible explanation when he wrote:

> The full faith and credit clause is one of the provisions incorporated into the Constitution by its framers for the purpose of transforming an aggregation of . . . independent, sovereign States into a nation. . . . If in its application local policy must at times be required to give way, such 'is part of the price of our federal system.'[142]

Out of this seemingly desultory picture of the rather uncomfortable position the concept of full faith and credit has placed our judicial system, from an appellate court in Tennessee comes a ray of clarification. In *Porter v. Daniels,*[143] Court of Appeals Judge Todd wrote that judicial decisions have two functions. Some are meant to guide judges and lawyers in the jurisdictions where the decision was made, and for those professionals in other jurisdiction - the "guidance" use. Others are for the purpose of determining disputes between the parties to the case in which the decision was rendered - the "conclusive" use. He opined that the erroneous decisions will probably be ignored by not only those professionals outside the jurisdiction in which the decision was rendered, but also those within it. They will be restricted for use among the parties, judges and lawyers directly involved in the case; a rather comforting thought. [144]

At times the U.S. Supreme Court tempers the seeming plusable statements above considered. In *Sun Oil Co. v. Wortman*[145] Justice Antonin Scalia wrote:

> To constitute a violation of the Full Faith and Credit Clause or the Due Process Clause, it is not enough that a state court misconstrue the law of another State. Rather, our cases make plain that the misconstruction must

---

[141] 334 U.S.343 (1948).

[142] *Id.* at 355.

[143] 1989 W.L. 14219 (Tenn. App. 1989).

[144] *Id.* at *4.

[145] 486 U.S. 717 (1988). *See infra* text accompanying notes 146, 667, 668 for additional reference to this case.

> contradict law of the other State that is clearly established and that has been brought to the court's attention.[146]

c. Credit Preclusive Effects of F-1 Judgment

While neither the Constitution nor any of its implementing statutes explicitly require deference to the preclusive principles (collateral estoppel and *res judicata*) an Ohio Court of Appeals in a Per Curiam Opinion in *Salver v. Eplion*[147] has proclaimed that they are just as compelling as they would be had they been specifically designated in those imperative documents, provided, of course, that the F-1 court met the subject-matter and personal jurisdiction requirements. Full faith and credit requires the use of both common law and statutory doctrines of F-1 for state-federal, and federal-state relations. Where F-1 has not clearly stated its law *Viking Pump, Inv. v. Century Indem. Co.*[148] teaches that F-2 will try to "predict" what it is from the "teachings" of F-1's courts.[149] For example, at times parties are involved in litigation in State B. One of the parties wants to establish a point that had already been established between the parties in State A. The Full faith and Credit Clause (Art. IV, § 1) and implementing statute (28 U.S.C. § 1738) not only permits, but requires, certain conditions being met, that some fact already established between the parties in one court will be recognized in another.[150] In that situation, therefore, State A becomes F-1, and State B becomes State F-2, not for enforcement purposes, but simply to be recognized, in order to establish a point, by precluding contradictions of it. In other cases the defendant may use preclusion to prevent the recognition and enforcement of a judgment entered by a foreign court. Of course the U.S. Eleventh Circuit Court of Appeals in *Green v. Jefferson County Com'n*,[151] teaches that even if a party does not raise the preclusion principle the trial or appellate court may raise it *sua sponte*. A plethora of cases has held that if such an issue arises, the preclusion law of F-1 must be

---

[146] *Id.* at 730, 731. *See also* Thompson v. Bayer, 2009 W.L. 362982 *2 (E.D. Ark. 2009).

[147] 2009 W.L. 891797, *7 (Ohio App. 2009).

[148] 2009 W.L. 3297559 (Del. Ch. 2009).

[149] *Id.* at *20.

[150] *See* Justice Ruth Bader Ginsburg's disquisition of the subject in Taylor v. Sturgell, 553 U.S. 880, in passim, (2008).

[151] 563 F.3d 1243, 1252 (11th Cir. 2009).

used for its resolution.[152] As we learn from *Tristani v. Richman*[153] the Constitution made the preclusionary principle applicable to the states, and the statute of 1790 (now 28 U.S.C. § 1738) made it applicable to the federal courts. Hence a set of preclusionary rules have been established, which apply, are now considered.

Another plethora of courts has held that the preclusionary rules apply whether the relationship is F-1 (state) – F-2 (federal) or F-1 (federal) – F-2 (state);[154] and whether or not the states in which the federal courts sit are the same or different. i.e. whether or not full faith applies or the two proceedings are tried in the same jurisdiction, where full faith and credit does not apply.

While *Baldwin v. Iowa State Traveling Men's Ass'n*[155] established that neither the Full Faith Clause, nor its implementing statutes apply to federal court-federal court relations, Justice Potter Stewart in *Allen v. McCurry*[156] made it clear that federal courts do give each other preclusive effect by writing that "federal courts may give each other preclusive effect by the use of the common law, or policies supporting *res judicata* and collateral estoppel."

---

[152] *See* Migra v. Warren Cty. School Dist., 465 U.S. 75, 81 (1984); Ross v. Alaska, 189 F. 3d 1107, 1110 (9th Cir. 1999); Jefftex Int'l. Ltd.,v. JPI Trading Corp., 2010 W.L. 915812 at *1 (2d Cir. 2010); Johnson v. McClure, 2009 W.L. 2356147 (N.D. N.Y. 2009); Lane v. Carpinello, 2009 W.L. 3074344 at 3, n.13 (N.D. N.Y. 2009); Rimkus Consulting Group, Inc. v. Cammarata, 257 R.F.D. 127 (S.D. Tex. 2009); Tokio Marine v. Carter, 2009 W.L. 2461048 (S.D. N.Y. 2009); Rinkus Consulting Group, Inc. v. Cammarata, 2010 W.L. 645253 at *41 (S.D. Tex. 2010).

[153] 609 F. Supp. 2d 423, 447 (W.D. Pa. 2009).

[154] Coleman v. America's Wholesale Lender, 2009 W.L. 761169 at *4 (E.D. Pa. 2009); Aaron v. Mahl, 674 S.E.2d 482, 486 (S.C. 2009); Reaves v. Roabike Housing Development Auth., 2009 W.L. 366045 at *4 (W.D. Va. 2009); Coatney v. City of Dearborn, 2009 W.L. 322032 at *3 (E.D. Mich. 2009); Baranowski v. Waters, 2009 W.L. 331597 at *4 (W.D. Pa. 2009); Douglas v. Smith, 2009 W.L. 789450 (N.D.N.Y. 2009); Dexter v. Tran, 654 F. Supp.2d 1253, 1260 (E.D. Wash 2009); Ford v. Krusan, 2009 W.L. 959534 at *7 (N.D. N.Y. 2009).

[155] 283 U.S. 522, 524 (1931). *See supra* text accompanying note 18, 19, 20.

[156] 449 U.S. 90, 96 (1980). *See also* Baldwin, *id,* where F-1 was a U.S. District Court in Iowa and F-2 was the U.S. Circuit Court of Appeals for the Eighth Circuit, and the issue was whether the District Court had jurisdiction of the cause.

i. Issue Preclusion

If either the plaintiff or the defendant in State A litigation wants to establish an issue that has already been established in another action in state B, he must assert collateral estoppel, or issue preclusion. He must prove to the court that (1) there occurred in State B, litigation in which he, or one in privity[157] with him; (2) and a party of record in this state A case, or one in privity with him, were parties of record in that state B case; (3) that an issue in this case is identical to an issue that was tried in the state B case;[158] (4) that there was a full and fair opportunity to litigate it there (i.e. state B), and it was actually litigated there;[159] (5) either a final judgment was entered in the state B action, or the determination of the issue was "sufficiently firm to be accorded conclusive effect;"[160] and (6) determination of the issue was essential to the resolution of the proceedings which occurred in state B.

Certainly one of the most important issues which an F-2 court will face is whether F-1 had jurisdiction of either the subject-matter of the case and/or personal jurisdiction of one or more parties in that F-1 action. Several courts have established that whether jurisdiction was actually litigated is immaterial in view of the necessary conclusion that there was full opportunity to litigate it and that it was adjudicated by the decree.[161] *Jackson v. Irving Trust Co.* [162] made it clear that if

---

[157] Privity is defined by Black's Law Dictionary, 8th Edition (2004) as "[t]he connection or relationship between two parties, each having a legally recognized interest in the same subject matter (such as a transaction, proceeding, or piece of property)."

[158] That requirement can produce some narrow determinations. In Government & Civic Employees Organizing Comm, C.I.O. v. Windsor, 353 U.S. 364, 366 (1957) the U.S Supreme Court held that a party's inquiry as to whether a statute applied to it was not the same issue as to whether the statute was constitutional.

[159] In Tilzer v. Davis, Bethume, & Jones, L.L.C., 204 P 3d 617, 625 (Ka. 2009), the court said that "[t]he doctrine applies only to those issues that were necessarily and unambiguously decided."

[160] Rest. 2d Judgments § 13. Comment g explains this rather obtuse explanation. If the jurist in F-1 makes a ruling on an issue it would be unnecessary to wait until she or he sign a final judgment, or an appellate court finishes reviewing the judgment for that issue to have been determined. Query: what would be the effect of that issue determination if the final judgment were reversed, is an intriguing issue, in itself. Ed.

[161] Cromwell v. County of Sac, 94 U.S. 351, 352, (1876); Grubb v. Public Utilities Commission, 281 U.S. 470, 478, (1930); Chicot County Drainage District v. Baxter State

the F-1 court had erred in dealing, or in failing to deal, with the issue of jurisdiction thus involved, the remedy would be by appeal in the F-1 jurisdiction, and not by collateral attack in the F-2 courts.

In *Hartford Life Ins. Co. v. Ibs,*[163] what must have been an early class action, though the court did not mention that term, it was held that Minnesota violated the Full Faith and Credit Clause by not honoring an issue decided by a Connecticut court, even though the causes of action before the two courts were not the same. U.S. Supreme Court Justice Joseph R. Lamar, in his Opinion of the Court, sans reference to collateral estoppel, made the point clear with his following words:

> [T]hough the form and causes of action be different, a decision by a court of competent jurisdiction in respect to any essential fact or question in the one . . . action is conclusive between the parties in all subsequent actions.[164]

Salovarra v. Eckart[165] has required that there be a final judgment to be entered before issue preclusion takes an effect.[166]

Calhoun v. Special Commitment Center[167] held that if the claim asserted in F-2 arose after the F-1 case was decided, neither claim nor issue preclusion would apply.[168]

Bank, 308 U.S. 371, 374, 375 (1940); Sunshine Anthracite Coal Co. v. Adkins, 310 U.S. 381, 403 (1940).

162 311 U.S. 494, 503 (1941).

163 237 U.S. 662 (1915).

164 *Id.* at 673, 674.

165 2002 W.L. 32507111 (N.J. Super. Ch. 2002). *See infra* text accompanying notes 166, 182, 183, dealing with other considerations of this case.

166 *Id.* at *5. This is a minority decision, but it sounds like a wise one despite the position taken by Restatement 2d of Judgments. *See supra* note 160.

167 2009 W.L. 674457 (W.D. Wash. 2009).

168 *Id.* at *6.

Griffen v. Crompton Corp.[169] found that if the issue of adequate notice to all members of a class, including the same party in two different actions, that party would be precluded from re-arguing the matter.[170]

Nazarchyk v. Talkington—Nazarchyk [171] clarified the difference between an action dissolving a marriage in one state, (F-1), and an action in another state, which merely attempts to compel one party to comply with the F-1 decree. The issues in the two actions are not the same.[172]

Gillis v. Srate[173] was a criminal case.[174] A person accused of murder was acquitted by Delaware, but was tried by Maryland when a dead body was found in that state. The Maryland Supreme Court held that the Full Faith and Credit Clause would not bind Maryland by the Delaware acquittal, where Maryland was not give an opportunity of being present at the proceeding in which the acquittal was decreed.[175]

Several courts have specifically ruled that the taking of an appeal does not adversely affect the preclutionary effect of issues decided in F-1.[176]

ii. Claim Preclusion

If litigation exists in state B attempting to have state B recognize and enforce, or simply recognize, a judgment that was entered in state A the plaintiff will want

---

169 2009 W.L. 4789230 (Tenn. App. 2009).

170 *Id.* at *5.

171 2010 W.L. 2080115 (Iowa App. 2010). *See infra* text accompanying notes 172, 192 and 193

172 *Id.* at *3.

173 633 A 2d 888 (Md. 1993).

174 *See infra* Chapter I. Section I, test accompanying notes 935-974.-

175 *Gillis*, 633 A. 2d at 893.

176 Dunham v. Board of Ed. of City School District of Cincinnati 99 N.E.2d 183, 185 (Ohio. Com Pl..1950); Luebke v. Marine Nat'l Bank of Neenah, 567 F. Supp. 1460, 1462 (D.C. Wis. 1983); Crockett & Brown, P.A. v. Wilson, 864 S.W.2d 244, 246 (1993): Gausvik v. Abbey, 107 P.3d 98 (Wash. App. 2005).

the state B court to give that state A judgment full faith and credit, rather than have to try the case all over again. The defendant will want to prevent the state B court from giving the state A judgment full faith and credit, unless, on the outside chance that he thinks the state A judgment was more in his favor than against him. The defendant may argue to the state B court that in State A, not long ago a judgment was entered against the plaintiff on the same claim.[177] The plaintiff would probably argue, that those cases involved different claims - the one in state A was for specific performance of a contract, in which he did not prevail, but in this case (in state B) he seeks damages against the same defendant. The defendant can prevail and require the court to deny plain full faith and credit by dismissing the case if the defendant proves to the court that (1) there was a case in state A involving the same parties or their privies; (2) in which a claim was made by this plaintiff arising out of the same transaction or occurrence as the transaction or occurrence out of which the claim in state B is being made; (3) upon which the court in state A decided that the plaintiff was not entitled to obtainl (4) a judgment so proclaiming, on the merits,[178] was entered by the court in state A which is final[179] and valid; and (5) even if the claim being made in state B was not made in state A, it could have been made there by the plaintiff. This would be claim preclusion in favor of the defendant.

In *Cieszkowska v. Gray Line, N.Y.*,[180] an action seeking damages for wrongful discharge, discharge without cause, and defamation of a professional reputation was held to be the same claim as being discharged for ethnic origin.[181] This was not a full faith and credit case, because F-1 and F-2 were the same court. It reveals, however, how at times two or more similar terms or issues can be so convoluted as to really form a whole.

---

[177] Black's Law Dictionary, 8th Edition (2004) defines a claim as "[t]he aggregate of operative facts giving rise to a right enforceable by a court;" in other words a chose-in-action or cause of action.

[178] A judgment "on the merits" has been described as one in which the jurist reviewed the facts, considered the arguments, and then ruled. *See* Davis v. Altman, 2009 W.L. 928063 at *3 (S.D. N.Y 2009).

[179] Rest. 2d Judgments § 13, Comment g states that the possibility of an appeal will effect the finality of the judgment.

[180] 295 F.3d 204 (2d Cir. 2002).

[181] *Id.* at 206.

In *Salovaara v. Eckart* [182] it was held that claim preclusion will not apply unless there was a final judgment in the F-1 case.[183]

In *Davis v. Altman*[184] It was held that: (1) if claims arise out of the same "factual grouping" they are deemed to be part of the same cause of action as was brought in the prior court even if the claim in the second court is based upon a different legal theory or seeks different relief; (2) the prior judgment must have been "on the merits;" and (3) that a claim for declaratory relief was not available in F-1 does not mean that it can be brought in F-2 because a declaratory judgment merely "creates a means by which rights and obligations may be adjudicated in cases involving an actual controversy that has not reached the stage at which either party may seek a coercive remedy or in which the party entitled to such a remedy fails to sue for it."[185]

In *Heiser v. Woodruff*[186] Chief Justice Harlan F. Stone proclaimed that: "[i]t has been held in non-diversity cases since *ErieR. Co. v. Tompkins*,[187] that the federal courts will apply their own rule of *res judicata*."[188]

In *El-Fil v. Countrywide Home Loans, Inc.*[189] a state court judgment concerning the foreclosure of a mortgage and the sale of the plaintiff's house will bar a federal court action concerning asserted violations of the Truth in Lending Act and RESPA, on the Rooker-Feldman doctrine[190] and the basis of claim preclusion.[191]

---

182 2002 W.L. 32507111 (N.J. Super. Ch. 2002).

183 *Id.* at *5.

184 2009 W.L. 928063 (S.D. N.Y).

185 *Id.* at *3.

186 327 U.S. 726 (1946). *See infra* text accompanying notes 188, 427, 505, 522, 757, 990, 991 for further reference to this case.

187 304 U.S. 64 (1938).

188 *Heiser*, 327 U.S. 64 (1938).

189 2009 W.L. 4946259 at *1 (E.D. Mich. 2009).

190 *See infra* text accompanying notes 278 and 405.

191 *El-Fil*, 2009 W.L. 4946259 at *1.

In *Nazarchyk v. Talkington—Nazarchyk*[192] it was held that an action in Iowa attempting to require a party in a Texas divorce action to comply with its decree is not barred by claim preclusion. The claims were entirely different. The one in Texas was to dissolve a marriage. The one in Iowa was to enforce the terms of the marriage dissolution.[193]

In *Adar v. Smith*[194] Judge Weiner gave a clear discussion of the distinction between full faith and credit and *res judicata*:

> [F]ull faith and credit is not merely a redundant reiteration of *res judicata.* At its core, the common law doctrine of *res judicata* is concerned with respecting the finality of litigation. . . . In contrast, even though the Clause does promote this laudatory end, . . . its primary purpose is to serve the *modus vivendi*[195] of federalism by harmonizing the competing sovereign interests of the several states
> . . . . A crucial difference between *res judicata* and the Clause is that *res judicata* is the *voluntary* restraint by a forum state from exercising its power . . . so as to respect the judgment of another state. Indeed, as to judgments, a forum state may and sometimes does choose to re-litigate issues as it sees fit. . . . In contrast, the Clause is a *mandatory,* constitutional curb on every state's sovereign power. With respect to judgments (although not to statutes), a state as a rule *has no discretion* to disregard a decision of another state on a matter over which that other state is competent to exercise jurisdiction. . . . [196]

---

[192] 2010 W.L. 2080115 (Iowa App. 2010).

[193] *Id.* at *3.

[194] 597 F. 3d 697 (5th Cir. 2010). *See infra* text accompanying notes 196, 249, 250, 523, 525, 536-538, 673, 674, 933, and 934 for other references to this case.

[195] Black's Law Dictionary, 8th Edition (2004) defines *modus vivendi* as "[n]ormally . . . used for provisional and interim arrangements which ultimately are to be replaced by a formal agreement of a more permanent and detailed character."

[196] *Id* at 709, 710.

2. What Should be Done as Compared to What Must be Done[197]

1. Verify that the judicial question with which the F-2 court is dealing was "fully and fairly" litigated and that a final judgment of the F-1 court was duly entered incorporating that issue.[198]

2. Check to determine whether you or your privies were involved with the opposite party or its privies in which issues or claims were established that will prevent the opposite party from re-litigating now.[199]

3. If you are a government official with the responsibility of imposing penalties upon other persons, verify that you have the authority to impose a penalty, otherwise you may be violating the Full Faith and Credit Clause.[200]

4. If you are a trial judge, use your own court's statute of limitations rather than the statute of limitations of some other court because the Full Faith and Credit Clause does not require using other jurisdiction's statute of limitations.[201]

5. If you were not a party to the original action in F-1, and such parties would not be allowed to contest the F-1 court's jurisdiction, do not attempt to contest that jurisdiction, because such action is not allowed.[202]

6. If in F-2 you argue a full faith and credit point, make certain that the point was argued in F-1.[203]

---

[197] There are certain matters which are not absolutely mandatorily required, but good sense dictates that they be done.

[198] American Express Co. v. Mullins, 212 U.S. 311, 313, 314 (1909) (though not using the term "fully and fairly"). Courts using the term "fully and fairly" are: Durfee v. Duke, 375 U.S. 106, 111, 112 (1963) (Mr. Justice Potter Stewart clearly proclaiming that jurisdiction of the F-1 court is an issue to be determined by the F-2 court); Russo v. Dear, 105 S.W. 3d 43, 47 (Tex. App. 2003); Playnation Play Systems, Inc. Gualardo, 2007 W.L. 1439740 at *3 (Tex. App. 2007); Scott v. Commonwealth of Virginia, 676 S.E. 2d 343, 345 (Va. App. 2009.)

[199] *See supra* text accompanying notes 147-196.

[200] As an example Altamira-Torres v. United States, 353 Fed. Appx. 386, 389 (11th Cir. 2009), established that whether Immigration officials violated the Full Faith and Credit Clause depended upon the nature of a court's vacation of a criminal conviction.

[201] Wells v. Simonds Abrasive Co., 345 U.S. 514, 517 (1953).

[202] Johnson v. Muelberger, 340 U.S. 581, 589 (1951), *See* text accompanying notes 49, 51, 592, 744 and 761 for further consideration of this case.

[203] Howell v. Mississippi, 543 U.S. 440, 446 (2005).

3. What Must Not Be Done

1. If you are governed by a federal statute don't deviate from its provisions. In *Sharifzarh. Farrazi v. I.N.S.*[204] the Ninth Circuit found that the Immigration & Nationality Act does not take into account the marital status of one of its subjects; hence where the Service was not concerned with its subject's annulment, its handling of a matter involving the subject was not affected by full faith and credit. principles.[205]

2. If you are a state, don't refuse to offer your courts for the trial of an issue under the statutes of another state. In *Hughes v. Fetter*[206] the U.S. Supreme Court held that Wisconsin was not permitted to refuse to allow the Administrator of an Illinois decedent to bring a Wrongful Death claim under an Illinois statute.[207]

3. If you are a corporate employer which holds a court ordered injunction prohibiting a former employee from testifying about trade secrets or other confidential information, don't attempt to prevent the courts of another state from requiring by subpoenaing the former employee's testimony in litigation concerning people who were not parties in the case producing the injunction. In *Baker by Thomas v. General Motors Corp.*[208] the U.S. Supreme Court held that a Michigan judgment containing such injunctive provisions would not prevent a Georgia court from subpoenaing a former employee of General Motors from testifying about General Motors' products involving people who were not parties to the Michigan proceeding.[209]

4. If you are a judge, don't enter an order decreeing title to land in another jurisdiction. In *Fall v. Eastin*[210] the U.S. Supreme Court ruled that a Washington state judgment decreeing that real property in Nebraska belonged to the wife in a

---

[204] 24 F.3d 249 (9th Cir. 1994).

[205] *Id.* at *1.

[206] 341 U.S. 609 (1951). *See supra* text accompanying note 73, and *infra* notes 206, 207, 411, 412, 594, 638-641, 676, 677, and 683 for further reference to this case.

[207] *Id.* at 620, 621.

[208] 522 U.S. 222 (1998). *See infra* text accompanying notes 209, 212, 245, 247, 248,396, 419, 415, 416, 462, 513, 532, 533, 541, 543-545, 537, 539, and 974 for further reference to this case.

[209] *Id.* at 224.

[210] 215 U.S.1 (1909). *See infra* text accompanying notes 211, 397, 586, 588, 589, 591 for further reference to this case.

divorce case was not entitled to full faith and credit, even though a court-appointed Commissioner delivered to the wife an executed deed to the property. The court made it clear, by dictum, that had the husband conveyed to the wife all his interest in the property, that conveyance would be recognized, but as the husband refused to do so, the Commissioner's Deed, which was created in the belief that the judgment conveyed title, was meaningless.[211]

5. If you are a judge do not enter orders you have no power to enforce, because they will not receive any full faith and credit from other jurisdictions and probably not even from the courts of your own jurisdiction.[212]

6. If you are a state don't use a statute of another state if it offends the public policy of your state.[213]

7. If you are an F-2 court do not attempt to examine the merits of the F-1 proceedings.[214]

8. If you hold a favorable judgment of an Indian tribal court, don't bother attempting to have it recognized and enforced under full faith and credit. Try comity.[215]

9. If you hold a favorable judgment from a foreign country, don't bother trying to have it recognized and enforced under full faith and credit. Try comity.[216]

---

[211] *Id.* at 7.

[212] Thomas v. Washington Gas Light Co., 448 U.S. 261, 282, 283 (1980); and *Baker by Thomas.,* 522 U.S.at 241. For additional comment about Thomas v. Washington Gas Light Co. *see infra* text accompanying notes 656, 657. 659, 663. For additional comment about Baker by Thomas v. General Motors Corp., *see supra* text accompanying notes 208, 209, and *infra* notes 245, 247, 248, 396, 419, 415, 416, 462, 513, 532, 533, 541, 543-545, 537, 539, 974.

[213] *See* Alaska Packers Ass'n v. Industrial Acc. Comm, 294 U.S. 532, 549, 550 (1935); Pacific Employers Ins. Co. v. Industrial Acc. Comm'n, 306 U.S. 493, 504, 505 (1939).

[214] Hawley v. Donaghue, 116 U.S. 1, 4 (1885); Milliken v. Meyer, 311 U.S. 457,463, 464 (1940); Hospital Underwriting Group, Inc. v. Summit Health, Ltd. 63 F.3d 486, 494, 495 (6th Cir. 1995); Bradley v. Holivay, 918 N.E.2d 166, 168 (Ohio App. 2009); Armtech Ins. Services, Ins. v. Hamilton, 2009 W.L. 498048 (Tex. App. 2009).

[215] *See infra* text accompanying notes 1031-1079.

[216] *See infra* text accompanying notes 1080-1094.

C. Recognition and Enforcement

1. General Statement

In 1839 the U.S. Supreme Court in *McElmoyle v. Cohen*,[217] held that a successful litigant could not take his judgment obtained in F-1 and enforce[218] it by executing on it in some other state. So lawyers had to get an authenticated copy of their judgment,[219] and send it to a lawyer in some other place, with a request to sue on it, using the judgment as a chose-in-action, requesting an F-2 judgment that could be basis of supplementary proceeding, levy and execution, in F-2, because the defendant had assets in F-2, but either no, or insufficient, assets in F-1 upon which to satisfy the F-1 judgment. Then in 1948 the National Conference of Commissioners on Unified Laws and the American Bar Association proposed a new uniform Act – the Uniform Enforcement of Foreign Judgments Act (UEFJA). It proposed legislation which would "streamline" the procedure for obtaining that F-2 judgment.[220] The former procedure using the F-1 judgment as the chose-in-action for the new, F-2 judgment, required a retrial of the F-1 trial. The new proposed uniform act did not complete the objective of saving time and expense - it allowed the judgment debtor to raise certain defenses against the F-1 judgment. That problem was corrected by a 1948 amendment to the UEFJA. It was called the Uniform Enforcement of Foreign Judgments Recognition Act (FMJRA).

In 1946 U.S. Supreme Court Justice John Marshall Harlan, II, wrote in *Banco Nacional de Cuba v. Sabbatino*[221] that "[p]olitical recognition is exclusively a function of the Executive. The possible incongruity of judicial 'recognition,' by

---

[217] 38 U.S. (13 Peter) 312, 325 (1839).

[218] Judicial enforcement of judgments, of course, is entirely different from the enforcement of the laws, rules and regulations of governments. *See* Mullin v. Municipal City of South Bend, 639 N.E. 2d 278, 283 (Ind. 1994).

[219] In general terms an "authenticated" copy means one signed and sealed by the Clerk of the rendering court, and also signed by a judge of that court proclaiming that the Clerk had the authority to do so.

[220] Usually referred to as a "domesticated" or at times an "enrolled" judgment. Some judges equate "domestication" with "recognition." *See* Judge Rodkowski's observation in Mike Smith Pontiac v. Mercedes-Benz of North America, 741 A.2d 462, 472 (Md. Ct. App. 1999).

[221] 376 U.S.398 (1964).

permitting suit, of a government not recognized by the Executive is completely . . . absent when merely diplomatic relations are broken."[222] He was writing about two forms of "recognition" - political and judicial. The Executive of the United States is concerned with the "political recognition" of the existence of other sovereign nations, and their compatibility with our nation. The judiciary of the United States is concerned with the "judicial recognition," about which he wrote - (1) that of permitting suit, in our courts, of a foreign government whether or not recognized by the Executive; and (2) that of a court of this country "recognizing" a judgment of another court (i.e. either federal or state), of this country, or even a court of a foreign nation. This Lexicon is concerned with the second form of judicial recognition. That form of "recognition" is most often considered in conjunction with the "enforcement" of those judgments. That "recognition," and its correlative "enforcement" Are both required to be given "full faith and credit," as that term is referred to in our Constitution and implementing statutes?[223] Of course, in order to be entitled to such recognition and enforcement the F-1 judgment must be "facially valid,"[224] i.e. a final judgment, adjudicating the litigation in a conclusive and definitive manner,[225] by a court of competent jurisdiction.[226]

In 1974 the distinction between the recognition of a judgment and its enforcement was clearly described by U.S. District Judge Pollack in *American Fidelity Fire Ins. Co. v. Paste-Ups Unlimited, Inc.*[227] where it was opined that:

> A foreign judgment is recognized . . . when it is given the same effect that it has in the State where it was rendered with respect to the parties, the subject matter of the action and the issues involved. A foreign judgment is enforced when, in addition to being recognized, a party is given the affirmative relief to which the judgment entitles him. Recognition of a

---

[222] *Id.* at 410, 411.

[223] Society of Lloyd's v. Reinhart , 402 F. 3d 982, 993 (10th Cir. 2005); Baker & McKenzie, Advokkatbyra, v. Thinkstream, Inc. 20 So.3d 1109, 1117 (La. App. 2009).

[224] Centre Equities, Inc. v. Tingley, 106 S.W.3d 143, 149, n.2 (Tex. App. 2003).

[225] Lee v. DeSheney, 457 N.E.2d 504, 607 (Ind. App. 1983); Gamas-Castellamas v. Gamas, 803 N.E. 2d 665, 666 (Ind. 2004).

[226] Brito v. Ryan, 864 A.2d 378, 380 (N.H. 2005).

[227] 368 F. Supp. 219 (S.D.N.Y. 1974).

> judgment is a condition precedent to its enforcement. Restatement (Second) of Conflict of Laws, ch. 5, Topic 2, at 277 (1969).[228]

As Judge Brock wrote in *Sainz v. Sain*:[229]

> A foreign judgment is recognized, as the term is used in the Restatement of this Subject, when it is given the same effect that it has in the state where it was rendered with respect to the parties, the subject matter of the action and the issues involved. A foreign judgment is enforced when, in addition to being recognized, a party is given the affirmative relief to which the judgment entitles him.[230]

In 1992 Judge Hallanan of the United States Court of Appeals for the Fourth Circuit in *Guinness PLC v. Ward*[231] wrote:

> While the goal of reciprocity might arguably not be advanced as far without mandatory enforcement, we nonetheless believe that such goal as well as the principles of comity are still sufficiently served by the fact that judgments which are not enforceable might still be entitled, . . . to recognition; for a finding of recognition establishes that such judgment is conclusive between the parties and will be given *res judicata* and collateral estoppel effect by the recognition court. Additionally maintaining the distinction between recognition and enforceability would also appear to enable courts to more adequately balance the interests of the rendering and recognition courts where such interests are arguably conflicting by allowing the recognition court to both respect principles of comity through recognition of the foreign judgment but yet avoid unnecessarily the subservience of its own laws and public policies otherwise applicable regarding the enforcement of such judgments. Thus, in close cases the ability of a recognition court to recognize a foreign judgment but yet refuse to enforce it might lead to the recognition of greater numbers of

---

[228] *Id.* at, 224.

[229] 245 S.E.2d 372 (N.C. App. 1978). *See infra* text accompanying notes 230, 422, 466, 467, 534, 535, 555-557 for additional decisions dealing with this case.

[230] *Id.* at 375.

[231] 955 F.2d 875 (4th Cir. 1992).

> foreign judgments and correspondingly fewer instances of recognition courts broadly and expansively [denying recognition].[232]

In 2006 District Judge Jenkins in *Richmond v. Wampanoag Tribal Court Cases*[233] wrote:

> [A] party seeking to enforce a federal or state court judgment in a federal or state court in another state or federal district. . . . generally must commence a recognition proceeding or a civil action upon that judgment in a court of the jurisdiction where he seeks its enforcement. Upon formal recognition of the judgment by the latter court, it may then be enforced as a judgment of that court by the officers having the duty to do so.[234]

In 2007 that explanation was further clarified by Tennessee Court of Appeals Judge Koch in *Bauman v. Williams*[235] when he wrote that "recognition and enforcement of a judgment involves a two-step process; 'recognition of a judgment is a condition precedent to its enforcement.'"[236]

In 2008 in *Manco Contracting Co. (W.W.L.) v. Bezdikian,*[237] a case dealing with a judgment from a foreign nation, California Supreme Court Justice Corrigan wrote that:

> There is an analytical difference between *recognition* of a foreign judgment and *enforcement* of that judgment. A foreign judgment must be recognized before it is enforced, making enforcement, perhaps, the most common reason for filing such an action. Of course, recognition may also be sought so that a . . . party may rely on *res judicata* or collateral estoppel principles unrelated to enforcement of a money judgment.[238]

---

232 *Id.* at 889 n.9.

233 431 F. Supp. 2d 1159 (D. Utah 2006).

234 *Id.* at 1175, 1176.

235 2007 W.L. 3375365. (Tenn. App. 2007).

236 *Id.* at *1.

237 85 Cal.Rptr.3d 233 (Cal. 2008).

238 *Id.* at 243.

Of course it must be remembered, as is stated in the Section concerning the exceptions to full faith, and credit,[239] that a dictum has proclaimed that a situation may arise in which the F-2 court must recognize a judgment, but only partially enforce it, i.e. grant full faith and credit to a portion of an F-1 judgment, yet deny full faith and credit to another portion of it. A prime example of a partial enforcement is the judgment which concerns a covenant not to compete, or restrictive covenant, as it is sometime called, where the restriction against competition is enforced only as to certain particulars. *Weiser, LLP v. Coopersmith*[240] is an example.

Mike Smith Pontiac v. Mercedes Benz of North America[241] is a case in which the prevailing plaintiff sought partial enforcement of the F-1 judgment in F-2, but was refused by the F-2 court. In that case Smith obtained a judgment, including federal post-judgment interest, against Mercedes-Benz (hereinafter "M-B") in a Florida based federal court. Smith, under Maryland's Uniform Enforcement of Foreign Judgments Act (UEFJA), domesticated the judgment there. Within days, however M-B paid the judgment and secured from Smith a Satisfaction of Judgment. Smith thereupon took the position that since Maryland's post-judgment interest was payable at a higher rate than federal post-interest, which M-B paid, he was entitled to a judgment for the differential in interest. His thesis was premised upon the theory that the Maryland, domesticated judgment was a new (ostensibly state) judgment that differed from the Florida based federal judgment. The Maryland Court of Appeals did not agree. It reasoned that the UEFJA was merely a "streamlined" method of obtaining a new judgment for enforcement purposes. That new judgment, while it may be different from the F-1 judgment in form, is not different in essence. Satisfaction of the F-1 judgment satisfies the F-2 judgment *in toto*. Smith would not be permitted to collect a certain amount of interest from the first judgment, and subsequently be allowed to collect a different amount of interest from the second judgment. Before concluding its Opinion the court pronounced a dictum to the effect that there is a difference between recognition and enforcement, in at least one regard, which involves a certain amount of partial enforcement. The F-2 court "may . . . inquire into post-judgment defenses in order to determine the extent to which the F-1 judgment is

---

[239] *See infra* text accompanying notes 258-463.

[240] 902 N.Y.S.2d 74 (N.Y. App. Div. 2010).

[241] 741 A.2d 462 (Md. Ct. App. 1999). *See infra* text accompanying notes 240-244. for additional reference to this case.

enforceable,"[242] and added that "M-B was entitled to all defenses against enforcement as would a judgment debtor under a judgment originally rendered in Maryland."[243]

Apparently finding no defenses to which M-B could assert, the court held that:

> [W]e hold, as a matter . . . of Maryland defense to a Maryland judgment, that satisfaction of a money judgment in a sister, judgment-rendering state, satisfies a Maryland enforcing judgment, and satisfaction in a sister, judgment-enforcing state satisfies a Maryland rendered . . . judgment, without regard to whether there is a post-judgment interest differential and without regard to the direction in which any differential might run. There is no unfairness in a judgment creditor's receiving the rate of post-judgment interest which a judgment carries either in the forum where the judgment was obtained or in the forum to which the creditor took the judgment for enforcement. Further, where the judgment-rendering state's post-judgment interest rate is less than Maryland's, the rule for which Smith contends encourages forum shopping. Creditors holding foreign judgments that carry a lower rate of post-judgment interest than do Maryland judgments would be encouraged immediately to record their judgments in Maryland in the hope that, even after the judgment has been satisfied in the judgment-rendering state, some asset of the debtor might be in, or be brought into, Maryland on which execution could be had for the post-judgment interest differential.[244]

In *Baker by Thomas v. General Motors Corp*[245] Justice Ruth Bader Ginsburg said, for a unanimous Court, that:

> Full faith and credit . . . does not mean that States must adopt the practices of other States regarding the time, manner, and mechanisms for enforcing judgments. Enforcement measures do not travel with the sister state judgment as preclusive effects do;[246] such measures remain subject to the

---

242 *Id.* at 472, 473.

243 *Id.* at 474.

244 *Id.* at 476.

245 522 U.S. 222 (1998).

246 *See supra* Subsection I, B. 3., texts accompanying notes 147-156.

> evenhanded control of forum law. *See McElmoyle ex rel. Bailey v. Cohen,* 13 Pet. 312, 325, 10 L.Ed. 177 (1839) (judgment may be enforced only as "laws [of enforcing forum] may permit"); see also Restatement (Second) of Conflict of Laws § 99 (1969) ("The local law of the forum determines the methods by which a judgment of another state is enforced.").[247]

> Justice Ginsburg added:

> As to judgments, the full faith and credit obligation is exacting. A final judgment in one State, if rendered by a court with adjudicatory authority over the subject matter and persons governed by the judgment, qualifies for recognition throughout the land. *See, e.g., Matsushita Elec. Industrial Co. v. Epstein,* 516 U.S. 367, 373, 116 S.Ct. 873, 877, 134 L.Ed.2d 6. A court may be guided by the forum State's "public policy" in determining the *law* applicable to a controversy, see *Nevada v. Hall,* 440 U.S. 410, 421-424, 99 S.Ct. 1182, 1188-1190, 59 L.Ed.2d 416, but this Court's decisions support no roving "public policy exception" to the full faith and credit due *judgments, see, e.g., Estin v. Estin,* 334 U.S. 541, 546, 68 S.Ct. 1213, 1217, 92 L.Ed. 1561. In assuming the existence of a ubiquitous "public policy exception" permitting one State to resist recognition of another's judgment, the District Court in the Bakers' action misread this Court's precedent.[248]

In *Adar v. Smith*[249] Judge Weiner clarified Justice Ginsburg's reference, in *Baker*, to the full faith and credit obligation being "exacting" by the following words:

> [T]he duty of recognition that is owed is "exacting," however, it is not absolute. For example, even though the forum state may not refuse to enforce the judgment of the adjudicating state, the forum state is not required to substitute the adjudicating state's provisions for the *enforcement* of judgments for their own. The substantive issues adjudicated in that state are afforded full faith and credit; within particular

---

[247] *Id.* at 235.

[248] *Id.* at 223.

[249] 597 F.3d 697 (5th Cir. 2010).

bounds, the provisions for enforcing that judgment are determined by the law of the forum state.[250]

There are three uniform Acts which have extended the theory of giving foreign judgments full faith and credit. The Uniform Enforcement of Foreign Judgment Act (UEFJA) has been in effect since 1948.[251] The Uniform Foreign Money Judgments Recognition Act (UFMJRA) has been in effect since 1962.[252] The Uniform Foreign-Country Money Judgments Recognition Act, (UFCMJRA), has been in effect since 2005.[253]

2. The Uniform Foreign Money Judgments Recognition Act (UFMJRA)[254]

§ 1. [Definitions].
As used in this Act:

(1) "foreign state" means any governmental unit other than the United States, or any state, district, commonwealth, territory, insular possession thereof, or the Panama Canal Zone, the Trust Territory of the Pacific Islands, or the Ryukyu Islands;

(2) "foreign judgment" means any judgment of a foreign state granting or denying recovery of a sum of money, other than a judgment for taxes, a fine or other penalty, or a judgment for support in matrimonial or family matters;

§ 2. [Applicability].
This Act applies to any foreign judgment that is final and conclusive and enforceable where rendered even though an appeal therefrom is pending or it is subject to appeal.

---

[250] *Id,* at 708.

[251] *See infra* text accompanying note 255.

[252] *See infra* text accompanying note 257.

[253] *See infra* text accompanying note 1091.

[254] As of Jan. 15, 2012, the District of Columbia, the Virgin Islands and the following 19 states have adopted the Uniform Foreign Money Judgments Recognition Act (UFMJRA): Alaska, Connecticut, Delaware, Florida, Georgia, Illinois, Iowa, Maine, Maryland, Massachusetts, Minnesota, Missouri, New Jersey, New York, North Dakota ,Ohio, Pennsylvania, Texas and Virginia.

§ 3. [Recognition and Enforcement].
Except as provided in section 4, a foreign judgment meeting the requirements of section 2 is conclusive between the parties to the extent that it grants or denies recovery of a sum of money. The foreign judgment is enforceable in the same manner as the judgment of a sister state which is entitled to full faith and credit.

§ 4. [Grounds for Non-recognition].

(a) A foreign judgment is not conclusive if

(1) the judgment was rendered under a system which does not provide impartial tribunals or procedures compatible with the requirements of due process of law;

(2) the foreign court did not have personal jurisdiction over the defendant; or

(3) the foreign court did not have jurisdiction over the subject matter.

(b) A foreign judgment need not be recognized if

(1) the defendant in the proceedings in the foreign court did not receive notice of the proceedings in sufficient time to enable him to defend;

(2) the judgment was obtained by fraud;

(3) the [cause of action] [claim for relief] on which the judgment is based is repugnant to the public policy of this state;

(4) the judgment conflicts with another final and conclusive judgment;

(5) the proceeding in the foreign court was contrary to an agreement between the parties under which the dispute in question was to be settled otherwise than by proceedings in that court; or (6) in the case of jurisdiction based only on personal service, the foreign court was a seriously inconvenient forum for the trial of the action.

§ 5. [Personal Jurisdiction].

(a) The foreign judgment shall not be refused recognition for lack of personal jurisdiction if

(1) the defendant was served personally in the foreign state;

(2) the defendant voluntarily appeared in the proceedings, other than for the purpose of protecting property seized or threatened with seizure in the proceedings or of contesting the jurisdiction of the court over him;

(3) the defendant prior to the commencement of the proceedings had agreed to submit to the jurisdiction of the foreign court with respect to the subject matter involved;

(4) the defendant was domiciled in the foreign state when the proceedings were instituted, or, being a body corporate had its principal place of business, was incorporated, or had otherwise acquired corporate status, in the foreign state;

(5) the defendant had a business office in the foreign state and the proceedings in the foreign court involved a [cause of action] [claim for relief] arising out of business done by the defendant through that office in the foreign state; or

(6) the defendant operated a motor vehicle or airplane in the foreign state and the proceedings involved a [cause of action] [claim for relief] arising out of such operation.

(b) The courts of this state may recognize other bases of jurisdiction.

§ 6. [Stay in Case of Appeal].

If the defendant satisfies the court either that an appeal is pending or that he is entitled and intends to appeal from the foreign judgment, the court may stay the proceedings until the appeal has been determined or until the expiration of a period of time sufficient to enable the defendant to prosecute the appeal.

§ 7. [Savings Clause].

This Act does not prevent the recognition of a foreign judgment in situations not covered by this Act.

§ 8. [Uniformity of Interpretation].

This Act shall be so construed as to effectuate its general purpose to make uniform the law of those states which enact it.

§ 9. [Short Title].

This Act may be cited as the Uniform Foreign Money-Judgments Recognition Act.

§ 10. Repealed.

[This section of the Act simply instruct the Legislature to insert the identification of the statutes which are repealed].

§ 11. [Time of Taking Effect].

This Act shall take effect _______.

3. The Uniform Enforcement of Foreign Judgments Act (UEFJA)[255]

In *W & T, Inc. v. Ham*[256] Judge Cottrell wrote that this statute was:

> [I]ntended to put the full faith and credit clause efficiently and uniformly into operation. Under the Act, if a copy of an authenticated foreign judgment is filed in a circuit or chancery clerk's office, then the clerk is to treat the foreign judgment in the same manner as a judgment rendered in this state.[257]

It provisions are as follows:

§ 1. Definition.
In this Act "foreign judgment" means any judgment, decree, or order of a court of the United States or of any other court which is entitled to full faith and credit in this state.

§ 2. Filing and Status of Foreign Judgments.
A copy of any foreign judgment authenticated in accordance with the act of Congress or the statutes of this state may be filed in the office of the Clerk of any [District Court of any city or county] of this state. The Clerk shall treat the foreign judgment in the same manner as a judgment of the [District Court of any city or county] of this state. A judgment so filed has the same effect and is subject to the same procedures, defenses and proceedings for reopening, vacating, or staying as a judgment of a [District Court of any city or county] of this state and may be enforced or satisfied in like manner.

§ 3. Notice of Filing.
(a) At the time of the filing of the foreign judgment, the judgment creditor or his lawyer shall make and file with the Clerk of Court an affidavit setting forth the

---

[255] This Act has been described as "implementing" the Full Faith and Credit Clause. *See* Ruff v. Splica, Inc., 923 N.E.2d 1250, 1252 (Ill. App. 2010). As of Jan. 15, 2012, all states have adopted the Uniform Enforcement of Foreign Judgments Act (UEFJA), with the exception of California, Indiana, Massachusetts and Vermont.

[256] 2009 W.L. 225256 (Tenn. App. 2009).

[257] *Id.* at *2.

name and last known post office address of the judgment debtor, and the judgment creditor.

(b) Promptly upon the filing of the foreign judgment and the affidavit, the Clerk shall mail notice of the filing of the foreign judgment to the judgment debtor at the address given and shall make a note of the mailing in the docket. The notice shall include the name and post office address of the judgment creditor and the judgment creditor's lawyer, if any, in this state. In addition, the judgment creditor may mail a notice of the filing of the judgment to the judgment debtor and may file proof of mailing with the Clerk. Lack of mailing notice of filing by the Clerk shall not affect the enforcement proceedings if proof of mailing by the judgment creditor has been filed.

(c) No execution or other process for enforcement of a foreign judgment filed hereunder shall issue until [ ] days after the date the judgment is filed.

(a) If the judgment debtor shows the [District Court of any city or county] that an appeal from the foreign judgment is pending or will be taken, or that a stay of execution has been granted, the court shall stay enforcement of the foreign judgment until the appeal is concluded, the time for appeal expires, or the stay of execution expires or is vacated, upon proof that the judgment debtor has furnished the security for the satisfaction of the judgment required by the state in which it was rendered.

(b) If the judgment debtor shows the [District Court of any city or county] any ground upon which enforcement of a judgment of any [District Court of any city or county] of this state would be stayed, the court shall stay enforcement of the foreign judgment for an appropriate period, upon requiring the same security for satisfaction of the judgment which is required in this state.

§ 5. Fees.

Any person filing a foreign judgment shall pay to the Clerk of Court ____________ dollars. Fees for docketing, transcription or other enforcement proceedings shall be as provided for judgments of the [District Court of any city or county of this state].

§ 6. Optional Procedure.

The right of a judgment creditor to bring an action to enforce his judgment instead of proceeding under this Act remains unimpaired.

§ 7. Uniformity of Interpretation.

This Act shall be so interpreted and construed as to effectuate its general purpose to make uniform the law of those states which enact it.

§ 8. Short Title.
This Act may be cited as the Uniform Enforcement of Foreign Judgments Act.

§ 9. Repealed.
[This section of the Act simply instruct the Legislature to insert the identification of the statutes which are repealed].

§ 10. Taking Effect.
This Act takes effect on ____________.

D. The Exceptions to Full, Faith and Credit

1. Introductory Statement

A jurisdiction, whether it be a state or the federal government, may perform a certain transaction, as an example, the entry of a judgment. The person performing that transaction probably thinks that it is performed properly, but if it is not, that transaction may be denied full faith and credit by some other jurisdiction, whether that be another state, or the federal government. There are other transactions that while they are performed properly have been judicially proclaimed to be not entitled to full faith and credit. These are the transaction known as the "exceptions" to full faith and credit. Those transactions which cause them to be denied full faith and credit are not specified in any statute. They have been formulated by judges, i.e. judicially constructed, and they absolutely prevent the transaction from being accorded full faith and credit; they are listed below in Section B[258] of this chapter.

San Remo Hotel, L.P. v. City and County of San Francisco, Cal.[259] exemplifies the procedure by which the exceptions are made, and ones which the

---

[258] Some courts opine that there are far fewer exceptions to full faith and credit than are listed in section B. As an example the court in Ice Stores, Inc. v. Holmes, 2008 W.L. 4981077 at * 4 (Tenn. Ct. App. 2008) said that there were only two exceptions, e.g. (1) lack of personal jurisdiction and (2) lack of subject matter jurisdiction. As displayed by this lexicon, that statement is grossly incorrect. See also text accompanying notes 41, 265, 311, 962 and 962 for other considerations of this case.

[259] 545 U.S. 323 (2005). *See infra* text accompanying notes 260-262, considering this case.

courts refuse to make. Hotel owners were incensed with fees being charged them by the City of San Francisco. Before they could present their federal "taking" claims under the Fifth Amendment the federal court held that those claims were required to be made ripe, by preventing state claims in state court. When the federal court reviewed the claims that had been "ripened" in state court, it determined that there were certain issues the hotel owners were precluded from rearguing, because of rulings in the state courts. When the case arrived in the U.S. Supreme Court the owners asked the court to create an exception to full faith and credit requirements under 28 U.S.C. § 1738 because they argued that it was unfair to impose upon them rulings by a state court which they were required to enter. The Court denied their request. Justice John Paul Stevens, in the Opinion of the Court, said initially that the owners' argument "assumes that courts may simply create exceptions to 28 U.S.C. § 1738 wherever courts deem them appropriate."[260] He added:

> Even conceding, *arguendo,* the laudable policy goal of making federal forums available to deserving litigants, we have expressly rejected petitioners' view. 'Such a fundamental departure from traditional rules of preclusion, enacted into federal law, can be justified only if plainly stated by Congress.' (Citation omitted). Our cases have therefore made plain that 'an exception to § 1738 will not be recognized unless a later statute contains an express or implied partial repeal.' (Citation omitted). Even when the plaintiff's resort to state court is involuntary and the federal interest in denying finality is robust, we have held that Congress must 'clearly manifest' its intent to depart from § 1738.' (Citation omitted).[261]
>
> The same concerns animate our decision here. Congress has not expressed any intent to exempt from the full faith and credit statute federal takings claims. Consequently, we apply our normal assumption that the weighty interests in finality and comity trump the interest in giving losing litigants access to an additional appellate tribunal.[262]

---

[260] *Id.* at 344. Exceptions to full faith and credit must be justly made and proved by clear and convincing evidence. Mindus Metal, Inc. v. Oilfield Motor & Control, Inc., 132 S.W. 3d 477, 485 (Tex. App. 2004).

[261] *Id.* at 345.

[262] *Id.*

There is a type of transaction which is not prohibited from being enforced, but is not required to receive full faith and credit. Those transactions are listed in subsection C. of this chapter.

2. Matters Which Must Not Be Given Full Faith and Credit

Because they are judicially determined, the "exceptions" to full faith and credit could be done away with, or repealed, but that procedure has seldom been accomplished. The U.S. Supreme Court has, rather reservedly, opined in *Kremer v. Chemical Const. Corp.*[263] that the exceptions will remain "unless a later statute contains an express or implied partial repeal."[264] In the following description of the various exceptions to the requirement of full faith and credit the symbol "F-1" refers to a court of a foreign jurisdiction which has rendered an order that is sought to be recognized, or recognized and enforced in a court of another jurisdiction, designated by the symbol "F-2." The symbol "S-1" refers to a jurisdiction, which though it does not have a court order sort to be recognized or recognized and enforced has a statute or record sought to be recognized or recognized and enforced in a court of another jurisdiction, which is designated by the symbol "FS-2."

The "exceptions" are ones in which:

(1) the F-1 court lacked subject-matter jurisdiction;[265]

Let us first consider the subject-matter jurisdiction of the courts. There are two criterions for the determination of a court's jurisdiction, federal or state. The first is the type of proceeding the court is asked to handle, e.g. award a sum of money for wrong done the plaintiff by the defendant, probate a Last Will and Testament, dissolve a marriage, and so forth. The second, far less complicated than the first, is the "amount in controversy," i.e. the amount of money damages is being sought by the plaintiff. The jurisdiction of federal courts is specified by the federal

---

263 456 U.S. 466 (1982).

264 *Id.* at 468.

265 D'Arcy v. Ketchum, 52 U.S. 165, 176 (1850); Boswell's Lessee v. Otis, 52 U.S. 336, 350, 351 (1850); Tufares v. Wright, 644 P.2d 522, 525 (N. Mex. 1982); Ice Stores, Inc. v. Holmes, 2003 W.L. 4981077 at *4 (Tenn. Ct. App. 2008). See text accompanying notes 41, 258, 311, and 962 for other considerations of this case.

constitution and statutes which the Constitution gives Congress the power to enact.[266] State legislatures specify the judicial power of their courts and sometimes give certain courts "general jurisdiction," which means that those courts have jurisdiction of all justiciable issues not exclusively vested in other courts.[267] Black's Law Dictionary defines "amount in controversy" as "[t]he damages claimed or relief demanded by the injured party in a lawsuit. For a federal court to have diversity jurisdiction, the amount in controversy must exceed $75,000. 28 USCA § 1332(a). — Also termed *jurisdictional amount*; *matter in controversy*."[268] The major prohibition of courts' jurisdiction are the following:

a. All Courts

No court has subject-matter jurisdiction when the statute of limitations on the claim has run; such situation is known as being "time barred."[269] Courts are forbidden by the First Amendment to the federal constitution from considering ecclesiastic problems,[270] and religious governance except under limited circumstanced.[271] Courts are forbidden by the Eleventh Amendment to the U.S. Constitution from commencing or prosecuting "any suit in law or equity . . . against one of the United States by Citizens of another State, or by Citizens or Subjects of any foreign State."[272] In cases where the plaintiff is seeking an award

---

[266] Hatcher v. Lowe's Home Centers, Inc., 2010 W.L. 2473804 at *1 (E.D. Va. 2010).

[267] Rita Spencer *et al.* v. Kentucky Tax Bill Servicing, Inc., 2010 W.L. 2428393 at *1 (Ky. App. 2010).

[268] *See* Black's Law Dictionary. 8th Edition. (2004).

[269] Sylla v. First Franklin Financial Corp., 2010 W.L. 1710948, at *3 (D. Md. 2010).

[270] Redwing v. Catholic Bishop for the Diocese of Memphis, 2010 W.L. 2106222 at *8 (Tenn. Ct. App. 2010); Protestant Episcopal Church In the Diocese of Virginia v. Truro Church, 2010 W.L. 2303389 (Va. 2010).

[271] Shaeriff v. Rahman, 787 N.E. 2d 72, 76 (Ohio App. 2003).

[272] *Ex Parte* Young, 209 U.S. 123, 155, 156 (1908) involved a habeas corpus proceeding brought by the Minnesota Attorney General for having been punished for his actions of having presented a mandamus action due to Minnesota allegedly having enacted and prosecuted an unconstitutional statute The U.S. Supreme Court held that the action against the state official did not offend the Eleventh Amendment because, in essence, the proceeding was against the state official in his individual capacity, and that he lost sovereign immunity under the Eleventh Amendment when he participated in the enactment

of money that person must allege the "mount in controversy," which is usually accepted by the court unless the amount stated is patently questionable or the defendant questions it.[273]

b. Federal Courts

"The district courts shall not enjoin, suspend or restrain the assessment, levy or collection of any tax under State law where a plain, speedy and efficient remedy may be had in the courts of such State."[274] "The district courts shall not have jurisdiction of any civil action by or against any corporation upon the ground that it was incorporated by or under an Act of Congress, unless the United States is the owner of more than one-half of its capital stock."[275] "A district court shall not have jurisdiction of a civil action in which any party, by assignment or otherwise, has been improperly or collusively made or joined to invoke the jurisdiction of such court."[276] "A court of the United States may not grant an injunction to stay proceedings in a State court except as expressly authorized by Act of Congress, or where necessary in aid of its jurisdiction, or to protect or effectuate its judgments."[277] Under the Rooker-Feldman doctrine, lower federal courts lack jurisdiction to review the rulings of a state court.[278] In *Ankenbrandt v. Richards*[279] the U.S. Supreme Court announced that "divorce, alimony, and child custody decrees remain outside federal jurisdictional bounds" and recognized "the special proficiency developed by state tribunals . . . in handling issues that arise in the

---

of an unconstitutional statute. Many courts frowned upon the decision, labeling it as having created a "fiction."

[273] *See* Walco Int'l, Inc. v. CSR Summit, Inc. 2010 W.L. 2331843 at *3 (N.D. Tex. 2010); Firemans' Fund Ins. Co v. Workers Compensation Appeals Board, 104 Cal. Rptr.3d 641, 650 (Cal. App. 2010).

[274] 28 U.S.C. § 1341.

[275] 28 U.S.C. § 1349.

[276] 28 U.S.C. § 1359.

[277] 28 U.S.C. § 2283.

[278] Rooker v. Fidelity Trust Co., 263 U.S. 413 (1923); District of Columbia Court of Appeals v. Feldman, 460 U.S. 462 (1983).

[279] 504 U.S. 689, 703-04 (1992).

granting of [divorce, alimony, and child custody] decrees."[280] In *Markham v. Allen*[281] the U.S. Supreme Court announced the "probate exception" for federal courts in the following words: "federal court has no jurisdiction to probate a will or administer an estate, the reason being that the equity jurisdiction conferred by the Judiciary Act of 1789, . . . which is that of the English Court of Chancery in 1789, did not extend to probate matters."[282] In *Kalb v. Feurstein*[283] the U.S. Supreme Court held that where Congress gave Bankruptcy Courts jurisdiction of certain subjects state courts lacked jurisdiction of those subjects.[284]

c. State Courts

It was opined in *Landreth v. Malik* [285] that state courts' jurisdiction is limited to the type of proceedings specified by state legislatures.[286] In *In re Estate of Gardiner*[287] the Supreme Court of Kansas held that Kansas courts had no jurisdiction to give full faith and credit to a birth certificate amended by Wisconsin to show that the subject was a female rather than a male in order to solemnize a marriage between a man and a transexual, because the state's marriage statutes proclaimed that a marriage is a procedure between a man and a woman.[288]

State statutes designating the jurisdiction of state courts might be abrogated by federal authorities preempting the subject matter of the state statute. Either Congress or the U.S. Supreme Court can preempt a subject. In *Int'l*

---

280 This so-called "domestic relations exception" was again approved in Marshall v. Marshall, 547 U.S. 293, 308 (2006).

281 326 U.S. 490 (1946).

282 *Id.* at 494.

283 305 U.S. 433 (1940).

284 *Id.*. at 444.

285 221 P.3d 1265 (Nev. 2009).

286 *Id.* at 1267.

287 42 P.3d 120 (Kan 2002).

288 *Id.* at 126. The issue in the case, which the state Supreme Court held that it was a legislative matter to resolve, was whether the statute's reference to gender of the parties referred to gender at birth, or gender post operative procedures.

Longshoremaens Ass'n v. Davis[289] the U.S. Supreme Court held that Congress by enacting the National Labor Relations Act (N.L.R.A.), preempted state labor law.[290] In *San Diego Bldg. Trade Council v. Garmon*[291] the U.S. Supreme Court preempted portions of the National Labor Relations Act so that henceforth federal courts rather than state courts will deal exclusively with activities that the Act protects, prohibits, or arguably attempts to protect or prohibit.[292] Because of the federal Constitution and implementing statutes[293] state courts do not have jurisdiction to hear bankruptcy cases.[294]

Unlike the above subjects of state court jurisdiction the area of states' jurisdiction dealing with child support and custody/visitation privileges the impact of a plethora of federal statutes and uniform Acts makes the subject-matter jurisdiction of state courts in these area extremely difficult to define. There follows a recitation of some of the more often pursued litigation in those areas.[295]

i. Custody Orders

The principal federal statute *vis-à-vis* custody of children 28 U.S.C. § 1738A, the Parental Kidnapping Prevention Act (PKPA), and the principal uniform Acts are the Uniform Child Custody Jurisdiction Act (UCCJA) and the Uniform Child Custody Jurisdiction Enforcement Act (UCCJEA).

---

[289] 476 U.S. 380 (1986).

[290] *Id.* at 398.

[291] 359 U.S. 236 (1959).

[292] *Id* at 245. *See also* Chamber of Commerce of the U.S. v. Brown, 554 U.S. 60 (2008).

[293] Notably Title 11 of the United States Code.

[294] U.S. Const. Art I, § 8, cl. 4 gave Congress the power to establish uniform laws on "the subject of Bankruptcies throughout the United States." Congress has followed this directive by enacting Chapter 11 of Title 28, U.S. Code, providing for Bankruptcy Courts and their Judges, who handle bankruptcy matters to the exclusion of the states.

[295] *See infra* text accompanying notes 296-301, 804-865 for additional material dealing with child custody, and text accompanying notes 302-310, 867-907 for additional material dealing with child support.

In *Tufares v. Wright*[296] three courts were involved. The first was the New Mexico court which granted a divorce and awarded custody. The jurisdiction of this court would have continued for the duration of the children's needs, but it was lost by the father having kept custody of them for a year in Utah, hence the second (Utah), court, and the third court, a New Mexico appellate court which held that its trial court could not modify a Utah judgment which modified the original New Mexico judgment. [297]

In *Rainbow v. Ransom*[298] the parents were divorced in their home state of Hawai'i, but thereafter the mother and child moved to Maine, where she filed for a judicial determination of parental rights and responsibilities. The father took the position that Hawai'i, as the home state, had jurisdiction, rather than Maine. The two judges conferred telephonically, and agreed that technically Hawai'i had jurisdiction, but that it would be more "appropriate" to try the parental issues in Maine. The Hawaiian judge, therefore, dismissed the father's proceedings which the father had commenced in Hawai'i.[299]

In *Ex parte Pierce*[300] the married couple moved from California, where they had lived, and settled in Alabama, where their child was born. Shortly after that event the mother and infant moved to Colorado, the husband remaining in Alabama. The wife sued for divorce and custody of the child in Colorado. Two weeks later the father sought custody from an Alabama court. During a telephone conference between the Alabama and Colorado judges and the parties, the judges agreed that the jurisdiction of the court to decide the custody issue should be governed by the UCCJEA, but the infant had not lived in either state for the UCCJEA's "home state" provisions to apply. They tentatively agreed that by virtue of the mother having filed first, Colorado should proceed. The Colorado judge, however, not being certain of the Colorado law upon the facts said that he would defer to the Alabama judge's opinion as to which state would make the most convenient forum. The Alabama judge decided that it would be no more

---

[296] 644 P.2d 522 (N. Mex. 1982).

[297] *Id.* at 523.

[298] 990.A.2d 535 (Me. 2010). *See infra* text accompanying notes 299, 858, 859 for additional cases considering this case.

[299] *Id.* at 536.

[300] 2010 W.L. 1740001 (Ala. Civ. App. 2010). *See infra* text accompanying notes 301, 860, 861 for further consideration of this case.

inconvenient for the mother to attend court in Alabama, than for the father to attend court in Colorado.[301]

ii. Support Orders.

The principal federal statute *vis-à-vis* support of children is 28 U.S.C. § 1738B, the Full Faith and Credit for Child Support Orders Act, (FFCCSOA), and the principal uniform Act is the Uniform Interstate Family Support Act (UIFSA) which was promulgated to improve the handling of problems found with the Uniform Reciprocal Enforcement of Support Act (URESA) and the Revised Uniform Reciprocal Enforcement of Support Act.[302]

In *In re Scott*[303] Massachusetts entered the initial child support. When New Hampshire modified it pursuant to the UIFSA, as the state with the greater interest, it became the "issuing state." Hence New Hampshire continued with jurisdiction over support concerns with which it was permitted to use its own substantive law.[304]

In *Evans v. Mississippi Dept. of Human Resources*[305] the child's mother and father were divorced in Louisiana, but subsequently the father moved to Mississippi due to employment opportunities. He petitioned in Mississippi for a modification of the child support payments, but the Mississippi court proclaimed that it did not have jurisdiction of the cause because Louisiana retained jurisdiction.[306]

---

[301] *Id.* at *9.

[302] "Under URESA, a state had jurisdiction to establish, vacate, or modify an obligor's support obligation even when that obligation had been created in another jurisdiction. . . . UIFSA was designed to correct this problem." Lacarrubba v. Lacarrubba, 688 S.E.2d 769, 774 (N.C. App. 2010). See infra text accompanying notes , 873, 899, 900 for additional consideration of Lacarrubba v. Lacarrubba

[303] 2010 W.L. 2196476 (N.H. 2010).

[304] *Id.* at *5.

[305] 2010 W.L. 2163809 (Miss. App. 2010).

[306] *Id.* at ** 304

In *Highfill v. Moody*[307] the court pointed out that the parties by stipulation may change the jurisdiction of the court called upon to modify a child support award.[308]

In *State v. Peteet*[309] the court made it clear that Ohio, which issued a child support order continued to have jurisdiction even though the parent ordered to make the payments changed her domicile to Louisiana.[310]

> (2) the F-1 court lacked personal jurisdiction over the defendant,[311] (unless the court is simply granting a dissolution of the marriage which existed between the defendant and the plaintiff[312]), or an indispensable party.[313]

Personal (*in personam*) jurisdiction is far more complicated than is subject-matter jurisdiction. Personal jurisdiction may be acquired by a court over a defendant by the defendant walking into the courtroom and informing the judge

---

[307] 2010 W.L. 2075698 (Tenn. Ct. App. 2010). *See infra* text accompanying notes 308, 848-855, 857 for further reference to this case.

[308] *Id.* at *5.

[309] 2010 W.L. 1909588 (La. App. 2010).

[310] *Id.* at *3.

[311] As has been stated by the U.S. Supreme Court, "a judgment in personam directing execution to issue against petitioner, and thus purporting to cut off all available defenses, could not be rendered on any theory of the state's power over him, without some form of notice by personal or substituted service." *See* Griffin v. Griffin 327 U.S. 220, 228 (1946). *See also* Baker & McKenzie, Advokatbyra v. Thinkstream, Inc., 20 So. 2d 1109, 1119 (La. App. 2009); Citibank, N.A. v. Soto, 2010 W.L. 2106087 at *4 (Conn. Super. 2010); Ice Stores, Inc. v. Holmes, 2003 W.L. 4981077 at *4 (Tenn. Ct. App. 2008). It should be remembered that personal jurisdiction is presumed when a foreign judgment appears on its face to be a record of a court of general jurisdiction, Law Firm of Paul L. Erickson, P.A. v. Boykin, 681 S.E.2d 575, 577 (S.C.2008).

[312] Williams v. North Carolina, 317 U.S. 287, 303 (1942). *See* text accompanying notes 45, 50, 51, 724, and 728-737 for further discussion of Williams, I.

[313] Hanson v. Denckla, 357 U.S. 235, 256 (1958) (the court finding that Delaware was correct in refusing to grant a Florida judgment full faith and credit concerning a controversy about trust property where the Florida court did not have personal jurisdiction over the trusts or the trustee).

that she or he agrees to be subject to the jurisdiction of the court over her or him;[314] or by authorizing her or his attorney in the case[315] to file with the court a written statement to that effect.[316] Otherwise a defendant must be "served by process."[317] If a plaintiff is seeking a personal judgment[318] the surest way in which to get personal service over a defendant is to have an official of the court or a certified process server hand the defendant in the territorial limits of the court a summons issued by the court, together with a true copy of the plaintiff's Complaint. This "in-hand" process was approved by the United States Supreme Court in *Pennoyer v. Neff.*[319] The territorial limits requirement was a holdover from the days when the colonies, eventually to become states, were true sovereigns. With society increasing in its mobility a procedure had to be crafted for serving a defendant outside the territorial limits of the court. Hence the development of "substituted service," in order to acquire personal jurisdiction over a defendant who cannot be found in the geographical limits of the forum for the application of in-hand service. Substituted service[320] takes many forms provided by the various Rules of Civil Procedure, e.g. publishing notice of the filing the suit in a newspaper, leaving the papers with a member of defendant's household of a certain age, or a responsible person in defendant's office, registered or certified mail, mailing the papers to the Secretary of State or an agent registered by the defendant, nailing copies to the papers on the door of defendant's last known address and mailing the same to that address. Justice Oliver Wendell Holmes in *McDonald v. Mabee*[321] observed that "substituted service" complied with due process and "fair play."[322]

---

[314] *In re* R.T.J.N., 2009 W.L. 3763782 at *2 (Tex. App. 2009). *See infra* text accompanying notes 922-924 for further consideration of this case.

[315] Usually referred to as the "attorney of record."

[316] A non-personal defendant may accomplish the same objective by appointing someone to do the same thing.

[317] Service by process is covered by Rules of Civil Procedure of the federal government for cases in federal court, and by state Rules of Civil Procedure for cases in state court.

[318] A personal judgment means that the defendant is personally liable for the orders imposed upon her, him or it, so that those assets which are at least partially unencumbered may be used to satisfy the obligations imposed by the court.

[319] 95 U.S. 714 (1877).

[320] It is sometimes referred to as "constructive service." or "conspicuous service."

[321] 243 U.S. 90 (1917).

[322] *Id.* at 91, 92.

Eventually substituted service was permitted to be applied in order to achieve personal service on people who were domiciled within the forum's territorial boundaries, but were temporarily not living there, or could not be located within those boundaries.[323]

In *Milliken v. Meyer*[324] Meyer was a resident of Wyoming, but not living there at the time a suit was filed against him by Milliken, so substituted service was used. Later litigation was commenced in Colorado to enforce the Wyoming judgment. The Colorado trial court found that service was proper, but the Colorado Supreme Court overruled, but not on the issue of service – on what it considered an incorrect ruling of the Wyoming court on the facts. Justice William O. Douglas writing the Opinion of the Court, reversed the Colorado court for considering the merits of the Wyoming judgment, and added that the substituted service in Colorado, was proper even if Meyer was a resident of Wyoming, but temporarily living elsewhere.[325] He specified that service of process, whatever form it takes, must be such as "not to offend notions of fair play and substantial justice."[326]

[323] Substituted service effects personal service as in-hand service. *See* Sheldon v. Fettig, 893 P 2d 1136, 1138 (Wash. App. 1995). Some states have statutes which permit substituted service on the Secretary of State if the defendant cannot be found for in-hand service where the defendant negligently drove upon the state's roadways. *See* Martin v. Triol, 847 P.2d 471, 479 (Wash. 1993). An Oklahoma court has indicated that certain statutes permitting substituted service on state officials is to comply with due process requirements. *See* Shamblin v. Beasley, 967 P.2d 1200, 11208 (Okla. 1998). Some decisions have indicated that the purpose of substituted service is merely to give the defendant notice of the pending litigation. *See* Shurman v. Atlantic Mortg. & Inv. Corp., 795 So.2d 952, 954 (Fla. 2001); Lovely v. Trembley, 2008 W.L. 4514148 at *2 (Conn. Super. 2008).

[324] 311 U.S. 457 (1940).

[325] *Id.* at 463. Douglas wrote that "the authority of a state over one of its citizens is not terminated by the mere fact of his absence of the state," adding that if the defendant was living in the forum state, but could not be located there substituted service by leaving the papers at his last known address within the state was acceptable. *Id.*

[326] *Id.* at 463. the phraseology used in International Shoe – *see infra* text accompanying notes 327-330.

In *International Shoe Co. v. Washington*[327] Chief Justice Harlan F. Stone, for the U.S. Supreme Court, used words from *Milliken v. Meyer*[328] that service of process made outside the boundaries of the forum state must be such that it "not offend the traditional notions of fair play and substantial justice."[329] The case concerned a Delaware corporation, headquartered in Missouri, which manufactured shoes at several locations, not including Washington state and sold them at several locations, including Washington. Stone made it clear that that rule, concerning substituted service, would apply whether the person served be individual or artificial and no mater the extent to which its activities affect commerce.[330]

The U.S. Supreme Court in *Mullane v. Hanover Bank & Trust Co.*[331] clearly proclaimed that whatever the method of substituted specified, the objective is to furnish the defendant with notice that the suit has been filed and giving the defendant an opportunity to respond and defend.[332]

In 1955 the Illinois legislature enacted a statute by which personal jurisdiction over non-residents of the forum state could be obtained if that person, in its state did something to the plaintiff it its state that caused damage. Its name is the "Long-arm statute." Service of process is made in the defending party's state, though it is issued by the plaintiff's state. Long-arm statutes have been interpreted as to require that even though the defending party may not have been physically in the forum state, there must be sufficient contact with it to justify this measure which appears to be halfway between in-hand service and substituted service. In *Kulko v. Superior Court,*[333] where such service was used, the U.S. Supreme Court Justice Thurgood Marshall proclaimed that it would make a mockery of the Due Process Clause if a man was required to travel 3,000 mile from New York to California to

327 326 U.S. 310 (1945).

328 311 U.S. 457 (1940).

329 *International Shoe Co.*, 326 U.S. at 316.

330 *Id.* at 313.

331 339 U.S. 306 (1950). *See infra* text accompanying notes 332, 368, 369, concerning additional consideration of this case.

332 *Id.* at 315. Justice Robert H. Jackson wrote that "when notice is a person's due, process which is a mere gesture is not due process." *Id.*

333 436 U.S. 84 (1978).

attend a child support hearing just because 13 years prior he paid two brief visits to the state.[334] There are other Supreme Court decisions recording the requirement of substantial contact.[335]

In 1963 a Uniform Interstate and International Procedure Act was proposed, but it was withdrawn in 1977 as being obsolete.

In 1990 the Supreme Court considering *Burnham v. Superior Court of California*[336] revisited in-hand service of process. A formerly married man was temporarily in California, visiting his children when his ex-wife had him personally served with process for a hearing concerning their former marriage. Justice Antonin Scalia, for the court, referred quickly to *Pennoyer v. Neff.*[337] Even though this man was but briefly in the state such "transient" appearance in the state[338] was held sufficient for in-hand service to give the court *in personam* jurisdiction. Justice Scalia almost eulogized the "in-hand" method of service of process by alleging that its validation was its "pedigree."[339]

In order for a judgment of F-1 to have personal jurisdiction over the defendant, either human or judicially recognized, the above rules must be complied with.[340]

In 1997 U.S. District Court Judge McLaughlin in *Zippo Manufacturing Co. v. Zippo Dot Com.*[341] found that his court had personal jurisdiction over a defendant who purposely availed itself of custom in Pennsylvania by its activities over the internet. Though several years have elapsed since that ruling it is probably accurate

---

334 *Id.* at 93.

335 *See* World Wide Volkswagen Corp. v. Woodson, 444 U.S..286 (1980); Helicopteros Nacionales de Columbia, S.A. v. Hall, 466 U.S. 408 (1983) and Asahi Metal Industry Co. v. Superior Court, 480 U.S. 102 (1987).

336 495 U.S. 604, 639, 640 (1990). *See infra* text accompanying notes 638, 639, 1226, and 1227 for further reference to this case.

337 95U.S. 714 (1877).

338 *See Burnham,* 495 U.S. at 610.

339 *Id.* at 621.

340 *See* Mezyk v. U.S. Bank Pension Plan, 2009 W.L. 3853878 (S.D. Ill. 2009).

341 952 F. Supp. 1119 (W.D. Pa. 1997).

to observe that personal jurisdiction acquired by use of the internet is still just in its seminal development.[342]

In addition to the above methods of a court acquiring personal jurisdiction over a defendant there is yet another method. It is the *quasi-in-rem* action. While *in-rem* cases seek to determine the status of property ownership, without seeking personal jurisdiction over the owner of that property, *quasi-in-rem* actions seek to obtain personal jurisdiction over the owner of proper which is located in the geographical bounds of the court, even though the owner is often not present there. The owner is named as a defendant in the action, even though that person, not being found within the state, cannot be served by in-hand process. The procedure following the filing of the Complaint is to attach, or sequester, the defendant's property. That property being in *custodia legis*[343] it will be available to be executed upon in the event the Plaintiff prevails in the suit. *Shaffer v. Heitner*[344] is an example of a *quasi-in-rem* action.[345]

(3) the F-1 court has subject matter jurisdiction over a marriage, and the moving party, but no personal jurisdiction over the defending party, yet it enters a judgment concerning financial affairs;[346]

---

342 *Id.* at 1128.

343 A legal term signifying that the property is in the physical or constructive possession of the court.

344 433 U. S. 186 (1977). *See infra* text accompanying notes 498, 811, 813, and 814 for further treatment of this case.

345 In Shaffer a disgruntled owner of stock in a Delaware corporation sued its officers and directors for their allegedly wrongful acts performed in Oregon. Since none of the defendants could be in-hand served in Delaware the plaintiff sequestered their stock, the certificate of which were also not in Delaware. The Delaware court found that personal jurisdiction existed over the absent defendants, despite their argument that: (1) the Delaware statute which authorized the sequestration of stock, even the certificate of which were not physically within the court's geographic location, violated the Due Process Clause, and (2) the International Shoe "minimum contacts" doctrine was violated by the procedure. It was the second argument upon which Justice Thurgood Marshall delivered his classic exposition for reversing the Delaware court.

346 Estin v. Estin, 334 U.S. 541 (1948). *See supra* note 248 in which a case quotes this decision, and see *infra* text accompanying notes 750, 754, 790-792 for further reference to this case.

(4) the F-1 judgment was entered due to fraud in the procurement of it;[347]

(5) the F-1 judgment was entered due to collusion in the procurement of it;[348]

(6) the F-1 judgment is interlocutory, (it is subject to modification) at the time it is sought to be recognized;[349]

Interlocutory is not exactly an antonym for "final," nor is it a synonym for "not final."[350] In most states before the UEFJA was promulgated if an appeal of the judgment were taken, the judgment was not final. The UEFJA provides that if an execution may issue, a judgment is final. In most states executions may not be issued if a supersedes bond has been posted, unless by state law an appeal automatically stays executions.[351]

---

[347] Levin v. Gladstein, 55 S.E. 371, 376 (N.C. 1906); Milwaukee County v. M.E. White Co., 296 U.S. 268, 276 (1935); Padron v. Lopez, 220 P.3d 345, 353 (Kan. 2009); Ullrich v. Walsh, 2010 W.L. 1372485 at *1 (Ark. App. 2010); Cutter v. Classic Fire Marine Ins. Co., 2010 W.L. 1790764 at *1 (Ind. App. 2010).

[348] Nevin v. Nevin, 149 A.2d 722, 727 (R.I. 1959); Erie Ins. Exchange v. Allstate Ins. Co., 1999 W.L. 33722349 at *5 (Va. Cir. Ct. 1999); In re Juck, 282 B.R. 753, 755 n.1 (Bankr D. Conn. 2002).

[349] Wilkerson v. Wilkerson, 418 So.2d 403, 404 (Fla. DCA (1982). What is "interlocutory," or "final" is determined by F-1 law. Grynberg v. Shaffer, 165 P.3d 234, 236 (Ariz. App 2007); Armtech Ins. Services, Inc. v. Hamilton, 2009 W.L. 498048 *2 (Tex. App. 2009).

[350] Black's Law Dictionary defines an interlocutory judgment as "[a]n intermediate judgment that determines a preliminary or subordinate point or plea but does not finally decide the case. A judgment or order given on a provisional or accessory claim or contention is generally interlocutory. — Also termed *interlocutory decree*." Black's Law Dictionary 8th Edition (2004).

[351] The following cases have held that the taking of an appeal does not constitute a judgment being "not final:" A. Coolot Co. v. L. Kahner & Co., 140 F.836 (9th Cir.1905); Maner v. Maner, 412 F.2d 449, (5th Cir.1969); Fidelity Standard Life Ins. Co. v. First Nat'l Bank & Trust Co., 510 F.2d 272 (5th Cir.1975); Faber v. Hovey, 117 Mass. 107 (Mass. 1875); Woodbridge & Turner Engineering Co. v. Ritter, 70 F. 677 (C.C. E.D.Pa.1895); Lonergan v. Lonergan, 76 N.W. 16, 317 (Neb. 1898); Sweetser v. Fox, 134 P.599 (Utah 1911); Ebner v. Steffanson, 172 N.W. 857 (N.D. 1919); Weiss v. Metalsalts Corp., 178 A.2d 240 (N.J. Super. 1962); Tarr v. Tarr, 391 F. Supp. 1053 (E.D. Tenn.1974); Armstrong

Marsden v. Arnett & Foster, L.L.C.[352] clearly established that a preliminary injunction is not a final order.[353]

Hanken v. Graphic Technology, Inc.[354] presents an interesting analysis of cognovit notes[355] and how they affect the finality of their judgments. The law of Pennsylvania, which gives legality to cognovit notes, considers judgments enforcing them to be appealed for modification of the judgment and still be considered to be final for full faith and credit purposes. Since the finality of an F-1 judgment is determined by F-1 law, a Kansas (F-2) trial court erred in using Kansas law in finding the judgment not final because it was on appeal.[356]

Worthley v. Worthley[357] proclaimed that even though a court is not required to recognize and/or enforce a prior, modifiable judgment, it is not prevented from doing so.[358]

(7) the F-1 court (a Bankruptcy court) has discharged the debtor of a claim;[359]

---

v. Armstrong, 130 N.E.2d 710 (Ohio App. 1954), aff'd, 350 U.S. 568 (1956); Schwartz v. Vecchiotti, 529 S.W.2d 603 (Tex.Civ.App.1975).

352 2009 W.L. 3246996 (S.D. W. Va. 2009).

353 *Id.* at *5. *See also* Padron v. Lopez, 220 P. 3d 345, 358 (Kan. 2009).

354 222 P.3d 523 (Kan. App. 2010).

355 Cognovit notes, at times called "confessed judgment notes" are recognized only in Alaska, Arizona, Ohio, Pennsylvania, New York, and the District of Columbia. They allow the maker to agree to a court entering judgment with few formalities in the event of default. Some states (Florida for example) statutorily prohibit their execution in the state, though full faith and credit requires them to be recognized by the state.

356 *Hanken*, 222 P. 3d at 531. The court did not mention the predicament that would occur if the F-2 court authorized payment to the Plaintiff, and subsequently the F-1 appellate court reversed the Plaintiff's favorable judgment.

357 288 P. 2d 19 (Cal. 1944).

358 *Id.* at 27.

359 Brouwer v. Superior Court, 19 P.2d 834, 835 (Cal . App. 1933).

(8) the F-1 court (a Bankruptcy court) has discharged the debtor of a judgment;[360]

(9) the F-1 court (a Bankruptcy Court) considering extent of the debtor's dischargeability has used *res judicata* (claim) preclusion rather than collateral estoppel (issue) preclusion law of the state in which it sits;[361]

(10) the F-1 judgment has been satisfied because it has been paid;[362]

(11) the F-1 case has been settled by the parties;[363]

(12) the F-1 court has not afforded the defendant due process, as the following cases elucidate;

The courts often look at full faith and credit jointly with attention to due process. The U.S. Court of Appeals for the Third Circuit in *Powers v. Lyoming Engines*[364] held that in class actions full faith and credit and due process must be considered.[365]

---

[360] Reitman v. Texas Exotic Feline Found., Inc., 152 F. 3d 341, 343, 344 (5th Cir. 1998); *In re* Bayhi, 528 F. 3d 393, 402 (5TH Cir. 2008).

[361] Brown v. Felsen, 442 U.S. 127, 139, 139 n.10 (1979), which did not say what state law should not be used, but specified that the state law to be used in a dischargeability proceeding is collateral estoppel (issue) preclusion. Hence *res judicata* (claim) preclusion law is not to be used. See iinfra text accompanying notes 997, 1006, 1013-1015., and 1018 for further reference to this case.

[362] Milwaukee County v. M.E. White Co., 296 U.S. 268, 275 (1935); TacCo Falcon Point, Inc. v. Clapper, 2007 W.L. 287173 at *7 (Mich. App. 2007).

[363] *See* Guiness v. Ward, 955 A.2d 875, 888, 889 (4th Cir. 1992), where the court discussed accord and satisfaction. It was established by that decision that the exception would apply only if the F-1 court would not recognize a settled case; and if no F-1 law can be found the F-2 court must extrapolate what F-1 decisions it can find in order to make a determination of what F-1 would do if presented with the issue.

[364] 328 Fed. App. 121 (3d Cir. 2009).

[365] *Id.* at 125.

In *United States v. Casciano*[366] it was made clear that due process requires that a person be given notice and an opportunity to be heard before a judgment or order can be given full faith and credit in another jurisdiction. The Due Process Clause requires that notice be "reasonably calculated, under all the circumstances, to apprise interested parties of the pendency of the action and afford them an opportunity to present their objections."[367]

In *Mullane v. Central Hanover Bank & Trust Co.*[368] Justice Robert H. Jackson wrote that "when notice is a person's due, process which is a mere gesture is not due process."[369]

In *Phifer v. Com. Dept of Social Sciences*[370] it was held that even if a party did not receive notice he was due because he had given the wrong address, he was deprived of due process because the sender, after the document was returned to it, should have taken steps to ascertain the correct address.[371]

In *Biglow v. Old Dominium Copper Mining & Smelting Co.*,[372] *Bagley v. General Fire Extinguisher Co.*,[373] and *Boltz v. Helvering*,[374] the so-called F-1 "defendants" were never parties in the F-1 proceeding. Hence they were deprived of due process of law.

In *Bradley v. Cantin*,[375] a mortgagor was subjected to charges without being allowed to defend himself by the F-1 court.[376]

---

[366] 124 F.3d 106 (2d Cir. 1997). *See infra* text accompanying notes 367, 946, and 947 for further reference to this case.

[367] *Id.* at 112.

[368] 339 U.S. 306 (1950).

[369] *Id.* at 314.

[370] 2009 W.L. 2997058 (Va. App. 2009).

[371] *Id.* at *8.

[372] 225 U.S. 111, 134 (1912).

[373] 212 U.S. 477, 480 (1909).

[374] 134 F.2d 538, 545 (8th Cir. 1943).

[375] 113 S.E.2d 878 (Va. 1961).

[376] *Id.* at 888.

In *Hansen v. Haagensen*[377] the F-1 judgment was an attempt to enter a personal judgment in a *quasi in rem* proceeding.[378]

In the Matter of Betty Warren[379] the hearing official in a Bar disciplinary proceeding was hired, paid, housed and trained by the state Bar, the prosecuting party, and a statute upon which a decision was rendered had been declared unconstitutional by a federal court.[380]

In *Pruett v. Eli Lilley*[381] the Plaintiff's residence and all facts in connection with a personal injury case had occurred in Alabama but the Plaintiff filed her suit in Minnesota because the Alabama statute of limitations had expired.[382]

In *West Virginia v. Madden*[383] a forum in a class action suit applied forum law which conflicted with the law of every other state involved.[384]

In *Mississippi State Dept of Human Services v. Fargo*[385] mailing a copy of a motion to an address from which the moving party knew the defendant had relocated.[386]

(13) the F-1 proceeding was non-adversarial, as the following cases elucidate;

---

377 178 N.W. 2d 325 (Iowa 1970).

378 *Id.* at 328.

379 1997 W.L. 33558225 (U.S. Supreme Court 1997).

380 *Id.* at *7.

381 2009 W.L. 2520641 (E.D. N.Y. 2009).

382 *Id.* at *1.

383 607 S.E.2d 772 (W. Va. 2004).

384 *Id.* at 780.

385 771 So.2d 935 (Miss. App. 2000).

386 *Id.* at 937.

Eisenenger v. Comm'r of the Internal Revenue [387] was a tax case. The Defendant Internal Revenue Commissioner was not a party, and was not even physically present at a state court hearing concerning the assessment of taxes. Consequently its determinations were found to be not binding on the Tax Court.[388]

In *New Century Financial Services, Inc. v. Shaheen,*[389] a stolen identity case, the defendant did not physically appear in the F-1 proceeding, and there was "no indication" that an Answer had been served for her and she never lived at the address to which a purported service in the F-1 proceeding was made.[390]

In *State of Arizona v. Yuen*[391] the "defendant" was not aware that she had been made a party.[392]

In *Reynolds v. Stockton*[393] the court had jurisdiction over the defendant, but its decree was "in no way responsive to the issues tendered by the pleadings and [it was] rendered in the absence of the defendant." In other words it was a figment of someone's imagination, and not entitled to full faith and credit.[394]

(14) the F-2 judgment is contrary to a prior judgment of F-1 involving the same issues and the same parties to which F-3 need not give full faith and credit; [395]

---

387 1943 W.L. 9226 (U.S. Tax Ct. 1943).

388 *Id.* at *(3).

389 2009 W.L. 5449218 (N.Y.C. Civ. Ct 2009).

390 *Id.* at *1.

391 101 Cal Rptr,3d 525 (Cal. App. 2009).

392 *Id.* at 537.

393 140 U.S. 254 (1891).

394 *Id.* at 264.

395 *See* Tinsley v. Tinsley, 431 So.2d 1304, 1308 (Ala. Civ. App. 1983), where Alabama was the F-1 court, Texas was the F-2 court and Alabama was the F-3 court; Smith v. Smith, 606 So.2d 164, 164 (Ala. Civ. App. 1992), where Alabama was the F -1 court, Florida was F-2 and Alabama was F-3; Tougas v. Tougas, 868 P.2d 437, 447 (Hawai'i 1994) where Hawai'i was the F-1 court, California was F-2 and Hawai'i was F-3. While none of the above courts so stated, it would seem that the objection to F-2's decision

(15) the F-1 judgment is recognized by F-2, but the portions of it dealing with the time, place and manner of enforcing it are not given full faith and credit;[396]

(16) a decree of F-1 attempts to directly affect (i.e. proclaim or quiet, title) real property in F-2, or some other state;[397]

Hood v. McGehee [398] established that if a statute deals only with property located in its state i.e. declaring the terms of the inheritance of such property, it is entitled to full faith and credit, even if it also refers to events occurring outside its state.[399]

Oyakawa v. Gillet[400] established that if two states have the form of property ownership, known as community property, and F-1 declares that community property in that state is liable for the separate debts of the spouses, if the F-1 judgment is recognized in State F-2 the community property in F-2 will be liable for the separate debts of the spouses.[401]

McQuay v. McQuay[402] established that if a court in one state orders a person to execute a deed which purports to convey to another person property located in another state that second state, by not rejecting the deed is not "enforcing it;" it is merely accepting it.[403]

---

conflicting with F-1's prior decision was that, in essence, it was an attempt of the F-2 court to modify a prior ruling of F-1's judgment. Ed.

[396] *See* Baker by Thomas v. General Motors Corp., 522 U.S. 222, 235 (1998).

[397] Fall v. Eastin, 215 U. S. 1 (1909); Durfee v. Duke, 375 U.S. 106 (1969). *See supra* text accompanying notes 210, 211, 297, and infra 550, 552,586, 588, 589 591 regarding Fall v..Eastin. *See supra* text accompanying notes 135, 137, 198 and infra note 427, 581-585, 587 regarding Durfee v. Duke.

[398] 237 U.S. 611 (1915).

[399] *Id.* at 615.

[400] 854 P.2d 1212 (Ariz. App. 1993).

[401] *Id.* at 1218.

[402] 2009 W.L. 2148424, (Minn. App. 2009).

[403] *Id.* at *3.

(17) the F-1 court normally had procedures available to parties that were denied to a party in the instant action, such unfairness, while not exactly a denial of due process is likely to affect the outcome of the cause of action;[404]

(18) F-1 is a state court and F-2 is a Federal District Court which is being asked to correct the F-1 judgment;[405]

(19) the S-1 state has a statute which pertains to a matter pending before an F-2 court, but that statute offends a public policy[406] of F-2;[407]

The exception to full faith and credit applies only to statutes. F-2 is required to render full faith and credit to judgments. When Justice Ruth Bader Ginsburg said

---

[404] Pennsylvania Truck Lines, Inc. v. Int'l Broth. of Teamsters, 1990 W.L. 59305 at *9 (E.D. Pa. 1990).

[405] The United States Supreme Court has held that one may not attempt to use federal courts as appellate courts for state court judgments. Rooker v. Fidelity Trust Co., 263 U.S. 413, 417 (1923) and District of Columbia Court of Appeals v. Feldma*n,* 460 U.S. 462, 488 (1983), giving rise to the "Rooker-Feldman Doctrine."

[406] It has been opined that the "public policy" of a jurisdiction is discerned from its constitutional, statutory and decisional law. Godfrey v. Spano, 13 N.Y.S.2d 358, 377 (N.Y. 2009). A Concurring Opinion in that case added that public policy may be discerned from "prevailing social and moral attitudes of the community." *Id.* at 380.

[407] Pacific Employers Ins. Co. v. Industrial Acc. Comm'n, 306 U.S. 493, 504, 505 (1939) (a Massachusetts employee of a Massachusetts employer was injured in California and sued for workers' compensation in California. Both employee and employer agreed that Massachusetts workers' compensation statute would apply. California, however, was not required by full faith and credit to apply Massachusetts statute which conflicted with its public policy of providing compensation to people injured or mortally wounded in California). Nevada v. Hall, 440 U.S. 410, 426, 427 (1979) (people injured on a California highway by an instrumentality of Nevada sued Nevada in a California court. Nevada had waived its sovereign immunity by a statute with a cap of $25,000.00. California had waived its sovereign immunity by a statute without any cap. California was not required, by full faith and credit, to use Nevada's statute waiving its immunity with a cap where that statute violated California's public policy of unlimited damages should the sovereign be proved liable); Miller v. Kingsley, 230 N.W.2d 472, 474, 475 (Neb. 1945).

in *Baker by Thomas v. General Motors Corp.*[408] "[w]e are "aware of [no] considerations of local policy or law which could rightly be deemed to impair the force and effect which the full faith and credit clause and the Act of Congress require to be given to [a money] judgment outside the state of its rendition,"[409] she was referring to the judicial determine-ation that there is no public policy exception to full faith and credit regarding judgments, even though there is as to statutes.[410]

When the issue is whether to apply another jurisdiction's statute the U.S. Supreme Court has held that courts should weigh the public policies of both states. In *Hughes v. Fetter*[411] in which Wisconsin had a statute forbidding wrongful death actions to be brought in its courts unless the death occurred in Wisconsin, before the Court abrogated that statute, finding found lacking the Wisconsin public policy giving rise to the statute.[412]

Public policy also may be used by an F-2 court in furnishing a reason for honoring full faith and credit. As an example in *In re Trust Created by Nixon*[413] the Nebraska (F-2) court used its state's public policy of rendering adopted children the same right as biological children, in recognizing and applying full faith and credit to a California adoption of an adult, despite a Nebraska statute which does not allow Nebraska adoption of adults except in specific circumstances.[414] Also remember that Justice Ginsburg in *Baker by Thomas v. General Motors Corp*[415]

---

[408] 522 U.S. 222 (1998)

[409] *Id.* at 234.

[410] To like effect *see* Miller v. Kingsley, 230 N.W. 2d 472, 474, 475 (Neb. 1945).

[411] 341 U.S. 609 (1951).

[412] *Id.* at 612. *See supra* note 73 and *infra* 590 and 677 for further reference to Hughes v. Fetter. The same ruling was made by the Supreme Court in First Nat. Bank of Chicago v. United Airlines, 342 U.S. 338, 689.393 (1952), even though one of the prerequisites of the rejected Illinois statute was that service of process could not be made in the state where the death occurred.

[413] 763 N.W.2d 404 (Neb. 2009).

[414] *Id.* at 404, in passim.

[415] 522 U.S. 222 (1998).

said that "[a] state may be guided by the forum [F-2] state's public policy in the law applicable to a controversy."[416]

As was apparent in *Houston v. Whittier*[417] if both states' statutes are "virtually identical" there should be no public policy or full faith and credit problem.[418] It must also be remembered that the full faith and credit exception for the public policy of F-2 applies only as to statutes of F-1, and not otherwise.[419]

In *Farabell v. Town of Macedon*[420] Florida had a statute that prohibited a person from holding a public position if that person had been involved in certain prohibited situations. That statute conflicted with a New York statute concerning the same subject matter. A New York court held that it was not required, by full faith and credit, to comply with the Florida statute.[421]

Despite the observations of some commentators that there is a "public policy" exception to the Full Faith and Credit Clause and implementing statutes, which will permit F-2 to ignore a judgment of F-1 if it violates the public policy of F-2,[422] such statements are just not correct. There is a public policy exception to full faith

---

416 *Id.* at 233.

417 216 P.3d 1272 (Idaho, 2009).

418 *Id.* at 1280.

419 *Baker by Thomas*, 522 U.S. at 232.

420 877 N.Y.S.2d 796 (N.Y. App. Div. 2009). *See infra* text accompanying notes 421, 964, 965 for further reference to this case.

421 *Id.* at 800.

422 *See* Sainz v. Sainz, 245 S.E.2d 372, 374 (N.C. App. 1978), in which it was stated: "[i]t being contrary to the public policy and Constitution of North Carolina to imprison for debt, this Court cannot grant full faith and credit to the judgment of the Supreme Court of New York ordering the defendant to specifically perform the contract of separation, and specifically its provisions for future support payments." *See also* Foster v. KNTV Television, Inc. 2009 WL 3047005, *2 (N.D. Cal. 2009) in which it was stated: "[t]he rare exceptions to the application of the full faith and credit clause arise only when there is a violation of some fundamental state public policy ..."

and credit, but is applies only to statutes.[423] There is no public policy" exception where an F-1 judgment is presented to F-2 for recognition and enforcement.[424]

Public policy has played an important part in the courts' keeping their schedules timely. In 1860 U.S. Supreme Court Justice Robert C. Grier in *Washington, A. & G. Steam Packet Co. v. Sickles*[425] said about it:

> This doctrine of estoppel is not a mere technical rule, tending to exclude truth, but it is based on sound principles of public policy. Society has an interest in putting an end to litigation, and preventing the unnecessary repetition of it. Courts are established for the benefit of the community, not to encourage the litigious spirit of individuals. This case is a striking illustration of the necessity of such a rule. The trial of the questions now disputed occupied the time of the court and jury below for fourteen business days.[426]

Justice Grier's words have been repeated by seven other Justices.[427]

(20) S-1 marriage certificate is between persons of the same gender;[428]

(21) S-1 marriage offends the public policy of F-2;[429]

---

[423] Alaska Packers Ass'n v Industrial Acc. Comm; 294 U.S. 532 (1935); Pacific Employers Ins. Co. v. Industrial Acc. Comm'n, 306 U.S. 493, 504, 505 (1939).

[424] Miller v. Kingsley, 230 N.W.2d 472, 374 (Neb. 1975).

[425] 65 U.S. 333 (1860).

[426] *Id.* at 339.

[427] Chief Justice Fuller in Hylton v. Guyot, 159 U.S. 113, 229 (1895); Justice Owen Roberts in Baldwin v. Iowa Traveling Men's Ass'n, 283 U.S. 522, 525 (1931); Chief Justice Stone in Heiser v. Woodruff, 327 U.S. 725, 733 (1946); Justice Frankfurter in Hoffman v. Blaski, 363 U.S. 335, 348 (1960); Justice Stewart in Durfee v. Duke, 375 U.S. 106, 111 (1963); Justice Rehnquist in Federated Department Stores, Inc. v. Moite, 452 U.S 394, 401 (1981); and Justice Stevens in James M. Bean Distilling Co. v. Georgia, 501 U.S. 529, 542 (1991).

[428] 28 U.S.C. § 1738C.

[429] Salucco v. Aldridge, 2004 W.L. 864459 at *3 (Mass. Super. 2004).

Some states refer to such marriages as being offensive to "a public sense of morality."[430]

(22) F-1 has accorded its residents certain benefits, but has not included them in An F-1 judgment. F-2, is not required by full faith and credit to accord those benefits to F-1 residents who may be in F-2 if such benefits do not comply with F-2's police power;[431]

In *Loughran v. Loughran*[432] Justice Louis D.Brandeis stated:

> It [a state] may, in the exercise of the police power, prohibit the enjoyment by persons within its borders of many rights acquired elsewhere and refuse to lend the aid of its courts to enforce them. . . . But when rights, however arising, have ripened into a judgment of a court of another state, the full faith . . . and credit clause (article 4, s 1) applies.[433]

(23) S-1 has a statute under which it has conducted judicial proceedings which impose obligations on F-2 residents when F-2 has the power to interpret the statute *vis-a-vis* its own residents;[434]

(24) S-1 has a statute governing its sovereign immunity (establishing a limitation on damages), which offends F-2's legislative policy governing its sovereign immunity (establishing a limitation on damages):[435]

(25) F-2 has more substantial contact with the case than does S-1.[436]

---

[430] *See* Martinez v. County of Monroe, 850 N.Y.S. 2d 740, 745 (N.Y. App. Div. 2008).

[431] Baltimore & O.S.W.R. Co. v. McDonald, 1904 W.L. 3727 at *4 (Ill. App. 1903).

[432] 292 U.S. 216 (1934).

[433] *Id.* at 227, 228.

[434] Pink v. A.A.A. Express, 314 U.S. 201, 209, 210 (1941).

[435] Nevada v. Hall, 440 U.S. 410, 424 (1979); Franchise Tax Bd. of Cal. v. Hyatt, 538 U.S. 488, 496 (2003). *See supra* text in notes 248 and 407 which refer to Nevada v. Hall, and *infra* text accompanying notes 462, 685, 686, and 1121.

[436] Allstate Ins. Co. v. Hague, 449 U.S. 302, 302 passim (1981).

In *Allstate Ins. Co. v. Hague.*[437] a resident of Wisconsin, who worked in Minnesota was killed in a vehicular accident occurring in Wisconsin. His widow, having remarried a resident of Minnesota, moved there and commenced estate proceeding for the decedent in Minnesota, under a Minnesota statute which permitted administration of the estates of non-domiciliaries if the Personal Representative were a Minnesota domiciliary. Discovering that the tortfeasor, who caused her former husband's death, had no insurance, she sought recompense from her late husband's uninsured motorist coverage with Allstate, which the deceased had purchased in Wisconsin. As Wisconsin did not allow the "stacking" of the three policies extant, she sought to have the law of Minnesota apply, because she could stack the policies under its law. The U.S. Supreme Court, the apogee of the courts considering the choice-of-law problem, ruled that on the basis of three contacts with Minnesota, that state's law would be applied. Those contacts were: (1) the decedent had a fifteen-year work record in Minnesota, (2) the insurance company did business in Minnesota; and (3) the decedent's widow, and Personal Representative of his estate, became a Minnesota resident prior to the litigation.[438] Justice William J. Brennan, Jr., made the following statement in the Court's plurality Opinion:

> In deciding constitutional choice-of-law questions, whether under the Due Process Clause or the Full Faith and Credit Clause, this Court has traditionally examined . . . the contacts of the State, whose law was applied, with the parties and with the occurrence or transaction giving rise to the litigation. (Citation omitted). In order to ensure that the choice of law is neither arbitrary nor fundamentally unfair, see *Alaska Packers Assn. v. Industrial Accident Comm'n*, 294 U.S. 532, 542, 55 S.Ct. 518, 521, 79 L.Ed. 1044 (1935), the Court has invalidated the choice of law of a State which has had no significant contact or significant aggregation of contacts, creating state interests, with the parties and the occurrence or transaction.[439]

---

[437] 449 U.S. 302 (1981).

[438] *Id.* at 319.

[439] *Id.* at 308. The ruling in that case was specifically approved by the Supreme Court in a class action, Phillips Petroleum Co/. v. Shutts, 472 U.S. 797, 818 (1985).

(26) F-2 is not required to use the statute of limitations of F-1; [440]

(27) the F-1 judgment is an attempt to enforce the penal laws of F-1;[441]

In *The Antelope*[442] Chief Justice John Marshall said that "[t]he courts of no country execute the penal laws of another."[443]

In *United States v. Castellon* [444] it was held that if a federal court uses a state criminal conviction merely for the purpose of enhancing[445] defendant's sentence for a federal criminal conviction such is not enforcing the state penal law.[446]

In *Brown v. Handgun Permit Review Bd.*[447] it was held that F-2 may deny the right to possess a regulated firearm to a person who was convicted and punished in

---

440 Wells v. Simonds Abrasive Co., 345 U.S. 514, 527 (1953); Nevada v. Hall, 440 U.S. 410, 426 (1979).

441 Huntington v. Attrill, 146 U.S. 657 (1892); Nelson v. George, 399 U.S. 224, 229 (1970); Paper Products Co. v. Doggrell, 261 S.W.2d 127, 131 (Tenn. 1953) (" Whether the full faith and credit clause requires the Courts of one state to enforce the law of another state's penal laws in some respects depends upon whether its purpose is to punish an offense against the public justice of the state, or to afford a private remedy to a person injured by the wrongful act."). *See also* Holbein v. Rigot, 245 So.2d 57, 59 (Fla.1971); Brown v. Handgun Permit Review Board, 982 A. 2d 830, 848 (Md. App. 2009); and Hall v. Phelps, 641 F. Supp. 2d 334, 347, 348 (D. Del. 2009).

442 23 U.S. (10 Wheat.) 66 (1825).

443 *Id.* at 123.

444 228 Fed. Appx. 494, 496, 497 (5th Cir. 2007). *See infra* text accompanying notes 446. 959 and 961 for further reference to this case.

445 Enhancing a sentence means increasing the severity of the sentence. Black's Law Dictionary, 8th Edition (2004) defines "enhancement" as "enhancement. The act of augmenting; the state of being enhanced <the use of a deadly weapon led to an enhancement of the sentence>."

446 *Castellon,* 228 Fed. Appx. at 496, 497.. *See also* Smart v. United States, 2008 W.L. 2902608 at *2 (S.D. Ga. 2008). *See infra* text accompanying note 852 regarding the Smart case. *See supra* text accompanying notes 402 and 403 regarding a court not enforcing a judgment – merely accepting it.

447 982 A.2d 830 (Md. App. 2009).

F-1 for possessing a firearm, differently than he would have been punished by F-2.[448]

In *Douglas v. Smith*[449] it was held that a guilty plea precludes litigation in a subsequent civil trial of all actions necessarily determined in the conviction following the guilty plea.[450]

(28) the F-1 judgment represents a criminal conviction which is constitutionally invalid;[451]

(29) taxes which S-1 has assessed against its citizens;[452]

The U.S. Supreme Court in *Milwaukee County v. M.E. White Co.*[453] has emphasized that a judgment in favor of a state for the collection of taxes is recognizable and enforceable under full faith and credit, whereas recognition and enforcement of the taxes, themselves, is not, because the state's cause of action for the collection of taxes is a different entity from a judgment which results from that cause of action.[454]

(30) the F-1 judgment does not require the defendant to take some affirmative action that F-2 requires the defendant to take;[455]

(31) the F-1 court is an Indian tribal court;[456]

---

[448] *Id.* at 847.

[449] 2009 W.L. 789450 (N.D.N.Y. 2009).

[450] *Id.* at *3.

[451] State v. Harrison, 2010 W.L. 94346 at *8 (Wash. App. 2010).

[452] Milwaukee County v. M.E. White Co., 296 U.S. 268, 268 in passim (1935).

[453] 296 U.S. 268 (1935).

[454] *Id.* at 268 in passim.

[455] Rosin v. Monken, 599 F.3d 574, 577 (7th Cir. 2010) (the Full Faith and Credit Clause did not prevent Illinois from requiring a sex-offender to register in that state simply because a New York judgment did not require that sex offender to register in New York.). *See infra* text accompanying notes 972-974 for additional decisions considering this case.

[456] *See infra* Section I, K. text accompanying notes 1030-1077.

(32) the F-1 court is a tribunal of a foreign country;[457]

It can be observed that there is a certain amount of over-lapping, in these "exceptions" proclaimed by the courts. Hence at times an F-2 court might assign more that one reason for denying recognition and enforcement of an F-1 judgment. At times, in fact, the courts proclaim their own list of exceptions, which is not identical to the above list compiled from reported decisions.[458]

The Full Faith and Credit Clause and its implementing statute, as amended, specify, in general terms, what is to be given full faith and credit; only the judicially created "exceptions" provide what is not to be given full faith and credit. The following Section considers those matters as to which courts have judicially determined that may be recognized and enforced even though not required to be. There appears to be no case or scholarly writing approving of judicial recognition and enforcement in the unusual event of a matter not being entitled to recognition and enforcement, but agreement thereto by the party against whom it is asserted. In other words could a defendant waive subject matter jurisdiction and personal service, just to name two "exceptions?" It would seem that a defendant might be permitted to waive the second, under certain circumstances, but would not be permitted to waive the first, under any circumstances.

3. Matters Which May Be, But Are Not Required to Be, Recognized and Enforced

Matters which may be, but are not required to be, recognized and enforced are a different form of "exception" to the Clause and its implementing statute than those matters which must not be recognized and enforced. They are not required to be recognized and enforced, but they are not prohibited from being accorded such benefit. Those are:

---

[457] *See infra* Section I. L. text accompanying notes 1080 -1093.

[458] As an example the Arizona Supreme Court in Phares v. Nutter, 609 P. 2d 561, 563 (Ariz. 1980), gave the following list: (1) lF-1's lack of jurisdiction over the subject matter; (2) lack of jurisdiction of the person of the defendant; (3) the judgment was obtained through lack of due process; (4) the F-1 court was "incompetent" to render the judgment; (5) the judgment was the result of "intrinsic fraud;" (6) the judgment was "invalid;" (7) the judgment was "unenforceable."

(1) judgments of Indian tribal courts;[459]

(2) judgments of foreign country courts,[460] including, but not limited to foreign adoptions of a foreign child;[461]

(3) judgments which violate the F-2 public policy, if F-2 chooses to honor it.[462]

(4) A forum is not required by full faith and credit to use a statute of another state merely because that other state has some connection with its proceedings.[463]

E. Money Judgments

Without doubt the greatest number of judgments that prompt a court to voice some opinion about the Full Faith and Credit Clause and/or its implementing statute are the money judgments – those requiring a defendant to pay to the plaintiff a certain amount of money. Judge Cuff in *Arnold, White & Durkee, Professional Corp. v. Gotcha Covered, Inc* [464] has written:

> Case law is replete with instances in which full faith and credit has been accorded to money judgments of other states, even though the original

---

459 Garcia v. Gutierrez, 217 P.3d 591, 608 (N. Mex. 2009). *See infra* text accompanying notes 1031-1079, regarding Indian Tribal courts, and notes 1068, 1069, 1073, 1074 for further reference to Garcia v. Gutierrez.

460 Petkov v. Petkov, 2009 W.L. 103701 at *2 (Mich. App. 2009). See infra text accompanying notes 1080-1094 regarding foreign country judgments.

461 *In re* Adoption of M.S., 103 Cal. Rptr 3d 715, 721 (Cal. App. 2010).

462 Nevada v. Hall, 440 U.S. 410, 426 (1979) (in which Justice John Paul Stevens said: "It may be wise policy, as a matter of harmonious interstate relations, for States to accord each other immunity or to respect any established limits on liability. They are free to do so.") He also said several times that under certain conditions a state would not be "required" to give another state full faith and credit. The Supreme Court in Baker by Thomas v. General Motors Corp., 522 U.S. 222, 233 (1998) made it clear that there is no compulsory exception to the Full Faith and Credit Clause and statute.

463 Pacific Employer's Ins. Co. v. Industrial Acc. Comiss., 306 U.S. 493 (1939) (the statute in that case authorizing worker's compensation). Query: if the only contact that the forum had with the accident was the worker's choice to use it as her or his forum, and all other contacts were with the other state, would full faith and credit require the forum to use the other state's worker compensation statute? Ed.

464 714 A.2d 360 (N.J. Super. A..D. 1998).

> claim is founded on a debt or a transaction contrary to the public policy of the state in which the money judgment is sought to be enforced.[465]

In *Sainz v. Sainz*[466] Judge Brock said that:

> Under the full faith and credit clause a valid judgment for the payment of money must, as a general rule, be recognized and enforced in a sister state. Restatement 2d, Conflict of Laws ss 93 and 100 (1971).[467]

The judicial opinions are not, moreover, of just recent origin, as the following examples of some of the more interesting money judgment-full faith and credit decisions will reveal. The first two cases considered did not refer to full faith and credit, but they did concern money judgments.

Phelps v. Holker,[468] a case in which the Pennsylvania Supreme Court considered whether it should recognize a Massachusetts judgment under the Articles of Confederation, which still governed[469] and which contained full faith and credit language. The court ruled that the Articles did not require recognition without further inquiry. Even though the Massachusetts' court entered what it considered to be a money judgment, the Pennsylvania court thought it to be a judgment *in rem*, since it was commenced by an attachment of the defendant's blanket,[470] and entered upon a default. The full faith and credit provisions of the Articles of Confederation, therefore, did not require Pennsylvania to enforce the Massachusetts' judgment.[471]

---

[465] *Id.* at 363.

[466] 245 S.E.2d 372 (N.C. App. 1978).

[467] *Id.* at 375.

[468] 1 U.S. 261 (Pa. Sup. Ct. 1788).

[469] The effective date of the Constitution was March 4, 1789.

[470] Sheriffs in those years must have been less discriminating than modern-day sheriffs. Ed.

[471] *Phelps,* 1 U.S. at 264.

Georgia v. Brailsford,[472] the U.S. Supreme Court's first case, decided slightly after its final Justice, James Iredell, was appointed. A native of Great Britain recovered a money judgment against an American citizen. A statute of Georgia authorized its Governor to bring an injunction against the British creditor from executing on American assets to satisfy his judgment. By a 4-2 vote the court authorized the issuance of the injunction.[473]

Chisholm v. Georgia[474] authorized an assumpsit action for money due against a state.[475] It aroused public condemnation to such an extent that five years after the decision was handed down the Eleventh Amendment was ratified.

Armstrong v. Carson's Executors,[476] the first case to expound upon the Full Faith and Credit Clause and statute, by U.S. Supreme Court Justices was not a case of that Court, but one of the Circuit Court for the District of Pennsylvania. In those early days of the Court it did not have an abundance of cases and its jurists often sat on Circuit Court cases. A money judgment was obtained in New Jersey, and it was attempted to be satisfied in Pennsylvania. The judgment debtor raised the defense of *Nil Debet*.[477] U.S. Supreme Court Justice James Wilson, the first Associate U.S. Justice to have been sworn in as a member of the Court, wrote the Opinion of the Court, stressing the Full Faith and Credit Clause and statute. He proclaimed: "[i]n the courts of New Jersey no such plea would be sustained and therefore it is inadmissible in any court sitting in Pennsylvania."[478] He added that *Nul Tiel Record*[479] was the only plea he would consider.[480]

---

472 2 U.S. 402 (1792).

473 *Id.* at 402, passim.

474 2 U.S. 419 (1793).

475 *Id.* at 419.

476 2 U.S. (2 Dall.) 302 (1794).

477 *Nil Debet* (improperly referred to as "*nil debent*" in the Opinion) was a common law defense of a judgment debtor proclaiming "I do not owe that debt."

478 Armstrong, 2 U.S. at 302.

479 *Nil Debet* is a common law defense stating that the validity or invalidity of the F-1 judgment was revealed by its record.

480 *Amstrong*, 2 U.S. at 302.

Mills v. Duryee[481] involved a judgment entered on a debt by a New York court which was attempted to be recognized and enforced in the District of Columbia. *Nil Debet*[482] was pled by the defendant and rejected by the Court, with an Opinion written by Justice Joseph Story, on full faith and credit grounds. He wrote that where the rendering state has "evidence of the highest nature, *viz. record evidence*, it must have the same faith and credit in every other Court. Congress have therefore declared the *effect* of the record by declaring what faith and credit shall be given to it."[483]

Hampton v. M'Connel[484] involved a decision of the U.S. Supreme Court with an Opinion by Chief Justice John Marshall, in which he said the legal principles involved were identical to those of *Mills v, Duryee.*[485]

McElmoyle for Use of Bailey v. Cohen[486] was a case in which a money judgment had been entered in South Carolina against one its residents, who subsequently moved to Georgia, and died there without satisfying the judgment. Upon his demise an action was brought in Georgia, against his estate, for payment of the debt. A defense was interposed on the ground that the judgment had been entered longer ago than five years, the time period specified in a Georgia statute of limitations applying to foreign judgments. The United States Supreme Court, with Justice James M. Wayne, coincidentally a Georgian, writing the Court's Opinion, held that Georgia was permitted to assert its own statute of limitations against the presentation of the South Carolina judgment. Wayne first analyzed the judgment as a "record" within the meaning of the Full Faith and Credit Clause and statute. As such, the judgment could not be assailed by the plea of *Nul Teil* [sic] *Record.*[487] An adverse statute of limitations could, however, be applied against it if it were asked to be recognized, "in virtue of the sovereignty by which it [the F-2 court] exercises its legislation for all persons and property within its jurisdiction."[488] In

[481] 11 U.S. (7 Cranch) 481 (1813).

[482] *See supra* note 477 for the meaning if *Nil Debet.*

[483] *Mills*, 11 U.S. at 484.

[484] 16 U.S. (3 Wheat.) 234 (1818).

[485] *Id.* at 234.

[486] 38 U.S. 312 (1839).

[487] *See supra* note 479 for the definition of *Nul Tiel Record.*

[488] *M'Elmoyle*, 38 U.S. at 327.

other words, the foreign judgment being a record it could not be attacked on the merits, but if it is asked to be recognized and enforced, the enforcing state could determine whether it was unworthy of recognition due to its age.[489]

Christmas v. Russell[490] involved liability on a promissory note given by Christmas, and assigned to Russell. Six years after the note had become dormant under the law of Mississippi, Christmas' home state, he traveled into Russell's home state, Kentucky, where Russell sued him on the note. The Kentucky court ignored Christmas' defense that the note had become dormant under Mississippi law, because it was still viable under Kentucky law, and subject to being enforced by a Kentucky judgment. When the Kentucky judgment was brought to a federal trial court in Mississippi for enforcement, the Mississippi court recognized it as an enforceable judgment under the full faith and credit statute.[491] The Supreme Court affirmed, Justice Nathan Clifford, writing the Opinion of the Court in which he said: "as the act expressly declares, that the record, when duly authenticated, shall have in every other court of the United States the same faith and credit as it has in the State court from whence [sic] it was taken."[492] – referring to *Mills v. Duryee.*[493] He added: "[i]f a judgment is conclusive in the State where it was pronounced, it is equally conclusive everywhere' in the courts of the United States."[494]

Harris v. Balk[495] is a complicated case in which the author of the Court's Opinion, Justice Rufus J. Peckham, did not give as much attention to full faith and credit as he did to the facts and how one's creditor can lose the money he is owed simply because he is another's debtor. Harris owed Balk, both North Carolinians; but Balk owed Epstein, a resident of Maryland. When Harris was temporarily in Maryland Epstein had him served with a Writ of Garnishment, though referred to

---

489 An almost duplicate of this case appeared in 1966 as Watkins v. Conway, 385 U.S. 188 (1966), with Florida as F-1 and Georgia as F-2.

490 72 U.S. (5 Wall.) 290 (1866).

491 The statute of 1790, today 28 U.S.C. § 1738.

492 *Christmas*, 72 U.S. at 302.

493 11 U.S. (7 Cranch) 481 (1813).

494 *Christmas,* 72 U.S. at 302.

495 198 U.S. 215 (1905).

by Peckham as a Writ of Attachment.[496] Harris did not remain long in Maryland, and upon his return to North Carolina he agreed that his Maryland lawyer would acknowledge that he owed Balk $180.00, A Maryland judgment, therefore, was entered in favor of Epstein against Harris for $180.00, which Harris paid. Shortly thereafter Balk sued Harris in North Carolina. Harris defended on the basis of the Maryland judgment which he paid – but not to Balk – to Epstein, Balk's creditor. Justice Peckham, for the Supreme Court, agreed that Harris no longer owed Balk, because the Maryland judgment requiring Harris' payment to Balk must be given full faith and credit. The balance of his Opinion was devoted to an explanation of why the Privileges and Immunities Clause[497] and the garnishment process justified the result. The Privileges and Immunities Clause would permit Balk to sue Harris in Maryland. Epstein, who is owed money by Balk is Balk's representative, and if Balk could sue Harris in Maryland, so can his representative, Epstein. Then the question arises, what would be the cause of action of the Epstein v. Harris suit? The debt Harris owed to Balk, which accompanied Harris on his trip to Maryland, no matter how short his stay,[498] was the cause of action, provided: (1) that Harris notified Balk of the situation (which he did), and (2) that Balk did not deny his indebtedness to Epstein (which he did not).[499]

---

[496] Justice Peckham appears to confuse garnishment with attachment, as many lawyers do. In this case the Writ that was served upon Harris was really a Writ of Garnishment.

[497] U.S. Const., art IV, § 2, CL 1.

[498] It must be remembered that this part of Harris v. Balk was overruled by Shaffer v. Heitner, in which Justice Thurgood Marshall, writing for the Court, said that "the International Shoe Court believed that the standard it was setting forth governed actions against natural persons as well as corporations, and we see no reason to disagree." *See* Shaffer v. Heitner 433 U.S. 186, 204, n.19 (1977). A short business trip might not be sufficient contact with the state in which process was served to satisfy the "fair play and substantial justice" of International Shoe. The following year Justice Marshall, for the Court in Kulko v. Superior Court, 436 U.S. 84, 92 (1978) noted that a defendant's "glancing presence in the state" would offer a plaintiff slim hope of obtaining personal jurisdiction over a defendant.

[499] *Harris*, 198 U.S. at 228. A debt is a thing or asset of value, which can be garnished, i.e. the garnishor (Epstein), is put in the place of the creditor (Balk), against the garnishee (Harris), the person who owes money to another person (Balk). The third meaning of "debt" as defined in Black's Law Dictionary, 8th Edition (2004) is that it is a "thing" of value. Black's Law Dictionary describes garnishment as "[a] judicial proceeding in which a creditor (or potential creditor) asks the court to order a third party who is indebted to, or is bailee for, the debtor to turn over to the creditor any of the debtor's property (such as wages or bank accounts) held by that third party." In this case the debtor's debtor (Harris)

Old Wayne Mut. Life Ass'n v. McDonough[500] was a case in which the U.S. Supreme Court placed itself virtually in the position of an F-2 court determining whether the F-1 court had subject matter jurisdiction. The case involved an action against an Indiana insurance company on a life insurance policy in a Pennsylvania court in obtaining a money judgment. Justice John Marshall Harlan, I made short shrift of the presumption to the effect that an F-1 court has jurisdiction. He alluded to *Galpin v. Page*[501] which held that the presumption applies only as to facts as to which the record is silent. Therefore he consulted the record to ascertain whether he could determine from it whether or not the Pennsylvania court had subject-matter jurisdiction. He did not need any testimony to determine that the initial forum did not have such jurisdiction, since the record established the following facts: (1) although it did some business in Pennsylvania; (2) the defendant had made no application with Pennsylvania authorities to establish an agent upon service of process could be made; (3) merely substituted service was made upon the defendant by serving only the Pennsylvania Insurance Commissioner, who apparently had no contact with the defendant; (4) at the trial the defendant did not appear, either personally, or by an attorney of its own selection; (5) the insurance company did not appear at the trial; (6) at the trial no pleadings nor testimony nor evidence were introduced by the defendant; (7) it was established at trial that the insurance coverage was negotiated, and the policy issued in Indiana; (8) that policy provided that if any litigation be brought against the insurer it must be commenced within six months of the insured's death, which was not complied with; (9) the policy provided that Indiana law would apply in the event of litigation; (10) Indiana law provided that if a suit is not brought upon an insurance policy timely, it is void and of no effect; (11) the Pennsylvania court defaulted the defendant, and entered a money judgment against it.[502] When the judgment was brought to Indiana for enforcement the Indiana court, based on full faith and credit, recognized it. Justice Harlan, writing for the Court, in disagreement, wrote that:

---

owes money to the debtor (Balk), so the debtor's creditor (Epstein) may ask the court to turn that debt over to him. Whatever the creditor receives from the garnishment is credited on the debtor's debt owed to the creditor.

[500] 204 U.S. 8 (1907).

[501] 85 U.S. (18 Wall.) 350, 366 (1873). See infra text accompanying notes 502-504 for further reference to this case.

[502] *Old Wayne Mut Life Ass'n*, 204 U.S. at 17-23.

> No state can, by any tribunal or representative, render nugatory a provision of the supreme law. And, if conclusiveness of a judgment of [sic] decree in a court of one state is questioned in a court of another government, Federal or state, it is open, under proper averments, to inquire whether the court rendering the decision had jurisdiction to render it.[503]

Having approved those words the Court found the Pennsylvania judgment void for lack of due process and not entitled to full faith and credit.[504]

Fauntleroy v. Lum[505] initially involved an arbitration award, in Mississippi, of money to a creditor on a futures transaction. The award was a mistake because incurring liability on futures was illegal in Mississippi. The creditor, nonetheless, took his award to Missouri, the home state of his debtor, and had it reduced to a Missouri judgment. When the now judgment-creditor took his Missouri judgment back to Mississippi to have it recognized and enforced, the Mississippi court refused, because the judgment was void under Mississippi law. The U.S. Supreme Court reversed the Mississippi refusal upon constitutional (i.e. full faith and credit) grounds, not very clearly stated by Justice Oliver Wendell Holmes, despite his usual cogency.[506]

American Express Co. v. Mullins[507] differs from the usual money judgment cases in that here a Kansas court instead of entering a judgment decreeing that the defendant owed the plaintiff money, declared that the defendant carrier did not owe its customer anything despite the fact that the boxes of liquor with which the customer entrusted it had been lost. The defendant's excuse was that the liquor had been seized by enforcement agents and destroyed. The customer tried again to obtain a judgment against its former carrier, this time in Kentucky. The defendant asserted that full faith and credit required the Kentucky court to honor the Kansas

---

503 *Id.* at 15.

504 *Id.* at 23.

505 210 U.S. 230 (1908). . For further consideration of this case *see* text accompanying notes 126, 508 and 512, and notes 506, 574, 589 and 1122.

506 *Id.* at 238. . For further consideration of this case *see* text accompanying notes 126, 5o5, 508 and 512, and notes 574, 589 and 1122 and *see infra* text accompanying notes 511-513 for Holmes' attempt to clarify his sketchy explanation in Fauntleroy.

507 212 U.S. 311, 314 (1909). *See supra* text accompanying note 198, and *infra* text accompanying notes 509, and 510 for further reference to thus case.

judgment; but the Kentucky court disagreed. The U.S. Supreme Court reversed. Justice David J. Brewer, writing the Opinion of the Court, explained that the Clause was just as effective in requiring a defendant's favorable judgment to be enforced as it is in requiring a plaintiff's favorable judgment to be enforced. As in *Fauntleroy*,[508] he said that even if the Kansas court was guilty of a mistake of law, such was not enough to discredit its judgment, as they will be discredited only for consent, connivance or fraud.[509] Justice Brewer ended his Opinion with these words: "this court will determine for itself whether there was anything in the record which shows any . . . consent, connivance or fraud."[510] One might question if instead of "this court" he meant to say "the court which was asked to recognize the judgment." A consanguine explanation would probably include both courts.

Chicago Life Ins. Co. v. Cherry[511] was an action entering a money judgment against an insurance company in Tennessee in which, when it was sought to be recognized and enforced in Illinois, the company complained that it had not been properly served. In affirming the Illinois court's recognition of the judgment, Justice Holmes took the opportunity to expound upon his rather limited explication in *Fauntleroy*[512] of the effect of a mistake by the F-1 court. He wrote:

> Whenever a wrong judgment is entered against a defendant, his property is taken when it should not have been; but whatever the ground may be, if the mistake is not so gross as to be impossible in a rational administration of justice, it is no more than the imperfection of man, not a denial of constitutional rights.[513]

---

[508] For further consideration of this case *see* text accompanying notes 126, 505 and 512, and notes 506, 574, 589 and 1122.

[509] *Id.* at 314.

[510] *Id.*

[511] 244 U.S. 25 (1917).

[512] For further consideration of this case *see* text accompanying notes 126, 505, and 508 and notes 506, 574, 589 and 1122.

[513] *Chicago Life Ins. Co.*, 244 U.S. at 30. Posterity will determine whether that explanation is satisfactory. Ed.

Adam v. Saenger[514] was a case involving a California money judgment on a cross-claim for goods sold and delivered. When the judgment was presented to a Texas court with a request that it be recognized and enforced, the court refused to give it full faith and credit on the ground that the California court lacked personal jurisdiction over the plaintiff-cross defendant, because of defective service of process, i.e. the cross-claim being served solely on plaintiff's counsel of record. The U.S. Supreme Court revered, finding that the method of service of process was valid. The then Justice Harlan F. Stone, writing the Opinion of the Court, made it clear that when determination of jurisdiction *vel non* of the F-1 court is made by the F-2 court, it is the court, itself, and not the jury that makes the inquiry.[515] He continued. The law of California, concerning serving of process on plaintiff's attorney of record in a Cross-Claim action was constitutionally valid; specifically not violating the Fourteenth Amendment. Justice Stone concluded his Opinion with the observation that the California method was "the price which the state may exact as the condition of opening the state's court to the plaintiff."[516]

Heiser v. Woodruff[517] is an interesting case revealing the treatment that can be received by a money judgment in a bankruptcy court, until halted by full faith and credit.[518] A money judgment was rendered by the U.S. District Court for the Southern District of California. Subsequently the judgment-debtor voluntarily filed for bankruptcy, under the Bankruptcy Act of 1898.[519] The bankrupt[520] objected to the judgment-creditor filing the judgment as a claim in the bankruptcy case on the basis that it was procured by fraud. Two proceedings had been held in the same District Court, which rendered the judgment, for determination of the fraud claim, both of which found that fraud had not been proved. The Ninth Circuit affirmed.[521] On the basis of full faith and credit the U.S. Supreme Court held the bankruptcy

---

[514] 303 U.S. 59, 62 (1938).

[515] *Id.* at 68.

[516] *Id.*

[517] 327 U.S. 726 (1946).

[518] *See infra* text accompanying notes 976-1029, dealing with Bankruptcy Court Judgments.

[519] *See infra* text accompanying notes 980-997.concerning the Bankruptcy Act of 1898.

[520] Under the Bankruptcy Act of 1898 debtors were referred to as "bankrupts."

[521] Jackson v. Heiser, 111 F. 2d 310, 313 (9th Cir 1940).

court was not permitted to re-litigate that issue. The final words of Chief Justice Stone, writing for the Court, were: "[t]hat [fraud] issue, having been twice litigated and decided in the court in which the judgment was rendered, in proceedings brought by the trustee in bankruptcy and the bankrupt, and by the bankrupt alone, may not now be relitigated in the bankruptcy court."[522]

In *Adar v. Smith*[523] Circuit Judge Wiener made it clear that there is no difference between money judgment cases and equity cases *vis-à-vis* full faith and credit when he wrote that:

> The Registrar's claim that adoptions fall within a "category" of judgments that are not owed full faith and credit is likewise unavailing. The dichotomy she purports to identify would describe judgments as either prospective or retrospective, with retrospective judgments being owed full faith and credit but prospective judgments *not* being owed such respect by forum states. According to this contention by the Registrar, the Clause would apply to such retrospective judgments as money judgments, but not to prospective judgments (to which subset she would assign adoption decrees). This assertion echoes the argument dismissed by the Supreme Court in *Baker*[524] that there is some *per se* difference under the Clause between money judgments and equitable judgments. The *Baker* Court held unequivocally that both kinds of judgments are afforded full faith and credit under the Constitution.[525]

Perhaps Judge Seymour's words in *Yeager v. Allstate Ins. Co.*[526] best describe the above cases:

> For a state's substantive law to be selected consistent with the Full Faith and Credit Clause and the Due Process Clause, the state must have a significant contact or significant aggregation of contacts, creating state

---

[522] *Heiser*, 327 U.S. at 740.

[523] 597 F.3d 697 (5th Cir 2010).

[524] *See* 522 U.S. 222 (1998).

[525] *Adar*, 597 F. 3d at 712.

[526] 2010 W.L. 680429 (D.S.C. 2010).

> interest, so that the choice of its law is neither arbitrary [n]or fundamentally unfair.[527]

F. Equitable Remedy Judgments

1. General Statement

In 1858 Mr. Justice Peter V. Daniel of the United States Supreme Court in *Barber v. Barber*,[528] speaking about federal courts, which just as correctly could have been said about state courts, wrote that:

> [I]n order to bar the jurisdiction of the courts of the United States in equity, the remedy at law must be as practical and efficacious to the ends of justice and its prompt administration as the remedy in equity; and it is not objection to such equity jurisdiction that there is a remedy under the local law.[529]

In 1934 Justice Lewis Brandeis, in *Loughran v. Loughran*[530] said, concerning equity, that: "[e]quity does not demand that its suitors shall have led blameless lives," even though the clean hands doctrine might, depending upon the facts hold a party accountable for its actions.[531]

In 1998 in *Baker by Thomas v. General Motors Corporation*[532] Justice Ruth Bader Ginsburg said that "[t]he Court has never placed equity decrees outside the full faith and credit domain. Equity decrees for the payment of money have long been considered equivalent to judgments at law entitled to nationwide recognition."[533]

---

[527] *Id.* *4. For a like pronouncement *see* Caldwell v. Geico General Ins. Co.,2010 W.L. 865773 at *4 (D. Colo. 2010).

[528] 62 U.S. (21 Haw.) 582 (1858).

[529] *Id.* at 583.

[530] 292 U.S. 216 (1934).

[531] *Id.* at 229, 230.

[532] 533 U.S. 222 (1998).

[533] *Id.* at 234.

In *Sainz v. Sainz* [534] Judge Brock said that:

> Under the full faith and credit clause a valid judgment for the payment of money must, as a general rule, be recognized and enforced in a sister state. Restatement 2d, Conflict of Laws ss 93 and 100 (1971). Likewise, a judgment in the nature of an equitable decree that orders the doing of an act is entitled to recognition to the same degree as another judgment. Id. at 102, Comment b.[535]

In *Adar v. Smith*[536] it was made clear that as far as full faith and credit is concerned, there is no difference between money judgments[537] and equitable judgments.[538]

In *Underwriters Nat. Assur. Co. v North Carolina Life & Acc. Health Ins. Guaranty Ass'n*[539] Justice Thurgood Marshall wrote that if an F-2 court were allowed an equitable argument concerning an F-1 judgment, the result would be to allow two state courts to reach mutually inconsistent positions on the same issue. Such, the Justice exclaimed, would be precisely the situation which the Full Faith and Credit Clause was designed to prevent.[540]

2. Judgments Granting Injunctions

Baker by Thomas v. General Motors Corporation[541] is a tale of three cases, all of which occurred in the same year - 1991. Early in the year a products liability case was filed against General Motors in Georgia. In November of that year a

---

534 245 S.E.2d 372 (N.C. App. 1978).

535 *Id.* at 375.

536 597 F.3d 697 (5th Cir, 2010).

537 *Id.* at 712.

538 *Id.*

539 455 U.S. 691 (1982).

540 *Id.* at 715.

541 522 U.S. 222 (1998).

wrongful death action was filed against General Motors in Missouri.[542] In December, 1991 a G.M. employee, Roland Elwell, sued G.M. in Michigan, for wrongful discharge. Elwell had testified against G.M in the Georgia action, no doubt prompting the corporation's counterclaim against him in his wrongful discharge action. Elwell and G.M. settled their dispute with Elwell receiving some undesignated funds and giving an agreement to his former employer to be bound by a permanent injunction prohibiting him from:

> [C]onsulting or discussing with or disclosing to any person any of General Motors Corporation's trade secrets[,] confidential information or matters of attorney-client work product relating in any manner to the subject matter of any products liability litigation whether already filed or [to be] filed in the future which Ronald Elwell received, had knowledge of, or was entrusted with during . . . his employments with General Motors Corporation. [543]

The stipulation excepted any subpoena-required testimony Elwell might give in the Georgia case.

In the Bakers' case against G.M. in Missouri the trial judge permitted Elwell to testify against G.M. because he did not believe that the Michigan stipulation between Elwell and G.M covered the Missouri case. The 8th Circuit reversed, and the U.S. Supreme Court reversed the 8th Circuit. Justice Ginsburg, writing for the Court, said that G.M.'s granting the exception for the Georgia litigation was not the result of "altruism." It was simply a recognition of the fact that the Michigan court had no power to reach into "the Missouri courtroom to displace the forum's own determination whether to admit or exclude evidence relative to the Bakers' wrongful death case before it."[544] The Court said, by dictum, that had Elwell volunteered his testimony, rather than being subpoenaed to give it, the Michigan injunction would have precluded him from doing so.[545] It was the attempt by G.M.

---

[542] The Missouri case is the one from which the title of the Supreme Court decision is derived. Two sons, named Baker, of a decedent, Mrs. Garner, brought an action against General Motors for their mother's wrongful death. One of the sons must have been a minor since he was represented in the case by his "next friend," a person named Thomas.

[543] *Baker,* 522 U.S. at 227, 228.

[544] *Id.* at 240.

[545] *Id*, at 239.

to assert the injunction into the Missouri courtroom to prevent the Missouri court from designating how testimony would be handled, that failed the full faith and credit test.

Olivares v. Performance Contracting Group [546] is a case in which Judges Hoekstra, Neff, and Davis gave the following lucid, even if subject to a few questions, Per Curiam explanation of the *Baker* decision:

> Plaintiff next cites *Baker v. General Motors Corp,* 522 U.S. 222; 118 S Ct 657; 139 L.Ed.2d 580 (1998), as support for his argument that injunctions are not entitled to full faith and credit to the same extent as other judgments. This is a misreading of Baker. Contrary to plaintiff's assertion, the *Baker* Court specifically held[547] that an injunction entered by a Michigan state court would be entitled to enforcement in Missouri under the Full Faith and Credit Clause, as between the same parties.[548] *Id.* at 239-241. In doing so, the Court rejected the argument that the Full Faith and Credit Clause does not apply to injunctive or other equitable orders. *Id.* at 234. In the present case, because the same parties were involved in the Indiana proceeding and the subsequent Michigan action, the trial court was required to afford full faith and credit to the Indiana injunction. *Poindexter, supra.* The trial court did not err by entering an injunction to enforce the Indiana decree.[549]

---

[546] 2005 WL 3479817 (Mich. App. 2005).

[547] We think the pronouncement was a dictum, rather than a holding. Ed. *See supra* text accompanying note 3.

[548] We are not certain that this requirement that the parties in the two actions be identical, as the court indicates, is accurate. Justice Ginsburg's statement at the top of page 239 ("[a]s the District Court recognized, Michigan's decree could operate against Elwell to preclude him from *volunteering* his testimony") does not indicate such restriction. The statement in n.12 on page 239, moreover, appears to refer only to "preclusive effect" application. It would seem that the case holds that volunteered testimony would be enjoinable whether or not the parties in the two cases are identical; and it is not a holding to the effect that the only time that testimony may be enjoined is where the testimony is volunteered and the parties in the two actions are identical. Ed.

[549] *Olivares,* 2005 WL 3479817 at *3.

3. Judgments Granting Specific Performance

The closest the U.S. Supreme Court has gotten to ruling on the application of full faith and credit to judgments awarding specific performance of contracts was a Concurring Opinion by Justice Oliver Wendell Holmes in *Fall v. Eastin,*[550] a case elsewhere considered in this work.[551] Justice Holmes agreed with the majority's approval of the Nebraska court denying full faith and credit to a Washington state judgment attempting to make a declaration of title concerning real property located in Nebraska, but for a different reason. He thought that if the Nebraska court had treated the Washington judgment as one granting specific performance of a contract officially agreeing to a transfer of title the court would have given it full faith and credit; but the Nebraska court did not so treat it. In effect the Nebraska court was not interested in acknowledging the equities of the situation, because the so-called "grantor" was not personally under the jurisdiction of the Washington court. Had he been so, the so-called "grantee" would have acquired equitable rights which she did not possess under the facts of the case. In such a situation it was not the Supreme Court's duty to tell the F-2 court how to treat the F-1 judgment. Nebraska's ruling, therefore, did not deny Washington's judgment full faith and credit.[552]

Donner v. Donner[553] is a tale of three states. Beatrice and Samuel, while in New York, contemplating a divorce, executed a written separation agreement in which Samuel agreed to make out a Will leaving 1/3 of his estate to Beatrice, provided she survived him unmarried. The agreement provided it would be "interpreted by New York law." Beatrice obtained her divorce in Alabama, her state of residency, agreed to by Samuel. The Alabama divorce decree "incorporated" the separation agreement, but did not merge it into the decree. Beatrice's attorneys informed the court that this omission was to protect her – while court orders, even final orders, can be modified, agreements cannot, except by the willing assent of the parties. The Alabama decree was domesticated in Florida. Thereafter in post-divorce proceeding in New York, instigated by Beatrice, Samuel, for the first time, attacked the separation agreement, claiming that it was, *inter alia*, procured by fraud. The New York trial judge rejected

---

550 215 U.S. 1 (1909).

551 *See* the Table of Cases of this work identifying reference to this case.

552 *Fall*, 215 U.S. at 15.

553 302 So2d 452 (Fla. 3d DCA 1974).

Samuel's position. Finding that he had prior opportunity to present his position, but having failed to do so, by the Full Faith and Credit Clause he was prevented from making that issue the basis of a collateral attack in New York. Samuel died while on his honeymoon with his third wife. His will was probated in Broward county, Florida, sans the provision concerning Beatrice, to which he had agreed in the separation agreement. A trial judge in Dade County, Florida granted Beatrice motion for summary judgment requiring that the separation agreements be specifically enforced. The Florida appellate court affirmed because the divorce decree, (1) entered in Alabama, (2) domesticated in Florida, and (3) judicially declared in New York was entitled to full faith and credit. The Florida appellate court found that even if the agreement was not subscribed by two witnesses, as required by Florida law, it was entitled to full faith and credit because of the numerous judicial proceeding which had approved it. Judge Hendry summarized the court's holding in the following words:

> [I]t is our conclusion that the judgments of the courts in Alabama, Florida and New York incorporating and construing provisions of the separation agreement between Beatrice and Samuel Donner preclude the appellants from raising the defense that the contract to make a will was unenforceable under principles of full faith and credit and *res judicata*.[554]

In *Sainz v. Sainz*[555] a married couple, who were residents of New York state, entered into a separation agreement. Subsequent to their divorce the former husband moved to North Carolina and ceased paying alimony. The former wife obtained an order from the New York court requiring the former husband to comply with the separation agreement. She wanted to domesticate the New York specific performance order in North Carolina in order to have her former husband held in contempt of court and incarcerated. The North Carolina court refused her request on the ground that the North Carolina public policy and Constitution forbid imprisonment for non payment of debts.[556] The appellate court affirmed, but remanded the case so that the trial court might consider the domestication of the New York judgment for arrearages.[557]

---

[554] *Id.* at 458.

[555] 245 S.E.2d 372 (N.C. App. 1978).

[556] *Id* at 374. *See supra* text accompanying notes 400, 401 and 422 for the courts' position on the viability of public policies as authorizing an exception to full faith and credit.

[557] *Id.* at 375.

4. Declaratory Judgments

The U.S. Court of Appeals for the Second Circuit in *United States. v. Doherty*[558] has defined a declaratory judgment as a procedure which:

> [E]nables a party who is challenged, threatened or endangered in the enjoyment of what he claims to be his . . . rights, to initiate the proceedings against his tormentor and remove the cloud by an authoritative determination of the plaintiff's legal right, privilege and immunity and the defendant's absence of right, and disability.[559]

It has also been said that a declaratory judgment:

> [C]reates a means by which rights and obligations may be adjudicated in cases involving an actual controversy that has not reached the stage at which either party may seek a coercive remedy, or in which the party entitled to such a remedy fails to sue for it.[560]

Injunctions may be issued in conjunction with a declaratory judgment. The U.S. Court of Appeals for the Second Circuit in *Kidder, Peabody & Co., Inc. v. Maxus Enerfy Corp.*[561] has declared that if the injunction exceeds the bounds of a proper declaratory judgment the court need not determine whether the injunction violated the Full Faith and Credit Clause.[562]

In *Pelczynski v. Dolatowski*[563] a declaratory judgment was rendered by the state of Wisconsin, declaring that automobile liability coverage was not available because the tortfeasor-driver had substantially deviated from the scope of the insured's permission to drive the vehicle in question. That declaratory judgment was given full force and credit, by Illinois despite the fact that the law of

---

[558] 786 F.2d 491,498,499 (2d Cir.1986).

[559] *Id.* at 498, 499.

[560] *Id.*

[561] 925 F.2d 556 (2d Cir. 1991).

[562] *Id.* at 565.

[563] 721 N.E.2d 196 (Ill. App. 1999).

Wisconsin conflicted with Illinois public policy of providing a broader scope of insurance coverage for those who technically violate the permission given them.[564]

In *Ponder Research Group. LLP v. Aquatic Navagation, Inc.*[565] a Texas court refused to enter a declaratory judgment to the effect that any judgment entered in the case which was then pending before it would be enforceable in Florida, under the Full Faith and Credit clause. The court declared that "there has been no showing that an actual controversy exists as to whether a judgment by this State may be enforced in Florida."[566]

Brown v. Progressive Direct Ins. Co.[567] involved an automobile accident which occurred in Hawai'i, injuring a passenger. Since the driver of the car was uninsured the passenger filed a declaratory judgment action in Massachusetts seeking a determination as to whether he could "stack" his uninsured coverage. The Massachusetts court rendered a judgment in the negative. The Hawai'i Supreme Court held that, under full faith and credit it was bound to honor the Massachusetts' declaratory judgment.[568]

In *Directory Assistants, Inc v. Cooke, Cameron, Travis & Co., P.C.*[569] an Alabama accounting firm contracted with a Connecticut business consulting firm, concerning business acumen. Before the contract was to expire the consulting firm was informed by the accounting firm that its services were no longer needed. The consulting firm promptly commenced arbitration proceeding in Connecticut, pursuant to the contract, and the accounting firm, taking a position naturally counter to the consulting firm, shortly thereafter filed for declaratory relief in Alabama. The arbitrators ruled in favor of the consulting firm, as did the Alabama court in the declaratory judgment action. The consulting firm obtained a Connecticut judgment confirming the arbitration award, and the accounting firm appealed the judgment rendered against it in Alabama. Thereupon the consulting

---

564 *Id.* at 199, 200.

565 2009 W.L. 2868456 (N.D. Tex. 2009).

566 *Id.* at *12. Query: if the parties had agreed that such a controversy, in fact, existed, would the court have rendered a declaration concerning that issue? Ed.

567 2010 W.L. 1806031 (Hawai'i App. 2010).

568 *Id.* at *4.

569 2010 W.L. 1541351 (Ala. Civ. App. 2010).

firm, under the UEFJA[570] obtained in Alabama registration of the Connecticut judgment in its favor. In Alabama the "registration" court found that under the UEFJA the only defense against registration of a foreign judgment is lack of personal and/or subject-matter jurisdiction of the F-1 court, and that there was a presumption in favor of that jurisdiction, and that even though there was little or no contact between Connecticut and the consulting firm's participation in fulfilling its contractual duties,[571] the contract specifically provided for arbitration to be performed in Connecticut, with Connecticut judicial approval of the award. The court, therefore affirmed the trial courts refusal to abrogate the registered Connecticut judgment. As to the appeal to the Alabama appellate court in the "declaratory judgment" part of the controversy, the court ruled that due to the Connecticut judgment which was given full faith and credit, there pended in the declaratory action no justiciable controversy to support a declaratory judgment and consequently the appeal must be dismissed.[572]

Martin v. SAIF Corp.[573] is an example of how a full faith and credit determination can, at times, become final without a final determination of a jurisdiction's highest court. A decision of Oregon's Workers' Compensation Board, concluded that Oregon's state-chartered workers' compensation insurance company was entitled to a certain distribution of proceeds from a claimant's third-party settlement with a tortfeasor, constituted a final judgment entitled to full faith and credit. The entitlement had been established in a declaratory judgment action in Montana commenced by the claimant seeking a declaration that Montana law governed distribution of the third-party settlement proceeds. The Montana judgment was against the claimant. The Oregon proceeding was final as the claimant dismissed his appeal.[574]

---

570 *See supra* text accompanying notes 255-257.

571 *See* text accompanying notes 59, 335, 345, 436, 438, 498, 503. 527, 571, 572, 846, 906, 1117, and 1119 concerning the importance of contacts with the jurisdiction from which the enforcement of a judgment (i.e. the rendering jurisdiction), is requested.

572 *Directory Assistants, Inc* , 2010 W.L.1541351 at *5.

573 167 P.3d 916 (Mont. 2007).

574 *Id.* at 920. It would appear that even had the claimant continued questioning the Montana decision it would have been upheld, and given full faith and credit, even if is were legally inaccurate. *See* Fauntleroy v. Lum (and for further consideration of this case

Manuel v. Convergys Corp.[575] was a non-competition and non-disclosure action, which was filed in Georgia by the former employee seeking a declaratory judgment to the effect that he had not breached his contract by leaving his employment and affiliating with a competitor, based in Ohio. The former employer defended the action in Georgia on the grounds that the forum for any litigation between the parties should be in Ohio. The Georgia court ruled in favor of its retaining jurisdiction on the basis that a declaratory judgment entered by the Georgia declaratory judgment court will have the same preclusive effect as a judgment entered by a Georgia court, and "under full faith and credit, *res judicata*, and collateral estoppel, the final judgment of Georgia courts [will] bind these parties as well as courts of other jurisdictions." The court added, almost as an afterthought, that it was problematical whether the Ohio district court could resolve this controversy because there are serious questions as to whether it would have personal jurisdiction over the plaintiff.[576]

5. Judgments Quieting Title

The full faith and credit concept has been recognized in connection with the establishment of the title to lands situate within a state at least since 1896 when the Circuit Court for the Eastern District of New York in *Roberts v. Brooks*[577] ruled that New Jersey law would apply to quieting title to land.[578] Other than that pronouncement there has been little to no enlightenment on the subject.

Hood v. McGehee[579] was an attempt by adopted children to quiet title to real property located in Alabama. The U.S. Supreme Court held that legally they were not permitted to do so. Alabama had a statute which prohibited children adopted in

---

see text accompanying notes 126, 5o5, 508 and 512, and notes 506, 589 and 1122) and the Treines case at notes 130, 131, 134, 135 and 137.

[575] 2004 W.L 5545025 (N.D. Ga. 2004).

[576] *Id.* at *4.

[577] 71 F. 914 (Cir. Ct. E. E.D. N.Y.1896).

[578] *Id.* at 916. In that case the court reviewed a prior action which quieted land foreclosed under a mortgage upon which no sums were due. The Court proclaimed that the prior judgment was not only correct, but was rendered in a proceeding "to whose proceedings full faith and credit are to be given."

[579] 237 U.S. 611 (1915).

other states to inherit property located in Alabama. The plaintiffs were adopted in Louisiana, and they had been devised land located in Alabama. Justice Oliver Wendell Holmes, writing for the Court said that such a statute does not offend the Full Faith and Credit Clause because Alabama recognized the foreign adoption, and allowed adopted children to take from the adoptive parent any gifts the parent wished to give them except for certain property located in Alabama at the time of the gift. As Alabama was the "sole mistress" of such property, it did not violate the Full Faith and Credit Clause.[580]

One of the most famous U.S. Supreme court decisions, *Durfee v. Duke*[581] concerned the quieting of land at the bottom of the Missouri River. It is most famous, however, for its dissertation as to subject-matter jurisdiction of the F-1 court. The course of the Missouri River is of serpentine character, subject to avulsion, and accretion,[582] which by its meandering course either adds to or takes away from land bordering it. In this case the states bordering the river were Nebraska and Missouri. Mr. & Mrs. Durfee filed a suit in Nebraska against Ms. Duke, asking that the land be quieted in their names. The Nebraska court recognized that it had subject-matter jurisdiction to make that decision only if the land were in Nebraska. As the result of a contested trial between the Durfees and Ms. Duke the Nebraska court found that the land was in Nebraska, and it entered a judgment quieting title in the Durfees. An appeal to the Nebraska Supreme Court resulted in an affirmance. Ms. Duke did not seek review in the U.S. Supreme Court, but several months later she asked a Missouri court to quiet title in her. The case was removed to a federal District Court, whose judge felt that the land was in Missouri, but that by the Full Faith and Credit Clause and its implementing statute he was bound by the determination of the Nebraska court. The Eighth Circuit didn't agree and reversed him because it felt that the full faith and credit principle did not apply to cases involving real property in foreign states. The U.S. Supreme Court reversed the Eighth Circuit, not only on this real property issue,[583] but also on the subject-matter jurisdiction inquiry. The Court, Justice Potter Stewart writing its Opinion, noted that there was no question about personal jurisdiction, both parties having appeared and participated in the case. The issue was: did the

---

[580] *Id.* at 615.

[581] 375 U.S.106 (1963).

[582] *Id.* at 108. Avulsion is a tearing away of land by the river; by accretion the river adds land to its borders.

[583] *Id.* at 115.

Nebraska court have subject-matter jurisdiction, which the Missouri court was bound to respect if it did. Justice Stewart said that for the full faith and concept to apply the F-1 court must have "fully litigated" the matter.[584] Unfortunately he did not live up to his usual attention to details as to what "fully litigated" really meant. His only comment was that "[t]he respondent [Ms. Duke] appeared in the Nebraska court and through counsel fully litigated the issue, explicitly contesting the court's jurisdiction over the subject matter of the controversy."[585] Perhaps that was sufficient, but it would have been helpful had we been favored with some details.

Another case, *Fall v. Eastin*,[586] long preceding *Durfee v. Duke*,[587] concerned quieting titles only peripherally, as it was more concerned with a court's ability to affect land in another state. In that Washington state case, a divorce proceeding, the judge proclaimed in the final decree that certain improved real property in Nebraska was henceforth to be owned by the wife, and directed the husband to execute a deed of that property to her. When the husband refused to execute and deliver such a deed the judge appointed a Commissioner, who did so. After the divorce proceedings were concluded the former wife without the former husband being served with process or appearing, asked a Nebraska court to quiet the title of the property in her name. The Nebraska court refused to do so on the basis that the Washington court lacked jurisdiction to proclaim title to land in another state. Justice Joseph McKenna, writing for the Court, in a dictum, made it clear that had the husband executed and delivered the deed, even though pursuant to an order of the court of equity which had personal jurisdiction over him, title would have passed from the husband to the wife. In this case, however, the Commissioner's deed, delivered in compliance with an order which the court did not have jurisdiction to make, was meaningless, of no effect, and not entitled to full faith and credit.[588] Justice Oliver Wendell Holmes raised an interesting point in his Concurring Opinion. Had the Nebraska court treated the action before it as one for recognition of a foreign judgment requiring specific performance of a contract such would have been entitled to full faith and credit. The Supreme Court,

[584] *Id.* at 112.

[585] *Id.* at 109.

[586] 215 U.S. 1 (1909).

[587] 375 U.S. 106 (1963).

[588] *Fall*, 215 U.S. at 7.

however, has no control over how an F-2 court treats an F-1 judgment which it is asked to recognize; and if the F-2 court makes a mistake in its treatment of the F-1 judgment, so be it.[589]

Higginbotham v. Higginbotham[590] is factually very similar to *Fall v. Eastin*[591] except for the fact that *Fall* was an account of what transpired in F-1 and F-2 by the U.S. Supreme Court, whereas *Higginbotham* was an account by F-2 of what transpired in that case. There, a couple lived in New Jersey, and accumulated some New Jersey property. Later they moved to Florida, and continued in business until the wife filed for divorce. The husband was served with process and actively participated in the divorce proceedings. The Florida judge decreed that the wife was to receive real property in New Jersey and ordered the husband to sign a deed conveying title to the wife. To insure compliance with court orders the Florida judge placed the husband under *Ne exeat* restrictions. The husband disobeyed both court orders and departed Florida for New Jersey. The former wife thereupon appeared in New Jersey, and requested a New Jersey Chancery Division court to grant her several forms of relief, including a declaration that pursuant to the Florida judgment, which she urged should receive full faith and credit, that she was the owner of the New Jersey real property, and that the former husband be ordered to sign a deed conveying the property to her. Though the former husband had been served with process, he disappeared before hearing, and was represented only by counsel. The chancellor denied the former wife's request for relief, based primarily on *Fall v. Eastin*, and New Jersey authority. The appellate court reversed. It distinguished *Fall*, primarily on a comparison between the Washington order in *Fall*, which in effect was a declaration that the property belongs to the wife, and the Florida judgment here, which merely provided that the New Jersey property was to become that of the wife. The court also referred to facets of the case similar to *Johnson v. Muelberger*,[592] where the husband participated actively in that Florida divorce proceeding, but never appealed. Here the husband never appealed the Florida decree and, in fact, accepted every ruling made by the Florida judge

---

[589] *Id.* at 15. It seems as though the author of Fauntleroy v. Lum (*see* supra text accompanying note 126, and other cases listed in the Table of Cases contained in this book).

[590] 222 A.2d 120 (N.J. Super A.D. 1966).

[591] 215 U.S.U.S.. 1 (1909).

[592] 340 U.S. 581 (1951). *See* text accompanying notes 49, 51, 202, 744 and 761 for further consideration of this case.

except the one concerning the New Jersey real property. In a pronouncement resounding of equitable principles the court declared that the Florida decree was entitled to full faith and credit.[593]

G. Statutes Sued Upon & Used in Defense & Causes of Action

1. Statutes

a. Statutes Sued Upon

Black's Law Dictionary defines "statute" as "[a] law passed by a legislative body; specif., legislation enacted by any lawmaking body, including legislatures, administrative boards, and municipal courts. The term *act* is interchangeable as a synonym."[594] Judge-made "law" may be the genesis of a cause of action, but a statute may also govern the right of a plaintiff to bring his suit.[595] This chapter shall deal with the latter of those two sources, as they comply with the full faith and credit concept. As a general proposition the Supreme Court of Massachusetts in *Heron v. Heron*[596] observed that the provisions of any statute yield to the Full Faith and Credit Clause.[597]

In *Bowles v. Barde Steel Co.*[598] Justice Brand opined that:

> [I]f a court of one state refuses to enforce the statute of another state in a case in which it ought to do so and in which the statute gives a right, it

---

[593] *Higginbottham*, 222 A. at 130.

[594] Black's Law Dictionary, 8th Edition (2004).

[595] Justice Oliver Wendell Holmes once wrote: "[i]t would seem a miscarriage of justice if a plaintiff should recover upon a statute that did not govern the case." *See* Atlantic Coast Line R. Co. v. Burnette, 239 U.S. 199, 200 (1915).

[596] 703 N.E.2d 712 (Mass. 1998). *See infra* text accompanying notes 597, 800-803 for further reference to this case.

[597] *Id.* at 714.

[598] 164 P.2d 692 (Ore. 1945).

> thereby denies the full faith and credit demanded by the Federal Constitution, because the statute is a public act of another state.[599]

It should be remembered that in *Chicot County Drainage District v. Baxter State Bank*[600] the U.S. Supreme Court established that parties who do not object to the constitutionality of a statute are bound by the preclusive effect of *res judicata*, in a decision governed by that statute which is later found to be unconstitutional.[601]

The U.S. Supreme Court has had its share of expounding upon that subject. We shall address some of the more prominent cases chronologically in order to answer the question posed by Justice Felix Frankfurter in his lengthy dissent in *Hughes v. Fetter*:[602] "[h]ow far the Full Faith and Credit Clause undercuts the purpose of the Constitution made explicit by the Tenth Amendment,[603] to leave the conduct of domestic affairs to the States."

Hawkins v. Barney's Lessees,[604] early in our country's history cautioned against imposing upon the fora a "state of vassalage."[605]

Williamson v. Berry[606] was a Supreme Court decision, reviewing a New York special Act in which Justice James M. Wayne, writing for the Court said:

> [T]he jurisdiction of any court exercising authority over a subject may be inquired into in every other court, when the proceedings in the former are relied upon, and brought before the latter, by a party claiming the benefit

---

599 *Id.* at 699.

600 308 U.S. 371 (1940).

601 *Id.* at 374, 375.

602 341 U.S. 609, 620 (1951). *See* the Table of Cases for further cases concerning this case.

603 The Tenth Amendment (1791) provides "[t]he powers not delegated to the United States by the Constitution, nor prohibited by it to the States, are reserved to the States respectively, or to the people."

604 30 U.S. (5 Pet.) 457 (1831).

605 *Id.* at 467.

606 49 U.S. (8 Howard) 495 (1850).

> of such proceedings. The rule prevails, whether the decree or judgment has been given in a court of admiralty, chancery, ecclesiastical court, or court of common . . . law, or whether the point ruled has arisen under the laws of nations, the practice in chancery, or the municipal laws of states.[607]

Chambers v. Baltimore & Ohio R. Co.[608] held that an Ohio statute which provided that wrongful death actions were permitted to be tried in Ohio courts only if the decedent had been a citizen of Ohio, was not unconstitutional because the only person differentiated is the decedent. There is no differentiation as to the decedent's surrogate who brings the suit, a right that is indeed precious. Anyone who brings the suit, whether an Ohio citizen or a citizen of another state, is subject to the same statutory provision.[609]

Converce v. Hamilton[610] concerned the refusal of Wisconsin courts to permit an action to enforce liability of stockholders of an insolvent Minnesota corporation to be maintained by the Receiver of such corporation. The Receiver had been given, by the Minnesota statute, greater rights than the usual Receiver, such as bringing actions in states other than Minnesota. Under the Minnesota statute the Receiver became a quasi assignee of creditors charged with the enforcement of stockholders' liability. The U.S. Supreme Court held that the action of Wisconsin, in refusing the Receiver access to its courts, denied full faith and credit to the laws of Minnesota and the judicial proceedings in that state.[611]

In *Pennsylvania Fire Ins. Co. of Philadelphia v. Gold Issue Min. & Mill. Co.*[612] the Court, through Justice Oliver Wendell Holmes, expressed responsibility imposed upon a party viewing a statute of a foreign jurisdiction in the following

---

[607] *Id.* at 540, 541.

[608] 207 U.S. 142 (1907).

[609] *Id.* at 148, 149. The Court said that the basis of this principle was the Privileges and Immunities principle (as expressed in U.S. Const art. IV, § 2 cl.1), which, in turn, was emphasized by Justice Bushrod Washington in Corfield v. Coryell, 6 F. Cas. 546 (Cir. Ct. E.D. Pa. 1823). *See infra* text accompanying notes 1303, 1340, 1341, regarding Corfield v. Coryell.

[610] 224 U.S. 243 (1912).

[611] *Id.* at 256.

[612] 243 U.S. 93 (1917).

words: "[t]here is nothing to suggest that it was not candidly construing the Colorado statutes to the best of its ability, and even if it was wrong, something more than an error of construction is necessary in order to entitle a party to come here under article 4, § 1."[613]

Douglas v. N.Y., N.H., & H. R. Co [614] emphasized the fact that a state may, by statute, prefer its citizens rather than citizens of other states, based not only upon attempting to achieve convenience for them in overly crowded courts, but also upon the fact that it is they who are burdened with the cost of such objectives.[615]

Brinkerhoff-Faris Trust & Savings Co. v. Hill[616] held that one need not attempt to use administrative remedies that are not provided for by the statute under which the plaintiff is proceeding.[617]

Alabama Pub. Service Comm. v. Southern R. Co.[618] made it clear that if in the forum a statute of another jurisdiction is complained of, all statutes which may be invoked in conjunction therewith, i.e. those requiring administrative procedures, must be considered.[619]

In *Bradford Electric Light & Power Co. v. Clapper*[620] legal action for common law damages (permitted by a New Hampshire statute), was brought in New Hampshire for the death, in New Hampshire, of employee Clapper, a citizen and resident of Vermont. The employer was also a resident and citizen of Vermont. The employer asserted that the New Hampshire court should use the Vermont statute, (which forbid actions for common law damages in like situations), applicable to the tort committed in New Hampshire because the employee was

---

613 *Id* at 96, 97.

614 279 U.S. 377 (1929).

615 *Id.* at 387.

616 281 U.S. 673 (1930).

617 *Id.* at 682. It seems that this case preceded in its admonition what the case which followed it had expounded upon.

618 341 U.S. 341 (1951).

619 *Id.* at 344, 345.

620 286 U.S. 145 (1932).

hired and the contract of employment was executed in Vermont. The Vermont statute specified that if an employee was hired in Vermont it applied even if an injury occurred outside the state. The New Hampshire statute gave the employee, or his legal representative an option of suing for common law damages. The trial judge applied New Hampshire law, apparently accepting the plaintiff's argument to the effect that if the Vermont statute were used New Hampshire's public policy would be abused. The U.S. Supreme Court reversed. Justice Lewis Brandeis, writing for the Court, opined that Vermont had the authority to enact an exclusive statute as to contracts executed in Vermont, and the Full Faith and Credit Clause required the New Hampshire forum to apply the Vermont statute, there being no damage to its public policy by doing so.[621]

Alaska Packers Ass'n v Industrial Acc. Comm.[622] held that California was free to use its own workers' compensation statute, in an employee-injured-in-Alaska case, to the exclusion of that of Alaska, even though a contract between the employer and the employee provided that the Alaska statute would be used in the event of an accident to the employee. The Alaska statute purported to give Alaska an exclusive remedy to all persons injured there, including the non-resident alien employee involved in the action under consideration.[623] The Court, however, discounted that position by the words of Justice Harlan F. Stone who wrote the Opinion of the Court:

> It has often been recognized by this Court that there are some limitations upon the extent to which a state will be required by the full faith and credit clause to enforce even the judgment of another state, in contravention of its own statutes or policy. . . . In the case of statutes, the extra-state effect of which Congress has not prescribed, where the policy of one state statute comes into conflict with that of another, the necessity of some accommodation of the conflicting interests of the two states is still more apparent. A rigid and literal enforcement of the full faith and credit clause, without regard to the statute of the forum, would lead to the absurd . . . result that, wherever the conflict arises, the statutes of each state must be

---

621 *Id.* at 161, 162. The holding of this case was modified by Crider v. Zurich Ins. Co., 380 U.S. 39 (1965). *See supra* text accompanying note 72 and infra notes 645, 646, 648-650 for further consideration of that case.

622 294 U.S. 532 (1935).

623 *Id.* at 549, 550.

> enforced in the courts of the other, but cannot be in its own. . . . [T]he conflict is to be resolved, not by giving automatic effect to the full faith and credit clause, compelling the courts of each state to subordinate its own statutes to those of the other, but by appraising the governmental interests of each jurisdiction, and turning the scale of decision according to their weight.[624]

Broderick v, Rosner[625] required New Jersey to provide a forum to corporate stockholders whose liability was governed by New York statutes.[626]

John Hancock Mut. Life Ins. Co. v. Yates [627] required a Georgia court to give full faith and credit to a parole evidence statute which prevented recovery on an insurance contract executed in New York, because the New York statute, though not having an extraterritorial effect, became a part of the insurance contract.[628]

Pacific Employers Ins. Co. v. Industrial Acc. Comm.[629] permitted California to reject a Massachusetts workers' employment statute even though Massachusetts was (1) the place of the execution of the contract of employment, (2) the usual place of the employee's work, and (3) the place of citizenship of the employee and the place of incorporation of the employer. Reason: the Full Faith and Credit Clause does not require states to abandon their own statutes just because other states have similar, but not identical, ones, and use of the other state's statute would offend the forum's public policy.[630]

---

624 *Id.* at 546, 547.

625 294 U.S. 629 (1935).

626 *Id.* at 647.

627 299 U.S. 178 (1936).

628 *Id.* at 182, 183.

629 306 U.S. 493 (1939). *See supra* notes 73, 213, 407 and 462 in which this case is mentioned, and *infra* text accompanying notes 630, 1118, and 1119 for further consideration of this case.

630 *Id.* at 504, 505. *See* the Table of Cases for a listing of other references to this case, and in particular *supra* note 407.

Griffin v. McCoach[631] authorized a forum's decline of enforcement of an insurance policy in favor of beneficiaries who had no insurable interest under the statutory law of the forum.[632]

In *Pink v. A.A.A.Highwar Exps*[633] New York state had statutes under which it took judicial proceedings to assess members of an insolvent mutual insurance company, some of whom were residents of Georgia. When the New York Commissioner of Insurance sued those persons in a Georgia court his petition was dismissed, by an order of the court affirmed by the Georgia Supreme Court. When the case reached the U.S. Supreme Court the issue was whether the Full Faith and Credit Clause obligated the Georgia courts to honor the New York statutes and judicial proceedings or, in effect, did this case represent an exception to the Clause. The Court held that these statutes and judicial proceedings were of a nature that the Georgia courts had the power to interpret for their residents, and not be compelled to obey the rulings of New York authorities. Chief Justice Harlan F. Stone, writing the Opinion of the Court said:

> To the extent that Georgia must give full faith and credit to the New York statutes and judicial proceedings, . . . it must be denied authority to adjudicate the meaning and domestic effect under its own laws of a contract entered into by its own inhabitants and containing no stipulation that they should be bound by obligations extrinsically imposed by New York law. But the full faith and credit clause is not an inexorable and unqualified command. It leaves some scope for state control within its borders of affairs which are peculiarly its own. This Court has often recognized that, consistent with the appropriate application of the full faith and credit clause, there are limits to the extent to which the laws and policy of one state may be subordinated to those of another. Alaska Packers Ass'n v. Industrial Accident Commission, 294 U.S. 532, 55 S.Ct. 518, 79 L.Ed. 1044, Pacific Employers Ins. Co. v. Industrial Accident Commission, 306 U.S. 493, 59 S.Ct. 629, 83 L.Ed. 940; Klaxon Co. v. Stentor Co., 313 U.S. 487, 497, 498, 61 S.Ct. 1020, 1022, 85 L.Ed. 1477;

---

[631] 313 U.S. 498 (1941).

[632] *Id.* at 504.

[633] 314 U.S. 201 (1941).

> *see* Milwaukee County v. M. E. White Co., 296 U.S. 268, 273, 56 S.Ct. 229, 232, 80 L.Ed. 220.[634]

Buford v. Sun Oil Co.[635] is a case which reveals that at times doctrines other than full faith and credit require action by courts which are similar, but not identical to, full faith and credit. This was an abstention[636] case. It held that where a Texas statute provided a unified method for the formation of a policy regarding the oil industry, and determination of cases by the Texas Railroad Commission and judicial review of the Commission's decision in state courts was expeditious and adequate, a sound respect for the independence of state action required a federal exercising its equity jurisdiction to refuse to take jurisdiction of a diversity of citizenship suit to enjoin enforcement of the Commission's order granting permits to drill oil wells, and allow state courts to consider the problems involved.[637]

In *Hughes v. Fetter*[638] a man was killed in Illinois. The administrator of his estate brought a wrongful death action in Wisconsin because the decedent, the administrator of his estate, and the corporate defendant were all Wisconsin residents. The action was based, however, on the Wrongful Death statute of Illinois the place of the death. The Wisconsin courts dismissed the action based on a Wisconsin statute which provided that its Wrongful Death statute was to be utilized only for deaths occurring in Wisconsin. The U.S. Supreme Court reversed based on the Full Faith and Credit Clause, which Justice Hugo L. Black, writing for the Court, described as "unifying."[639] The Court reasoned that such a statute violates the spirit of full faith and credit: (1) Wisconsin, having its own Wrongful Death statutes has no antagonism to the procedure; (2) though service of process was possible in this case, it might not be so in all cases brought before the Wisconsin courts, which, if Wisconsin would not permit the action the moving

---

[634] *Id.* at 209, 210.

[635] 319 U.S. 315 (1943).

[636] Abstention is a judge-made doctrine which provides that under certain circumstances a federal court should abstain from hearing a case and defer to the state courts in that particular.

[637] *Buford*, 319 U.S. at 333, 334.

[638] 341 U.S. 609 (1951). *See supra* text accomplishing notes 73, 405, 590 and infra 677 for further consideration of Hughes v. Fetter.

[639] *Id.* at 612.

party would go forth without a remedy.[640] Justice Black concluded the Court's Opinion, stating "we conclude that Wisconsin's statutory policy which excludes this Illinois cause of action is forbidden by the national policy of the Full Faith and Credit Clause."[641]

Carroll v. Lanza[642] concerned injuries to an employee of a subcontractor. They were both residents of Missouri, and their contract was executed in Missouri. The employee, however, did not elect to be bound by the Missouri compensation Act, but he received compensation under the Missouri Act after he received injuries in Arkansas while working for the general contractor. While he was receiving compensation from Missouri the employee sued the general contractor in Arkansas and recovered a general damage award. It was reversed by the appellate court on full faith and credit grounds, i.e. that the exclusivity of the compensation statute of the home state (Missouri) must be followed. The U.S. Supreme Court reversed, permitting Arkansas, where the injury occurred, to grant common law damages for an employee's injuries, even though Missouri, the residence of the employer and employee had a worker's compensation Act which purported to be exclusive.[643] Justice William O. Douglas, in the Opinion of the Court, said that:

> Whatever deprives the remedy of the home State of its exclusive character qualifies or contravenes the policy of that State and denies it full faith and credit, if full faith and credit is due. But the Pacific Employers Insurance Co. case teaches that in these personal injury cases the State where the injury occurs need not be a vassal to the home State and allow only that remedy which the home State has marked as the exclusive one. The State of the forum also has interests to serve and to protect.[644]

In *Crider v. Zurich Ins. Co.*[645] an employee was a resident of Alabama who was employed by a resident of Georgia. He was injured while working in Alabama. The court states that both the employee and the employer were "under" a

---

640 *Id.* at 12.

641 *Id.*

642 349 U.S. 408 (1955).

643 *Id*, at 413, 414.

644 *Id.* at 412.

645 380 U.S. 39 (1965).

Georgia worker's compensation statute.[646] The employee sued his employer in an Alabama state court "under" the Georgia statute, and recovered a default judgment. Then the employee sued the employer's insurance carrier in federal court in Alabama. The District Judge dismissed the suit against the carrier and the Fifth Circuit affirmed. The reason for the dismissal and the affirmance was that the Georgia statute is an exclusive statute which may be invoked only by the Georgia Compensation Board, and not by the courts. The U.S. Supreme Court reversed, Justice William O. Douglas writing the Opinion of the Court. The thrust of the decision was that *Clapper*,[647] which held that a state was free to enact a statute which it considered "exclusive," meaning that if other courts had to deal with it they must yield and give it full faith and credit, was wrongly decided by giving a statute that extraterritorial effect.[648] Douglas made it clear that even though Georgia enacted a statute, which if utilized within Georgia must be explicitly followed, when utilized outside of Georgia its "remedy" could be "supplemented" or "displaced."[649] Reason: "[t]he state where the employee lives and where he was injured has a large and considerable interest in the event."[650]

Hanner v. Plumer[651] was a full faith and credit case involving differences between Massachusetts and federal Rules for the service of process. Chief Justice Earl Warren, writing the Opinion of the Court made it plain that under *Erie v. Thompkins*[652] if there is no distinction as to the procedure between state and federal court in the same state, the state rule will apply. Where there is conflict, however, the Rules Enabling Act[653] controls and the federal Rule is applied. In his writing Chief Justice Warren made the Court's position clear with the following words:

---

646 *Id*, at 39.

647 Bradford Electric Light & Power Co. v. Clapper, 286 U.S. 145 (1932). *See* Table of Cases for a listing of other cases concerning this case.

648 *Crider,* 380 U.S. at 40. Justice Douglas seemed to indicate that Alaska Packers (*see supra* text accompanying note 60 and Pacific Employers *see* text accompanying note 72) which were the cases that overruled Clapper (*see supra* text accompanying note 61.

649 *Id.* at 41.

650 *Id.* at 42.

651 380 U.S. 460 (1965).

652 304 U.S. 64 (1938).

653 28 U.S.C. § 2072.

> Erie and its offspring cast no doubt on the long-recognized power of Congress to prescribe housekeeping rules for federal courts even though some of those rules will inevitably differ from comparable state rules. (Citation omitted). 'When, because the plaintiff happens to be a non-resident, such a right is enforceable in a federal as well as in a State court, the forms and mode of enforcing the right may at times, naturally enough, vary because the two judicial systems are not identic.' (Citations omitted). Thus, though a court, in measuring a Federal Rule against the standards contained in the Enabling Act and the Constitution, need not wholly blind itself to the degree to which the Rule makes the character and result of the federal litigation stray from the course it would follow in state courts, (citation omitted), it cannot be forgotten that the Erie rule, and the guidelines suggested in York,[654] were created to serve another purpose altogether. To hold that a Federal Rule of Civil Procedure must cease to function whenever it alters the mode of enforcing state-created rights would be to disembowel . . . either the Constitution's grant of power over federal procedure or Congress' attempt to exercise that power in the Enabling Act.[655]

In *Thomas v. Washington Gas & Light Co.*[656] a worker, resident of the District of Columbia, was hired by a District of Columbia employer, but was injured, while working for that employer in Virginia. He obtained workers' compensation from Virginia, but subsequently applied for a supplemental award from his home base, the District of Columbia. His employer objected on the ground that the Full Faith and Credit Clause required the District to deny a second award. An administrative order granting his request was overruled by the Fourth Circuit. The U.S. Supreme Court revered the Fourth Circuit. Justice John Paul Stevens, joined by three other Justices in a plurality Opinion said that the Full Faith and Credit Clause does not preclude successive awards of workers' compensation since states have no legitimate interest in the "context of the federal system" as that system does not allow F-1 to object to F-2 granting a supplemental award, under its compensation

---

654 Guranty Trust Co. of New York v. York, 324 U.S. 99 (1945).

655 *Hanna*, 389 U.S. at 473, 474.

656 448 U.S. 261 (1980).

statute when F-2 would have the power to do so in the first instance.[657] Specifically Stevens said for the plurality:

> The Full Faith and . . . Credit Clause "is one of the provisions incorporated into the Constitution by its framers for the purpose of transforming an aggregation of independent, sovereign States into a nation."[658] To vest the power of determining the extraterritorial effect of a State's own laws and judgments in the State itself risks the very kind of parochial entrenchment on the interests of other States that it was the purpose of the Full Faith and Credit Clause and other provisions of Art. IV of the Constitution to prevent.[659]

The judgment of the Court, therefore, was to the effect that a second state was permitted to authorize, by statute, a supplemental workers' compensation Act, which must be accorded full faith and credit, even if there were no Opinion of the Court to support it. The judgment was in conformity with a prior Supreme Court decision, *Industrial Comm. of Wisconsin v. McCartin*[660] which held that a state was permitted to take such a position if it did so by some "unmistakable" language of its legislature or judiciary.[661] The judgment, however, was in conflict with *Magnolia Petroleum Co. v. Hunt*[662] which the plurality said should be overruled,[663] but wasn't.

In *Trauger v. A.J. Spagnol Lumber Co., Inc.*[664] the Florida Supreme Court held that while the state legislature may prohibit the courts of its state from recognizing

---

657 *Id.* at 286.

658 Quoting from Sherrer v. Sherrer, 334 U.S. 343, 355 (1948). *See supra* text accompanying note 58, 141, 142, infra notes 658, 752-755.

659 *Thomas*, 448 U.S. at 272. The Court referred to Nevada v. Hall, 440 U.S. 410, 424-425 (1979).

660 330 U.S. 622 (1947).

661 *Id.* at 628.

662 320 U.S 430 (1943).

663 *See Thomas*, 448 U.S. at 286.

664 442 So. 2d 182 (Fla. 1983).

and enforcing judgments based on cognovit notes,[665] it may not attempt to prohibit courts of other states from entering such judgments by prohibiting the recognition and enforcement thereof.[666]

Sun Oil Co. v. Wortman[667] was a class action suit involving royalties on gas deposits in Texas, Oklahoma and Louisiana; the forum was located in Kansas. The forum applied the substantive law of the three states which involved the royalties, but its own statute of limitations as to the rights to royalties. The issue before the U.S. Supreme Court was whether the Kansas court had violated the Full Faith and Credit Clause by ignoring the other states' statutes of limitations and applying its own. The Court, with Justice Antonin Scalia writing the Court's Opinion, gave no definitive answer as to whether a statute of limitations was substantive or procedural. It concentrated on a pragmatic approach. As long as state legislatures have been deciding, for 200 years, what are stale claims for their courts to apply when deciding choice-of-law questions, the courts will continue to abide by that method of resolving viability disputes. Justice Scalia phrased it in his Opinion, as follows:

> A State's interest in regulating the work load of its courts and determining when a claim is too stale to be adjudicated certainly suffices to give it legislative jurisdiction to control the remedies available in its courts by imposing statutes of limitations. Moreover, petitioner could in no way have been unfairly surprised by the application to it of a rule that is as old as the Republic. There is, in short, nothing in Kansas' action here that is "arbitrary or unfair, . . . "[668]

In *Midwest Title Loans, Inc. v. Ripley*[669] Judge Sarah Evans Parker opined that: "[a] state may not directly regulate conduct or events beyond its own borders, no matter its motivation for doing so."[670] In *Farnham v. Farnham*,[671] however, the

---

665 *See supra* note 355 for a definition of *cognovit* notes.

666 *Trauger*, 442 U.S. at 183.

667 486 U.S. 717 (1988).

668 *Id.* at 730.

669 616 F .Supp.2d 897 (S.D. Ind. 2009).

670 *Id.* at 907.

671 2009 W. L 5125123, (Tenn. Ct. App. 2009).

court approved the following statement rendered by an unidentified New York court:

> We feel that the Massachusetts statute has extraterritorial effect and can be applied to parties who are married and live outside of Massachusetts. Such recognition is consistent with giving full faith and credit to the interlocutory nature of the foreign decree. . . . The Massachusetts statute is remedial in nature and should be applied for its intended purpose of protecting persons who marry innocently in good faith and to avoid the stigma of illegitimacy for innocent children when one parent is blameless of any conscious violation of the marriage laws.[672]

In *Adar v. Smith*[673] the U.S. Court of Appeals for the Fifth Circuit followed the U.S. Supreme Court's directive that full faith and credit does not require a state to use statutes of another state in place of its own.[674]

b. Statutes Used in Defense

In *Roche v. McDonald*[675] one Dart sued and recovered against McDonald a money judgment in Washington state. Dart thereupon assigned the judgment to Roche. Thereupon Roche attempted to convert the Washington judgment into an Oregon judgment. McDonald resisted Roche's attempt on the ground that under a Washington statute the Washington judgment became dormant upon the elapse of six years. Roche's response to this defense was the Washington judgment must be recognized as a cause of action for the creation of a new judgment under the Full Faith and Credit Clause. The Oregon court agreed, and domesticated the Washington judgment into an Oregon judgment. When the case reached the U.S. Supreme Court it held that Washington (now F-2), must recognize the Oregon (now F-1) judgment even if its doing so was repugnant to its statute of the dormancy of judgments.[676]

---

[672] *Id.* at *8. Chief Justice John Marshall in Church v. Hubbart, 6 U.S. (2 Cranch) 187, 234 (1804) suggested that Congress be authorized to enact extraterritorial statutes.

[673] 597 F.3d 697 (5th Cir 2010).

[674] *Id.* at 709.

[675] 275 U.S. 449 (1928).

[676] *Id* at 455.

2. Causes of Action

Black's Law Dictionary defines "cause of action"[677] as "[a] group of operative facts giving rise to one or more bases for suing; a factual situation that entitles one person to obtain a remedy in court from another person."[678] The question of whether a cause of action must be entitled to full faith and credit can be answered quickly. It must be.

While the courts have not expounded upon which of the three categories referred to in the Full Faith and Credit Clause,[679] causes of action fit, such differentiation is not all that important, as they must fit somewhere in the constitutional wording. Probably as "judicial Proceedings."

Before exploring cases recognizing and enforcing causes of action, it would be well to briefly review the distinction between a cause of action and the judgment it encompasses, if a judgment is entered on it. They are distinct, and something different from each other. This point was made eminently clear by Chief Justice Harlan F. Stone in *Milwaukee County v. M.E. White Co.*[680] While, at times, full faith and credit does not demand recognition and enforcement of a matter, such as another state's taxes, as in the *Milwaukee County* case, full faith and credit will demand that a judgment of that state for their collection must be recognized and enforced.[681]

There appear to have been three lines of defense asserted against including causes of action within the aegis of full faith and credit: (1) allowing a cause of action arising out of F-1 law in F-2 violates the public policy of F-2; (2) enforcing an F-1 cause of action in F-2 violates the exclusivity provisions giving rise to a similar cause of action in the enforcing (F-2) state; and (3) the venue provisions of the F-1 statute giving rise to the cause of action attempted to be enforced require that the cause of action must be brought in F-1.

---

677 At times referred to as a "chose-in-action," or a "right-of-action."

678 Black's Law Dictionary, 8th Edition (2004).

679 To wit: "public Acts." Records," or "judicial Proceedings."

680 296 U.S. 268, 278 (1935), which discredited Wisconsin v. Pelican Ins. Co., 127 U.S. 265, 292, 293 (1888), to the extent that it said anything different.

681 *Millwaukee County*, 296 U.S. at 268 in passim.

With regard to the first line of defense, i.e. offense of F-2's public policy the U.S. Supreme Court in the 1952 case of *First Nat. Bank of Chicago v. United Air Lines, Inc.*[682] held that an Illinois statute which allowed the trial of wrongful death actions arising in another state where service of process could not be obtained, but did not allow those cases to be tried where service of process could be obtained in the foreign state. The court offered no explanation other that the public policy of Illinois violated the Full Fait and Credit Clause. The author of the Court's Opinion, Justice Hugo L. Black, did point out that as was mentioned in *Hughes v. Fetter*, [683] the inability to serve process in other states is not of major significance.[684] Although Justice Black did not expound upon the reason for the court's decision, it might have been that while the Illinois statute permitted the bringing of wrongful death actions in Illinois if service of process may not be obtainable in other states may have been a benevolent gesture on the part of the Illinois legislature, its giving importance to something which the Court had said was not of importance, and differentiating states on that basis. If so, such explanation just does not square with the equality attempted to be achieved by the framers when they used the term in the Constitution. In 1979 Justice John Paul Stevens, for the U.S. Supreme Court in *Nevada v. Hall*[685] wrote that "the Full Faith and Credit Clause does not require a State to apply another State's law in violation of its own legitimate public policy.".[686] It is, therefore, incontestable that from the *First Nat. Bank* and *Nevada v. Hall* cases, a postulate has been established to the effect that a public policy which violates the Full Faith and Credit Clause is not a legitimate public policy worth considering.

Certain (F-2) state statutes permitting a cause of action to arise, under various conditions, specify that trial of the cause of action shall be tried exclusively in that state. Such provisions have given rise to the second line of defense where a cause of action accruing in state F-1 is attempted to be brought in state F-2. The Supreme Court of the United States has not dealt with this defense, but the Illinois Supreme Court in *Blount v. Stroud*[687] has offered a plausible reason as to why the defense is

---

682 342 U.S. 396, 397, 398 (1952).

683 341 U.S. 609 (1951).

684 *First Nat. Bank Of Chicago*, 342 U.S. at 397.

685 440 U.S. 410 (1979).

686 *Id.* at 422.

687 904 N.E.2d 1 (Ill. 2009).

not sustainable. It was there held that an exclusionary provision, providing that an action on a specified cause of action may be brought in that state, refers to a cause of action arising in that state.[688] Such holding is plausible, because, even though the court did not mention it, any statute which attempted to outlaw a foreign cause of action would violate the Court's holding in *Hughes v. Fetter.*[689] This holding of the Illinois Supreme Court was followed in *Ferreri v. Hewitt Associates,*[690] in which an Illinois court permitted a discharged employee to file in Illinois a human rights cause of action, based on Missouri law.[691]

Certain (F-1) state statutes which authorize a cause of action that is attempted to be enforced in F-2 contain provisions specifying that the trials of those causes of action are limited to certain venues in F-1, thus ostensibly eliminating trial is an F-2 venue. This is the source from which the third defense to using F-1 causes of action in F-2 is taken.

In *Tennessee Coal, Iron, & R.R. Co. v. George*[692] the plaintiff brought, in Georgia, a suit based on the Alabama worker's compensation statute. The defendant employer moved to dismiss the suit, citing an Alabama venue provision that required all actions under the worker's compensation statute to be "brought in a court of competent jurisdiction within the state of Alabama, and not elsewhere." The United States Supreme Court held that the venue provision could not be enforced to prevent suit in Georgia. Justice Joseph Lamar, in the Opinion of the Court, wrote that:

> The courts of the sister [s]tate trying the case would be bound to give full faith and credit to all those substantial provisions of the statute which inhered in the cause of action or which name conditions on which the right to sue depend. *But venue is no part of the right;* and a [s]tate cannot create a transitory cause of action and at the same time destroy the right to sue on that transitory cause of action in any court having jurisdiction. That jurisdiction is to be determined by the law of the court's creation [that is,

---

688 *Id.* at 1.

689 *See* Hughes v. Fetter, 341 U.S. 609 (1951).

690 909 N.E.2d 1073 (Ill. App. 2009).

691 *Id.* at 1077.

692 233 U.S. 354 (1914).

> the law of the forum state,] and cannot be defeated by the extraterritorial operation of a statute of another [s]tate, even though it created the right of action.[693]

The Illinois Supreme Court, moreover has proclaimed in *Williams v. Illinois State Scholarship Comm'n*,[694] that "statutory venue provisions are procedural only, and have no relation to the power of a court to decide the merits of a case."[695]

H. Judgments Dealing With Family Matters

1. Celebrating a Marriage

The U.S. Supreme Court has always spoken, not only approvingly, but almost eloquently of that sacred institution we call marriage.

Perhaps the most eloquent statement about marriage was composed by Justice Stephen Johnson Field, the first and only tenth member of the U.S. Supreme Court, and a member of the prominent Field family[696] when in *Maynard v. Hill*[697] he wrote:

> Marriage, as creating the most important relation in life, as having more to do with the morals and civilization of a people than any other institution, has always been subject to the control of the legislature. That body prescribes the age at which parties may contract to marry, the procedure or

---

693 *Id.* at 360. *See also* James v. Grand Trunk Western R.R. Co., 152 N.E. 2d 858, 864 (Ill. 1958).

694 563 N.E.2d 465 (Ill. 1990).

695 *Id.* at 472. In Union National Bank v. Lamb, 337 U.S. 38, 43 (1949) it was held that a judgment revived in state F-1 was required to be enforced in state F-2 under full faith and credit, even though it would not have been revivable in state F-2 because the F-1 cause of action was a judgment and not to have enforced it would be an "undermining" of a judgment.

696 He graduated first in his class at the prestigious Williams College. His brother, David, was the creator of the Field Code, and his brother Cyrus developed the first trans-Atlantic cable.

697 125 U.S. 190 (1888).

> form essential to constitute MARRIAGE, the duties and obligations it creates, its effects upon the property rights of both, present and prospective, and the acts which may constitute grounds for its dissolution.
>
> It is conceded that to determine the propriety of dissolving the marriage relation may involve investigations of a judicial nature, which can properly be conducted by the judicial tribunals. Yet, such investigations are no more than those usually made when a change of the law is designed. They do not render the enactment, which follows the information obtained, void as a judicial act because it may recite the cause of its passage. Many causes may arise, physical, moral, and intellectual, such as the contracting by one of . . . the parties of an incurable disease like leprosy, or confirmed insanity, or hopeless idiocy, or a conviction of a felony, which would render the continuance of the marriage relation intolerable to the other party, and productive of no possible benefit to society. When the object of the relation has been thus defeated, and no jurisdiction is vested in the judicial tribunals to grant a divorce, . . . it is not perceived that any principle should prevent the legislature itself from interfering, and putting an end to the relation in the interest of the parties as well as of society.[698]

In 1967 Chief Justice Earl Warren in *Loving v. Virginia*[699] described marriage as being "one of the 'basic civil rights of man,'" fundamental to our very existence and survival.[700] Two years prior thereto Justice William O. Douglas, for the Court in *Griswold v. Connecticut*[701] made it clear that the intimate activities of marital couples were within the constitutional right of privacy.[702]

In 1787 the framers of the U.S. Constitution, while not explicitly mentioning "marriage" in their work, implicitly made it clear (in Art. IV. § 1) were to solemnize a marriage, other states were to honor that solemnization.

---

[698] *Id.* at 205-206.

[699] 388 U.S. 1 (1965).

[700] *Id.* at 12.

[701] 381 U.S. 479 (1965).

[702] *Id.* at 530.

In 1971 the American Law Institute in § 283 of the Second Restatement of Conflict of Laws made explicit what states were to have the authority to determine the validity of marriage in the following words: [703]

> (1) The validity of a marriage will be determined by the local law of the state which, with respect to the particular issue, has the most significant relationship to the spouses and the marriage under the principles stated in § 6.
> (2) A marriage which satisfies the requirements of the state where the marriage was contracted will everywhere be recognized as valid unless it violates the strong public policy of another state which had the most significant relationship to the spouses and the marriage at the time of the marriage.

Over the years there have been alterations in what jurisdictions have the authority to solemnize a marriage, but in 1996 there occurred a sea change in the constitutional directive of to what extent those jurisdictions' determinations of the validity of a marriage must be recognized and enforced. On the 21st of September of that year Congress enacted 28 U.S.C. § 1738C, which proclaims:

> No State, territory, or possession of the United States, or Indian tribe, shall be required to give effect to any public act, record, or judicial proceeding of any other State, territory, possession, or tribe respecting a relationship between persons of the same sex that is treated as a marriage under the laws of such other State, territory, possession, or tribe, or a right or claim arising from such relationship.

This "defense of marriage" amendment (DOMA) has not been accepted unanimously by all of the states and the District of Columbia. Some jurisdictions accepted it, some rejected it and some seemed to straddle the fence.

In *Wilson v. Ake*[704] a U.S. District Court in Florida refused to preempt the U.S. Supreme Court's ruling as to whether DOMA conflicts with the Constitution. Judge Moody's words cogently explains the court's position:

---

[703] Section 6 of the Second Restatement is a list of Choice-of-Law principles.

[704] 354 F. Supp. 2d 1298 (M.D. Fla. 2003).

> In short, Plaintiffs' argument is that, given their recent "civil rights revolution," the United States Supreme Court is likely to declare that same-sex marriage is a fundamental right that is protected by the Constitution. Plaintiffs are asking this Court to create such a fundamental right immediately, before the Supreme Court revisits the issue of same-sex marriage. But that is not this Court's role. This Court is bound to follow the precedent established by the Eleventh Circuit Court of Appeals and the United States Supreme Court. None of their precedent acknowledge or establish a constitutional right to enter into a same-sex marriage. The legislatures of the individual states may decide to permit same-sex marriage or the Supreme Court may decide to overturn its precedent and strike down DOMA. But, until then, this Court is constrained to hold DOMA and Florida Statutes § 741.212 constitutionally valid.[705]

In *Jackson v. District of Columbia Board of Elections and Ethics*[706] the District of Columbia Court of Appeals affirmed a lower court's refusal to order the District's Board of Elections and Ethics to define marriage as a proceeding between a man and a woman. Judge Thompson's concluding remarks in his Opinion of the Court were the following:

> Although, theoretically, it is possible that heterosexuals of the same gender would enter into a same-sex marriage, there can be no dispute that the impact of District agencies' refusal to recognize same sex-marriage would fall most heavily on gay and lesbian residents, denying them the ability to participate fully in an important aspect of life in the District.[707]

In *Martinez v. County of Monroe*[708] a New York appellate court held that even though New York does not recognize a same-sex marriage attempted to be solemnized in New York the state will recognize such a proceeding performed in the Province of, Ontario where it is recognized. Judge Persdotto's words in his Opinion of the court are revealing of the thinking of the court:

---

[705] *Id.* at 1309.

[706] 2010 W.L. 2771743 (D.C. Ct. App. 2010).

[707] *Id.* at *16.

[708] 850 N.Y.S. 2d 740 (N.Y. App. Div. 2008).

> [W]e conclude that plaintiff's marriage to Golden, valid in the Province of Ontario, Canada, is entitled to recognition in New York in the absence of express legislation to the contrary. As the Court of Appeals indicated in *Hernandez* [*v. Robles*], the place for the expression of the public policy of New York is in the Legislature, not the courts (see 7 N.Y.3d at 361, 366, 821 N.Y.S.2d 770, 855 N.E.2d 1). The Legislature may decide to prohibit the recognition of same-sex marriages solemnized abroad. Until it does so, however, such marriages are entitled to recognition in New York.[709]

On August 4, 2010 U.S. District Court Judge Walker held in *Perry v. Schwarzenegger*[710] that an amendment to the California Constitution entitled "Proposition 8" was unconstitutional because it proclaimed that the only valid marriage recognized in California was that between a man and a woman, and therefore violated the due process and equal protection clauses[711] of the U.S. Constitution. Judge Walker in the Conclusion of his Opinion explained his rationale as follows:

> Proposition 8 fails to advance any rational basis in singling out gay men and lesbians for denial of a marriage license. Indeed, the evidence shows Proposition 8 does nothing more than enshrine in the California Constitution the notion that opposite-sex couples are superior to same-sex couples. Because California has no interest in discriminating against gay men and lesbians, and because Proposition 8 prevents California from fulfilling its constitutional obligation to provide marriages on an equal basis, the court concludes that Proposition 8 is unconstitutional.[712]

It would seem that the *Perry* case will eventually be reviewed by the U.S. Supreme Court. If the Court affirms, DOMA would appear to be in jeopardy.

---

[709] *Id.* at 743.

[710] 2010 W.L. 3025614 (N.D. Cal. 2010).

[711] U.S. Const.Aamend XIV, § 1.

[712] *Perry*, W.L. 3025614 at * 79.

2. Granting A Divorce or Annulment

a. Divorce

The most emphatic thing that can be said about divorce and full faith and credit is that a divorce, like a Last Will and Testament, if executed properly in F-1, because of full faith and credit, will usually be recognized in F-2.[713]

Some of the cases dealing with divorce use terms not readily understandable to laymen, such as divorce *a vinculo*[714] and divorce *a mensa et thoro*.[715]

In *Cheever v. Wilson*[716] it was opined that a divorce entered in one state in which the moving party was domiciled and in which the court had personal jurisdiction over the other was as conclusive in other states as it was in the rendering state.[717]

In *Atherton v. Atherton*[718] it was said that a divorce granted in the state of the marital domicile with personal jurisdiction over the defending spouse who is not a domiciliary of that state is as conclusive in other states as it is in that state,

---

[713] Brown v. Brown, 925 N.E.2d 572 *1 (Mass. App. 2010).

[714] Black's Law Dictionary, 8th Edition, (2004) defines divorce *a vinculo* as " . . . [Latin "(divorce) from the chains of marriage"] A total divorce of husband and wife, dissolving the marriage tie and releasing the parties wholly from their matrimonial obligations. At common law, but not always in canon law, this type of divorce bastardized any children from the marriage and was granted on grounds that existed before the marriage. In England, the Matrimonial Causes Act of 1857 introduced statutory divorce *a vinculo matrimonii*. — Usu. shortened to *divorce.*"

[715] Black's Law Dictionary, 8th Edition (2004) defines divorce *a mensa et thoro* as " . . . [Latin "(divorce) from board and hearth"] *Hist.* A partial or qualified divorce by which the parties were separated and allowed or ordered to live apart, but remained technically married. This type of divorce, abolished in England in 1857, was the forerunner of modern judicial separation. — Also termed *separation a mensa et thoro*; *separation from bed and board*; *limited divorce*; *legal separation*; *judicial separation.*"

[716] 76 U.S. (9 Wall.) 108 (1869).

[717] *Id.* at 123, 124.

[718] 181 U.S. 155 (1901).

providing the defending souse is given notice reasonably certain to reach her or him, regardless of whether or not it does in fact.[719]

In *Bell v. Bell*[720] a wife sued her husband for divorce on grounds of adultery. The husband defended on the ground that his acts did not constitute adultery because he had been divorced in Pennsylvania prior to his intimate relations with another woman. The U.S. Supreme Court held that no "divorce" is entitled to full faith and credit where such proceeding took place in a state of which neither party was a domiciliary.[721]

In *Haddock v. Haddock*[722] a husband left his wife in New York, their marital domicile, moved to Connecticut, established his domicile there. His wife sued for separate maintenance. The husband defended on the ground that he had obtained Connecticut divorce from his wife. The U.S. Supreme Court held that New York in the separate maintenance case need not give the Connecticut divorce full faith and credit because the husband wrongfully left the wife at their marital domicile, and service upon the wife was only by publication to which she did not respond.[723] The decision was overruled in the first *Williams* case.[724]

In *Davis v. Davis*[725] a husband as a domiciliary of the District of Columbia obtained a decree of separation there. He subsequently filed a divorce action in Virginia, as a Virginia domiciliary. The wife entered the Virginia cause and contested the court's jurisdiction with a rigorous attack. Even though her plea was to the effect that she was appearing specially to contest the Virginia court's subject matter jurisdiction because of an alleged flaw in the husband's residence, her participation in the case caused the court to conclude that she had made a general

---

719 *Id.* at 172, 175.

720 181 U.S. 175 (1901).

721 *Id.* at 177.

722 201 U.S. 562 (1906).

723 *Id.* at 632, 633.

724 Williams v. North Carolina, 317 U.S. 287, 304 (1942).

725 305 U.S. 32 (1939).

appearance.[726] The Virginia court found for the husband, and that finding was accorded full faith and credit. by the U.S. Supreme Court in the *Davis* case.[727]

In *Williams v. North Carolina*, I[728] O.B. Williams and his wife Carrie were residents of North Carolina, as were Thomas Hendricks, and his wife, Lillie. In 1940, however O.B. and Lillie decided to move to Las Vegas, where they would divorce their spouses and get married to each other, which is just what they did. O.B. and Lilley lived at a motor court[729] during their stay in Nevada, and after a period of time that has never been definitely established, they each filed for divorce. Lillie had Thomas served by publishing notice of her divorce action in a newspaper published only in Las Vegas. O.B. had Carrie served by having a North Carolina Deputy Sheriff serve her in North Carolina with copies of the Nevada summons and his Complaint. Shortly thereafter the Nevada court, finding that both plaintiffs had lived in Nevada for more than 6 weeks, immediately preceding the action "in a manner prescribed by law,"[730] divorced both from their respective spouses. Lillie and O.B. were married in Las Vegas, and retuned to North Carolina, where they took up housekeeping. They did not enjoy a peaceful existence, however, since North Carolina convicted both of them for bigamy; in other words that each contracted marriages while still being married to other persons. The North Carolina Supreme Court had ruled that North Carolina was not required under the Full Faith and Credit Clause to recognize the Nevada divorce decree. The U.S. Supreme Court, when the case reached that level, said that North Carolina admitted that there was probably sufficient evidence of the fact that the defendants had met the Nevada residence requirement.[731] It was this admission that caused the Court not to further address the issue as to whether O.B. and Lilley met the Nevada residence requirements. At that point, therefore, it seemed as though the only fault of Lillie and O.B. was going through divorce proceedings without their spouses being present. The Court, therefore, turned to an issue of whether an exception to Full Faith and Credit should be created by the Court which would

---

[726] *Id.* at 41, 42.

[727] *Id.* at 43.

[728] 317 U.S. 287 (1942). *See* a list of other cases, in the Table of Cases, which considered this case.

[729] *Id.* at 313.

[730] *Id.* at 290.

[731] *Id.* at 291.

provide that a divorce decree may be ignored, and not given full faith and credit, if the defending spouse was not present, and such a decree might offend the policy of other states.[732] While admitting that courts may carve out such exceptions to full faith and credit, this Court was not going to do so. Justice William O. Douglas summarized the Court's position in the following words:

> Each state as a sovereign has a rightful and legitimate concern in the marital status of persons domiciled within its borders. The marriage relation creates problems of large social importance. Protection of offspring, property interests, and the enforcement of marital responsibilities are but a few of commanding problems in the field of domestic relations with which the state must deal. Thus it is plain that each state by virtue of its command over its domiciliaries and its large interest in the institution of marriage can alter within its . . . own borders the marriage status of the spouse domiciled there, even though the other spouse is absent. There is no constitutional barrier if the form and nature of the substituted service . . . meet the requirements of due process.[733]

Nor would this Court determine which states have the better divorce law.[734] That is for the states to decide.[735] Justice Douglas did not specifically say what North Carolina was to do with the two prisoners, but his Opinion left no doubt about that matter - free them. Justice Felix Frankfurter concurred with a written Opinion,[736] but Justices Murphy and Jackson dissented with stinging Dissenting Opinions.[737]

Eisenwein v. Comm'wlth of Pennsylvania ex rel. Eisenwein[738] is similar to *Williams* I;[739] in fact the moving party, the former husband, based his position on

---

[732] *Id.* at 303.

[733] *Id.* at 298, 299.

[734] *Id.* at 302, 303.

[735] *Id.* at 303.

[736] *Id.* at 304-307.

[737] *Id.* at 308-311 (Justice Murphy); 311-324 (Justice Jackson).

[738] 325 U.S. 279 (1945).

[739] *See supra* note 728.

Williams, I. He and his wife had lived in Pennsylvania until he moved to Nevada and obtained a divorce; afterward he took up residence in Ohio. He asked the Pennsylvania court to cancel a prior-obtained support order, on the basis of his having obtained a divorce in Nevada, and a Pennsylvania law to the effect that the obligation of support payments does not survive divorce. The Pennsylvania courts denied his prayer for relief on the ground that he had not established sufficient residence in Nevada to give its court subject matter jurisdiction. The U.S. Supreme Court affirmed, Justice Felix Frankfurter, in the Court's Opinion stating that: "[t]he Pennsylvania courts have viewed their Constitutional duty correctly. It is not for us to retry the facts, and we cannot say that in reaching their conclusion the Pennsylvania courts did not have warrant in evidence and did not fairly weigh the facts."[740] The problem with the case is that there is nothing which reveals the details of the Nevada court's alleged lack of subject matter jurisdiction due to the husband not establishing his residence in that state..

In *Williams v. North Carolina* II[741] the Court, in *Williams* I, having held that Nevada could dissolve a marriage if it had jurisdiction over only one spouse, even if such a divorce offended the policy of North Carolina, now took up the question of whether North Carolina had the power, under the Full Faith and Credit Clause, to refuse full faith and credit to that Nevada divorce. The Court held that North Carolina had that power ! It not only said it could; it said it should.[742] And that was unfortunate. After apparently approving of Mrs. Hendrix and Mr. Williams untying their marital knots, and tying new ones in Nevada, and taking up housekeeping in North Carolina,[743] the Court now allowed North Carolina to throw them in jail ! Not having contested the verities of the Nevada divorce in 1942, allowing it to do so three years later seems entirely too late and imminently without due process being shown to the parties...

Almost six years after *Williams* II the Court held that a husband not having made a direct attack against a Florida court's having jurisdiction over his wife, and

---

740 *Eisenwein*, 325 U.S. at 281.

741 325 U.S. 226 (1945). See infra text accompanying notes 742, 747-749, 752 for additional reference to this case.

742 *Id.* at 239.

743 To the ire of Justices Murphy and Jackson, who wrote such compelling dissents in Williams I. *See supra* note 737.

hence of their divorce, could not collaterally attack it. Justice Stanley Reed, writing for the Court in *Johnson v. Muelberger*[744] wrote that:

> When a divorce cannot be attacked for lack of jurisdiction by parties actually before the court or strangers in the rendering state, it cannot be attacked by them anywhere in the Union. The Full Faith and Credit Clause forbids.[745]

Comparing *Williams, II,* with *Johnson v. Muelberger*, it would appear that the Court had returned to its senses by the tome it reached *Muelberger*. If a divorce proceeding cannot be collaterally attacked for lack of jurisdiction by strangers or by the parties who participated in it because they did not attack it directly, by what right does a state have the authority to collaterally attack it? It is unfortunate that Justice Reed, who was on the Court at the time of Williams, II, did not have more persuasion when the Court considered that case.. As a matter of fact he was a member of the Williams, II majority. It is surprising that Justices Murphy and Jackson, who attacked *Williams* I, with their dissenting Opinions[746] did not do so in *Williams* II. Justice Black, who was in the *Williams* I majority, wrote a dissenting Opinion in II,[747] which was joined in by Justice Douglas,[748] the author of the majority Opinion in *Williams* I. Justice Wiley Rutledge, who was not on the Court for *Williams* I, wrote a dissenting Opinion in II.[749]

Humpty Dumpty sat on a wall and had a great fall; but all the king's horses and all the king's men couldn't put Humpty back together again.

In *Estin v. Estin*[750] Mr. and Mrs. Estin were married in New York state and made that their home until Mr. Estin moved to Nevada, and established it as his home. When that occurred Mrs. Estin filed, in New York, for separate

---

744 340 U.S. 581 (1951). *See* text accompanying notes 49, 51, 202, 592, and 761 for further consideration of this case.

745 *Id.* at 589.

746 *See supra* note 737.

747 *Williams*, 325 U.S. at 261-278.

748 *Id.* at 278.

749 *See Id.* at 244-261.

750 334 U.S. 541 (1946).

maintenance, in which proceeding Mr. Estin appeared. The court awarded Mrs. Estin alimony or separate maintenance.[751] Subsequently Mr. Estin sought a divorce in Nevada, having Mrs. Estin served by publication. She did not appear in the Nevada proceedings, and the Nevada court dissolved the marriage. Though informed of the New York separation proceeding the Nevada court did not award the wife any financial support. Mr. Estin thereupon stopped paying his ex-wife the separate maintenance which he had paid up to that point. Hence Mrs. Estin commenced a proceeding in New York for the arrearages that had accumulated. Mr. Estin appeared and argued that the separate maintenance should cease because of the Nevada divorce. The trial court disagreed, and rendered a judgment for the arrearages. The Appellate Division and Court of Appeals agreed. When the case arrived in the U.S. Supreme Court the author of the *Williams v. North Carolina II*[752] Opinion of the Court (Justice Frankfurter), was assigned the writing of the Court's Opinion in this case. He lost no time in pointing up the significance of a court's *in personam* jurisdiction by personal service and/or personal appearance. Without that *in personam* jurisdiction over the other spouse all that the forum can do is dissolve the marriage. Reason: a divorce or dissolution of marriage is considered "divisible," i.e. the two sides of the marriage are divided[753] into the marital status and the financial aspects of the marriage. If a court has jurisdiction over the subject-matter (i.e. the marriage) and the moving party, it has the jurisdiction (power) to dissolve the bands of matrimony, but not financial affairs. Any attempt to do so is not entitled to full faith and credit.[754]

Sherrer v. Sherrer,[755] one of the most often cited Supreme Court cases in connection with divorce and the impact of full faith and credit involved a Massachusetts couple in which the wife left the husband and moved to Florida where she ostensibly established residence and filed for divorce. The husband appeared personally[756] and by counsel. The Florida court considered the matter and

---

751 The term "separate maintenance is applied to monetary awards from one spouse to another who while they are living separate and apart their marriage is still intact.

752 Williams v. North Carolina, 325 U.S. 226 (1945). *See supra* text accompanying notes 728-737.

753 The term "bifurcated" is also used.

754 *Estin,* 334 U.S. at 549.

755 334 U.S. 343 (1948).

756 Though curiously sat in a side room while the proceedings were going on. *Id* at 372.

ruled against him, apparently the court perfunctorily finding that it had jurisdiction by the wife having established her prerequisite residence. Subsequent to the divorce the husband filed in a Massachusetts court claiming that the Florida divorce was a nullity, the wife having failed to establish her residence, and the Massachusetts court agreed. The U.S. Supreme Court reversed, Chief Justice Fred Vinson writing the Opinion of the Court. The two reasons assigned were first - that Massachusetts violated the federal Constitution since it is equally important that there be an end to litigation as that there be a beginning;[757] but more importantly, second - that

> [T]he requirements of full faith and credit bar a defendant from collaterally attacking a [judgment] on jurisdictional grounds in the courts of a sister State where there has been participation by the defendant in the divorce proceedings, where the defendant has been accorded full opportunity to contest the jurisdictional issues, and where the decree is not susceptible . . . to such collateral attack in the courts of the State which rendered the decree.[758]

Thus, even if there were not a contest over jurisdiction in the Florida court, that tribunal having noted the point in its decree, it could have been contested by the husband, in the Florida appellate courts, but he failed to do so.

Apropos of *Sherrer* something should be said about the extent of contest that is made about the moving party's residence in a divorce case. It should be concerted that just as the Florida trial court's perfunctory finding that it had jurisdiction due to the wife probably having testified about the time that such residence commenced, a perfunctory attack on residence conceivably would not suffice on appeal; but how often is jurisdiction attacked by appeal? *Osorio v. Gonzalez*[759] aptly described the extent of review that probably most appellate courts give to

---

[757] *Sherrer*, 334 U.S. at 350. Justice Stanley Reed made the same point in Stoll v. Gottlieb, 305 U.S. 165, 172 (1938). Chief Justice Harlan Stone opined that bringing an end to litigation is a matter of public policy. *See* Heiser v. Woodruff, 327 U.S. 726, 733 (1946).

[758] *Sherrer,* 334 U.S. at 351, 352.

[759] 2008 W.L.4646914 (N.J. Super. 2008). *See infra* text accompanying notes 760, 1071, and 1090, concerning additional reference to this case.

family court decisions concerning the areas of their expertise. It is due deference,[760] which is not really an in-depth approach.

Johnson v. Muelberger[761] tells the story about an attack on a jurisdictional finding not only in a divorce case, but any case in general. Mr. Johnson and wife No.2 lived in New York City until she went to Florida to obtain a divorce. Mr. Johnson was represented by counsel who attacked the grounds of cruelty alleged, but did not attack subject matter jurisdiction, based on the wife's residence for sufficiently long to comply with the Florida statute. Mr. Johnson married wife No. 3 and died leaving his entire estate to his daughter, Mrs. Muelberger. wife No.3, having been left out of the Will, opted for dower.[762] Mrs. Muelberger entered the New York probate court with a plan to defeat the quest for dower: she claimed that wife No. 2 had not resided in Florida prior to filing for divorce to give the Florida court jurisdiction to sever the marriage; hence there could not have been a marriage to so-called wife No. 3 because Mr. Johnson was not divorced from wife No.2. The probate court and the Appellate Division held that Mrs. Muelberger was prevented from attacking the Florida divorce decree because of the Full Faith and Credit Clause, but New York's highest court (the Court of Appeals), reversed, though holding that perhaps Mr. Johnson could not have attacked it, his daughter, being a stranger to the Florida proceeding, could. The U.S. Supreme Court reversed New York's highest court. Justice Stanley F. Reed, writing the Opinion of the Court, made it clear that Mr. Johnson could not have collaterally attacked, after the time for appeal had elapsed,[763] the finding of jurisdiction by the Florida Court. Reason: full faith and credit constituted the Florida judgment inviolate, not attackable by anyone, anywhere – not because the defendant attacked it and lost, but because he could have attacked it but didn't. Justice Reed concluded the Opinion with the following words:

> We conclude that Florida would not permit Mrs. Muelberger to attack the Florida decree of divorce between her father and his second wife as

---

[760] *See Id.* at *2.

[761] 340 U.S. 581 (1951). *See* text accompanying notes 49, 51, 202, 592, 744 and 744 for further consideration of this case.

[762] By the common law right of dower wife No. 3 would get 1/3 of the Johnson probatable estate despite not having been mentioned in the Will.

[763] Not having contested jurisdiction in the trial court Johnson probably would not have been able to make a direct attack on the court's finding of jurisdiction.

> beyond the jurisdiction . . . of the rendering court. In that case New York cannot permit such an attack by reason of the Full Faith and Credit Clause. When a divorce cannot be attacked for lack of jurisdiction by parties actually before the court or strangers in the rendering state, it cannot be attacked by them anywhere in the Union. The Full Faith and Credit Clause forbids.[764]

b. Annulment

The most emphatic thing that can be said about annulment and full faith and credit is that an annulment, like a Last Will and Testament, if executed properly in F-1, because of full faith and credit it must generally be recognized in F-2.[765]

In *Dodds v. Pittsburgh M. & B.Rys. Co.*[766] a Pennsylvania appellate court applied what appears to be the majority rule - the law of the place of the marriage governs in determining whether an annulment is recognizable. The holding, however, was somewhat unusual because (1) the place of the marriage was Mexico, and the forum proclaiming the annulment was California, which applied its own law instead that of Mexico, to attempt an invalidation of the annulment; and (2) the rationale given by the Pennsylvania court, in holding that the attempted annulment was a nullity, was full faith and credit rather than comity.[767]

Sutton v. Lieb[768] is one of those complex tales of three states, which though very informative, taxes the ability of the reader to fully understand its ramifications. Verma, before her marriage to Mr. Sutton was married to A. Wells Lieb. In 1939 they were divorced in Illinois where the decree required Mr. Lieb to pay Verna alimony until she remarried. She was remarried in Nevada to Walter, on July 3, 1944, the same day his divorce decree from Dorothy, a New York resident, became final. Dorothy, not having been served with process, and not knowing of the Nevada divorce, filed in her home state of New York, for separate maintenance. Walter appeared and defended on the ground the he had obtained a

---

[764] *Johnson,* 340 U.S. at 589.

[765] Brown v. Brown, 29 S.W.3d 491, 494 (Tenn. App. Ct. 2000).

[766] 162 A. 486 (Pa. Super. 1932).

[767] *Id.* at 488, 489.

[768] 342 U.S. 402 (1952).

divorce from Dorothy in Nevada. Ultimately the New York court ruled that Walter's divorce from Dorothy was invalid, due to her never having received notice. Verna, in January, 1945 filed suit in New York to annul her marriage to Walter on the ground of his having been married at the time of her supposed marriage to him. In 1957 the New York Court agreed with Verna and annulled her marriage to Walter. Verna then sued A. Wells Lieb in the Federal District Court for the Southern District of Illinois for accrued installments of unpaid alimony, and was successful. The Seventh Circuit affirmed on April 26, 1951, reasoning that it is the Nevada marriage which must be given full faith and credit, rather than the New York judgment of annulment. That meant that Walter's divorce from Dorothy and marriage to Verna terminated A. Well's obligation to continue paying alimony to Verna. The U.S. Supreme Court reversed the Seventh Circuit. The Court, with Justice Reed writing the Opinion of the Court, envisioned two issues in the case. The first, being: what was the full faith and credit effect of the New York annulment judgment? That issue, being one of federal law, was to be decided by the Federal courts, ultimately the Supreme Court. That Court's decision was that full faith and credit must be given to the New York judgment of annulment by all states, including Nevada and Illinois. The second issue was one of state law, i.e. how would a New York annulment of a Nevada marriage affect an Illinois divorce decree's obligations which depended on whether a re-marriage had occurred.? That state issue could be decided by a federal court,[769] and need not be remanded to state courts. The case, therefore, was remanded to the Seventh Circuit for a determination of how Illinois would resolve the issue. Justice Frankfurter, concurring, suggested a quick, declaratory submission to the Illinois Supreme Court, as the final arbiter of what Illinois law would be.[770] This suggestion must have been welcomed by A. Wells Lieb who had been waiting eight years[771] for a determination of his liability, *vel non*, to Verna Sutton.[772]

In *In re Estate of Rifkin*[773] a Florida court pronounced that since a Colorado court had subject-matter jurisdiction, as well as jurisdiction of both parties and the

---

[769] Obviously under Erie R. Co v. Tompkins 304 U.S. 64 (1938).

[770] *Sutton*, 342 U.S. at 413.

[771] March 3, 1952 was the date of the U.S. Supreme Court's concluding decision of a controversy which began July 3, 1944.

[772] The only date cutting off his obligation to Verna, of which he could be certain, was her New York marriage to Mr. Sutton. *Sutton,* 342 U.S. at 403.

[773] 359 So.2d 1197 (3d DCA 1978).

decree appeaered to be otherwise regular on its face, pursuant to the Full Faith and Credit Clause the Florida court would recognize the Colorado Decree of Annulment.[774]

In *Brawer v. Pinkins*[775] New York state recognized a Nevada annulment, even though the Nevada court had never been informed that a New York divorce case was in process. The New York judge, probably perplexedly, dismissed the New York proceeding, with the exception of custody and child support matters.[776]

3. Awarding Alimony & Special Maintenance

Barber v. Barber.[777] In the year 1847, the court of chancery of New York granted Huldah B. Barber a separation from Hiram Barber, and directed the payment of alimony in quarterly installments. Although the separation was decreed to be forever, the power to modify was reserved by a provision that the parties might at any time thereafter, by their joint petition, apply to the court to have the decree modified or discharged. It was provided that unpaid installments of alimony should bear interest, "and that execution might issue therefore." The husband failed to pay where he procured an absolute divorce. Subsequently an action was brought by Mrs. Barber upon the common-law side of the District Court of the United States in the territory of Wisconsin, to recover the arrears of alimony, but relief was denied "for the reason that the remedy for the recovery of alimony was in a court of chancery, and not at law." A suit in equity to recover the overdue alimony was then commenced by Mrs. Barber in the district court of the United States for the District of Wisconsin. The proceedings culminated in a decree in favor of Mrs. Barber. The decree was affirmed. In the course of the opinion it was declared, among other things, that courts of equity possessed jurisdiction to interfere to prevent the decree of the court of another state from being defeated by fraud, and reference was made to English decisions asserting the power of chancery to compel the payment of overdue alimony. Considering the nature and character of a decree of separation and for alimony, and the operation

---

774 *Id.* at 1200.

775 626 N.Y.S.2d 674 (N.Y. S. Ct. 1995).

776 *Id.* at 679.

777 62 U.S. (21 How.) 582 (1858). *See infra* text accompanying notes 778-780 for further reference to this case.

and effect upon such a decree as to past-due installments of the full faith and credit clause, Justice Wayne, in the Opinion of the Court said:

> The parties to a cause for a divorce and . . . for alimony are as much bound by a decree for both, which has been given by one of our state courts having jurisdiction of the subject-matter and over the parties, as the same parties would be if the decree had been given in the ecclesiastical courts of England. The decree in both is a judgment of record, and will be received as such by other courts. And such a judgment or decree, rendered in any state of the United States, the court having jurisdiction, will be carried into judgment in any other state, to have there the same binding force that it has in the state in which it was originally given.[778]
>
> Alimony decreed to a wife in a divorce of separation from bed and board is as much a debt of record, until the decree has been recalled, as is any other judgment for money.[779]
>
> Justice Wayne concluded his Opinion with the following words:
>
> The general rule is, that a voluntary separation will not give to the wife a different domiciliation in law from that of her husband. But if the husband, as is the fact in this case, abandons their domicile [sic] and his wife, to get rid of all those conjugal obligations which the marriage relation imposes upon him, neither giving to her the necessaries nor the comforts suitable to their condition and his fortune, and relinquishes altogether his marital control and protection, he yields up that power and authority over her which alone makes his domicil [sic] hers, and places her in a situation to sue him for a divorce *a mensa et thoro*, and to ask the court having jurisdiction of her suit to allow her from her husband's means, by way of alimony, a suitable maintenance and support. When that has been done, it becomes a judicial debt of record against the husband, which may be enforced by execution or attachment against his person, issuing from the court which gave the decree; and when that cannot be done on account of the husband having left or fled from that jurisdiction to another, where the

---

[778] *Id.* at 591.

[779] *Id.* at 595.

> process of that court cannot reach him, the wife, by her next friend, may sue him wherever he may be found, or where he shall have acquired a new domicil, [sic] for the purpose of recovering the alimony due to her, or to *carry the decree into a judgment there with the same effect that it has in the State in which the decree was given.*[780]

Sistare v. Sistare[781] was another case of a decree *a mensa et thoro*; this time by a court of New York. The same court, at a later time entered a decree for arrearages of the alimony awarded at the time of the original decree.[782] A Connecticut court denied recognition and enforcement on the ground that the money awarded, though arrearages, were subject to modification. The U.S. Supreme Court, with Justice Edward D. White,[783] writing the Opinion of the Court, reversed. The Court announced the general proposition that a decree for installments past due and unpaid, are within the protection of the Full Faith and Credit Clause of the federal Constitution. The court, however, added a proviso, consisting of two elements: (1) the final decree must have been made prior to the maturity of such installments; and (2) unless by the law of the state in which the decree was rendered, its enforcement is so completely within the discretion of the courts of that state that they may annul or modify the decree, even as to overdue and unsatisfied installments. The Court found that the decrees of the New York courts for the future payment of alimony are not subject to annulment or modification by those courts as to overdue and unsatisfied installment so as to deprive such decrees of the protection, as to past-due and unpaid installments, of the Full Faith and Credit Clause of the Federal Constitution.[784]

---

[780] *Id.* at 595.

[781] 218 U.S. 1 (1910). *See infra* text accompanying notes 782-784 for further reference to this case.

[782] The original decree was for $22.50 per week for the wife's and child's alimony. The arrearages amounted to $5,85.00, revealing a 258 week default in payments.

[783] Justice White was one of the most interesting members of the high Court. Though a devout Roman Catholic, in his early years he was a member of Ku Klux Klan and originally believed in slavery. He volunteered for the Confederate infantry during the Civil War, rising to officership as a Lieutenant. After the war he became a United States Senator from Louisiana, Associate Justice of the U.S. Supreme Court, and just after the Sistare case, its Chief Justice.

[784] *Sistare*, 218 U.S. at 26.

In *Loughran v. Loughran*[785] a married woman, who had committed adultery, was divorced from her husband pursuant to a District of Columbia statute requiring that as punishment for her wrong the woman was to receive no alimony and she was prohibited from re-marrying. After the divorce she and her paramour traveled to Florida and married, but then took up residence in Virginia. She later obtained a divorce in Virginia under a decree of divorce *a mensa et thoro* which awarded her alimony. When her ex-husband No.2 died, he owed unpaid alimony installments, and the busy lady sued his estate for dower[786] and accrued alimony in the District of Columbia where she and husband No. 2 had resumed residence, The estate defended on the ground that since she was prohibited from re-marrying by the absolute divorce from Husband No.1, her reputed marriage to husband No. 2 was a nullity and her demand for relief from his estate was apocryphally asserted. The reply to that position of the estate, by Justice Lewis Brandeis, writing for the court, was: "while a statute of the . . . District provides for forfeiture of dower in case of the wife's adultery during marriage, . . . none denies dower to a widow because she had been guilty of adultery prior to the marriage with her late husband."[787]

In *Barber v. Barber*[788] a judgment for accrued alimony was entered in North Carolina, but refused o be recognized and enforced in Tennessee because, as contended by defendant it was subject to modification. The U.S. Supreme Court reversed. Even though under the North Carolina law an award of alimony is subject to modification, once unpaid installments are accrued and reduced to judgment modification is not allowed. Chief Justice Harlan F. Stone, writing the Opinion of the Court, opined that:

---

785 292 U.S. 216 (1934).

786 Black's Law Dictionary 8th Edition (2004) describes dower as "at common law, a wife's right, upon her husband's death, to a life estate in one-third of the land that he owned in fee. With few exceptions, the wife could not be deprived of dower by any transfer made by her husband during his lifetime. Although most states have abolished dower, many states retaining the concept have expanded the wife's share to a life estate in all the land that her husband owned in fee." As the divorce was *a mensa et thoro*, (See supra note 703 for a definition of *a mensa et thoro*) dower was technically available to her since she was not divorced *a vincula* (see supra note 702 for a definition of divorce *a vinvula*).

787 *Loughran* , 292 U.S. at 226.

788 323 U.S. 77 (1944).

> [E]very reasonable implication must be resorted to against the existence of' a power to modify or revoke installments of alimony already accrued 'in the absence of clear language manifesting an intention to confer it.' The admonition is none the less to be heeded when the debt has been reduced to a judgment upon which execution has been directed to issue.[789]

Estin v. Estin[790] involved a New York couple, the husband, having left the wife, settled in Nevada, and promptly stopped sending the wife any financial support. Such treatment prompted the wife to obtain an action for separate maintenance - divorce *a mensa et thoro*. Thereupon the husband filed for divorce *a vinculo* in Nevada, serving the wife with notice by publication, as to which the wife took no heed, and did not attend the hearing. The Nevada divorce court severed the bonds of matrimony, but rendered no alimony. The wife filed in New York for collection of the arrearages of her separate maintenance. The former husband appeared in the New York proceeding and defended on the ground that the couple were divorced by Nevada, with no alimony being granted to the wife, The U.S. Supreme Court recognized the efficacy of the Nevada divorce, it being "divisible;"[791] but found that because of the Full Faith and Credit Clause the New York court was not required to heed the Nevada decree, which failed to award alimony.[792]

In *Armstrong v. Armstrong*[793] a husband and wife were apparently happily residents of Florida until the husband decided to sue for divorce. The wife then decided to move the Ohio and took up residence there. She was served by constructive notice of the Florida proceeding, but did not appear. With reference to alimony the husband took an almost clairvoyant position. His Complaint did not allege that his wife does not deserve alimony, but simply that she does not need any. His pleading added, "nevertheless the plaintiff hereby offers to do equity and to abide by such orders or decrees with reference to the settlement of the property affairs as to this court may be deemed equitable."[794] The Florida court entered a

---

789 *Id.* at 82.

790 334 U.S. 541 (1948).

791 *Id.* at 549.

792 *Id.*

793 350 U.S. 568 (1956).

794 *Id.* at 570.

decree dissolving the marriage. As to alimony the court provided in the decree: "Mrs. Armstrong has not come into this court in good faith or made any claim to the equitable conscience of the court and has made no showing of any need on her part for alimony. It is, therefore, specifically decreed that no award of alimony be made to the defendant."[795] Mrs. Armstrong subsequently sued for divorce in Ohio. The Ohio court denied the prayer for divorce because the Florida court had already dissolved the marriage, but granted the prayer for alimony. The former husband complained that the Ohio ruling, granting alimony, denied full faith and credit to the Florida decree which failed to award any. The U.S. Supreme Court did not see it the same way as Mr. Armstrong did. Justice Sherman Minton, writing the Opinion of the Court, said that "[t]aken literally, [the Florida court's] language means only that, for the reasons it gave, the . . . court would refrain from making an affirmative award of alimony to the wife, not that it . . . adjudicated in favor of the husband that his wife was not entitled to alimony."[796] Justice Minton concluded the Court's Opinion, saying that "[t]he Florida judgment was given full faith and credit as far as the judgment in Florida went, and no other questions are presented here."[797]

Vanderbilt v. Vanderbilt[798] was quit similar to *Entin v. Entin.* Cornelius Vanderbilt and his wife lived in California, until his wife left him to reside in New York. Mr. Vanderbilt thereupon obtained a Nevada divorce, without alimony being awarded to his wife. The former Mrs. Vanderbilt thereupon filed for separate maintenance alimony and secured a New York decree in her favor. Mr. Vanderbilt objected on the ground that the New York decree was invalid under the Full Faith and Credit Clause. When the case arrived in the U.S. Supreme Court it was determined that the Clause was not violated because, as in *Entin,* the wife not having been before the Nevada court, it, the Nevada court, had no power to deprive her of alimony. The only major difference between this case and *Entin* was that Mrs. Entin had obtained an order for alimony prior to the marriage dissolution, whereas Mrs. Vanderbilt had not. Justice Hugo L. Black, writing for the court,

---

[795] *Id.* at 569, 570.

[796] *Id.*

[797] *Id.* at 572. This case possibly could be extended to hold that an F-1court's finding that a potential recipient of alimony does not need alimony at the time the marriage is dissolved, and nothing more, that recipient is not foreclosed from asking the F-1 court, or an F-2 court if there has been a change of residence, to grant alimony now because of need. Ed.

[798] 354 U.S. 416 (1957).

noted that such a distinction was insignificant to the resolution of the matter before the Court.[799]

In *Heron v. Heron* [800] the parties were married, divorced, re-married, and divorced again; for the second time in Nevada, which awarded alimony to the wife, both parties appearing before the Nevada court. A Massachusetts trial court modified the terms of the Nevada decree, but a Massachusetts appellate court reversed on the basis of *res judicata*. With regard to alimony the court said: "[i]n order to satisfy full faith and credit, the effect of the Nevada decree must be determined by Nevada law. A Nevada court interpreting Nevada law would not permit modification of the decree."[801] With regard to the property of the parties the Massachusetts court observed that while it could not determine the extent to which the Nevada court divided the marital assets, it thought the issue immaterial; because the wife could have contested the property division in the Nevada proceeding. The court added that in Nevada, "a judgment is conclusive not only on the questions actually contested and determined, but on all matters which might have been litigated and decided in the suit."[802] Nevada could have affected all the marital assets. Even out-of-State real property could have been addressed indirectly through an *in personam* decree because the court had personal jurisdiction over both parties. Further, the Nevada decree was a final judgment on the merits.[803]

4. Awarding Custody/Visitation Privileges

We commence our inquiry on a negative note - "[c]ustody litigation is full of injustice - let there be no doubt about that." At least that was the opinion of the Supreme Court of Michigan in a Per Curiam Opinion in *In re Clausen*.[804] The court, however, quickly added the following palliative:

---

[799] *Id.* at 418. By dictum Justice Black pointed out that the same ruling would be made if the husband were not before the court, yet it required him to pay alimony. Id. at 419. It is the financial obligation, either for or against, which may not be decreed in the absence of one of the parties.

[800] 703 N.E.2d 712 (Mass. 1998).

[801] *Id.* at 714.

[802] *Id.* at 715.

[803] *Id.*

[804] 502 N.W.2d 649, 660 (Mich.1993).

> No system of laws is perfect. Consistency in the application of the laws, however, goes a long way toward curing much of the injustice. While the laws of the fifty states may vary as to the substantive rules in custody determinations, at least there is a uniform standard imposed equally on all the states by the PKPA for determining which court makes that determination. The PKPA and its preemptive effect can no longer be avoided.[805]

It is almost certain that the framers of the Constitution who drew the Full Faith and Credit Clause and the Congressmen who wrote the 1790 statute never envisioned the circumstances in which children grow up in this twenty-first century, e.g. unwed parents, parents who live apart from each other, parents who are of the same gender, children who are conceived by someone they will never know, parents who were once in love with each other eventually became each other's worst enemy, children who would be neglected by their parents and/or kidnapped by them and/or living with a family member or non-related custodian, whom they hardy know, rather than their parents. Children living in "tattered and unclean clothes," shoes not of the correct size, and with teeth in their mouths requiring care.[806] With such milieu in which they are expected to develop into normally adjusted human beings it is no wonder that Congress in 1980 amended 28 U.S.C. § 1738, by enacting 28 U.S.C. § 1738A, the Anti Kidnapping Prevention Act (PKPA), and 28 U.S.C. § 1738B, the Full Faith and Credit for Child Support Orders Act" (FFCCSOA) and the Commissioners on uniform laws devised statutes to compensate for some of the shortfalls of the Full Faith and Credit Clause and original statute. They were the Uniform Child Custody Jurisdiction Act (UCCJA) of 1968,[807] and the Uniform Child Custody Jurisdiction Enforcement Act

---

[805] *Id.*

[806] *See In re* Guardianship of T.H., 589 N.W.2d 67, 68 (Iowa 1999). It is a blessing that the courts have an interest in the wellbeing of children The U.S. Supreme Court on March 23, 2011, while the preparation of this book was being concluded, heard oral argument in J.D.B. v. North Carolina, 2011 W.L. 588826 (2011), which involved the rights of juveniles who are being questioned about a burglary. As of Jan. 15, 2012, no decision has been rendered.

[807] The UCCJA at one time was adopted by every state of the Union, but as of Jan. 15, 2012, there are only four states which have retained it – Massachusetts, Missouri, New Hampshire and Vermont.

(UCCJEA) of 1997,[808] which on April 28, 2002 replaced the prior (1968) Act. Virginia Court of Appeals Judge Powell has written about the purpose of the UCCJEA in the following words:

> Although the PKPA mandates that "[t]he appropriate authorities of every State shall enforce according to its terms . . . any custody determination or visitation determination," there is no further mention of enforcement within the Act. . . . Thus, it does not specifically address registration. The UCCJEA was promulgated and adopted by a majority of the states to address the mechanics of enforcement, including registration.[809]

The purpose of the UCCJEA, which has become the most significant statute in connection with insuring Constitutional and statutory requirement that full faith and credit be extended when more than one state is involved has been described by the Commission on uniform Acts in the following words:

> This Act revisits the problem of the interstate child almost thirty years after the Conference promulgated the Uniform Child Custody Jurisdiction Act (UCCJA). The UCCJEA accomplishes two major purposes.
>
> First, it revises the law on child custody jurisdiction in light of federal enactments and almost thirty years of inconsistent case law. Article 2 of this Act provides clearer standards for which States can exercise original jurisdiction over a child custody determination. It also, for the first time, enunciates a standard of continuing jurisdiction and clarifies modification jurisdiction. Other aspects of the article harmonize the law on simultaneous proceedings, clean hands, and *forum non conveniens*.
>
> Second, this Act provides in Article 3 for a remedial process to enforce interstate child custody and visitation determinations. In doing so, it brings a uniform procedure to the law of interstate enforcement that is currently producing inconsistent results. In many respects, this Act accomplishes for custody and visitation determinations the same uniformity that has

---

808 As of Jan. 15, 2012, the District of Columbia, the Virgin Islands and all states except the four states which have retained the UCCJA, to wit: Massachusetts, Missouri, New Hampshire and Vermont have adopted the UCCJEA.

809 Prashad v. Copeland 685 S.E.2d 199, 205 n.4 (Va. App. 2009).

occurred in interstate child support with the promulgation of the Uniform Interstate Family Support Act (UIFSA).

It can be best understood by examining some actual situations that have been resolved by the courts.

Initially a dynamic and enlightening observation must be recalled. It was opined in *Hines v. Tilimon*[810] that custody cases are precisely the type of "status" cases that were alluded to in *Shaffer v. Heitner*[811] in which Justice Thurgood Marshall emphasized the importance of "personal status."[812] Justice Marshall, at three places in his Shaffer Court's Opinion referred to the importance of the "personal status" in litigation. He observed that because of personal status the moving party may obtain a divorce in her or his "home state" even though the defendant was not served with process in that state. He emphasized that "personal status" comports with fairness.[813] He observed that the plaintiff in Shaffer was moving against those who were in a fiduciary position in their relationship toward him.[814] How true this same importance applies in a custody case, where not only the moving party, but his or her adversary, could very likely, and probably will, mold the future of the little human being whose custody they seek.

In *People of New York ex rel. Halvey v. Halvey*[815] a married couple and their child lived in New York until the wife and their child moved to Florida, where the wife filed for divorce. On the day prior to hearing the father possessed the child and took her with him to New York. At the hearing, of which the father had been served by publication, but did not appear, the Florida court dissolved the marriage and gave the mother child custody. The mother promptly filed habeas corpus proceedings in New York, to retrieve possession of the child. Both parents attended the hearing. The New York court awarded custody to the mother, but with reasonable visitation privilege in the father, including vacation periods. The court also required the mother to file a $5,000 bond guaranteeing delivery of the child to

---

[810] 2001 W.L. 44026 (Tenn. Ct. App. 2001).

[811] 433 U.S. 186 (1977).

[812] *Hines*, 2001 W.L. at *8.

[813] *Shaffer*, 433 U.S. at.30.

[814] *Id.* at 214.

[815] 330 U.S. 610 (1947).

the father in Florida when his visitation periods were to commence. The New York Appellate Division and the Court of Appeals affirmed. The U.S. Supreme Court granted certiorari to determine whether the New York modification of the Florida judgment violated the Full Faith and Credit Clause. In holding that it did not Justice Douglas, writing for the Court opined that under the Full Faith and Credit Clause an F-2 court has the same power to modify a custody award as the rendering state possesses.[816]

In *May v. Anderson*[817] a mother from whom custody of her children was taken away by an Ohio court even though she was not a domiciliary or resident of Ohio and had not received notice of the hearing was able to have the U.S. Supreme Court reverse the award. The Court proclaimed that the right of notice concerning custody awards is of equal importance as alimony awards.[818]

In *Thompson v. Thompson*[819] the U.S. Supreme Court held that the Parental Kidnapping Prevention Act (PKPA) did not provide an implied cause of action for federal courts to determine which of two conflicting state custody decrees is valid. Rather, the context, language and history of the Act demonstrate that it was intended to have the same operative effect as the full faith and credit statute (28 U.S.C.A. §1738A) for child custody determinations. Justice Thurgood Marshall, in the Opinion of the Court, wrote that:

> The Parental Kidnapping Prevention Act (PKPA or Act) imposes a duty on the States to enforce a child custody determination entered by a court of a sister State if the determination . . . is consistent with the provisions of the Act. In order for a . . . state court's custody decree to be consistent with the provisions of the Act, the State must have jurisdiction under its own local law and one of five conditions set out in . . . § 1738A(c)(2) must be met. Briefly put, these conditions authorize the state court to enter a custody decree if the child's home is or recently has been in the State, if the child has no home State and it would be in the child's best interest for the State to assume jurisdiction, or if the child is present in the State and has been abandoned or abused. Once a State exercises jurisdiction

[816] *Id.* at 615, 616.

[817] 345 U.S.528 (1953).

[818] *Id.* at 534, 535.

[819] 484 U.S. 174 (1988).

> consistently with the provisions of the Act, no other State may exercise concurrent jurisdiction over the custody dispute, § 1738A(g), even if it would have been empowered to take jurisdiction in the first instance. And all States must accord full faith and credit to the first State's ensuing custody decree.[820]

The UCCJEA[821] provides for what is known as the "home state" to have jurisdiction to try custody matters. Of course there may not be a "home state." In *In re S.W.*[822] the father, apparently having a wander lust, was nowhere to be found. The mother, for reasons of her own moved to California with the couple's two children, and had been there for seven months when she commenced an action to terminate parental rights. The "no home state" provisions were applied by a California court.[823] These provisions require two basic situations: first, the child and the child's parents, or the child and at least one parent, or a person acting as parent must have a "significant connection" with a state which is to take jurisdiction of the custody matter, and that "significant connection" must be other than mere physical presence.[824] Second, "Substantial evidence" concerning the child's care, protection, training and personal relationships must be available in the state which is to take jurisdiction.[825] Inconvenience may be considered by the replacement court, but it must be raised by at least one of the parties.[826]

In *In re Marriage of Hamilton*.[827] the child's mother left her husband in Texas to visit their seven year old son who was living at her parents' home in Washington state. She remained there and five months later, she sued in Washington for dissolution of the marriage and for child custody. The mother had lived in Washington for seven years as a child and had attended one year of college

---

[820] *Id.* at 177.

[821] *See infra* text accompanying note 863.

[822] 56 Cal.Rptr.3d 665 (2007). *See infra* text accompanying notes 823-826 for additional decisions considering this case.

[823] *Id.* at 667.

[824] *Id.* at 670.

[825] *Id.* at 671.

[826] *Id.*

[827] 84 P.3d 259 (Wash. 2004).

in that state. The seven-year old had serious medical problems in Texas, and while in Washington he received extensive medical treatment there, where he was covered by Medicaid. These facts furnished a sufficient factual basis for jurisdiction by the Washington court to consider the divorce and custody.[828]

In *Staats v. McKinnon*[829] a husband and wife were divorced in Florida, the wife being granted custody of the parties' minor child. The ex-husband moved to Tennessee due to his employment, and petitioned the Florida court to award him custody of the child, the ex-wife and the child having moved to Massachusetts. The Florida trial court granted the father's petition for a change of custody, but that decree was reversed by the Florida District Court of Appeal. Thereupon the ex-husband asked a Tennessee court to modify the custody award, the parties having moved from Florida. The former wife promptly petitioned the Florida court to enforce its original order, and almost simultaneously appeared in the Tennessee action asking for the court's jurisdiction. The Tennessee court, ignoring the mother's petition, granted the father's petition for a change of custody. The Tennessee appellate court ruled that pursuant to the UCCJEA the Florida court lost jurisdiction of the custody controversy as the "home court" under the UCCJEA because the divorced parties and their child no longer lived in Florida: and that, under the UCCJEA Tennessee had become the new "home state," hence the father was not required to give the Florida court's custody decree full faith and credit by returning to the mother, in Massachusetts, their child who at the time was living with her father in Tennessee.[830]

In *Lippman v. Perham-Lippman*[831] the court applied the "inconvenient forum" analysis, in finding that Connecticut was the proper forum state for resolution of child custody issues, pursuant to Uniform Child Custody Jurisdiction Enforcement Act (UCCJEA). The following factors persuaded the judge: (1) the husband was employed full-time in Connecticut; (2) he was his family's sole wage-earner; (3) the distance between Connecticut and Colorado, state of wife's residence, was too great to allow commuting to court appearances; (4) the marital home was located in Connecticut and was available to the wife during the course of the proceedings;

---

828 *Id.* at 264.

829 206 S. W. 3d 533 (Tenn. Ct. App. 2006).

830 *Id.* at 549.

831 2006 WL 852169 (Conn. Super. 2006).

(5) Connecticut was the children's home state; and (6) the parties were long-term residents of Connecticut.[832]

In *Carl v. Tirado*,[833] a boy who was born to unmarried parents in Maryland. When the boy was four days old, he was taken by his mother to Virginia. The father sued for custody in the District of Columbia when the child was nine days old. The infant, therefore, had no home state. The District of Columbia judge decided that his court had jurisdiction, however, under the following "substantial," if not entirely wholesome facts: (1) the father resided in the District; (2) the infant had been baptized there; (3) the toddler had been cared for during the day by his father who returned the child to the mother in the evenings; (4) there were extended family members in the District of Columbia: and (5) the mother was suing the father for child support in the District.[834]

The UCCJEA encourages the judges of the various states involved in a custody case to confer about the jurisdiction dispute; and the judges often do so, usually telephonically. In one case, *Krebs v. Krebs*,[835] the husband and wife and their two children lived in Arizona, but the husband left them to live in Maryland due to his employment. During the children's visit to him he filed for divorce in Maryland, seeking custody of the children. Even though the wife appeared in the Maryland proceeding, testified and was represented by counsel, custody was awarded to the husband. Upon the former wife's return to Arizona she instituted a legal action through an attorney to contest the custody award, on the ground that Arizona was the "home state," and that the determination should have been made there. During a telephone conference between the Arizona judge and the Maryland master in chancery it was agreed that while Arizona was the home state, Maryland was the more convenient forum, and the Arizona judge dismissed the former wife's case.[836]

---

[832] *Id.* at *1 in passim.

[833] 945 A.2d 1208 (D.C. App. 2008).

[834] *Id.* at 1210.

[835] 960 A.2d 637 (Md. App. 2008).

[836] *Id.* at 640. There is a plethora of cases in which jurists confer about their cases, but reference to three will establish the extent to which such communication between jurists is being used. Mayer v. Barrow, 2010 W.L. 1225153 at *5 (Conn. Super 2010) (the court referring to discussions between judges from Connecticut and Colorado); Custody of Brandon, 551 N.E. 2d 506, 507 (Mass. 1990) (discussions between a probate judge in Massachusetts and a trial judge in Mississippi); and MacDougall v. Acres, 693 N.E.2d

The UCCJEA contains provisions attempting to prevent a state court's modification of another state court's "initial child-custody determination." In *Ullrich* v. *Walsh*[837] even though an apparently unmarried couple were living in Arkansas with their child, the mother took her to Texas to have the child's paternity established The Texas court determined that the man was the father of the child and established rights and duties of each parent. The father filed for "emergency custody" in Arkansas because the mother had threatened to take the child, who was living with her grandmother, to Texas permanently. The Arkansas court, pursuant to PKPA and UCCJEA considered that the Texas order, that used Arkansas (F-2) law,[838] was the "initial child-custody determination" which was required to be given full faith and credit by Arkansas.[839]

Preshad v. Copeland[840] had its share of uniqueness. A married man was a homosexual. His wife, being aware of her husband's "partner," agreed to being artificially inseminated by the sperm of both men. When the child was born, the husband was, naturally enough, shown on the Birth Certificate as the child's father. Upon the married couple obtaining a divorce in their home state of Minnesota, the ex-wife consented to the homosexual couple, and the infant child, moving to North Carolina. Though the relationship of the three adults was initially cordial, it eventually cooled, and virtually disintegrated when the homosexuals moved to California, where they obtained a "Declaration of Domestic Partnership." Upon their return to North Carolina the man who was shown on the Birth Certificate to be the father, (the reputed father), filed for custody.

The court determined that it had jurisdiction because North Carolina was the last state in which the homosexual couple and the child lived. The father's "partner," for reasons perhaps known only to himself, petitioned to be allowed to intervene in the custody proceeding. The mother, having notice of the custody proceeding, entered into an agreement with the homosexual couple allowing the

---

663, 665 (Mass. 1998) (discussions between judges from Massachusetts and Louisiana about "what should happen next").

837 2010 W.L. 1372485 (Ark. App. 2010). *See supra* note 347 in which this case is mentioned, and *infra* text accompanying notes 838-839 for additional consideration of the case.

838 *Id* at *1.

839 *Id.*

840 685 S.E. 2d 199 (Va. App. 2009).

"partner" to intervene. The judge, for reasons perhaps known only to himself, entered a *sua sponte* order allowing the putative father to "intervene" in the custody proceeding which had been commenced in his court. Subsequently the homosexual couple and the mother signed an agreement allowing the court to enter a consent order giving the couple primary and "physical custody" of the child, and the mother secondary custody. A year and three months later the mother, presumable having moved to Virginia, filed in a Virginia court having jurisdiction, seeking sole physical custody. That court denied her request and a Virginia appellate court affirmed. The thinking of the Virginia appellate court was that the North Carolina award having been made consistent with PKPA and the UCCJEA, was entitled to full faith and credit.[841] The appellate court touched upon DOMA.[842] Because the Virginia court had not been asked to determine the legitimacy of the prevailing couple's relationship DOMA had no application to the case.[843]

Reis v. Zmmer[844] illustrates the problems which may arise post-divorce where children are involved, and the two full faith and credit statutes[845] apply. The husband and wife lived in Massachusetts, where at first a Separation Agreement was entered into, followed by a divorce, with attendant orders of the Massachusetts court concerning custody and child support. The father remained living in Massachusetts, but the mother and their two children, with the father's consent, moved to Buffalo, N.Y., the city in which they were married. The mother remarried and moved with their two children to Portland, Oregon, and continued to live there with the two children of her first marriage, her second husband, and their two children. The father filed in Massachusetts to prevent the children from being moved to Oregon, and wanted him to have custody of them in Massachusetts. A week later he filed for the same relief in New York. The mother wanted the New York proceeding dismissed, per 28 U.S.C. § 1738 A (PKPA), and the Uniform Child Custody Jurisdiction Act (UCCJA). The father resisted on two grounds: (1) the children having lived for several years in New York state, New York was now their "home state," and (2) he was not attempting a "modification" of the

---

841 *Id.* at 205.

842 *See supra* text accompanying notes 37, 38.

843 *Preshad*, 685 S.E. 2d at 207.

844 700 N.Y.S.2d 609 (N.Y. App. Div. 2000). *See infra* text accompanying notes 846, 847, and 874 for additional cases considering this case.

845 28 U.S.C. §§ 1738 A and B.

children's custody, but attempting to maintain the "status quo." At that point, the mother, probably believing that the New York court would not dismiss the case, sought a modification of the Massachusetts custody award. The New York trial court seemed to be satisfied with the father's representation that he was withdrawing his Complaint in Massachusetts, and the mother's counsel's representation to the judge that the Massachusetts court had "declined" jurisdiction. He thereupon approved of the children's move to Oregon, the mother retaining primary custody, with the father having liberal visitation privileges. The New York trial court also made a modification in child support – not in the amount of payment - but directing the father to open a special bank account for the processing of the payments - and in providing the children with a toll free telephone number by which they could contact him. Even though the mother prevailed on most of her requests before the trial court, she appealed to the Appellate Division on two grounds: (1) her visitation privileges were reduced, and (2) she did not like the establishment of a separate bank account. Even though the father did not get his request for a change of custody, he did not appeal. The Appellate Division reversed, but not on the grounds argued by the mother. As to custody the Appellate Division said that under 28 U.S.C. § 1738A (PKPA) and the Uniform Child Custody Jurisdiction Act (UCCJA), Massachusetts, having made the initial custody award, retains jurisdiction as long as the father resided there, and the fact that the children may have acquired a new "home state" is immaterial. The court also chided its lower court in having established virtually no communications with the Massachusetts court. With regard to support, the court held that regardless of the fact that the amounts were not altered, under the provisions of the Uniform Interstate Family Support Act (UIFSA), and the Full Faith and Credit for Child Support Orders Act (U.S.C. § 1738B, or FFCCSOA) the lower court entered an impermissible modification order.[846] To elucidate, Judge Lawton expounded upon the goal of the UIFSA:

> The goal of the UIFSA is to eliminate the problems arising from multiple support orders from various states by providing for one tribunal to have continuing and exclusive jurisdiction to establish or modify a child support order (citations omitted); once a court enters a support order, no court may modify it as long as the obligee, obligor or child for whose benefit the order was issued continues to reside within the jurisdiction of the court unless each party consents in writing to the other jurisdiction.[847]

---

[846] *Reis* 700 N.Y.S.2d at 609 in passim.

[847] *Id.* at 613.

Highfill v. Moody[848] describes some of the basic principles of the Uniform Child-Custody Jurisdiction and Enforcement Act (UCCJEA). F-2 may modify a Custody order entered by F-1 only if F-1 has lost its "exclusive, continuing" jurisdiction, or has declined to use it.[849] F-1 loses it if (1) neither the child nor at least one parent or a person acting as a parent substitute has a connection with F-1; or (2) a state court in F-1 determines that neither the child, parent, nor parent substitute resides in the state.[850] F-2 is permitted to make a determination as to whether or not the child, parent or parent substitute has left F-1.[851] The court touched upon a very important uniform statute in custody matters – the Uniform Interstate Family Support Act (UIFSA). Even though the mother was given custody by F-1 (Arkansas in this case), F-2 (Tennessee in this case) may determine that it is the more "convenient jurisdiction" to modify a ruling under UIFSA. In fact, certain conditions existing in F-2 may authorize custody and support modifications, if it determines that there were changes in F-1, as indicated above.[852] It must be remembered that the parties may agree to whatever changes they deem suitable.[853] Observing the flexibility of both statutes, the court pointed out that there may be a custody proceeding in one state at the same time that a support proceeding is being conducted in another state.[854] Since both the custody and support statutes use the word "residence," rather than "domicile" of the parties, the court gave a clear definition of those terms, i.e. domicile being a place in which a person, having arrived there sometime in the past, intends to make it her or his permanent abode,[855] whereas "residence" s simply a place where a person lives, for

---

848 2010 W.L. 2075698 (Tenn. Ct. App. 2010).

849 *Id.* at *4.

850 *Id.*

851 *Id.*

852 *Id.* at *7. Both the UCCJEA and the UIFSA contain the same wording about the "exclusive, continuing" jurisdiction.

853 *Id.* at *5.

854 *Id.* at *6.

855 *Id.* at *10. In Arendale v. Arendale, 2008 W.L. 481943 at *5 (Tenn. Ct. App. 2008), the retention of the following items were found to be evidence of permanency: (1) one's house, (2) one's driver's license, (3) one's car registration, and (4) one's voter's registration. In Jordan v. Jordan, 2003 W.L. 1092877 (Tenn. Ct. App. 2003) the court

the present, often because of employment.[856] The use of "residence" instead of "domicile" adds to the flexibility of the statutes.[857]

In *Rainbow v. Ransom*[858] the parties' home state was Hawai'i, but the mother and children moved to Maine where the mother filed for a determination of parental rights and responsibilities. The father filed a similar petition in Hawai'i. The two judges conferred telephonically. They agreed that while Hawai'i was the "home state" it would be more convenient to try the issues in Maine. Consequently, Hawai'i declined to exercise its jurisdiction.[859]

In *Ex parte Pierce*[860] while the parties were living in California they decided to move to Alabama, where their child was born. The mother moved to Colorado, where she also filed for divorce; and two weeks later the father filed for divorce in Alabama. The judge in Alabama believed that he lacked subject matter jurisdiction over the divorce, but that he had jurisdiction over custody of the two children since Alabama was their home state. The Alabama and Colorado judges conferred telephonically and agreed that technically there was no "home state" as to the children because they had not lived in any state the requisite six months; but maybe Colorado should exercise jurisdiction because the mother had filed first. Before ending their conversation the Colorado judge deferred to the Alabama judge to decide which of the two jurisdictions was the more convenient. The Alabama judge chose Alabama because Alabama would not be more inconvenient for the mother than Colorado would be for the father.[861]

In *In re T.D.*[862] a child was born in Nevada, but was removed from his parental home due to inability to care for him. A Nevada agency first placed him in a foster

---

considered those same factors, together with (1) Union membership and (2) having been employed in the state until being discharged.

[856] As an example *see* Jordan, 2003 W.L. 1092877 at *1 in passim) where a man was domiciled in Alabama, but resided in Massachusetts due to his employment.

[857] *See Highfill,* 2010 W.L. 2075698. at **9, 10.

[858] 990 A.2d 535 (Me. 2010).

[859] *Id.* at 536.

[860] 2010 W.L. 1740001 (Ala. Civ. App. 2010).

[861] *Id.* at *9.

[862] 781 N.W. 2d 100 (Iowa App. 2010).

home, but shortly thereafter allowed him to stay with his maternal grandmother and step-grandfather in South Carolina, where he stayed for five months. He was then placed with his paternal aunt and uncle in Iowa. They wanted to adopt him, and his biological parents agreed. A Nevada court approved of this arrangement, and gave the child's grandparents visitation privileges. The aunt and uncle filed for adoption in Iowa. The Nevada court appointed a Guardian ad Litem, who filed a report, acknowledging the child's good relationship with his grandparents and adoptive parents, but informed the court of disharmony between the grandparents and the adoptive parents. The Nevada judge became impatient with the Iowa proceeding and that the grandparents were attempting to gain custody of T.D. in Iowa. The Nevada judge, therefore, removed the child from their care. The Iowa court approved of the adoption, and denied the grandparents' visitation privileges. The Iowa judge ruled that the Nevada decree was not final as it was subject to modification to comply with T.D.'s best interests, and that under Iowa law an adoption terminates all visitation privileges. An Iowa appellate court held that this ruling of the Iowa trial judge was error, as denying full faith and credit to the Nevada primary order awarding the grandparents visitation privileges. The case was remanded with instructions to award the grandparents visitation privileges due to full faith and credit.[863]

Though the UCCJEA does not require the courts to seek the child's best interest[864] the courts usually seek that element in their deliberations.[865]

---

[863] *Id.* at 700.

[864] The Commission's prefatory notes state that "[t]he UCCJEA eliminates the term 'best interests' in order to "clearly distinguish between the jurisdictional standards and the substantive standards relating to custody and visitation of children."

[865] *See* Hightower v. Myers, 304 S.W.3d 727, 729 (Mo. 2010); S.C. v. J.T.C., 2010 W.L. 1265188 at *4 (Ala. Civ. App. 2010); Hindle v. Fuith, 33 So.2d 782, 785 (Fla. 5th DCA 2010); Rennie v.Rosenthol, 2010 W.L. 1951697 at *5 n.4 (Pa. Super. 2010); Sutton v. Flores, 2010 W.L. 2006243 at *4 (Ariz. App. Div. 2010).

5. The Uniform Child-Custody Jurisdiction and Enforcement Act (UCCJEA)[866]

(a) Notice required for the exercise of jurisdiction when a person is outside this State may be given in a manner prescribed by the law of this State for service of process or by the law of the State in which the service is made. Notice must be given in a manner reasonably calculated to give actual notice but may be by publication if other means are not effective.

(b) Proof of service may be made in the manner prescribed by the law of this state or by the law of the state in which the service is made.

(c) Notice is not required for the exercise of jurisdiction with respect to a person who submits to the jurisdiction of the court.

§ 109. Appearance and Limited Immunity.

(a) A party to a child-custody proceeding, including a modification proceeding, or a petitioner or respondent in a proceeding to enforce or register a child-custody determination, is not subject to personal jurisdiction in this State for another proceeding or purpose solely by reason of having participated, or of having been physically present for the purpose of participating, in the proceeding.

(b) A person who is subject to personal jurisdiction in this State on a basis other than physical presence is not immune from service of process in this State. A party present in this State who is subject to the jurisdiction of another State is not immune from service of process allowable under the laws of that State.

(c) The immunity granted by subsection (a) does not extend to civil litigation based on acts unrelated to the participation in a proceeding under this [Act] committed by a**§ 101. Short Title.**

This [Act] may be cited as the Uniform Child-Custody Jurisdiction and Enforcement Act.

---

[866] As of Jan. 15, 2012, the District of Columbia, the Virgin Islands, and the following 42 states have adopted the Uniform Child Custody Jurisdiction and Enforcement Act (UCCJEA): Alabama, Alaska, Arizona, Arkansas, California, Colorado, Connecticut, Delaware, Florida, Georgia, Hawai'i, Idaho, Illinois, Indiana, Iowa, Kansas, Kentucky, Louisiana, Maine, Maryland, Michigan, Minnesota., Mississippi, Missouri, Nebraska, Nevarda, New Hampshire, New Jersey, New Mexico, New York, North Carolina, North Dakota, Ohio, Oklahoma, Oregon, Pennsylvania, Rode Island, South Carolina, South Dakota, Tennessee, Texas, and Utah. In other words, as of the date indicated, all but Massachusetts, Montana, Vermont, Virginia, Washington, West Virginia, Wisconsin and Wyoming have adopted the Act.

§ 102. Definitions.

In this [Act]:

(1) "Abandoned" means left without provision for reasonable and necessary care or supervision.

(2) "Child" means an individual who has not attained 18 years of age.

(3) "Child-custody determination" means a judgment, decree, or other order of a court providing for the legal custody, physical custody, or visitation with respect to a child. The term includes a permanent, temporary, initial, and modification order. The term does not include an order relating to child support or other monetary obligation of an individual.

(4) "Child-custody proceeding" means a proceeding in which legal custody, physical custody, or visitation with respect to a child is an issue. The term includes a proceeding for divorce, separation, neglect, abuse, dependency, guardianship, paternity, termination of parental rights, and protection from domestic violence, in which the issue may appear. The term does not include a proceeding involving juvenile delinquency, contractual emancipation, or enforcement under [Article] 3.

(5) "Commencement" means the filing of the first pleading in a proceeding.

(6) "Court" means an entity authorized under the law of a State to establish, enforce, or modify a child-custody determination.

(7) "Home State" means the State in which a child lived with a parent or a person acting as a parent for at least six consecutive months immediately before the commencement of a child-custody proceeding. In the case of a child less than six months of age, the term means the State in which the child lived from birth with any of the persons mentioned. A period of temporary absence of any of the mentioned persons is part of the period.

(8) "Initial determination" means the first child-custody determination concerning a particular child.

(9) "Issuing court" means the court that makes a child-custody determination for which enforcement is sought under this [Act].

(10) "Issuing State" means the State in which a child-custody determination is made.

(11) "Modification" means a child-custody determination that changes, replaces, supersedes, or is otherwise made after a previous determination concerning the same child, whether or not it is made by the court that made the previous determination.

(12) "Person" means an individual, corporation, business trust, estate, trust, partnership, limited liability company, association, joint venture, government;

governmental subdivision, agency, or instrumentality; public corporation; or any other legal or commercial entity.

(13) "Person acting as a parent" means a person, other than a parent, who:

(A) has physical custody of the child or has had physical custody for a period of six consecutive months, including any temporary absence, within one year immediately before the commencement of a child-custody proceeding; and

(B) has been awarded legal custody by a court or claims a right to legal custody under the law of this State.

(14) "Physical custody" means the physical care and supervision of a child.

(15) "State" means a State of the United States, the District of Columbia, Puerto Rico, the United States Virgin Islands, or any territory or insular possession subject to the jurisdiction of the United States.

(16) "Tribe" means an Indian tribe or band, or Alaskan Native village, which is recognized by federal law or formally acknowledged by a State.]

(17) "Warrant" means an order issued by a court authorizing law enforcement officers to take physical custody of a child.

§ 103. Proceedings Governed by Other Law.

This [Act] does not govern an adoption proceeding or a proceeding pertaining to the authorization of emergency medical care for a child.

§ 104. Application to Indian Tribes.

(a) A child-custody proceeding that pertains to an Indian child as defined in the Indian Child Welfare Act, 25 U.S.C. § 1901 et seq., is not subject to this [Act] to the extent that it is governed by the Indian Child Welfare Act.

[(b) A court of this State shall treat a tribe as if it were a State of the United States for the purpose of applying [Articles] 1 and 2.]

[(c) A child-custody determination made by a tribe under factual circumstances in substantial conformity with the jurisdictional standards of this [Act] must be recognized and enforced under [Article] 3.]

§ 105. International Application of [Act].

(a) A court of this State shall treat a foreign country as if it were a State of the United States for the purpose of applying [Articles] 1 and 2.

(b) Except as otherwise provided in subsection (c), a child-custody determination made in a foreign country under factual circumstances in substantial conformity with the jurisdictional standards of this [Act] must be recognized and enforced under [Article] 3.

(c) A court of this State need not apply this [Act] if the child custody law of a foreign country violates fundamental principles of human rights.

§ 106. Effect of Child-Custody Determination.
A child-custody determination made by a court of this State that had jurisdiction under this [Act] binds all persons who have been served in accordance with the laws of this State or notified in accordance with Section 108 or who have submitted to the jurisdiction of the court, and who have been given an opportunity to be heard. As to those persons, the determination is conclusive as to all decided issues of law and fact except to the extent the determination is modified.

§ 107. Priority.
If a question of existence or exercise of jurisdiction under this [Act] is raised in a child-custody proceeding, the question, upon request of a party, must be given priority on the calendar and handled expeditiously.

§ 108. Notice to Persons Outside State.
an individual while present in this State.

§ 110. Communication Between Courts.

(a) A court of this State may communicate with a court in another State concerning a proceeding arising under this [Act].

(b) The court may allow the parties to participate in the communication. If the parties are not able to participate in the communication, they must be given the opportunity to present facts and legal arguments before a decision on jurisdiction is made.

(c) Communication between courts on schedules, calendars, court records, and similar matters may occur without informing the parties. A record need not be made of the communication.

(d) Except as otherwise provided in subsection (c), a record must be made of a communication under this section. The parties must be informed promptly of the communication and granted access to the record.

(e) For the purposes of this section, "record" means information that is inscribed on a tangible medium or that is stored in an electronic or other medium and is retrievable in perceivable form.

§ 111. Taking Testimony in Another State.

(a) In addition to other procedures available to a party, a party to a child-custody proceeding may offer testimony of witnesses who are located in another State, including testimony of the parties and the child, by deposition or other means allowable in this State for testimony taken in another State. The court on its own motion may order that the testimony of a person be taken in another State and may prescribe the manner in which and the terms upon which the testimony is taken.

(b) A court of this State may permit an individual residing in another State to be deposed or to testify by telephone, audiovisual means, or other electronic means before a designated court or at another location in that State. A court of this State shall cooperate with courts of other States in designating an appropriate location for the deposition or testimony.

(c) Documentary evidence transmitted from another State to a court of this State by technological means that do not produce an original writing may not be excluded from evidence on an objection based on the means of transmission.

§ 112. Cooperation Between Courts; Preservation of Records

(a) A court of this State may request the appropriate court of another State to:

(1) hold an evidentiary hearing;

(2) order a person to produce or give evidence pursuant to procedures of that State;

(3) order that an evaluation be made with respect to the custody of a child involved in a pending proceeding;

(4) forward to the court of this State a certified copy of the transcript of the record of the hearing, the evidence otherwise presented, and any evaluation prepared in compliance with the request; and

(5) order a party to a child-custody proceeding or any person having physical custody of the child to appear in the proceeding with or without the child.

(b) Upon request of a court of another State, a court of this State may hold a hearing or enter an order described in subsection (a).

(c) Travel and other necessary and reasonable expenses incurred under subsections (a) and (b) may be assessed against the parties according to the law of this State.

(d) A court of this State shall preserve the pleadings, orders, decrees, records of hearings, evaluations, and other pertinent records with respect to a child-custody proceeding until the child attains 18 years of age. Upon appropriate request by a court or law enforcement official of another State, the court shall forward a certified copy of those records.

§ 201. Initial Child-Custody Jurisdiction.

(a) Except as otherwise provided in Section 204, a court of this State has jurisdiction to make an initial child-custody determination only if:

(1) this State is the home State of the child on the date of the commencement of the proceeding, or was the home State of the child within six months before the commencement of the proceeding and the child is absent from this State but a parent or person acting as a parent continues to live in this State;

(2) a court of another State does not have jurisdiction under paragraph (1), or a court of the home State of the child has declined to exercise jurisdiction on the ground that this State is the more appropriate forum under Section 207 or 208, and:

(A) the child and the child's parents, or the child and at least one parent or a person acting as a parent, have a significant connection with this State other than mere physical presence; and

(B) substantial evidence is available in this State concerning the child's care, protection, training, and personal relationships;

(3) all courts having jurisdiction under paragraph (1) or (2) have declined to exercise jurisdiction on the ground that a court of this State is the more appropriate forum to determine the custody of the child under Section 207 or 208; or

(4) no court of any other State would have jurisdiction under the criteria specified in paragraph (1), (2), or (3).

(b) Subsection (a) is the exclusive jurisdictional basis for making a child-custody determination by a court of this State.

(c) Physical presence of, or personal jurisdiction over, a party or a child is not necessary or sufficient to make a child-custody determination.

§ 202. Exclusive, Continuing Jurisdiction.

(a) Except as otherwise provided in Section 204, a court of this State which has made a child-custody determination consistent with Section 201 or 203 has exclusive, continuing jurisdiction over the determination until:

(1) a court of this State determines that neither the child, nor the child and one parent, nor the child and a person acting as a parent have a significant connection with this State and that substantial evidence is no longer available

in this State concerning the child's care, protection, training, and personal relationships; or

(2) a court of this State or a court of another State determines that the child, the child's parents, and any person acting as a parent do not presently reside in this State.

(b) A court of this State which has made a child-custody determination and does not have exclusive, continuing jurisdiction under this section may modify that determination only if it has jurisdiction to make an initial determination under Section 201.

§ 203. Jurisdiction to Modify Determination.

Except as otherwise provided in Section 204, a court of this State may not modify a child-custody determination made by a court of another State unless a court of this State has jurisdiction to make an initial determination under Section 201(a)(1) or (2) and:

(1) the court of the other State determines it no longer has exclusive, continuing jurisdiction under Section 202 or that a court of this State would be a more convenient forum under Section 207; or

(2) a court of this State or a court of the other State determines that the child, the child's parents, and any person acting as a parent do not presently reside in the other State.

§ 204. Temporary Emergency Jurisdiction.

(a) A court of this State has temporary emergency jurisdiction if the child is present in this State and the child has been abandoned or it is necessary in an emergency to protect the child because the child, or a sibling or parent of the child, is subjected to or threatened with mistreatment or abuse.

(b) If there is no previous child-custody determination that is entitled to be enforced under this [Act] and a child-custody proceeding has not been commenced in a court of a State having jurisdiction under Sections 201 through 203, a child-custody determination made under this section remains in effect until an order is obtained from a court of a State having jurisdiction under Sections 201 through 203. If a child-custody proceeding has not been or is not commenced in a court of a State having jurisdiction under Sections 201 through 203, a child-custody determination made under this section becomes a final determination, if it so provides and this State becomes the home State of the child.

(c) If there is a previous child-custody determination that is entitled to be enforced under this [Act], or a child-custody proceeding has been commenced in a court of a State having jurisdiction under Sections 201 through 203, any order issued by a court of this State under this section must specify in the order a period that the court considers adequate to allow the person seeking an order to obtain an order from the State having jurisdiction under Sections 201 through 203. The order issued in this State remains in effect until an order is obtained from the other State within the period specified or the period expires.

(d) A court of this State which has been asked to make a child-custody determination under this section, upon being informed that a child-custody proceeding has been commenced in, or a child-custody determination has been made by, a court of a State having jurisdiction under Sections 201 through 203, shall immediately communicate with the other court. A court of this State which is exercising jurisdiction pursuant to Sections 201 through 203, upon being informed that a child-custody proceeding has been commenced in, or a child-custody determination has been made by, a court of another State under a statute similar to this section shall immediately communicate with the court of that State to resolve the emergency, protect the safety of the parties and the child, and determine a period for the duration of the temporary order.

§ 205. Notice; Opportunity to be Heard; Joinder.

(a) Before a child-custody determination is made under this [Act], notice and an opportunity to be heard in accordance with the standards of Section 108 must be given to all persons entitled to notice under the law of this State as in child-custody proceedings between residents of this State, any parent whose parental rights have not been previously terminated, and any person having physical custody of the child.

(b) This [Act] does not govern the enforceability of a child-custody determination made without notice or an opportunity to be heard.

(c) The obligation to join a party and the right to intervene as a party in a child-custody proceeding under this [Act] are governed by the law of this State as in child-custody proceedings between residents of this State.

§ 206. Simultaneous Proceedings.

(a) Except as otherwise provided in Section 204, a court of this State may not exercise its jurisdiction under this [article] if, at the time of the commencement of the proceeding, a proceeding concerning the custody of the child has been commenced in a court of another State having jurisdiction substantially in conformity with this [Act], unless the proceeding has been terminated or is stayed by the court of the other State because a court of this State is a more convenient forum under Section 207.

(b) Except as otherwise provided in Section 204, a court of this State, before hearing a child-custody proceeding, shall examine the court documents and other information supplied by the parties pursuant to Section 209. If the court determines that a child-custody proceeding has been commenced in a court in another State having jurisdiction substantially in accordance with this [Act], the court of this State shall stay its proceeding and communicate with the court of the other State. If the court of the State having jurisdiction substantially in accordance with this [Act] does not determine that the court of this State is a more appropriate forum, the court of this State shall dismiss the proceeding.

(c) In a proceeding to modify a child-custody determination, a court of this State shall determine whether a proceeding to enforce the determination has been commenced in another State. If a proceeding to enforce a child-custody determination has been commenced in another State, the court may:

(1) stay the proceeding for modification pending the entry of an order of a court of the other State enforcing, staying, denying, or dismissing the proceeding for enforcement;

(2) enjoin the parties from continuing with the proceeding for enforcement; or

(3) proceed with the modification under conditions it considers appropriate.

§ 207. Inconvenient Forum.

(a) A court of this State which has jurisdiction under this [Act] to make a child-custody determination may decline to exercise its jurisdiction at any time if it determines that it is an inconvenient forum under the circumstances and that a court of another State is a more appropriate forum. The issue of inconvenient forum may be raised upon motion of a party, the court's own motion, or request of another court.

(b) Before determining whether it is an inconvenient forum, a court of this State shall consider whether it is appropriate for a court of another State to exercise jurisdiction. For this purpose, the court shall allow the parties to submit information and shall consider all relevant factors, including:

(1) whether domestic violence has occurred and is likely to continue in the future and which State could best protect the parties and the child;

(2) the length of time the child has resided outside this State;

(3) the distance between the court in this State and the court in the State that would assume jurisdiction;

(4) the relative financial circumstances of the parties;

(5) any agreement of the parties as to which State should assume jurisdiction;

(6) the nature and location of the evidence required to resolve the pending litigation, including testimony of the child;

(7) the ability of the court of each State to decide the issue expeditiously and the procedures necessary to present the evidence; and

(8) the familiarity of the court of each State with the facts and issues in the pending litigation.

(c) If a court of this State determines that it is an inconvenient forum and that a court of another State is a more appropriate forum, it shall stay the proceedings upon condition that a child-custody proceeding be promptly commenced in another designated State and may impose any other condition the court considers just and proper.

(d) A court of this State may decline to exercise its jurisdiction under this [Act] if a child-custody determination is incidental to an action for divorce or another proceeding while still retaining jurisdiction over the divorce or other proceeding.

§ 208. Jurisdiction Declined by Reason of Conduct.

(a) Except as otherwise provided in Section 204 [or by other law of this State], if a court of this State has jurisdiction under this [Act] because a person seeking to invoke its jurisdiction has engaged in unjustifiable conduct, the court shall decline to exercise its jurisdiction unless:

(1) the parents and all persons acting as parents have acquiesced in the exercise of jurisdiction;

(2) a court of the State otherwise having jurisdiction under Sections 201 through 203 determines that this State is a more appropriate forum under Section 207; or

(3) no court of any other State would have jurisdiction under the criteria specified in Sections 201 through 203.

(b) If a court of this State declines to exercise its jurisdiction pursuant to subsection (a), it may fashion an appropriate remedy to ensure the safety of the child and prevent a repetition of the unjustifiable conduct, including staying the proceeding until a child-custody proceeding is commenced in a court having jurisdiction under Sections 201 through 203.

(c) If a court dismisses a petition or stays a proceeding because it declines to exercise its jurisdiction pursuant to subsection (a), it shall assess against the party seeking to invoke its jurisdiction necessary and reasonable expenses including costs, communication expenses, attorney's fees, investigative fees, expenses for witnesses, travel expenses, and child care during the course of the proceedings, unless the party from whom fees are sought establishes that the assessment would be clearly inappropriate. The court may not assess fees, costs, or expenses against this State unless authorized by law other than this [Act].

§ 209. Information to be Submitted to Court.

(a) [Subject to [local law providing for the confidentiality of procedures, addresses, and other identifying information], in] [In] a child-custody proceeding, each party, in its first pleading or in an attached affidavit, shall give information, if reasonably ascertainable, under oath as to the child's present address or whereabouts, the places where the child has lived during the last five years, and the names and present addresses of the persons with whom the child has lived during that period. The pleading or affidavit must state whether the party:

(1) has participated, as a party or witness or in any other capacity, in any other proceeding concerning the custody of or visitation with the child and, if so, identify the court, the case number, and the date of the child-custody determination, if any;

(2) knows of any proceeding that could affect the current proceeding, including proceedings for enforcement and proceedings relating to domestic violence, protective orders, termination of parental rights, and adoptions and, if so, identify the court, the case number, and the nature of the proceeding; and

(3) knows the names and addresses of any person not a party to the proceeding who has physical custody of the child or claims rights of legal custody or physical custody of, or visitation with, the child and, if so, the names and addresses of those persons.

(b) If the information required by subsection (a) is not furnished, the court, upon motion of a party or its own motion, may stay the proceeding until the information is furnished.

(c) If the declaration as to any of the items described in subsection (a)(1) through (3) is in the affirmative, the declarant shall give additional information under oath as required by the court. The court may examine the parties under oath as to details of the information furnished and other matters pertinent to the court's jurisdiction and the disposition of the case.

(d) Each party has a continuing duty to inform the court of any proceeding in this or any other State that could affect the current proceeding.

[(e) If a party alleges in an affidavit or a pleading under oath that the health, safety, or liberty of a party or child would be jeopardized by disclosure of identifying information, the information must be sealed and may not be disclosed to the other party or the public unless the court orders the disclosure to be made after a hearing in which the court takes into consideration the health, safety, or liberty of the party or child and determines that the disclosure is in the interest of justice.]

§ 210. Appearance of Parties and Child.

(a) In a child-custody proceeding in this State, the court may order a party to the proceeding who is in this State to appear before the court in person with or without the child. The court may order any person who is in this State and who has physical custody or control of the child to appear in person with the child.

(b) If a party to a child-custody proceeding whose presence is desired by the court is outside this State, the court may order that a notice given pursuant to Section 108 include a statement directing the party to appear in person with or without the child and informing the party that failure to appear may result in a decision adverse to the party.

(c) The court may enter any orders necessary to ensure the safety of the child and of any person ordered to appear under this section.

(d) If a party to a child-custody proceeding who is outside this State is directed to appear under subsection (b) or desires to appear personally before the court with or without the child, the court may require another party to pay reasonable and necessary travel and other expenses of the party so appearing and of the child.

§ 301. Definitions.

In this [article]:

(1) "Petitioner" means a person who seeks enforcement of an order for return of a child under the Hague Convention on the Civil Aspects of International Child Abduction or enforcement of a child-custody determination.

(2) "Respondent" means a person against whom a proceeding has been commenced for enforcement of an order for return of a child under the Hague Convention on the Civil Aspects of International Child Abduction or enforcement of a child-custody determination.

§ 302. Enforcement Under Hague Convention.

Under this [article] a court of this State may enforce an order for the return of the child made under the Hague Convention on the Civil Aspects of International Child Abduction as if it were a child-custody determination.

§ 303. Duty to Enforce.

(a) A court of this State shall recognize and enforce a child-custody determination of a court of another State if the latter court exercised jurisdiction in substantial conformity with this [Act] or the determination was made under factual circumstances meeting the jurisdictional standards of this [Act] and the determination has not been modified in accordance with this [Act].

(b) A court of this State may utilize any remedy available under other law of this State to enforce a child-custody determination made by a court of another State. The remedies provided in this [article] are cumulative and do not affect the availability of other remedies to enforce a child-custody determination.

§ 304. Temporary Visitation.

(a) A court of this State which does not have jurisdiction to modify a child-custody determination, may issue a temporary order enforcing:

(1) a visitation schedule made by a court of another State; or

(2) the visitation provisions of a child-custody determination of another State that does not provide for a specific visitation schedule.

(b) If a court of this State makes an order under subsection (a)(2), it shall specify in the order a period that it considers adequate to allow the petitioner to obtain an order from a court having jurisdiction under the criteria specified in [Article] 2. The order remains in effect until an order is obtained from the other court or the period expires.

§ 305. Registration of Child-Custody Determination.

(a) A child-custody determination issued by a court of another State may be registered in this State, with or without a simultaneous request for enforcement, by sending to [the appropriate court] in this State:

(1) a letter or other document requesting registration;

(2) two copies, including one certified copy, of the determination sought to be registered, and a statement under penalty of perjury that to the best of the knowledge and belief of the person seeking registration the order has not been modified; and

(3) except as otherwise provided in Section 209, the name and address of the person seeking registration and any parent or person acting as a parent who has been awarded custody or visitation in the child-custody determination sought to be registered.

(b) On receipt of the documents required by subsection (a), the registering court shall:

(1) cause the determination to be filed as a foreign judgment, together with one copy of any accompanying documents and information, regardless of their form; and

(2) serve notice upon the persons named pursuant to subsection (a)(3) and provide them with an opportunity to contest the registration in accordance with this section.

(c) The notice required by subsection (b)(2) must state that:

(1) a registered determination is enforceable as of the date of the registration in the same manner as a determination issued by a court of this State;

(2) a hearing to contest the validity of the registered determination must be requested within 20 days after service of notice; and

(3) failure to contest the registration will result in confirmation of the child-custody determination and preclude further contest of that determination with respect to any matter that could have been asserted.

(d) A person seeking to contest the validity of a registered order must request a hearing within 20 days after service of the notice. At that hearing, the court shall confirm the registered order unless the person contesting registration establishes that:

(1) the issuing court did not have jurisdiction under [Article] 2;

(2) the child-custody determination sought to be registered has been vacated, stayed, or modified by a court having jurisdiction to do so under [Article] 2; or

(3) the person contesting registration was entitled to notice, but notice was not given in accordance with the standards of Section 108, in the proceedings before the court that issued the order for which registration is sought.

(e) If a timely request for a hearing to contest the validity of the registration is not made, the registration is confirmed as a matter of law and the person requesting registration and all persons served must be notified of the confirmation.

(f) Confirmation of a registered order, whether by operation of law or after notice and hearing, precludes further contest of the order with respect to any matter that could have been asserted at the time of registration.

§ 306. Enforcement of Registered Determination.

(a) A court of this State may grant any relief normally available under the law of this State to enforce a registered child-custody determination made by a court of another State.

(b) A court of this State shall recognize and enforce, but may not modify, except in accordance with [Article] 2, a registered child-custody determination of a court of another State.

§ 307. Simultaneous Proceedings.
If a proceeding for enforcement under this [article] is commenced in a court of this State and the court determines that a proceeding to modify the determination is pending in a court of another State having jurisdiction to modify the determination under [Article] 2, the enforcing court shall immediately communicate with the modifying court. The proceeding for enforcement continues unless the enforcing court, after consultation with the modifying court, stays or dismisses the proceeding.

§ 308. Expedited Enforcement of Child-Custody Determination.

(a) A petition under this [article] must be verified. Certified copies of all orders sought to be enforced and of any order confirming registration must be attached to the petition. A copy of a certified copy of an order may be attached instead of the original.

(b) A petition for enforcement of a child-custody determination must state:

(1) whether the court that issued the determination identified the jurisdictional basis it relied upon in exercising jurisdiction and, if so, what the basis was;

(2) whether the determination for which enforcement is sought has been vacated, stayed, or modified by a court whose decision must be enforced under this [Act] and, if so, identify the court, the case number, and the nature of the proceeding;

(3) whether any proceeding has been commenced that could affect the current proceeding, including proceedings relating to domestic violence, protective orders, termination of parental rights, and adoptions and, if so, identify the court, the case number, and the nature of the proceeding;

(4) the present physical address of the child and the respondent, if known;

(5) whether relief in addition to the immediate physical custody of the child and attorney's fees is sought, including a request for assistance from [law enforcement officials] and, if so, the relief sought; and

(6) if the child-custody determination has been registered and confirmed under Section 305, the date and place of registration.

(c) Upon the filing of a petition, the court shall issue an order directing the respondent to appear in person with or without the child at a hearing and may enter any order necessary to ensure the safety of the parties and the child. The hearing must be held on the next judicial day after service of the order unless that date is impossible. In that event, the court shall hold the hearing on the first judicial day possible. The court may extend the date of hearing at the request of the petitioner.

(d) An order issued under subsection (c) must state the time and place of the hearing and advise the respondent that at the hearing the court will order that the petitioner may take immediate physical custody of the child and the payment of fees, costs, and expenses under Section 312, and may schedule a hearing to determine whether further relief is appropriate, unless the respondent appears and establishes that:

(1) the child-custody determination has not been registered and confirmed under Section 305 and that:

(A) the issuing court did not have jurisdiction under [Article] 2;

(B) the child-custody determination for which enforcement is sought has been vacated, stayed, or modified by a court having jurisdiction to do so under [Article] 2;

(C) the respondent was entitled to notice, but notice was not given in accordance with the standards of Section 108, in the proceedings before the court that issued the order for which enforcement is sought; or

(2) the child-custody determination for which enforcement is sought was registered and confirmed under Section 304, but has been vacated, stayed, or modified by a court of a State having jurisdiction to do so under [Article] 2.

§ 309. Service of Petition and Order.
Except as otherwise provided in Section 311, the petition and order must be served, by any method authorized [by the law of this State], upon respondent and any person who has physical custody of the child.

§ 310. Hearing and Order.

(a) Unless the court issues a temporary emergency order pursuant to Section 204, upon a finding that a petitioner is entitled to immediate physical custody of the child, the court shall order that the petitioner may take immediate physical custody of the child unless the respondent establishes that:

(1) the child-custody determination has not been registered and confirmed under Section 305 and that:

(A) the issuing court did not have jurisdiction under [Article] 2;

(B) the child-custody determination for which enforcement is sought has been vacated, stayed, or modified by a court of a State having jurisdiction to do so under [Article] 2; or

(C) the respondent was entitled to notice, but notice was not given in accordance with the standards of Section 108, in the proceedings before the court that issued the order for which enforcement is sought; or

(2) the child-custody determination for which enforcement is sought was registered and confirmed under Section 305 but has been vacated, stayed, or modified by a court of a State having jurisdiction to do so under [Article] 2.

(b) The court shall award the fees, costs, and expenses authorized under Section 312 and may grant additional relief, including a request for the assistance of [law enforcement officials], and set a further hearing to determine whether additional relief is appropriate.

(c) If a party called to testify refuses to answer on the ground that the testimony may be self-incriminating, the court may draw an adverse inference from the refusal.

(d) A privilege against disclosure of communications between spouses and a defense of immunity based on the relationship of husband and wife or parent and child may not be invoked in a proceeding under this [article].

§ 311. Warrant to Take Physical Custody of Child.

(a) Upon the filing of a petition seeking enforcement of a child-custody determination, the petitioner may file a verified application for the issuance of a warrant to take physical custody of the child if the child is immediately likely to suffer serious physical harm or be removed from this State.

(b) If the court, upon the testimony of the petitioner or other witness, finds that the child is imminently likely to suffer serious physical harm or be removed from this State, it may issue a warrant to take physical custody of the child. The petition must be heard on the next judicial day after the warrant is executed unless that date is impossible. In that event, the court shall hold the hearing on the first judicial day possible. The application for the warrant must include the statements required by Section 308(b).

(c) A warrant to take physical custody of a child must:

(1) recite the facts upon which a conclusion of imminent serious physical harm or removal from the jurisdiction is based;

(2) direct law enforcement officers to take physical custody of the child immediately; and

(3) provide for the placement of the child pending final relief.

(d) The respondent must be served with the petition, warrant, and order immediately after the child is taken into physical custody.

(e) A warrant to take physical custody of a child is enforceable throughout this State. If the court finds on the basis of the testimony of the petitioner or other witness that a less intrusive remedy is not effective, it may authorize law enforcement officers to enter private property to take physical custody of the child.

If required by exigent circumstances of the case, the court may authorize law enforcement officers to make a forcible entry at any hour.

(f) The court may impose conditions upon placement of a child to ensure the appearance of the child and the child's custodian.

§ 312. Costs, Fees, and Expenses.

(a) The court shall award the prevailing party, including a State, necessary and reasonable expenses incurred by or on behalf of the party, including costs, communication expenses, attorney's fees, investigative fees, expenses for witnesses, travel expenses, and child care during the course of the proceedings, unless the party from whom fees or expenses are sought establishes that the award would be clearly inappropriate.

(b) The court may not assess fees, costs, or expenses against a State unless authorized by law other than this [Act].

§ 313. Recognition and Enforcement.

A court of this State shall accord full faith and credit to an order issued by another State and consistent with this [Act] which enforces a child-custody determination by a court of another State unless the order has been vacated, stayed, or modified by a court having jurisdiction to do so under [Article] 2.

§ 314. Appeals.

An appeal may be taken from a final order in a proceeding under this [article] in accordance with [expedited appellate procedures in other civil cases]. Unless the court enters a temporary emergency order under Section 204, the enforcing court may not stay an order enforcing a child-custody determination pending appeal.

§ 315. Role of [Prosecutor or Public Official].

(a) In a case arising under this [Act] or involving the Hague Convention on the Civil Aspects of International Child Abduction, the [prosecutor or other appropriate public official] may take any lawful action, including resort to a proceeding under this [article] or any other available civil proceeding to locate a child, obtain the return of a child, or enforce a child-custody determination if there is:

(1) an existing child-custody determination;

(2) a request to do so from a court in a pending child-custody proceeding;

(3) a reasonable belief that a criminal statute has been violated; or

(4) a reasonable belief that the child has been wrongfully removed or retained in violation of the Hague Convention on the Civil Aspects of International Child Abduction.

(b) A [prosecutor or appropriate public official] acting under this section acts on behalf of the court and may not represent any party.

§ 316. Role of [Law Enforcement].
At the request of a [prosecutor or other appropriate public official] acting under Section 315, a [law enforcement officer] may take any lawful action reasonably necessary to locate a child or a party and assist [a prosecutor or appropriate public official] with responsibilities under Section 315.
Enforcement (Refs & Annos)

§ 317. Costs and Expenses.
If the respondent is not the prevailing party, the court may assess against the respondent all direct expenses and costs incurred by the [prosecutor or other appropriate public official] and [law enforcement officers] under Section 315 or 316.

§ 401. Application and Construction.
In applying and construing this Uniform Act, consideration must be given to the need to promote uniformity of the law with respect to its subject matter among States that enact it.

§ 402. Severability Clause.
If any provision of this [Act] or its application to any person or circumstance is held invalid, the invalidity does not affect other provisions or applications of this [Act] which can be given effect without the invalid provision or application, and to this end the provisions of this [Act] are severable.

§ 403. Effective Date.
This [Act] takes effect ....

§ 404. Repeals.
The following acts and parts of acts are hereby repealed:

(1) The Uniform Child Custody Jurisdiction Act;
(2) ....
(3) ....

§ 405. Transitional Provision.
A motion or other request for relief made in a child-custody proceeding or to enforce a child-custody determination which was commenced before the effective date of this [Act] is governed by the law in effect at the time the motion or other request was made.

6. Awarding Child Support

a. The Cases

In 1992 Congress enacted the Child Support Recovery Act[867] and amended it in 1998 by the statute bearing the uncomplimentary, but perhaps appropriate, name of the "Deadbeat Parents Punishment Act of 1998."[868] Those pieces of legislation were codified as the criminal statute, 18 U.S.C. § 228, which provides that anyone who willfully fails to pay a support obligation with respect to a child who resides in another State, is subject to punishment if the obligation is of a specified amount and remains unpaid for a specified period of time.[869] These criminal statutes will not be further considered,[870] except as may be mentioned by cases dealing with the subject of this lexicon, full faith and credit.

The primary statutes, which *inter alia*, contain civil penalties for failure to abide by child support orders are the Full Faith and Credit for Child Support Orders Act (FFCCSOA of 1994) which was codified as 28 U.S.C. § 1738B[871] and

---

[867] Codified as 18 U.S.C. § 228(e).

[868] Pub. L. No. 105-187, 112 Stat. 618 (1998), codified as 18 U.S.C. § 228(a)(3).

[869] 18 U.S.C. § 228(a) and (c). The House record reveals that the 1992 Act was intended by Congress to strengthen state efforts to enforce child support obligations against parents who flee across state lines. Specifically, the Act "addresses the growing problem of interstate enforcement of child support by punishing certain persons who intentionally fail to pay their child support obligations." See H.R. Rep. No. 102-771, at 4 (1992).

[870] *See* an informative expose of them in United States v. Berner, 587 F.Supp.2d 1105, 1106 (D.S.D. 2008).

[871] *See supra* text accompanying note 36. FFCCSOA (28 U.S.C. § 1738B) has been described as "the paradigm for enforcing child support orders." *See* Witowski v. Roosevelt, 199 P.3d 1072, 1077 (Wyo. 2009). At *infra* text accompanying notes 875-877 that case is further discussed.

the Uniform Interstate Family Support Act (UIFSA).[872] FFCCSOA and UIFSA, working in tandem, have severely limited the circumstances under which a state may modify a child support order issued by another state.[873]

Reis v. Zimmer[874]

In *Yarborough v. Yarborough*[875] the family lived in Atlanta, Georgia. The husband and wife underwent a divorce and after it Mr. Yarborough continued living there, but their daughter moved to South Carolina, to live with her grandfather. At about the time she wanted to enter college she filed, in South Carolina, for an increase in child support, as she had insufficient funds with which to pay her increased expenses. The U.S. Supreme Court held that she was not permitted to obtain an increase. Justice Lewis Brandeis, writing the majority Opinion, while admitting that custody is ordinarily alterable, pointed out that the Georgia statutes do not permit alteration. His second point was that by permitting South Carolina to alter the Georgia decree would violate the Full Faith and Credit Clause which applies to custody awards.[876] It would seem that Justice Stone had the stronger position. He thought that with regard to such sensitive areas of the custody of children, the Full Faith and Credit Clause should be a bit more expansive. In his Dissenting Opinion he wrote that: "full faith and credit does not command that the obligations attached to a status, because once appropriately imposed by one state, shall be forever placed beyond the control of every other state, without regard to the interest in it and the power of control which the other may later acquire."[877]

In *In re Welfare of S.R.S*[878] an unmarried couple had a child, born in Colorado. A Colorado court gave custody of the child to the mother, required the father to

---

872 Neither the legislative history nor the wording of FFCCSOA (28 U.S.C. § 1738B) indicate an intention to preempt UIFSA. FFCCSOA, moreover, was intended to follow the contours of UIFSA. Basileh v. Alghusain, 912 N.E.2d 814, 820 (Ind. 2009).

873 Lacarrubba v. Lacarrubba, 688 S.E.2d 769, 770 (N.C. App. 2010).

874 *See supra* text accompanying notes 844, 846, and 847.

875 290 U.S.202 (1933).

876 *Id.* at 212, 213.

877 *Id.* at 219, 220.

878 756 N.W.2d 123 (Minn. App. 2008).

pay child support, gave him visitation rights, and subsequently authorized the mother's request to move, with the child, to Minnesota. When the father requested the Colorado court to modify his visitation rights the court, after a status conference, ordered the case transferred to Minnesota, as in its opinion Colorado would be an inconvenient place to try the issues involved. Upon physically receiving the case, the Minnesota court found that it did not have jurisdiction and dismissed the case. The mother, arguing that she was denied her rights under the Full Faith and Credit Clause, appealed. The Minnesota Court of Appeals affirmed, for the primary reason that the case differed from *Durfee v. Duke*, [879] which held that once F-2 was assured that F-1 had considered and determined that it had jurisdiction it must give the F-1 judgment full faith and credit. This case and *Durfee* are distinguishable because, referring to the Minnesota statute's exact words, it is not the jurisdiction of the Colorado (F-1) court that is in question here, but the jurisdiction of the Minnesota (F-2) court. Here, the question of jurisdiction was summarily addressed by the Colorado (F-1) court in response to respondent's request for a status conference to clarify the issue of jurisdiction, but it was not fully and fairly litigated by the Colorado court. The court did not address the issue of whether Minnesota had jurisdiction or the basis for its transfer of jurisdiction of the support order at this status conference. Its previous order, which it clarified at the status conference, was an order transferring jurisdiction of a motion to modify visitation based on its finding that Colorado was an inconvenient forum. The first jurisdictional transfer was based on the need to determine the child's bests interests with information and evidence available in Minnesota, not Colorado, relating to decisions regarding parenting time, i.e. visitation privileges. Colorado was found to be an "inconvenient" forum to try such issues, and Minnesota apparently agreed, by accepting jurisdiction to try the visitation matter. Until the Colorado court issued its order after the status conference, there was no indication that the court also intended to transfer jurisdiction of the support order when it transferred jurisdiction with respect to visitation. Nor did the Colorado court state a legal basis for transferring jurisdiction of the support order. Hence there was no violation of the Full Faith and Credit Clause.[880] This case indicates that if F-1 believes it should transfer a case to another (F-2) court based on its being inconvenient to try it, and

---

[879] 375 U.S. 106 (1963). *See supra* text accompanying notes 135, 137, 198, 427, 581-585, and 587 for further consideration of this case.

[880] *S.R.S., In re Welfare of* 75N.W. 2d at 129.

F-2 agrees and takes it (i.e. assumes jurisdiction of it), voluntarily, no full faith and credit considerations are involved.[881]

In *Witowski v. Roosevelt*,[882] a father complained to the effect that Wyoming (F-2) should not have given full faith and credit to a Virginia (F-1) support order because it was modifiable. The Wyoming court observed that under Virginia law the order was modifiable only prospectively, and not retroactively, and as such there was no violation of full faith and credit. The Wyoming court implicitly opined that if this prospective-retroactive dichotomy were not an exception to the modifiable exception,[883] 28 U.S.C. § 1738 B would be ineffective.[884] The court added, with a rather convoluted explanation to the effect that even if the law of the two states differed, as long as the complaining father did not assert in Virginia that the Virginia court's refusal to modify the required support payments violated 28 U.S.C. § 1738 B, the Supremacy Clause[885] obligates Wyoming to enforce the Virginia order.[886]

In *Meether v. Meether*[887] the mother and father were divorced in Utah, where they lived. The mother subsequently moved to California where she remarried. The father moved to Iowa, where he did not re-marry. When the mother attempted to enforce a Utah (F-1) judgment for post-due child support in the Iowa (F-2) court the father objected on the ground that the Utah judgment was not entitled to full faith and credit because of the Utah court's lack of subject-matter and personal jurisdiction. The Iowa court ignored the father's objection and enforced the Utah

---

[881] Query: is this another exception to full faith and credit (*see supra* text accompanying notes 265-444.)? Probably not, as exceptions exist where there would have been full faith and credit except for the exceptions, which absolves the problem. Here there is no problem, because full faith and credit never existed because of the agreement of the courts. Ed.

[882] 199 P.3d 1072 (Wyo. 2009).

[883] *See supra* text accompanying note 349.

[884] *Witowsk*i, 199 P.3d at 1077.

[885] U.S. Const art. VI, Cl. 2.

[886] *Witowski*, 199 P.3d at 10787. If the Wyoming courts' explanation is not convoluted, perhaps further inquiry of the relationship of the Full Faith and Credit Clause and the Supremacy Clause is called for. Ed.

[887] 771 N.W. 2d 651 (Iowa Ct. App. (2009).

judgment. Judge Sackett registered a strong dissent on the basis that not one of the Meether family had been in Utah for the past 26 years.[888]

In *DeSantis v. Lara*,[889] a Settlement Agreement which had been incorporated into a New York divorce decree did not contain a choice-of-law provision requiring modifications to the father's child support obligations to be calculated under New York law, and thus Ohio law applied to father's motion to modify filed after mother and child had moved to Ohio and the father had moved to Tennessee. The divorce decree did recite that the parties would annually recalculate child support in accordance with a formula set forth in New York's Child Support Standards Act, but the court found that the Agreement's reference to the New York' law contemplated only the first year of the child support. The Ohio court, therefore, made a choice-of-law decision, without specifically so indicating, on the "most significant Relationship" approach of the Restatement (Second) of Conflict of Laws).[890] In sort of a *renvoi*[891] approach, the court decreed that the matter of the duration of the child support should be determined by New York law.[892]

Basileh v. Alghusain[893] demonstrated the interplay between the FFCCSOA and the UIFSA. The subject couple were from Jordan, but were divorced in Indiana, where they were living at the time. After the divorce, the wife and their children moved to California. The husband returned to Jordan, and experienced difficulties in returning to this country. The Indiana trial court found that it had lost jurisdiction of the support case pursuant to the FFCCSOA, since none of the persons involved continued to live in that state. Pursuant to the UIFSA the Indiana court relinquished its jurisdiction to a trial court in California, where the mother and children lived. The Indiana appellate court affirmed.[894]

---

[888] *Id.* at *7.

[889] 2009 W.L. 1565068 (Ohio App. 2009).

[890] *Id* at *5.

[891] *Renvoi* is the Conflicts-of-law doctrine under which a court in resorting to foreign law adopts the foreign law's choice-of-laws principles, as well as its substantive law, which may in turn refer the court back to the law of the forum. Black's Law Dictionary, 8th Edition, (2004).

[892] *DeSantis*, 2009 W.L 1565068 at *6.

[893] 912 N.E.2d 814 (Ind. 2009).

[894] *Id.* at 821, 822.

In *Hamilton v. Hamilton*[895] a Florida court had required the father to pay $1,473-per-month child support and held him in contempt for not complying. An Indiana court, as enforcing court, required him to avoid incarceration by paying $150-per-month. The Indiana appellate court held that this was not an impermissible modification of the Florida order, which would be forbidden by full faith and credit. It did not alter "the amount, scope, or duration" of the Florida order as it was forbidden to do by 28 U.S.C. § 1738B(b). The arrearages continue to accrue in accordance with the Florida order. To be sure, the Indiana trial court issued a contempt order requiring the father to pay only $150 per month to avoid incarceration. As a responding tribunal, the Indiana trial court held that it had discretion to "specify the amount and the manner of compliance" with the original support order, and to fashion a remedy that would most effectively compel payment.[896]

In *Clarke v. Clarke*[897] a Petition was filed by a daughter, of adult age, who was a New York resident, seeking an order directing her New York resident mother to pay directly to her any moneys that were tendered to the mother by the father pursuant to the order of a California court for her support. A New York court held that the Petition constituted a *de novo* application for child support, rather than one for modification of the prior, out-of-state support order issued by the California (F-1) court. As such neither the FFCCSOA nor the UIFSA prevented the New York (F-2) court from considering the Petition.[898]

In *Lacarrubba v. Lacarrubba*[899] it was held by a North Carolina appellate court that a North Carolina trial court lacked authority to modify a foreign order for child support. The child support order was originally entered in New York and later registered in Florida, the state to which the mother and both children moved after the parties were divorced in New York. The father remained in New York, but after one child joined him there they moved to North Carolina, where the mother again registered the New York support order, but this time specifically for

---

[895] 914 N.E.2d 747 (Ind. 2009).

[896] *Id.* at 753.

[897] 889 N.Y.S.2d 766 (N.Y. App. Div. 2009).

[898] *Id.* at 768.

[899] 688 S.E.2d 769 (N.C. App. 2010).

"enforcement only," which she was permitted to do under UIFSA. Apparently simultaneously the mother sought over $30,000 of arrearages in child support payments, acquiring the title of "plaintiff" to which the appellate court referred to her in its Opinion. The "defendant" father contested, taking the position that Florida and North Carolina had "concurrent jurisdiction to modify the amount of arrearages. His position was agreed to by two North Carolina judges on the same day.[900] In reversing the trial court the appellate court made findings that:

> [I[t is undisputed that: (1) the child support order was issued in New York, and later registered in Florida; (2) Plaintiff registered the child support order in North Carolina for enforcement only; (3) North Carolina did not have personal jurisdiction over Plaintiff, who lived in Florida;[901] and (4) the parties did not consent to North Carolina's jurisdiction to modify the child support order.[902] We conclude that the trial court lacked authority to modify the order or reduce arrearages. We reject Defendant's arguments to the contrary.[903]

As grounds for its decision the North Carolina appellate court assigned 28 U.S.C.A. § 1738B(a, e, i); UIFSA, and the fact that the parties did not consent to North Carolina's jurisdiction to modify the child support order.[904]

Maya B. v. Omar Anthony L.[905] established that under state law a court may prospectively suspend a non-custodial parent's obligation to pay child support under two different circumstances. First, a parent's obligation to pay child support may be suspended where there is proof that a custodial parent has deliberately frustrated or actively interfered with a non-custodial parent's visitation rights. Second, child support may be prospectively suspended where it is established that a child of employable age has actively abandoned his or her parent by refusing all

---

900 *Id.* at 770.

901 The court did not explain how the trial court did not have personal jurisdiction over the Plaintiff who commenced proceedings to collect $30,000 in arrearages.

902 The court did not explain how the parties could consent to the trial court having subject matter jurisdiction.

903 *See* Lacarrubbaa, 688 S.E. 2d at 773.

904 *Id.* at 774.

905 2010 WL 2089281 (N.Y. Fam. Ct. 2010).

contact and visitation without just cause. The proof of such a state of affairs, however, must substantiate the claim.[906]

b. The Uniform Interstate Family Support Act

(UIFSA)[907] (2001 Amendment)
§ 101. Short Title.
This [Act] may be cited as the Uniform Interstate Family Support Act.

§ 102. Definitions.
In this [Act]:

(1) "Child" means an individual, whether over or under the age of majority, who is or is alleged to be owed a duty of support by the individual's parent or who is or is alleged to be the beneficiary of a support order directed to the parent.

(2) "Child-support order" means a support order for a child, including a child who has attained the age of majority under the law of the issuing State.

(3) "Duty of support" means an obligation imposed or imposable by law to provide support for a child, spouse, or former spouse, including an unsatisfied obligation to provide support.

(4) "Home State" means the State in which a child lived with a parent or a person acting as parent for at least six consecutive months immediately preceding the time of filing of a [petition] or comparable pleading for support and, if a child is less than six months old, the State in which the child lived from birth with any of them. A period of temporary absence of any of them is counted as part of the six-month or other period.

(5) "Income" includes earnings or other periodic entitlements to money from any source and any other property subject to withholding for support under the law of this State.

(6) "Income-withholding order" means an order or other legal process directed to an obligor's [employer] [or other debtor], as defined by [the income-withholding law of this State], to withhold support from the income of the obligor.

---

906 *Id.* at *4.

907 As of Jan. 15, 2012, The District of Columbia and the following 21 states have adopted the Uniform Interstate Family Support Act (UIFSA) (2001 Amendment): Arizona, California, Colorado, Connecticut, Delaware, Idaho, Illinois, Maine, Maryland, Mississippi, Nebraska, Nevada, New Mexico, Oklahoma, Rhode Island, South Carolina, Texas, Utah, Virginia, and Washington. The 2001 list is the same as the prior (1996) list with the omission of West Virginia, and Wyoming, and the addition of Washington.

(7) "Initiating State" means a State from which a proceeding is forwarded or in which a proceeding is filed for forwarding to a responding State under this [Act] or a law or procedure substantially similar to this [Act]~~, the Uniform Reciprocal Enforcement of Support Act, or the Revised Uniform Reciprocal Enforcement of Support Act~~.

(8) "Initiating tribunal" means the authorized tribunal in an initiating State.

(9) "Issuing State" means the State in which a tribunal issues a support order or renders a judgment determining parentage.

(10) "Issuing tribunal" means the tribunal that issues a support order or renders a judgment determining parentage.

(11) "Law" includes decisional and statutory law and rules and regulations having the force of law.

(12) "Obligee" means:

(A) an individual to whom a duty of support is or is alleged to be owed or in whose favor a support order has been issued or a judgment determining parentage has been rendered;

(B) a State or political subdivision to which the rights under a duty of support or support order have been assigned or which has independent claims based on financial assistance provided to an individual obligee; or

(C) an individual seeking a judgment determining parentage of the individual's child.

(13) "Obligor" means an individual, or the estate of a decedent:

(A) who owes or is alleged to owe a duty of support;

(B) who is alleged but has not been adjudicated to be a parent of a child; or

(C) who is liable under a support order.

(14) "Person" means an individual, corporation, business trust, estate, trust, partnership, limited liability company, association, joint venture, government, governmental subdivision, agency, or instrumentality, public corporation, or any other legal or commercial entity.

(15) "Record" means information that is inscribed on a tangible medium or that is stored in an electronic or other medium and is retrievable in perceivable form.

(16) "Register" means to [record; file] a support order or judgment determining parentage in the [appropriate location for the recording or filing of foreign judgments generally or foreign support orders specifically].

(17) "Registering tribunal" means a tribunal in which a support order is registered.

(18) "Responding State" means a State in which a proceeding is filed or to which a proceeding is forwarded for filing from an initiating State under this [Act]

or a law or procedure substantially similar to this [Act]~~, the Uniform Reciprocal Enforcement of Support Act, or the Revised Uniform Reciprocal Enforcement of Support Act.~~

(19) "Responding tribunal" means the authorized tribunal in a responding State.

(20) "Spousal-support order" means a support order for a spouse or former spouse of the obligor.

(21) "State" means a State of the United States, the District of Columbia, Puerto Rico, the United States Virgin Islands, or any territory or insular possession subject to the jurisdiction of the United States. The term includes:

(A) an Indian tribe; and

(B) a foreign country or political subdivision ~~jurisdiction~~ that:

(i) has been declared to be a foreign reciprocating country or political subdivision under federal law;

(ii) has established a reciprocal arrangement for child support with this State as provided in Section 308; or

(iii) has enacted a law or established procedures for the issuance and enforcement of support orders which are substantially similar to the procedures under this [Act]~~, the Uniform Reciprocal Enforcement of Support Act, or the Revised Uniform Reciprocal Enforcement of Support Act~~.

(22) "Support enforcement agency" means a public official or agency authorized to seek:

(A) enforcement of support orders or laws relating to the duty of support;

(B) establishment or modification of child support;

(C) determination of parentage; ~~or~~

(D) ~~to locate~~ location of obligors or their assets; or

(E) determination of the controlling child-support order.

(23) "Support order" means a judgment, decree, ~~or~~ order, or directive, whether temporary, final, or subject to modification, issued by a tribunal for the benefit of a child, a spouse, or a former spouse, which provides for monetary support, health care, arrearages, or reimbursement, and may include related costs and fees, interest, income withholding, attorney's fees, and other relief.

(24) "Tribunal" means a court, administrative agency, or quasi-judicial entity authorized to establish, enforce, or modify support orders or to determine parentage.

§ 103. Tribunal of State.
The [court, administrative agency, quasi-judicial entity, or combination] [is the tribunal] [are the tribunals] of this State.

§ 104. Remedies Cumulative.

(a) Remedies provided by this [Act] are cumulative and do not affect the availability of remedies under other law, including the recognition of a support order of a foreign country or political subdivision on the basis of comity.

(b) This [Act] does not:

(1) provide the exclusive method of establishing or enforcing a support order under the law of this State; or

(2) grant a tribunal of this State jurisdiction to render judgment or issue an order relating to [child custody or visitation] in a proceeding under this [Act].

§ 201. Bases for Jurisdiction Over Nonresident.

(a) In a proceeding to establish~~,~~ or enforce a support order or to determine parentage, a tribunal of this State may exercise personal jurisdiction over a nonresident individual [or the individual's guardian or conservator] if:

(1) the individual is personally served with [citation, summons, notice] within this State;

(2) the individual submits to the jurisdiction of this State by consent in a record, by entering a general appearance, or by filing a responsive document having the effect of waiving any contest to personal jurisdiction;

(3) the individual resided with the child in this State;

(4) the individual resided in this State and provided prenatal expenses or support for the child;

(5) the child resides in this State as a result of the acts or directives of the individual;

(6) the individual engaged in sexual intercourse in this State and the child may have been conceived by that act of intercourse; ~~[or]~~

(7) [the individual asserted parentage in the [putative father registry] maintained in this State by the [appropriate agency]; or

(8) there is any other basis consistent with the constitutions of this State and the United States for the exercise of personal jurisdiction.

(b) The bases of personal jurisdiction set forth in subsection (a) or in any other law of this State may not be used to acquire personal jurisdiction for a tribunal of the State to modify a child support order of another State unless the requirements of Section 611 or 615 are met.

§ 202. ~~Procedure When Exercising Jurisdiction Over Nonresident~~ **Duration of Personal Jurisdiction.**

Personal jurisdiction acquired by a tribunal of this State in a proceeding under this [Act] or other law of this State relating to a support order continues as long as a tribunal of this State has continuing, exclusive jurisdiction to modify its order or continuing jurisdiction to enforce its order as provided by Sections 205, 206, and 211.

~~A tribunal of this State exercising personal jurisdiction over a nonresident under Section 201 may apply Section 316 (Special Rules of Evidence and Procedure) to receive evidence from another State and Section 318 (Assistance with Discovery) to obtain discovery through a tribunal of another State. In all other respects, Articles 3 through 7 do not apply and the tribunal shall apply the procedural and substantive law of this State, including the rules on choice of law other than those established by this [Act].~~

§ 203. Initiating and Responding Tribunal of State.

Under this [Act], a tribunal of this State may serve as an initiating tribunal to forward proceedings to another State and as a responding tribunal for proceedings initiated in another State.

§ 204. Simultaneous Proceedings ~~in Another State~~**.**

(a) A tribunal of this State may exercise jurisdiction to establish a support order if the [petition] or comparable pleading is filed after a pleading is filed in another State only if:

(1) the [petition] or comparable pleading in this State is filed before the expiration of the time allowed in the other State for filing a responsive pleading challenging the exercise of jurisdiction by the other State;

(2) the contesting party timely challenges the exercise of jurisdiction in the other State; and

(3) if relevant, this State is the home State of the child.

(b) A tribunal of this State may not exercise jurisdiction to establish a support order if the [petition] or comparable pleading is filed before a [petition] or comparable pleading is filed in another State if:

(1) the [petition] or comparable pleading in the other State is filed before the expiration of the time allowed in this State for filing a responsive pleading challenging the exercise of jurisdiction by this State;

(2) the contesting party timely challenges the exercise of jurisdiction in this State; and

(3) if relevant, the other State is the home State of the child.

§ 205. Continuing, Exclusive Jurisdiction to Modify Child-Support Order.

(a) A tribunal of this State ~~issuing~~ that has issued a child-support order consistent with the law of this State has and shall exercise continuing, exclusive jurisdiction ~~over a~~ to modify its child-support order if the order is the controlling order and:

(1) ~~as long as~~ at the time of the filing of a request for modification this State ~~remains~~ is the residence of the obligor, the individual obligee, or the child for whose benefit the support order is issued; or

(2) ~~until all of the parties who are individuals have filed written consents with the tribunal of this State for a tribunal of another State to modify the order and assume continuing, exclusive jurisdiction~~ even if this State is not the residence of the obligor, the individual obligee, or the child for whose benefit the support order is issued, the parties consent in a record or in open court that the tribunal of this State may continue to exercise jurisdiction to modify its order.

(b) A tribunal of this State ~~issuing~~ that has issued a child-support order consistent with the law of this State may not exercise ~~its~~ continuing, exclusive jurisdiction to modify the order if ~~the order has been modified by a tribunal of another State pursuant to this [Act] or a law substantially similar to this [Act].~~:

(1) all of the parties who are individuals file consent in a record with the tribunal of this State that a tribunal of another State that has jurisdiction over at least one of the parties who is an individual or that is located in the State of residence of the child may modify the order and assume continuing, exclusive jurisdiction; or

(2) its order is not the controlling order.

~~(c) If a child-support order of this State is modified by a tribunal of another State pursuant to this [Act] or a law substantially similar to this [Act], a tribunal of this State loses its continuing, exclusive jurisdiction with regard to prospective enforcement of the order issued in this State, and may only:~~

~~(1) enforce the order that was modified as to amounts accruing before the modification;~~

~~(2) enforce nonmodifiable aspects of that order; and~~

~~(3) provide other appropriate relief for violations of that order which occurred before the effective date of the modification.~~

~~(d)~~ (c) ~~A tribunal of this State shall recognize the continuing, exclusive jurisdiction of~~If a tribunal of another State ~~which~~ has issued a child-support order pursuant to ~~this~~ [the Uniform Interstate Family Support Act] or a law substantially similar to ~~this [~~that Act~~]~~ which modifies a child-support order of a tribunal of this State, tribunals of this State shall recognize the continuing, exclusive jurisdiction of the tribunal of the other State.

(d) A tribunal of this State that lacks continuing, exclusive jurisdiction to modify a child-support order may serve as an initiating tribunal to request a tribunal of another State to modify a support order issued in that State.

(e) A temporary support order issued ex parte or pending resolution of a jurisdictional conflict does not create continuing, exclusive jurisdiction in the issuing tribunal.

~~(f) A tribunal of this State issuing a spousal support order consistent with the law of this State has continuing, exclusive jurisdiction over a spousal support order throughout the existence of the support obligation. A tribunal of this State may not modify a spousal support order issued by a tribunal of another State having continuing, exclusive jurisdiction over that order under the law of that State.~~

§ 206. ~~Enforcement and Modification of Support Order by Tribunal Having~~ **Continuing Jurisdiction to Enforce Child-Support Order.**

(a) A tribunal of this State that has issued a child-support order consistent with the law of this State may serve as an initiating tribunal to request a tribunal of another State to enforce ~~or modify a support order issued in that State~~:

(1) the order if the order is the controlling order and has not been modified by a tribunal of another State that assumed jurisdiction pursuant to [the Uniform Interstate Family Support Act]; or

(2) a money judgment for arrears of support and interest on the order accrued before a determination that an order of another State is the controlling order.

(b) A tribunal of this State having continuing~~, exclusive~~ jurisdiction over a support order may act as a responding tribunal to enforce ~~or modify~~ the order. ~~If a party subject to the continuing, exclusive jurisdiction of the tribunal no longer resides in the issuing State, in subsequent proceedings the tribunal may apply Section 316 (Special Rules of Evidence and Procedure) to receive evidence from another State and Section 318 (Assistance with Discovery) to obtain discovery through a tribunal of another State.~~

~~(c) A tribunal of this State which lacks continuing, exclusive jurisdiction over a spousal support order may not serve as a responding tribunal to modify a spousal support order of another State.~~

§ 207. ~~Recognition~~ Determination of Controlling Child-Support Order.

(a) If a proceeding is brought under this [Act] and only one tribunal has issued a child-support order, the order of that tribunal controls and must be so recognized.

(b) If a proceeding is brought under this [Act], and two or more child-support orders have been issued by tribunals of this State or another State with regard to the same obligor and same child, a tribunal of this State having personal jurisdiction over both the obligor and individual obligee shall apply the following rules ~~in determining~~ and by order shall determine which order controls ~~to recognize for purposes of continuing, exclusive jurisdiction~~:

(1) If only one of the tribunals would have continuing, exclusive jurisdiction under this [Act], the order of that tribunal controls and must be so recognized.

(2) If more than one of the tribunals would have continuing, exclusive jurisdiction under this [Act]:

(A) an order issued by a tribunal in the current home State of the child controls; ~~and must be so recognized,~~ but

(B) if an order has not been issued in the current home State of the child, the order most recently issued controls ~~and must be so recognized~~.

(3) If none of the tribunals would have continuing, exclusive jurisdiction under this [Act], the tribunal of this State ~~having jurisdiction over the parties~~ shall issue a child-support order, which controls ~~and must be so recognized~~.

(c) If two or more child-support orders have been issued for the same obligor and same child, ~~and if the obligor or the individual obligee resides in this State, an individual~~ upon request of a party who is an individual or a support enforcement agency, ~~may request~~ a tribunal of this State having personal jurisdiction over both the obligor and the obligee who is an individual shall ~~to~~ determine which order controls ~~and must be so recognized~~ under subsection (b). ~~The request must be accompanied by a certified copy of every support order in effect. The requesting party shall give notice of the request to each party whose rights may be affected by the determination.~~ The request may be filed with a registration for enforcement or registration for modification pursuant to Article 6, or may be filed as a separate proceeding.

(d) A request to determine which is the controlling order must be accompanied by a copy of every child-support order in effect and the applicable record of payments. The requesting party shall give notice of the request to each party whose rights may be affected by the determination.

~~(d)~~ (e) The tribunal that issued the controlling order under subsection (a), (b), or (c) ~~is the tribunal that~~ has continuing~~, exclusive~~ jurisdiction ~~under Section~~ to the extent provided in Section 205 or 206.

~~(e)~~ (f) A tribunal of this State ~~which~~ that determines by order ~~the identity of~~ which is the controlling order under subsection (b)(1) or (2) or (c), or ~~which~~ that issues a new controlling order under subsection (b)(3), shall state in that order:

(1) the basis upon which the tribunal made its determination;

(2) the amount of prospective support, if any; and

(3) the total amount of consolidated arrears and accrued interest, if any, under all of the orders after all payments made are credited as provided by Section 209.

~~(f)~~ (g) Within [30] days after issuance of an order determining ~~the identity of~~ which is the controlling order, the party obtaining the order shall file a certified copy of it ~~with~~ in each tribunal that issued or registered an earlier order of child support. A party ~~who obtains~~ or support enforcement agency obtaining the order ~~and~~ that fails to file a certified copy is subject to appropriate sanctions by a tribunal in which the issue of failure to file arises. The failure to file does not affect the validity or enforceability of the controlling order.

(h) An order that has been determined to be the controlling order, or a judgment for consolidated arrears of support and interest, if any, made pursuant to this section must be recognized in proceedings under this [Act].

§ 208. ~~Multiple~~ Child-Support Orders for Two or More Obligees.
In responding to ~~multiple~~ registrations or [petitions] for enforcement of two or more child-support orders in effect at the same time with regard to the same obligor and different individual obligees, at least one of which was issued by a tribunal of another State, a tribunal of this State shall enforce those orders in the same manner as if the ~~multiple~~ orders had been issued by a tribunal of this State.

§ 209. Credit for Payments.
~~Amounts~~ A tribunal of this State shall credit amounts collected ~~and credited~~ for a particular period pursuant to ~~a support order~~ any child-support order against the amounts owed for the same period under any other child-support order for support of the same child issued by a tribunal of this or another State ~~must be credited against the amounts accruing or accrued for the same period under a support order issued by the tribunal of this State.~~

§ 210. Application of [Act] to Nonresident Subject to Personal Jurisdiction.
A tribunal of this State exercising personal jurisdiction over a nonresident in a proceeding under this [Act], under other law of this State relating to a support order, or recognizing a support order of a foreign country or political subdivision on the basis of comity may receive evidence from another State pursuant to

Section 316, communicate with a tribunal of another State pursuant to Section 317, and obtain discovery through a tribunal of another State pursuant to Section 318. In all other respects, Articles 3 through 7 do not apply and the tribunal shall apply the procedural and substantive law of this State.

§ 211. Continuing, Exclusive Jurisdiction to Modify Spousal-Support Order.

(a) A tribunal of this State issuing a spousal-support order consistent with the law of this State has continuing, exclusive jurisdiction to modify the spousal-support order throughout the existence of the support obligation.

(b) A tribunal of this State may not modify a spousal-support order issued by a tribunal of another State having continuing, exclusive jurisdiction over that order under the law of that State.

(c) A tribunal of this State that has continuing, exclusive jurisdiction over a spousal-support order may serve as:

(1) an initiating tribunal to request a tribunal of another State to enforce the spousal-support order issued in this State; or

(2) a responding tribunal to enforce or modify its own spousal-support order.

§ 301. Proceedings Under [Act].

(a) Except as otherwise provided in this [Act], this article applies to all proceedings under this [Act].

(b) ~~This [Act] provides for the following proceedings:~~

~~(1) establishment of an order for spousal support or child support pursuant to Article 4;~~

~~(2) enforcement of a support order and income-withholding order of another State without registration pursuant to Article 5;~~

~~(3) registration of an order for spousal support or child support of another State for enforcement pursuant to Article 6;~~

~~(4) modification of an order for child support or spousal support issued by a tribunal of this State pursuant to Article 2;~~

~~(5) registration of an order for child support of another State for modification pursuant to Article 6;~~

~~(6) determination of parentage pursuant to Article 7; and~~

~~(7) assertion of jurisdiction over nonresidents pursuant to Article 2, Part 1.~~

~~(c)~~ (b) An individual [petitioner] or a support enforcement agency may initiate a proceeding authorized under this [Act] by filing a [petition] in an initiating tribunal for forwarding to a responding tribunal or by filing a [petition] or a comparable pleading directly in a tribunal of another State which has or can obtain personal jurisdiction over the [respondent].

§ 302. ~~Action~~ Proceeding by Minor Parent.
A minor parent, or a guardian or other legal representative of a minor parent, may maintain a proceeding on behalf of or for the benefit of the minor's child.

§ 303. Application of Law of State.
Except as otherwise provided ~~by~~ in this [Act], a responding tribunal of this State shall:

(1) ~~shall~~ apply the procedural and substantive law~~, including the rules on choice of law,~~ generally applicable to similar proceedings originating in this State and may exercise all powers and provide all remedies available in those proceedings; and

(2) ~~shall~~ determine the duty of support and the amount payable in accordance with the law and support guidelines of this State.

§ 304. Duties of Initiating Tribunal.

(a) Upon the filing of a [petition] authorized by this [Act], an initiating tribunal of this State shall forward ~~three copies of~~ the [petition] and its accompanying documents:

(1) to the responding tribunal or appropriate support enforcement agency in the responding State; or

(2) if the identity of the responding tribunal is unknown, to the State information agency of the responding State with a request that they be forwarded to the appropriate tribunal and that receipt be acknowledged.

(b) If ~~a responding State has not enacted this [Act] or a law or procedure substantially similar to this [Act], a~~ requested by the responding tribunal, a tribunal of this State ~~may~~ shall issue a certificate or other document and make findings required by the law of the responding State. If the responding State is a foreign country or political subdivision ~~jurisdiction~~, upon request the tribunal ~~may~~ shall specify the amount of support sought ~~and~~, convert that amount into the equivalent amount in the foreign currency under applicable official or market exchange rate as publicly reported, and provide any other documents necessary to satisfy the requirements of the responding State.

§ 305. Duties and Powers of Responding Tribunal.

(a) When a responding tribunal of this State receives a [petition] or comparable pleading from an initiating tribunal or directly pursuant to Section 301(b)~~ (c) (Proceedings Under this [Act])~~, it shall cause the [petition] or pleading to be filed and notify the [petitioner] where and when it was filed.

(b) A responding tribunal of this State, to the extent ~~otherwise authorized~~ not prohibited by other law, may do one or more of the following:

(1) issue or enforce a support order, modify a child-support order, determine the controlling child-support order, or ~~render a judgment~~ to determine parentage;

(2) order an obligor to comply with a support order, specifying the amount and the manner of compliance;

(3) order income withholding;

(4) determine the amount of any arrearages, and specify a method of payment;

(5) enforce orders by civil or criminal contempt, or both;

(6) set aside property for satisfaction of the support order;

(7) place liens and order execution on the obligor's property;

(8) order an obligor to keep the tribunal informed of the obligor's current residential address, telephone number, employer, address of employment, and telephone number at the place of employment;

(9) issue a [bench warrant; capias] for an obligor who has failed after proper notice to appear at a hearing ordered by the tribunal and enter the [bench warrant; capias] in any local and State computer systems for criminal warrants;

(10) order the obligor to seek appropriate employment by specified methods;

(11) award reasonable attorney's fees and other fees and costs; and

(12) grant any other available remedy.

(c) A responding tribunal of this State shall include in a support order issued under this [Act], or in the documents accompanying the order, the calculations on which the support order is based.

(d) A responding tribunal of this State may not condition the payment of a support order issued under this [Act] upon compliance by a party with provisions for visitation.

(e) If a responding tribunal of this State issues an order under this [Act], the tribunal shall send a copy of the order to the [petitioner] and the [respondent] and to the initiating tribunal, if any.

(f) If requested to enforce a support order, arrears, or judgment or modify a support_order stated in a foreign currency, a responding tribunal of this State shall convert the amount stated in the foreign currency to the equivalent amount in dollars under the applicable official or market exchange rate as publicly reported.

§ 306. Inappropriate Tribunal.
If a [petition] or comparable pleading is received by an inappropriate tribunal of this State, ~~it~~ the tribunal shall forward the pleading and accompanying documents to an appropriate tribunal in this State or another State and notify the [petitioner] where and when the pleading was sent.

§ 307. Duties of Support Enforcement Agency.
(a) A support enforcement agency of this State, upon request, shall provide services to a [petitioner] in a proceeding under this [Act].

(b) A support enforcement agency of this State that is providing services to the [petitioner] ~~as appropriate~~ shall:

(1) take all steps necessary to enable an appropriate tribunal in this State or another State to obtain jurisdiction over the [respondent];

(3) make a reasonable effort to obtain all relevant information, including information as to income and property of the parties;

(4) within [two] days, exclusive of Saturdays, Sundays, and legal holidays, after receipt of ~~a written~~ notice in a record from an initiating, responding, or registering tribunal, send a copy of the notice to the [petitioner];

(5) within [two] days, exclusive of Saturdays, Sundays, and legal holidays, after receipt of ~~a written~~ communication in a record from the [respondent] or the [respondent's] attorney, send a copy of the communication to the [petitioner]; and

(6) notify the [petitioner] if jurisdiction over the [respondent] cannot be obtained.

(c) A support enforcement agency of this State that requests registration of a child-support order in this State for enforcement or for modification shall make reasonable efforts:

(1) to ensure that the order to be registered is the controlling order; or

(2) if two or more child-support orders exist and the identity of the controlling order has not been determined, to ensure that a request for such a determination is made in a tribunal having jurisdiction to do so.

(d) A support enforcement agency of this State that requests registration and enforcement of a support order, arrears, or judgment stated in a foreign currency shall convert the amounts stated in the foreign currency into the equivalent amounts in dollars under the applicable official or market exchange rate as publicly reported.

(e) A support enforcement agency of this State shall [issue or] request a tribunal of this State to issue a child-support order and an income-withholding order that redirect payment of current support, arrears, and interest if requested to do so by a support enforcement agency of another State pursuant to Section 319 of the Uniform Interstate Family Support Act.

~~(e)~~ (f) This [Act] does not create or negate a relationship of attorney and client or other fiduciary relationship between a support enforcement agency or the attorney for the agency and the individual being assisted by the agency.

§ 308. Duty of [~~Attorney General~~ State Official or Agency].

(a) If the ~~Attorney General~~ [appropriate state official or agency] determines that the support enforcement agency is neglecting or refusing to provide services to an individual, the ~~Attorney General~~ [state official or agency] may order the agency to perform its duties under this [Act] or may provide those services directly to the individual.

(b) The [appropriate state official or agency] may determine that a foreign country or political subdivision has established a reciprocal arrangement for child support with this State and take appropriate action for notification of the determination

§ 309. Private Counsel.

An individual may employ private counsel to represent the individual in proceedings authorized by this [Act].

§ 310. Duties of [State Information Agency].

(a) The [Attorney General's Office, State Attorney's Office, State Central Registry or other information agency] is the state information agency under this [Act].

(b) The state information agency shall:

(1) compile and maintain a current list, including addresses, of the tribunals in this State which have jurisdiction under this [Act] and any support enforcement agencies in this State and transmit a copy to the state information agency of every other State;

(2) maintain a register of names and addresses of tribunals and support enforcement agencies received from other States;

(3) forward to the appropriate tribunal in the ~~place~~ [county] in this State in which the ~~individual~~ obligee who is an individual or the obligor resides, or in

which the obligor's property is believed to be located, all documents concerning a proceeding under this [Act] received from an initiating tribunal or the state information agency of the initiating State; and

(4) obtain information concerning the location of the obligor and the obligor's property within this State not exempt from execution, by such means as postal verification and federal or state locator services, examination of telephone directories, requests for the obligor's address from employers, and examination of governmental records, including, to the extent not prohibited by other law, those relating to real property, vital statistics, law enforcement, taxation, motor vehicles, driver's licenses, and social security.

§ 311. Pleadings and Accompanying Documents.

(a) ~~A~~ In a proceeding under this [Act], a [petitioner] seeking to establish ~~or modify~~ a support order, ~~or~~ to determine parentage ~~in a proceeding under the [Act]~~, or to register and modify a support order of another State must ~~verify the~~ file a [petition]. Unless otherwise ordered under Section 312 ~~(Nondisclosure of Information in Exceptional Circumstances)~~, the [petition] or accompanying documents must provide, so far as known, the name, residential address, and social security numbers of the obligor and the obligee or the parent and alleged parent, and the name, sex, residential address, social security number, and date of birth of each child for ~~whom~~ whose benefit support is sought or whose parentage is to be determined. ~~The~~ Unless filed at the time of registration, the [petition] must be accompanied by a ~~certified~~ copy of any support order ~~in effect~~ known to have been issued by another tribunal. The [petition] may include any other information that may assist in locating or identifying the [respondent].

(b) The [petition] must specify the relief sought. The [petition] and accompanying documents must conform substantially with the requirements imposed by the forms mandated by federal law for use in cases filed by a support enforcement agency.

§ 312. Nondisclosure of Information in Exceptional Circumstances.

~~Upon a finding, which may be made ex parte, that the health , safety, or liberty of a party or child would be unreasonably put at risk by the disclosure of identifying information, or if an existing order so provides, a tribunal shall order that the address of the child or party or other identifying information not be disclosed in a pleading or other document filed in a proceeding under this [Act].~~ If a party alleges in an affidavit or a pleading under oath that the health, safety, or liberty of a party or child would be jeopardized by disclosure of specific identifying information, that information must be sealed and may not be disclosed to the other party or the public. After a hearing in which a tribunal takes into consideration the health, safety, or liberty of the party or child, the tribunal may order disclosure of information that the tribunal determines to be in the interest of justice.

§ 313. Costs and Fees.

(a) The [petitioner] may not be required to pay a filing fee or other costs.

(b) If an obligee prevails, a responding tribunal may assess against an obligor filing fees, reasonable attorney's fees, other costs, and necessary travel and other reasonable expenses incurred by the obligee and the obligee's witnesses. The tribunal may not assess fees, costs, or expenses against the obligee or the support enforcement agency of either the initiating or the responding State, except as provided by other law. Attorney's fees may be taxed as costs, and may be ordered paid directly to the attorney, who may enforce the order in the attorney's own name. Payment of support owed to the obligee has priority over fees, costs and expenses.

(c) The tribunal shall order the payment of costs and reasonable attorney's fees if it determines that a hearing was requested primarily for delay. In a proceeding under Article 6 ~~(Enforcement and Modification of Support Order After Registration)~~, a hearing is presumed to have been requested primarily for delay if a registered support order is confirmed or enforced without change.

§ 314. Limited Immunity of [Petitioner].

(a) Participation by a [petitioner] in a proceeding under this [Act] before a responding tribunal, whether in person, by private attorney, or through services provided by the support enforcement agency, does not confer personal jurisdiction over the [petitioner] in another proceeding.

(b) A [petitioner] is not amenable to service of civil process while physically present in this State to participate in a proceeding under this [Act].

(c) The immunity granted by this section does not extend to civil litigation based on acts unrelated to a proceeding under this [Act] committed by a party while physically present in this State to participate in the proceeding.

§ 315. Nonparentage as Defense.

A party whose parentage of a child has been previously determined by or pursuant to law may not plead nonparentage as a defense to a proceeding under this [Act].

§ 316. Special Rules of Evidence and Procedure.

(a) The physical presence of ~~the [petitioner]~~ a nonresident party who is an individual in a ~~responding~~ tribunal of this State is not required for the establishment, enforcement, or modification of a support order or the rendition of a judgment determining parentage.

(b) ~~A verified [petition],~~ An affidavit, a document substantially complying with federally mandated forms, ~~and~~ or a document incorporated by reference in any of them, which would not be excluded under the hearsay rule if given in person, is admissible in evidence if given under ~~oath~~ penalty of perjury by a party or witness residing in another State.

(c) A copy of the record of child-support payments certified as a true copy of the original by the custodian of the record may be forwarded to a responding tribunal. The copy is evidence of facts asserted in it, and is admissible to show whether payments were made.

(d) Copies of bills for testing for parentage, and for prenatal and postnatal health care of the mother and child, furnished to the adverse party at least [ten] days before trial, are admissible in evidence to prove the amount of the charges billed and that the charges were reasonable, necessary, and customary.

(e) Documentary evidence transmitted from another State to a tribunal of this State by telephone, telecopier, or other means that do not provide an original ~~writing~~ record may not be excluded from evidence on an objection based on the means of transmission.

(f) In a proceeding under this [Act], a tribunal of this State ~~may~~ shall permit a party or witness residing in another State to be deposed or to testify under penalty of perjury by telephone, audiovisual means, or other electronic means at a designated tribunal or other location in that State. A tribunal of this State shall cooperate with tribunals of other States in designating an appropriate location for the deposition or testimony.

(g) If a party called to testify at a civil hearing refuses to answer on the ground that the testimony may be self-incriminating, the trier of fact may draw an adverse inference from the refusal.

(h) A privilege against disclosure of communications between spouses does not apply in a proceeding under this [Act].

(i) The defense of immunity based on the relationship of husband and wife or parent and child does not apply in a proceeding under this [Act].

(j) A voluntary acknowledgment of paternity, certified as a true copy, is admissible to establish parentage of the child.

§ 317. Communications Between Tribunals.

A tribunal of this State may communicate with a tribunal of another State or foreign country or political subdivision in ~~writing~~ a record, or by telephone or other means, to obtain information concerning the laws ~~of that State~~, the legal effect of a judgment, decree, or order of that tribunal, and the status of a proceeding in the other State or foreign country or political subdivision. A tribunal of this State may furnish similar information by similar means to a tribunal of another State or foreign country or political subdivision.

§ 318. Assistance with Discovery.

A tribunal of this State may:

(1) request a tribunal of another State to assist in obtaining discovery; and

(2) upon request, compel a person over whom it has jurisdiction to respond to a discovery order issued by a tribunal of another State.

§ 319. Receipt and Disbursement of Payments.

(a) A support enforcement agency or tribunal of this State shall disburse promptly any amounts received pursuant to a support order, as directed by the order. The agency or tribunal shall furnish to a requesting party or tribunal of another State a certified statement by the custodian of the record of the amounts and dates of all payments received.

(b) If neither the obligor, nor the obligee who is an individual, nor the child resides in this State, upon request from the support enforcement agency of this State or another State, [the support enforcement agency of this State or] a tribunal of this State shall:

(1) direct that the support payment be made to the support enforcement agency in the State in which the obligee is receiving services; and

(2) issue and send to the obligor's employer a conforming income-withholding order or an administrative notice of change of payee, reflecting the redirected payments.

(c) The support enforcement agency of this State receiving redirected payments from another State pursuant to a law similar to subsection (b) shall furnish to a requesting party or tribunal of the other State a certified statement by the custodian of the record of the amount and dates of all payments received.

§ 401. [Petition] to Establish Support Order.

(a) If a support order entitled to recognition under this [Act] has not been issued, a responding tribunal of this State may issue a support order if:

(1) the individual seeking the order resides in another State; or

(2) the support enforcement agency seeking the order is located in another State.

(b) The tribunal may issue a temporary child-support order if the tribunal determines that such an order is appropriate and the individual ordered to pay is:

(1) a presumed father of the child;
(2) petitioning to have his paternity adjudicated;
(3) identified as the father of the child through genetic testing;
(4) an alleged father who has declined to submit to genetic testing;
(5) shown by clear and convincing evidence to be the father of the child;
(6) an acknowledged father as provided by [applicable state law];
(7) the mother of the child; or
(8) an individual who has been ordered to pay child support in a previous proceeding and the order has not been reversed or vacated.

~~(1) the [respondent] has signed a verified statement acknowledging parentage;~~

~~(2) the [respondent] has been determined by or pursuant to law to be the parent; or~~

~~(3) there is other clear and convincing evidence that the [respondent] is the child's parent.~~

(c) Upon finding, after notice and opportunity to be heard, that an obligor owes a duty of support, the tribunal shall issue a support order directed to the obligor and may issue other orders pursuant to Section 305 ~~(Duties and Powers of Responding Tribunal)~~.

§ 501. Employer's Receipt of Income-Withholding Order of Another State.
An income-withholding order issued in another State may be sent by or on behalf of the obligee, or by the support enforcement agency, to the person ~~or entity~~ defined as the obligor's employer under [the income-withholding law of this State] without first filing a [petition] or comparable pleading or registering the order with a tribunal of this State.

§ 502. Employer's Compliance With Income-Withholding Order of Another State.

(a) Upon receipt of an income-withholding order, the obligor's employer shall immediately provide a copy of the order to the obligor.

(b) The employer shall treat an income-withholding order issued in another State which appears regular on its face as if it had been issued by a tribunal of this State.

(c) Except as otherwise provided in subsection (d) and Section 503, the employer shall withhold and distribute the funds as directed in the withholding order by complying with terms of the order which specify:

(1) the duration and amount of periodic payments of current child-support, stated as a sum certain;

(2) the person ~~or agency~~ designated to receive payments and the address to which the payments are to be forwarded;

(3) medical support, whether in the form of periodic cash payment, stated as a sum certain, or ordering the obligor to provide health insurance coverage for the child under a policy available through the obligor's employment;

(4) the amount of periodic payments of fees and costs for a support enforcement agency, the issuing tribunal, and the obligee's attorney, stated as sums certain; and

(5) the amount of periodic payments of arrearages and interest on arrearages, stated as sums certain.

(d) An employer shall comply with the law of the State of the obligor's principal place of employment for withholding from income with respect to:

(1) the employer's fee for processing an income-withholding order;

(2) the maximum amount permitted to be withheld from the obligor's income; and

(3) the times within which the employer must implement the withholding order and forward the child-support payment.

§ 503. Employer's Compliance With ~~Multiple~~ Two or More Income-Withholding Orders.

If an obligor's employer receives ~~multiple~~ two or more income-withholding orders with respect to the earnings of the same obligor, the employer satisfies the terms of the ~~multiple~~ orders if the employer complies with the law of the State of the obligor's principal place of employment to establish the priorities for withholding and allocating income withheld for ~~multiple~~ two or more child-support obligees.

§ 504. Immunity from Civil Liability.

An employer who complies with an income-withholding order issued in another State in accordance with this article is not subject to civil liability to an individual or agency with regard to the employer's withholding of child support from the obligor's income.

§ 505. Penalties for Noncompliance.

An employer who willfully fails to comply with an income-withholding order issued by another State and received for enforcement is subject to the same penalties that may be imposed for noncompliance with an order issued by a tribunal of this State.

§ 506. Contest by Obligor.

(a) An obligor may contest the validity or enforcement of an income-withholding order issued in another State and received directly by an employer in this State by registering the order in a tribunal of this State and filing a contest to that order as provided in Article 6, or otherwise contesting the order in the same manner as if the order had been issued by a tribunal of this State. ~~Section 604 (Choice of Law) applies to the contest.~~

(b) The obligor shall give notice of the contest to:

(1) a support enforcement agency providing services to the obligee;

(2) each employer that has directly received an income-withholding order relating to the obligor; and

(3) the person ~~or agency~~ designated to receive payments in the income-withholding order or, if no person ~~or agency~~ is designated, to the obligee.

§ 507. Administrative Enforcement of Orders.

(a) A party or support enforcement agency seeking to enforce a support order or an income-withholding order, or both, issued by a tribunal of another State may send the documents required for registering the order to a support enforcement agency of this State.

(b) Upon receipt of the documents, the support enforcement agency, without initially seeking to register the order, shall consider and, if appropriate, use any administrative procedure authorized by the law of this State to enforce a support order or an income-withholding order, or both. If the obligor does not contest administrative enforcement, the order need not be registered. If the obligor contests the validity or administrative enforcement of the order, the support enforcement agency shall register the order pursuant to this [Act].

§ 601. Registration of Order for Enforcement.

A support order or ~~an~~ income-withholding order issued by a tribunal of another State may be registered in this State for enforcement.

§ 602. Procedure to Register Order for Enforcement.

(a) A support order or income-withholding order of another State may be registered in this State by sending the following ~~documents~~ records and information to the [appropriate tribunal] in this State:

(1) a letter of transmittal to the tribunal requesting registration and enforcement;

(2) two copies, including one certified copy, of ~~all orders~~ the order to be registered, including any modification of ~~an~~ the order;

(3) a sworn statement by the ~~party seeking~~ person requesting registration or a certified statement by the custodian of the records showing the amount of any arrearage;

(4) the name of the obligor and, if known:

(A) the obligor's address and social security number;

(B) the name and address of the obligor's employer and any other source of income of the obligor; and

(C) a description and the location of property of the obligor in this State not exempt from execution; and

(5) except as otherwise provided in Section 312, the name and address of the obligee and, if applicable, the ~~agency or~~ person to whom support payments are to be remitted.

(b) On receipt of a request for registration, the registering tribunal shall cause the order to be filed as a foreign judgment, together with one copy of the documents and information, regardless of their form.

(c) A [petition] or comparable pleading seeking a remedy that must be affirmatively sought under other law of this State may be filed at the same time as the request for registration or later. The pleading must specify the grounds for the remedy sought.

(d) If two or more orders are in effect, the person requesting registration shall:

(1) furnish to the tribunal a copy of every support order asserted to be in effect in addition to the documents specified in this section;

(2) specify the order alleged to be the controlling order, if any; and

(3) specify the amount of consolidated arrears, if any.

(e) A request for a determination of which is the controlling order may be filed separately or with a request for registration and enforcement or for registration and modification. The person requesting registration shall give notice of the request to each party whose rights may be affected by the determination.

§ 603. Effect of Registration for Enforcement.

(a) A support order or income-withholding order issued in another State is registered when the order is filed in the registering tribunal of this State.

(b) A registered order issued in another State is enforceable in the same manner and is subject to the same procedures as an order issued by a tribunal of this State.

(c) Except as otherwise provided in this article, a tribunal of this State shall recognize and enforce, but may not modify, a registered order if the issuing tribunal had jurisdiction.

§ 604. Choice of Law.

(a) ~~The~~ Except as otherwise provided in subsection (d), the law of the issuing State governs:

(1) the nature, extent, amount, and duration of current payments ~~and other obligations of support and~~ under a registered support order;

(2) the computation and payment of arrearages and accrual of interest on the arrearages under the support order; and

(3) the existence and satisfaction of other obligations under the support order.

(b) In a proceeding for ~~arrearages~~ arrears under a registered support order, the statute of limitation ~~under the laws~~ of this State or of the issuing State, whichever is longer, applies.

(c) A responding tribunal of this State shall apply the procedures and remedies of this State to enforce current support and collect arrears and interest due on a support order of another State registered in this State.

(d) After a tribunal of this or another State determines which is the controlling order and issues an order consolidating arrears, if any, a tribunal of this State shall prospectively apply the law of the State issuing the controlling order, including its law on interest on arrears, on current and future support, and on consolidated arrears.

§ 605. Notice of Registration of Order.

(a) When a support order or income-withholding order issued in another State is registered, the registering tribunal shall notify the nonregistering party. The notice must be accompanied by a copy of the registered order and the documents and relevant information accompanying the order.

(b) ~~The~~ A notice must inform the nonregistering party:

(1) that a registered order is enforceable as of the date of registration in the same manner as an order issued by a tribunal of this State;

(2) that a hearing to contest the validity or enforcement of the registered order must be requested within [20] days after notice;

(3) that failure to contest the validity or enforcement of the registered order in a timely manner will result in confirmation of the order and enforcement of the order and the alleged arrearages; and

(4) of the amount of any alleged arrearages.

(c) If the registering party asserts that two or more orders are in effect, a notice must also:

(1) identify the two or more orders and the order alleged by the registering person to be the controlling order and the consolidated arrears, if any;

(2) notify the nonregistering party of the right to a determination of which is the controlling order;

(3) state that the procedures provided in subsection (b) apply to the determination of which is the controlling order; and

(4) state that failure to contest the validity or enforcement of the order alleged to be the controlling order in a timely manner may result in confirmation that the order is the controlling order.

~~(c)~~ (d) Upon registration of an income-withholding order for enforcement, the registering tribunal shall notify the obligor's employer pursuant to [the income-withholding law of this State].

§ 606. Procedure to Contest Validity or Enforcement of Registered Order.

(a) A nonregistering party seeking to contest the validity or enforcement of a registered order in this State shall request a hearing within [20] days after notice of the registration. The nonregistering party may seek to vacate the registration, to assert any defense to an allegation of noncompliance with the registered order, or to contest the remedies being sought or the amount of any alleged arrearages pursuant to Section 607 ~~(Contest of Registration or Enforcement)~~.

(b) If the nonregistering party fails to contest the validity or enforcement of the registered order in a timely manner, the order is confirmed by operation of law.

(c) If a nonregistering party requests a hearing to contest the validity or enforcement of the registered order, the registering tribunal shall schedule the matter for hearing and give notice to the parties of the date, time, and place of the hearing.

§ 607. Contest of Registration or Enforcement.

(a) A party contesting the validity or enforcement of a registered order or seeking to vacate the registration has the burden of proving one or more of the following defenses:

(1) the issuing tribunal lacked personal jurisdiction over the contesting party;

(2) the order was obtained by fraud;

(3) the order has been vacated, suspended, or modified by a later order;

(4) the issuing tribunal has stayed the order pending appeal;

(5) there is a defense under the law of this State to the remedy sought;

(6) full or partial payment has been made; ~~or~~

(7) the statute of limitation under Section 604 ~~(Choice of Law)~~ precludes enforcement of some or all of the alleged arrearages; or

(8) the alleged controlling order is not the controlling order.

(b) If a party presents evidence establishing a full or partial defense under subsection (a), a tribunal may stay enforcement of the registered order, continue the proceeding to permit production of additional relevant evidence, and issue other appropriate orders. An uncontested portion of the registered order may be enforced by all remedies available under the law of this State.

(c) If the contesting party does not establish a defense under subsection (a) to the validity or enforcement of the order, the registering tribunal shall issue an order confirming the order.

§ 608. Confirmed Order.

Confirmation of a registered order, whether by operation of law or after notice and hearing, precludes further contest of the order with respect to any matter that could have been asserted at the time of registration.

§ 609. Procedure to Register Child-Support Order of Another State for Modification.

A party or support enforcement agency seeking to modify, or to modify and enforce, a child-support order issued in another State shall register that order in this State in the same manner provided in Part 1 if the order has not been registered. A [petition] for modification may be filed at the same time as a request for registration, or later. The pleading must specify the grounds for modification.

§ 610. Effect of Registration for Modification.

A tribunal of this State may enforce a child-support order of another State registered for purposes of modification, in the same manner as if the order had been issued by a tribunal of this State, but the registered order may be modified only if the requirements of Section 611, 613, or 615 ~~(Modification of Child Support Order of Another State)~~ have been met.

§ 611. Modification of Child-Support Order of Another State.

(a) ~~After~~ If Section 613 does not apply, except as otherwise provided in Section 615, upon [petition] a tribunal of this State may modify a child-support order issued in another State ~~has been~~ which is registered in this State~~, the responding tribunal of this State may modify that order only if Section 613 does not apply and~~ if, after notice and hearing ~~it~~, the tribunal finds that:

(1) the following requirements are met:

(A) neither the child, nor the ~~individual~~ obligee who is an individual, ~~and~~ nor the obligor ~~do not~~ resides in the issuing State;

(B) a [petitioner] who is a nonresident of this State seeks modification; and

(C) the [respondent] is subject to the personal jurisdiction of the tribunal of this State; or

(2) ~~the child, or~~ this State is the State of residence of the child, or a party who is an individual is subject to the personal jurisdiction of the tribunal of this State, and all of the parties who are individuals have filed ~~a written~~ consents in a record in the issuing tribunal for a tribunal of this State to modify the support order and assume continuing, exclusive jurisdiction ~~over the order. However, if the issuing State is a foreign jurisdiction that has not enacted a law or established procedures substantially similar to the procedures under this [Act], the consent otherwise required of an individual residing in this State is not required for the tribunal to assume jurisdiction to modify the child-support law~~.

(b) Modification of a registered child-support order is subject to the same requirements, procedures, and defenses that apply to the modification of an order issued by a tribunal of this State and the order may be enforced and satisfied in the same manner.

(c) ~~A~~ Except as otherwise provided in Section 615, a tribunal of this State may not modify any aspect of a child-support order that may not be modified under the law of the issuing State, including the duration of the obligation of support. If two or more tribunals have issued child-support orders for the same obligor and same child, the order that controls and must be so recognized under Section 207 establishes the aspects of the support order which are nonmodifiable.

(d) In a proceeding to modify a child-support order, the law of the State that is determined to have issued the initial controlling order governs the duration of the obligation of support. The obligor's fulfillment of the duty of support established by that order precludes imposition of a further obligation of support by a tribunal of this State.

~~(d)~~ (e) On the issuance of an order by a tribunal of this State modifying a child-support order issued in another State, ~~a~~ the tribunal of this State becomes the tribunal having continuing, exclusive jurisdiction.

§ 612. Recognition of Order Modified in Another State.

~~A~~ If a child-support order issued by a tribunal of this State ~~shall recognize a modification of its earlier child-support order~~ is modified by a tribunal of another

State which assumed jurisdiction pursuant to ~~this [Act] or a law substantially similar to this [Act] and, upon request, except as otherwise provided in this [Act], shall~~ the Uniform Interstate Family Support Act, a tribunal of this State:

(1) may enforce ~~the~~ its order that was modified only as to ~~amounts~~ arrears and interest accruing before the modification;

(2) ~~enforce only nonmodifiable aspects of that order;~~

~~(3)~~ may provide ~~other~~ appropriate relief ~~only~~ for violations of ~~that~~ its order which occurred before the effective date of the modification; and

~~(4)~~ (3) shall recognize the modifying order of the other State, upon registration, for the purpose of enforcement.

§ 613. Jurisdiction to Modify Child-Support Order of Another State When Individual Parties Reside in this State.

(a) If all of the parties who are individuals reside in this State and the child does not reside in the issuing State, a tribunal of this State has jurisdiction to enforce and to modify the issuing State's child-support order in a proceeding to register that order.

(b) A tribunal of this State exercising jurisdiction under this section shall apply the provisions of Articles 1 and 2, this article, and the procedural and substantive law of this State to the proceeding for enforcement or modification. Articles 3, 4, 5, 7, and 8 do not apply.

§ 614. Notice to Issuing Tribunal of Modification.

Within [30] days after issuance of a modified child-support order, the party obtaining the modification shall file a certified copy of the order with the issuing tribunal that had continuing, exclusive jurisdiction over the earlier order, and in each tribunal in which the party knows the earlier order has been registered. A party who obtains the order and fails to file a certified copy is subject to appropriate sanctions by a tribunal in which the issue of failure to file arises. The failure to file does not affect the validity or enforceability of the modified order of the new tribunal having continuing, exclusive jurisdiction.

§ 615. Jurisdiction to Modify Child-Support Order of Foreign Country or Political Subdivision.

(a) If a foreign country or political subdivision that is a State will not or may not modify its order pursuant to its laws, a tribunal of this State may assume jurisdiction to modify the child-support order and bind all individuals subject to the personal jurisdiction of the tribunal whether or not the consent to modification of a child-support order otherwise required of the individual pursuant to Section

611 has been given or whether the individual seeking modification is a resident of this State or of the foreign country or political subdivision.

(b) An order issued pursuant to this section is the controlling order.

§ 701. Proceeding to Determine Parentage.

(a) A ~~tribunal~~ court of this State authorized to determine parentage of a child may serve as ~~an initiating or~~ a responding tribunal in a proceeding to determine parentage brought under this [Act] or a law or procedure substantially similar to this [Act]. ~~, the Uniform Reciprocal Enforcement of Support Act, or the Revised Uniform Reciprocal Enforcement of Support Act to determine that the [petitioner] is a parent of a particular child or to determine that a [respondent] is a parent of that child.~~

~~(b) In a proceeding to determine parentage, a responding tribunal of this State shall apply the [Uniform Parentage Act;] [procedural and substantive law of this State,] and the rules of this State on choice of law.~~

§ 801. Grounds for Rendition.

(a) For purposes of this article, "governor" includes an individual performing the functions of governor or the executive authority of a State covered by this [Act].

(b) The governor of this State may:

(1) demand that the governor of another State surrender an individual found in the other State who is charged criminally in this State with having failed to provide for the support of an obligee; or

(2) on the demand ~~by~~ of the governor of another State, surrender an individual found in this State who is charged criminally in the other State with having failed to provide for the support of an obligee.

(c) A provision for extradition of individuals not inconsistent with this [Act] applies to the demand even if the individual whose surrender is demanded was not in the demanding State when the crime was allegedly committed and has not fled therefrom.

§ 802. Conditions of Rendition.

(a) Before making a demand that the governor of another State surrender an individual charged criminally in this State with having failed to provide for the support of an obligee, the governor of this State may require a prosecutor of this State to demonstrate that at least [60] days previously the obligee had initiated proceedings for support pursuant to this [Act] or that the proceeding would be of no avail.

(b) If, under this [Act] or a law substantially similar to this [Act], ~~the Uniform Reciprocal Enforcement of Support Act, or the Revised Uniform Reciprocal Enforcement of Support Act~~ the governor of another State makes a demand that the governor of this State surrender an individual charged criminally in that State with having failed to provide for the support of a child or other individual to whom a duty of support is owed, the governor may require a prosecutor to investigate the demand and report whether a proceeding for support has been initiated or would be effective. If it appears that a proceeding would be effective but has not been initiated, the governor may delay honoring the demand for a reasonable time to permit the initiation of a proceeding.

(c) If a proceeding for support has been initiated and the individual whose rendition is demanded prevails, the governor may decline to honor the demand. If the [petitioner] prevails and the individual whose rendition is demanded is subject to a support order, the governor may decline to honor the demand if the individual is complying with the support order.

§ 901. Uniformity of Application and Construction.

~~This [Act] shall be applied and construed to effectuate its general purpose to make uniform~~ In applying and construing this Uniform Act consideration must be given to the need to promote uniformity of the law with respect to ~~the~~ its subject ~~of this [Act]~~ matter among States ~~enacting~~ that enact it.

§ 902. ~~903~~. Severability Clause.

If any provision of this [Act] or its application to any person or circumstance is held invalid, the invalidity does not affect other provisions or applications of this [Act] which can be given effect without the invalid provision or application, and to this end the provisions of this [Act] are severable.

§ 903. ~~904~~. Effective Date.

This [Act] takes effect ....

§ 904. ~~905~~. Repeals.

The following acts and parts of acts are hereby repealed:

(1)

(2)

(3)

7. Awarding An Adoption

The cases dealing with the adoption of another human being are a real mélange, ranging from those which contain the simplest factual situation to those which present such a labyrinth of interconnecting and interlocking situations that they are difficult to decipher. Thy pertain to people who are heterosexual, as well as those who are homosexual, who have children without bothering to enter the marital state; people who get married to other people of the same gender, people who don't get married to those of the same gender, but simply live with them, grandparents, aunts and uncles, who fret over the treatment their progeny are receiving, people who are so young they cannot defend themselves against mistreatment. All of this and full faith and credit, too, are what is to be found in many of the cases dealing with adoptions. After reading them one is prompted to wonder whether the bourgeoisie live on the same planet as the rest of the people.

The U.S. Supreme Court has not entered this area since 1915, when in *Hood v. McGehee*[908] it held that an Alabama statute which provided that children adopted in other states are not entitled to the same rights of inheritance as to property located within Alabama as are all other children, did not offend the Full Faith and Credit Clause. Justice Oliver Wendell Holmes, writing for the Court, made it clear that Alabama recognizes the Louisiana adoption and that it allows the adoptive parent to give her or his adopted children all the benefits which any parent may give to her or his children except for property located in Alabama. "Alabama is the sole mistress of the devolution of Alabama land by descent."[909] No such statute offends the Full Faith and Credit Clause.[910]

In *Finstuen v. Cautcher*[911] a "same-sex" couple was permitted to adopt a child in California. Oklahoma would not recognize the adoption based on a statute of the state prohibiting that type of adoption. The U.S. Court of Appeals for the Tenth Circuit held that Oklahoma's refusal constituted a violation of the Full Faith and Credit Clause.[912]

---

[908] 237 U.S. 611 (1915).

[909] *Id.* at 615.

[910] *Id*

[911] 496 F.3d 1139 (10th Cir. 2007).

[912] *Id.* at 1156.

Embry v. Ryan[913] is a factually simple case. A lesbian gave birth to a child in Washington state. Her partner adopted the child in Washington. After moving to Florida they ended their relationship and entered into an agreement about the partner's visitation with the child; but later the gestational mother refused to allow the adoptive mother any rights of visitation, and the latter sued. The gestational mother's defense was based on the position that the adoptive mother had no rights under the Washington adoption because of Florida's public policy prohibiting adoptions by same gender couples. The Florida court ruled against that defense based on full faith and credit.[914]

In re Adoption of Sebastian[915] is a complicated case. Two lesbians, one of Dutch-Italian extraction (Ingrid), and the other of Somali-Yemen parentage (Mona) were married to each other in the Netherlands. They wanted a child who would bear physical characteristics of their diverse backgrounds. In order to achieve this objective they had performed an *in vitro* procedure.[916] Ingrid delivered Sebastian while Mona observed at her side. Ingrid was shown as the "parent" on the birth certificate. While New York law would recognize Sebastian as having two parents, Mona having a genetic relationship to the child, the ladies were concerned that with their intercontinental lifestyle,[917] problems might arise in areas which would not recognize their marriage, or the form of Sebastian's conception. Even in this country with 44 states prohibiting same gender marriages, 29 of which have constitutional provisions to that effect,[918] full faith and credit problems could arise here, as well as within other countries. The Surrogate judge understood the problem, but was not sure as to how to solve it. She phrased the issue as follows:

---

913 11 So.3d 408 (Fla. 2d DCA 2009) Pet for Cert. den'd 26 So. 3d 590 (Fla. 2d DCA 2010).

914 *Id.* at 49. An added reason for the court's ruling was that Florida has a statute which requires recognition of adoptions in other states. *Id.* at 410.

915 879 N.Y.S.2d 677 (N.Y. Surr. 2009).

916 *Id.* at 678 n.2. An *in vitro* procedure differs form artificial insemination, in that even though a male donor is required, one of the females must donate her ova which is fertilized under the supervision of a physician.

917 The court described it as "a transient cross-border society." *See Id. at 678.*

918 *Id.* at 683. The statistics are as of the date of the decision.

> Whether adoption is appropriate and/or permitted where as here the party petitioning for adoption [Mona] was legally married to the child's mother [Ingrid] at the time of conception and birth and where she is also the child's genetic mother.[919]

Judge Kirstin Glen concluded that allowing the genetic mother, Mona, who was married to the gestational mother, Ingrid, to adopt Sebastian was the solution to the problem in the following words:

> Unless there is some other basis, grounded on genetic connection, upon which Mona's parentage of Sebastian can be legally established, adoption is the sole means by which their parent/child relationship and the rights and obligations incident thereto can be fully protected.[920]

The judge ended her Opinion implicitly observing that there should be no full faith and credit problems by explicitly saying that the adoption will be recognized "throughout the United States."[921]

In re R.T.J.N.[922] is another complicated case. An unmarried father filed an action in his home state of Teas to grant him a divorce, and establish parental rights to his child. Attached to his Complaint was an affidavit of the parents' termination of parental rights in favor of his parents – the child's grandparents. The Plaintiff's "former partner"[923] contested the "divorce" and *inter alia* the termination of parental rights on the ground that her so-called signature was a forgery. She soon took and child and departed for Arkansas, where she and the child established a home, the father and his parents remaining in Texas. Three years after the father had filed for a "divorce" in Texas the mother and her newly acquired husband filed for adoption in Arkansas. The father and his father (the grandfather), joined this proceeding and signed an agreed order to the effect that Arkansas was the child's home state. The grandfather agreed to the mother's husband being permitted to adopt the child in consideration of his being granted

---

[919] *Id.* at 682.

[920] *Id.* at 692.

[921] *Id.* at 692.

[922] 2009 W.L. 3763782 (Tex. App. 2009).

[923] Quoting from the court's designation of the child's mother. *See id.* at *1.

visitation privileges. Meanwhile the Texas court entered an order specifying that though the divorce action should be dismissed since the parents were never married, and though the court had continuing jurisdiction over the termination of the parental rights matter, Arkansas was the more convenient forum to try the adoption proceeding commenced by the mother, and her new husband, in that state. Shortly thereafter the grandmother, without the grandfather joining her, filed for visitation rights in the same court that heard the "divorce" action. She was subsequently joined by the grandfather. The trial court ruled against them. On appeal the Texas appellate court found that the issue was not whether the Texas court should have given full faith and credit to the Arkansas adoption proceedings, or whether the Texas court erred in finding that it no longer had jurisdiction, because it never relinquished jurisdiction. The issue was: did the Texas court abuse its discretion in finding that Arkansas was the more convenient forum. The appellate court could find no abuse of the trial court's discretion.[924]

In *Giancaspro v. Congleton*[925] this all-female couple, who were never married to each other, initially lived in the Peoples' Republic of China. One of the "partners" adopted three children in that country. When the couple moved to Illinois they jointly adopted the children. When they moved to Michigan the relationship dissolved and a custody dispute arose in the Michigan courts. The decision of Michigan was that full faith and credit must be given to the Illinois adoption proceeding, and hence the children had two parents. The plain language of Michigan's Child Custody Act[926] required the conclusion that each of the parties was a "parent;" and because that fact was binding, the parties' relationship with each other simply did not matter, and, as a consequence, the Michigan action was a child custody dispute between parents, under which the best interests of the child controlled.[927]

In *Palazzolo v. Mire*[928] two lesbians lived together in Louisiana while they acquired advanced academic degrees. Upon obtaining the decrees the two moved

---

[924] *Id.* at *4.

[925] 2009 WL 416301 (Mich. App. 2009).

[926] The Michigan Act was patterned after the Uniform Child Custody Judgment and Enforcement Act (UCCJEA). *See supra* text accompanying note 863.

[927] *Giancaspro*, 2009 W.L. 416301, at *4. (Mich. App. 2009).

[928] 10 So. 3d 748 (La. App. 2009).

to California. There they decided that, after having lived together for 17 years it would be nice to have a child by artificial insemination. After the child's birth the non-biological mother filed in California, under one of its "Second Parent Adoption" proceedings, for a Birth Certificate. A new Birth Certificate was issued, terminating all parental rights of the male sperm donor in the insemination proceeding, naming the biological mother as the child's "mother," and her homosexual partner as the "father." About two years later the "parents" returned to Louisiana with their child, and purchased a house in the New Orleans area. Unfortunately for them their house was destroyed by Hurricane "Katrina's" flooding. The "father," according to the "mother" began acting in a strange sexual manner, toward the child, probably being the cause of her to attempt a termination of the California adoption. Her grounds: Louisiana would not recognize the California adoption because (1) under Louisiana law adopting parents must be married: (2) the "mother" and "father" were not, and could not be, married under Louisiana law because they were of the same gender. The "father" countered with a full faith and credit argument. The Louisiana trial judge, after in-depth psychological testing of the "father" must have had doubts about her stability, since he terminated her visitation rights. The appellate judge must have analyzed the scientific reports differently because while he affirmed the "mother" having sole custody, due to full faith and credit which must be shown the California adoption, he gave the "father" visitation rights,[929] remanding the case to the trial court for the determination of its parameters.[930]

In *In re Trust Created by Nixon*[931] a well-to-do resident of Nebraska had a trust in which Wells Fargo Bank was the trustee. He executed his Will which provided that his estate be divided into two trusts upon his demise. One trust would be in favor of his daughter, and the other would be in favor of his son. In the event his daughter should die unmarried and without issue, her trust would go to his son. The daughter, a 64-year-old maiden lady, never having borne a child, did not like her brother. In order to prevent the brother or his family from inheriting her share of her father's estate she asked her 50-year-old maternal cousin if he would agree to her adopting him. When he agreed, the daughter obtained an adoption judgment in California. Upon the father's demise and his daughter's death without having married or borne children her brother's children took the position that the

---

[929] *Id.* at 778.

[930] *Id.* at 780.

[931] 763 N.W. 2d 404 (Neb. 2009).

California adoption had no merit since the Will concerned property located in Nebraska and a statute of Nebraska provided that adults may not be adopted except under specific conditions, not extant in this matter. The bank in Nebraska asked a Nevada court to make a determination of the legitimacy of a California court authorizing the adoption of an adult. The Nebraska court ruled that its state must recognize the California adoption based on (1) the Full Faith and Credit Clause, (2) a Nebraska public policy that adopted children are entitled to the same rights as biological children, and (3) the fact that the Will referred to "persons legally adopted."[932]

In *Adar v. Smith*[933] two unmarried adult males obtained a joint adoption decree, of a young child, in New York state. When they moved to Louisiana they sought from the state's Registrar a birth certificate showing them as the child's parents and giving him a new name. The Registrar refused, under legal advice from the state's chief legal advisor, to the effect that a state statute prohibits in-state adoption of children by unmarried couples. The men filed suit in federal court. After a careful examination of the state's statutes and the Full Faith and Credit Clause, the court entered an order requiring the Registrar to issue the birth certificate, and the Fifth Circuit affirmed.[934]

I. Judgments Imposing Penal Sanctions

One of the exceptions to the concept of full faith and credit[935] is to the effect that one state is not obliged to give full faith and credit to the penal statutes of another state.[936] Before we attempt to define to what extent this exception to full faith and credit applies to criminal cases it would be wise to determine what is the federal equivalent of the state. *Henderson v. Keefer*[937] held that in a criminal case a state order is not binding on the federal Bureau of Prisons.[938]

---

932 *Id.* at 410.

933 597 F.3d 697 (5th Cir. 2010).

934 *Id.* at 718.

935 *See supra*, Subsection I. D, text accompanying notes 258-463.

936 *See supra* notes 441, 451.

937 2009 W.L. 3294844 (W.D. La. 2009).

938 *Id.* at *3.

In *State of Wisconsin v. Pelican Ins. Co.*[939] the U.S. Supreme Court proclaimed that even though it had original jurisdiction of certain actions involving states, pursuant to the Constitution and the Judiciary Act of September 24, 1789 it did not have jurisdiction of an action by the state of Wisconsin to enforce the payment of a judgment obtained in a court of its state, which was authorized by a Wisconsin penal statute. Justice Horace Gray, writing the Opinion of the Court made that point eminently clear with the following concluding words:

> The statute of Wisconsin, under which the state recovered in one of her own courts the judgment now and here sued on, was, in the strictest sense, . . . a penal statute, imposing a penalty upon any insurance company of another state doing business in the state of Wisconsin without having deposited with the proper officer of the state a full statement of its property and business during the previous year. . . . The cause of action was not any private injury, but solely the offense committed against the state by violating her law. . . . If this court has original jurisdiction of the present case, it must follow that any action upon a judgment obtained by a state in her own courts against a citizen of another state for the recovery of any sum of money, however small, by way of a fine for any offense, however petty, against her laws, could be brought in the first instance in the supreme court of the United States. That cannot have been the intention of the convention in framing, or of the people in adopting, the federal constitution. Judgment for the defendant on the demurrer.[940]

In *Huntington v. Attril*[941] the U.S. Supreme Court had before it a case in which a plaintiff recovered a judgment in a court of New York against a defendant upon his personal liability as a director and stockholder in a New York corporation, under a New York statute. The grounds of liability were that the defendant, as a director, made and filed a false certificate that the stock was fully paid in (in which

---

[939] 127 U.S. 265 (1888).

[940] *Id.* at 299, 300. It must be noted that this decision was called into question by the Supreme Court in Milwaukee County v. M.E. White Co. 296 U.S. 268, 278 (1935) to the extent that the decision could be taken to suggest that a judgment is not to be given full faith and credit unless the cause of action upon which it is based would be entitled to like credit. *See supra* text accompanying notes 677-695, dealing with causes of action.

[941] 146 U.S. 657 (1892).

case the statute makes him personally liable for all the debts contracted by the corporation while he was an officer thereof), and that the debt was incurred before the stock was fully paid (in which case defendant, as a stockholder, was liable to the amount of his stock). Plaintiff thereafter brought a bill in a state court of Maryland to set aside an alleged fraudulent transfer of property by defendant, and to charge the same with the payment of the New York judgment. This case was taken to a Maryland appellate court which decided against the plaintiff's claim upon the ground that the New York judgment was for a penalty under the New York statute, and therefore could not be enforced in Maryland. The U.S. Supreme Court reversed. The New York judgment was the enforcement of a statute which made a corporate officer liable for a sum of money because of his defalcations. If there was a feature of punishment, as there is in every penal statute, it was only as a byproduct of the remedy akin to retribution owed by the defendant to the plaintiff in the New York court. The prohibition encompassed by the New York statute was not universal, but was limited to persons who occupied the positions designated by the statute. Justice Horace Gray, the author of the *Pelican Insurance Co.* case,[942] described the decision with the following words:

> The test whether a law is penal, in the strict and primary sense, is whether the wrong sought to be redressed is a wrong to the public or a wrong to the individual, according to the familiar classification of Blackstone: 'Wrongs are divisible into two sorts or species: private wrongs and public wrongs. The former are an infringement or privation of the private or civil rights belonging to individuals, considered as individuals, and are thereupon frequently termed 'civil injuries;' the latter are a breach and violation of public rights and duties, which affect the whole community, considered as a community, and . . . are distinguished by the harsher appellation of 'crimes and misdemeanors.' 3 Bl. Comm. 2.[943]
>
> The test is not by what name the statute is called by the legislature or the courts of the state in which it was passed, but whether it appears, to the tribunal which is called upon to enforce it, to be, in its essential character and effect, a punishment of an offense against the public, or a grant of a civil right to a private person.[944]

---

[942] *Wisconsin v. Pelican Ins. Co*, 127 U.S. 265.

[943] *Huntington*, 146 U.S. at 668, 669.

[944] *Id.* at 683.

The Violence Against Women Act (VAWA), enacted as Title IV of the Violent Crime Control Act of 1994.[945] It is a comprehensive statute designed to provide women nationwide greater protection and recourse against violence and to impose accountability on abusers. Subtitle B of VAWA is entitled "Safe Homes for Women." The subtitle created two new federal domestic violence crimes, directed that full faith and credit be given by the states to protection orders, and mandated restitution related to the federal crimes. The subtitle also provided for millions of dollars for shelters and youth education programs, and to encourage pro-arrest policies.

In *United States v. Casciano*[946] it was made clear that the validity of a protective order under the Violence Against Women Act is a matter for the judge, and not the jury, to decide.[947]

Holbein v. Rigot[948] was a suit on foreign judgment. The Florida trial court entered final judgment in favor of plaintiffs for the full amount of a Texas default judgment, and defendant appealed. The appellate court held that Texas judgment was entitled to full faith and credit for actual damages but not for exemplary or punitive damages, and the parties cross-appealed. The U.S. Supreme Court reversed and held that where the judgment was not based on a Texas penal statute but was based on general common-law liability for false, fraudulent and malicious representations on part of defendant who wrongfully induced plaintiffs to their injury to enter into a franchising agreement with defendant, and the award of punitive damages was not to punish defendant for an offense against the state of Texas or the general public, but to give the plaintiffs redress or reparation by way of punitive or exemplary damages for private wrong they suffered. The entire Texas judgment for both compensatory and punitive damages was entitled to full faith and credit in the Florida courts, as it was not for the enforcement of a penal statute.[949]

---

945 108 Stat. 1796, Pub. L. 103-322.

946 124 F.3d 106 (2d Cir. 1997).

947 *Id.* at 110.

948 245 So.2d 57 (Fla. 1971).

949 *Id.* at 62.

In *Hall v. Phelps*[950] Judge Robinson opined about the preclusive effects of criminal judgments. She said that "although the doctrine of *res judicata* applies to both criminal and civil proceedings, . . . a judgment in a criminal case operates as *res judicata* in another criminal case only when the parties to both cases are identical. . . . Consequently, the doctrine does not apply to successive prosecutions by different sovereigns."[951]

In *People v. Laino*[952] the defendant was convicted in California, of aggravated assault upon an elderly person. He urged upon the court that his conviction of an assault upon his wife in Arizona should not be counted pursuant to the Full Faith and Credit Clause as a conviction within California's "three strikes" rule because his conviction in Arizona had been dismissed after he completed a successful domestic violence "diversion" program. The California court disagreed. Under full faith and credit California was required to count the Arizona conviction, and was not required, by full faith and credit, to give the convict the same credit that Arizona does. California limited its own deferred entry of judgment program to certain nonviolent drug offenders, and specifically excluded such a benefit where the offender committed a crime involving domestic violence.[953]

In *Gillis v. State*[954] a person accused of murder had been acquitted of the crime by Delaware, but he was arrested and tried again for the same murder when a dead body was found in Maryland. His defense was twofold – (1) the Fifth Amendment Double Jeopardy defense, and (2) the Full Faith and Credit Clause required Maryland to honor Delaware's judgment of acquittal. The Maryland Supreme Court, in denying both objections, first referred to the U.S. Supreme Court decision in *Heath v. Alabama*[955] which held that if a defendant, in a single act violates the peace and dignity of two sovereigns by breaching the laws of each, and both sovereigns try him, he has not been twice punished for the same offense, because each of those acts of breaching the peace and dignity is a separate

---

[950] 641 F.Supp.2d 334 (D Del. 2009).

[951] *Id.* at 347, 348.

[952] 87 P.3d 27 (Cal. 2004).

[953] *Id.* at 40.

[954] 633 A.2d 888 (Md. 1993).

[955] 474 U.S. 82 (1985).

offense.[956] As to the second defense, the court said that while the Court in *Heath* did not mention full faith and credit, the dual sovereignty doctrine "may be viewed as equally applicable to full faith and challenges."[957] Summarizing the court's holding, Justice Chasanow wrote the following:

> [F]ull faith and credit cannot be used to deny Maryland the power to enforce its criminal laws and thereby thwart this State's obligation to 'maintain peace and order within [its] confines.' (Citation omitted). We hold that, with respect to successive criminal prosecutions by different states, the dual sovereignty rationale is applicable to the Full Faith and Credit Clause as well as the Double Jeopardy Clause.[958]

In *United States v. Castellon*[959] a defendant pled guilty to a four-Count Indictment of selling drugs. A federal District Court sentenced him to concurrent sentences of 48 months in prison and 4 years of suspended release on each Count. He complained that the Federal Court should not have considered a prior Texas adjudicatory proceeding for the purpose of enhancing[960] his sentence because it allegedly violated the Full Faith and Credit Clause. The Fifth Circuit denied his defense, and answered it, *Per Curiam*, as follows:

> The Full Faith and Credit Act obligates federal courts to give effect to the judgments of state courts, but the principles that underlie the Full Faith and Credit Act are simply not implicated when a federal court endeavors to determine how a particular state criminal proceeding is to be treated, as a matter of federal law, for the purpose of sentencing the defendant for a distinct and unrelated federal crime.[961]

---

956 *Id.* at 88.

957 *Gillis*, 633 A.2d at 891.

958 *Id. See also* Abbate v. United States, 359 U.S. 187, 195, 196 (1959).

959 228 Fed. Appx. 494 (5th Cir. 2007).

960 Enhancing a sentence apparently means increasing the severity of the sentence. Black's Law Dictionary, 8th Edition (2004) defines "enhancement" as "enhancement. The act of augmenting; the state of being enhanced <the use of a deadly weapon led to an enhancement of the sentence>."

961 *Castellon, 228 Fed. Appx. at* 496, 497. To like effect *see* Smart v. United States, 2008 W.L. 2902608 at *2 (S.D. Ga. 2008).

In *Ice Stores, Inc. v. Holmes*[962] a man pled *nolo contendere* to a criminal charge, and was required to pay restitution to a business enterprise known as "Lone Star Ice & Foods" in the amount of $144,839.56. Some time later Ice Stores, Inc. attempted to enforce the Texas judgment in Tennessee under the Full Faith and Credit Clause as there was still a bit still due, to wit: $144, 493.03, the defendant having paid only $346.53. The defendant defended on the basis that the plaintiff in the Tennessee enforcement proceeding (Ice Stores, Inc.) was not the same entity as the entity to whom the Texas court decreed restitution should be paid – Lone Star Ice & Foods. The plaintiff prevailed, however, by proving that the name designated in Texas was only the "doing business as" (d/b/a) name of the Tennessee plaintiff.[963]

In *Farabell v. Town of Macedon*[964] an applicant for a position as a police officer in New York had entered a plea of *nolo contendere* in Florida, with adjudication withheld, to a charge of dealing in stolen property. Had the applicant been convicted of the charge he would have been guilty of a felony, but under the plea of *nolo contendere* he was not considered a felon in Florida. Under Florida law, however, the applicant would not have been permitted to serve as a police officer. The New York Appellate Division held that New York is not required, under the Full Faith and Credit Clause, to prohibit the applicant from serving because New York has its own statutory scheme to determine what events disqualify an individual from serving as police officer in the state.[965]

In *Scott v. Commonwealth of Virginia* [966] it was determined that a Virginia trial court order which found that a defendant had violated the terms and conditions of his probation and imposed a sentence for that violation did not violate the Full Faith and Credit Clause, even though, according to the defendant, Ohio courts had already sentenced him for the probation violation. The transcript from the Ohio trial court revealed that the court had not addressed whether it had jurisdiction to

---

[962] 2008 W.L. 4981077 (Tenn. Ct. App. 2008).

[963] *Id.* at *6. *See* text accompanying notes 41, 258, 265, and 311 for other considerations of this case.

[964] 877 N.Y.S.2d 796 (N.Y. App. Div. 2009).

[965] *Id.* at 800.

[966] 676 S.E.2d 343 (Va. App. 2009).

adjudicate the defendant's Virginia probation violation, and thus the jurisdiction issue was not fully and fairly litigated in the Ohio courts.[967] Consequently the Full Faith and Credit Clause was not violated.

State v. Maddox[968] held that Washington state is not required, under the Full Faith and Credit Clause to give a prisoner credit for time served in Oregon for a crime separate and apart from the crime committed by him in Washington.[969]

Altamirano-Torres v. United States[970] established that if a Circuit Court vacates a criminal conviction for a procedural or substantive defect in the underlying conviction proceeding the accused no longer has a "conviction" for immigration purposes; but if the conviction is vacated for reasons unrelated to the merits of the conviction, e.g. rehabilitation or immigration purposes, then under those circumstances the conviction remains intact as a matter of record. It is not a violation of full faith and credit for the Board of Immigration Appeals to deny an immigrant's motion to reopen a determination by an Immigration Judge that the immigrant is not eligible for reentry to the United States.[971]

In *Rosin v. Monken*[972] New York state entered a judgment accepting a plea agreement acknowledging that a man was a sex offender, but the sex-offender registration provision was stricken from the standard sex offender form, and nothing inserted in its place. When the man took up residence in Illinois the state police and the supervisor of sex-offender registration required that he relocate and register in Illinois as a sex-offender for life. The U.S. Court of Appeals for the Seventh Circuit held that the Full Faith and Credit Clause did not prevent the Illinois action because the New York judgment had merely stricken the registration provision and was silent regarding registration in any other state. There was no judgment regarding registration to which Illinois was required to give effect, and New York lacked power to dictate means by which Illinois could protect its public,

---

[967] *Id.* at 348.

[968] 2009 W.L. 390033 (Wash. App. 2009).

[969] *Id.* at *3.

[970] 353 Fed. Appx. 386 (11th Cir. 2009).

[971] *Id.* at 389.

[972] 599 F.3d 574 (7th Cir. 2010).

even if provision had not been stricken. In the Opinion of the Court, Judge Cudahy stated the following:

> Illinois need not dispense with its preferred mechanism for protecting its citizenry by virtue merely of a foreign judgment that envisioned less restrictive requirements' being imposed on the relevant sex offender. Illinois, as a state of the Union, has police power over the health and welfare of its citizens. *See Barbier v. Connolly,* 113 U.S. 27, 31, 5 S.Ct. 357, 28 L.Ed. 923 (1885) (observing that a state's police power permits it to enact laws promoting "the health, peace, morals, education, and good order of the people"); *United States v. Salerno,* 481 U.S. 739, 747, 107 S.Ct. 2095, 95 L.Ed.2d 697 (1987) ("There is no doubt that preventing danger to the community is a legitimate regulatory goal."). The Supreme Court has regularly upheld states' exercise of their police powers to protect their citizens against sexual predators. *See, e.g., Smith v. Doe,* 538 U.S. 84, 123 S.Ct. 1140, 155 L.Ed.2d 164 (2003); *Kansas v. Hendricks,* 521 U.S. 346, 117 S.Ct. 2072, 138 L.Ed.2d 501 (1997). As in *Baker*, the New York court in the present case "cannot command obedience elsewhere on a matter the [New York] court lacks authority to resolve." *Baker,* 522 U.S. at 240, 118 S.Ct. 657. New York has no authority to dictate to Illinois the manner in which it can best protect its citizenry from those convicted of sex offenses.[973]
>
> Nor is this a case in which a state's police power conflicts with the U.S. Constitution or an Act of Congress, for this would require state law to give way by virtue of the Supremacy Clause. *See, e.g., Morris v. Jones,* 329 U.S. 545, 552-53, 67 S.Ct. 451, 91 L.Ed. 488 (1947). The Full Faith and Credit Clause was enacted to preclude the same matters' being relitigated in different states as recalcitrant parties evade unfavorable judgments by moving elsewhere. It was never intended to allow one state to dictate the manner in which another state protects its populace. This being the case, there is no tension between Illinois's police power and the Full Faith and Credit Clause here. As a result, New York could promise Rosin only that he would never have to register as a sex offender within its own jurisdiction. Rosin could not bargain for a promise from New York as to

[973] *Id.* at 577.

what other states would do based on his guilty plea to sexual abuse in the third degree, for New York had no power to make such a promise.[974]

J. Bankruptcy Court Judgments

The United States has not always had a bankruptcy Act,[975] despite the Constitution giving Congress the power "[t]o establish . . . uniform Laws on the subject of Bankruptcies throughout the United States."[976] During the periods that the country did not have a national Bankruptcy Act insolvency problems were governed by state. insolvency law. Today, because Congress, pursuant to its Constitutional authorization,[977] has enacted one of its authorized "Laws on the subject of Bankruptcies," to quote from the Constitution, we no longer have state insolvency laws by which a debtor might seek protection from creditors; we must look to the orders of the national, and only, "Bankruptcy Courts" for such relief.

A Bankruptcy Court might have involvement with the Full Faith and Credit statute,[978] but it would never be involved with the Full Faith and Credit Clause,[979] because a Bankruptcy Court is a federal court.

There follows some of the representative bankruptcy cases dealing with full faith and credit.

---

974 *Id.*

975 The dates of the Bankruptcy Acts and their intervening interstices are as follows: 1800-1803; 1841-1843; 1867-1878; 1898-1979; 1979-present. In 1978 Congress amended the 1898 Act with legislation known as "The Code," effective October 1, 1979. In the new bankruptcy statute the subjects of the proceedings, formerly known as "bankrupts" are now known as "debtors," the jurists are no longer "Bankruptcy Referees;" they are now "Bankruptcy Judges," with 14 year terms of office, who sit in their own courts, the "Bankruptcy Courts," as adjuncts of District Courts in their own quarters rather than as divisions of the District Courts, crowded into whatever space could be found for them.

976 U.S. Const. Art I, § 8, Cl. 4.

977 *See supra* note 975.

978 28 U.S.C. § 1738.

979 U.S. Const. Art. IV, § 1.

1. Decisions Under the 1898 Bankruptcy Act

Reily v. Lamar,[980] an early decision concerning a discharge under a state's insolvency laws in which Chief Justice John Marshall said that even if a procedure known today as an assignment for the benefit of creditors[981] had been perfected, the debtor would not receive the benefit of Maryland's insolvency laws, where at the time of his assignment he was no longer a citizen of Maryland because that state had conveyed away the land in which the debtor lived in order to partially create the District of Columbia.[982]

In *Davis v. Friedlander*[983] the U.S. Supreme Court ruled that if a Trustee in bankruptcy litigates an issue outside the bankruptcy court a decision against her or him is binding in the bankruptcy court.[984]

In *Stoll v. Gottlieb*[985] a United States District Court handling bankruptcy matters, entered an order relieving a guarantor of his guaranty of certain of the bankrupt's obligations in a proceeding for the reorganization of a company. Subsequently a creditor sued the guarantor in an Illinois Municipal Court, which granted the creditor the relief it sought. Though a state appellate court reversed, that decision was, in turn, reversed by the Illinois Supreme Court, giving the creditor his judgment, by approving the ruling of the Municipal court. In reversing the Illinois Supreme Court the U.S. Supreme Court said that Illinois' ruling ran counter to the full faith and credit provision of the statute which implemented the constitutional Clause.[986] Justice Stanley F. Reed, the author of the Court's Opinion, said, however, that the problem before the Illinois Supreme Court was not one of

---

980 6 U.S. (2 Cranch) 344 (1805).

981 An "A.B.C." is a form of debtor protection in which if a debtor assigns all of his assets to a person separate from the debtor, known as a "trustee," the debtor will be relieved of answering to creditors, since the "trustee" will have all of his assets with which to satisfy their claims.

982 *Reily* 6 U.S. at 357.

983 104 U.S. 570 (1881).

984 *Id.* at 577. To the same effect *see* Fischer v. Pauline Oil Co., 309 U.S. 294, 302, 303 (1940).

985 305 U.S. 165 (1938).

986 Presently 28 U.S.C. § 1738.

full faith and credit, but of *res judicata*.[987] The Supreme Court was not going to attempt a determination of the Federal court's jurisdiction to make its ruling in bankruptcy.[988] It was plain to Justice Reed and the Court that the Illinois court erred when it refused to honor the federal court's pronouncement. It was a ruling of a federal court under a federal statute which must be honored by a state in which the federal court sits. Even if the federal court's determination that it had the power to make its ruling was erroneous, and not binding in other actions involving other parties, it will bind these parties, no matter in what court the issue arises.[989]

In *Heiser v. Woodruff*[990] the U.S. Supreme Court held that once a proceeding in bankruptcy has decided that a debt was not fraudulent because of perjured evidence in its inception, a federal appellate court is not at liberty, under the aegis of the Full Faith and Credit Clause to countermand the decision. Chief Justice Harlan F. Stone wrote:

> [T]he alleged fraud was put in issue and the issue was decided against the trustee, the bankrupt and those whom they represent or who claim under them, for failure of proof. After two proceedings, in one of which the bankrupt and in the other of which the bankrupt and his trustee, sought, and were free, to prove that the judgment was based on fraudulently alleged, fictitious values, and in both of which the decision was against them, the principles of *res judicata* preclude the revival of the litigation in the bankruptcy court.[991]

As there is a list of exceptions to the Full Faith and Credit Clause and statute[992] there was in the 1898 Act a list of exceptions to the debts which may be discharged in bankruptcy. It was contained in Section 17 of the Act.[993] One subsection of § 17

---

987 *Stoll*, 305 U.S. at 171.

988 *Id.* Seemingly it did not consider that issue dispositive of the proper determination of the case before this court, as all courts making decisions, tacitly if not explicitly, proclaim that they have jurisdiction, both subject-matter and personal. Ed.

989 *Id.* at 173, 175.

990 327 U.S. 726 (1946).

991 *Id* at 736.

992 *See supra* text accompanying notes 258-463.

993 11 U.S.C. § 17.

provided that any claim for obtaining money by false pretenses would not be discharged in bankruptcy.[994] Another subsection provided that debts created by fraud, embezzlement, misappropriation or defalcation while acting as an officer or in any fiduciary capacity would not be discharged.[995] Those courts with bankruptcy jurisdiction left to state courts most of the questions in their cases as to whether the debts of their bankrupts were excepted from discharge. In 1970, however, Congress amended the Act to require creditors to apply to the courts with bankruptcy jurisdiction for the answers to these questions, rather than going to state courts for the decision. The first appellate court to rule upon the newly amended rule, the Tenth Circuit, held that the federal court must resolve: (1) a *res judicata* inquiry (2) by limiting its review to the record of the state court decision and its judgment. This became the law of the land.

In re Georgia Air, Inc.[996]decided seven years before the new Bankruptcy "Code" went into effect, was the last case decided under the 1898 Act which involved bankruptcy and full faith and credit. The state of Georgia filed a claim against the "bankrupt," Georgia Air, Inc. for taxes allegedly due the state. The bankruptcy Referee allowed the claim. On review to the U.S. District Judge, he reversed the ruling of the Referee. Judge Moye, in his Opinion said that Section 64(a)(4) of the Bankruptcy Act confers jurisdiction on the bankruptcy court to settle questions as to the amount or legality of any taxes and the bankruptcy court must give "full faith and credit" to state laws in determining validity of taxes assessed by state authorities who present claims for such taxes in bankruptcy proceedings. In viewing the bankruptcy court's decisions, the federal courts must also give "full faith and credit" to state law in determining the validity of the imposition of state taxes. In reviewing the Georgia state law the District Judge found an exemption to which the bankrupt was entitled; and he reversed the ruling of the Referee.[997]

---

[994] 11 U.S.C. § 17(2).

[995] 11 U.S.C. § 17(4).

[996] 345 F. Supp. 636 (N.D. Ga. 1972).

[997] *Id.* at 637.

2. Decisions Under The 1978 Code

In 1991 the U.S. Supreme Court ruled in *Grogan v. Garner*[998] that in dischargeability litigation the proper standard is the preponderance of evidence.[999] That ruling resolved a split of decisions not only among state courts but among some Bankruptcy Courts; so henceforth all Bankruptcy courts will use the preponderance of evidence standard.[1000]

In *In re Sasson*[1001] it was held that the doctrine of full faith and credit did not deprive the Bankruptcy Court of jurisdiction to enter a money judgment in a nondischargeability adversary proceeding, even though the underlying debt had already been reduced to judgment in state court proceedings.[1002] It was also held that the doctrine of full faith and credit does preclude, in dischargeability proceedings, by the bankruptcy court, relitigation of factual and legal issues actually decided in state court.[1003]

In *In re Siller* [1004] Bankruptcy Judge Klein wrote:

> [T]he Full Faith and Credit Statute requires that the [B]ankruptcy [C]ourt recognize the state-court judgment as fixing the amount of the debtor's liability, treat the attorney's fees incontestable on state-law grounds, and apply the state's rules of res judicata in determining the preclusive effect of its judgment. The Full Faith and Credit Statute must, however, also be construed so as to honor the Supremacy Clause.[1005]

---

998 498 U.S. 279 (1991).

999 *Id.* at 279 in passim.

1000 As Bankruptcy Judge Paskay, of the Middle District of Florida has said, the ruling of the Supreme Court has thus made it clear that "collateral estoppel is applicable not only as to the liability established by the state court judgment, but also the character of the liability." *See* In re Dowdell, 406 B.R. 106, 113 (Bankr. M.D. Fla. 2009).

1001 424 F.3d 864 (9th Cir. 2005).

1002 *Id.* at 876.

1003 *Id.* at 872.

1004 2010 W.L 1434324, (Bankr. E.D. Cal. 2010).

1005 *Id.* at * 8.

In 2001 the U.S. Court of Appeals for the Fourth Circuit made it clear that *Brown v. Felsen,*[1006] one of the last cases decided under the Bankruptcy Act of 1898, establishing an exception to the Full Faith and Credit statute was restricted to dischargeability considerations when Circuit Judge Widener wrote in *In re Heckert*[1007] that:

> [T]he authority granted the bankruptcy court under 28 U.S.C. § 157(b)(1) and 11 U.S.C. § 105(a) to enter orders, and the authority granted by 28 U.S.C. § 1334(b), 11 U.S.C. § 523(a) and Bankruptcy Rule 4007 to determine the dischargeability of a debt does not either explicitly or implicitly amend the provisions of 28 U.S.C. § 1738, which requires the courts of the United States to give full faith and credit to the judgments of state courts. By altering the amount of the judgment in this case by changing the interest rate and changing the initial effective execution date on the judgment of the state court by substituting its own judgment, the bankruptcy and district courts did exactly what § 1738 forbids. Even conceding that the bankruptcy court had the abstract authority to enter orders in a proper case, it had no authority to enter an order in violation of § 1738, the full faith and credit statute.[1008]

As the 1898 Bankruptcy Act contained a list of exceptions to discharge in bankruptcy, so also does the Bankruptcy Code.[1009] As with the 1898 Act[1010] this list has not been compiled judicially, but being a part of the legislation, it was compiled by Congress. One exception to discharge, specified in the bankruptcy list is that if a debt was incurred by fraud it will not be discharged.[1011] Another exception is that a debt incurred by willful and malicious injury will not be discharged.[1012] Dischargeability of a debt is an area of bankruptcy law that takes into account the aspect of full faith and credit that is so prevalent, yet at times not

---

[1006] 442 U.S. 127, 139 (1979).

[1007] 272 F.3d 253 (4th Cir. 2001).

[1008] *Id.* at 260.

[1009] It is 11 U.S.C. § 523.

[1010] *See supra* text accompanying notes 980-997 for cases decided under the 1898 Act.

[1011] 11 U.S.C. § 523(a)(2).

[1012] 11 U.S.C. § 523(a)(6).

specifically observed the law of preclusion. The debt that the debtor urges should be discharged, and the creditor, usually just as diligently urges should not be discharged, was incurred, in final order or settlement form, in a court other than the Bankruptcy Court, either federal or state. At the proceeding resulting in the alleged debt becoming fixed there usually are several facts established. Should the establishment of those facts preclude the Bankruptcy Judge from relitigating the issues which established the "facts" at a hearing before her or him to determine dischargeability?

Brown v. Felsen[1013] is one of the most well respected U.S. Supreme Court decisions providing an answer to this question. The pertinent facts of that case are as follows: Brown sued Felsen in state court seeking money which Brown alleged was owed him by Felsen because Felsen obtained it by fraud; the state court entered a consent decree embodying a stipulation providing that Felsen would pay Brown a certain amount; neither the decree nor the stipulation indicated the payment was for fraud; Felsen did not pay the debt, but entered bankruptcy; and in the Bankruptcy Court he requested the Judge to look behind the decree and stipulation and to hold that the debt was nondischargeable because it was a debt for money obtained by fraud. Brown had made that same claim in state court, but those courts held against him. They pointed out that the relevant debt was for money owed pursuant to a consent judgment; they noted that the relevant judgment related documents did not refer to fraud. It was at least the semble of the state courts that were Felsen to seek the protection of a Bankruptcy Court the doctrine of *res judicata* would prevent that court from looking behind those documents to uncover the nature of the claim that had led to their creation. The Supreme Court unanimously rejected the lower court's reasoning. The Court conceded that the state law of claim preclusion would bar Brown from making any claim "based on the same cause of action" that Brown had brought in state court.[1014] The court added that this aspect of *res judicata* would prevent Brown from litigating "all grounds for recovery" previously available to Brown, whether or not Brown had previously "asserted" those grounds in the prior state-court "proceeding."[1015] Those principles of law, however, would not prevent the Bankruptcy Court from looking beyond the record of the state-court proceeding and the documents that terminated that proceeding (the stipulation and consent judgment) in order to decide whether

---

1013 442 U.S. 127 (1979).

1014 *Id.* at 131.

1015 *Id.*

the debt at issue (namely, the debt embodied in the consent decree and stipulation) was a debt for money obtained by fraud.[1016] The Court rejected the theory of the lower court, the Fourth Circuit, to the effect that the settlement of the fraud claim into a consent decree novated[1017] the fraud claim into a liquidated debt, having no aspect which would authorize denying it discharge. What Congress intended by its creation and amendments of that portion of the Bankruptcy Code authorizing non-dischargeability under proper circumstances was to allow the relevant determination (whether a debt arises out of fraud) to take place in bankruptcy court, not to force it to occur earlier in state court at a time when nondischargeability concerns "are not directly in issue and neither party has a full incentive to litigate them."[1018] It would appear then that the Supreme Court has said that preclusion as to dischargeability of debts in bankruptcy is not quite the same, despite its development under full faith and credit, as it is in non-bankruptcy-discharge situations. In bankruptcy-non-discharge situations, courts not having discharge of debts firmly in mind might not see the situation as clearly as Bankruptcy Courts which do look at those facts with their consequence precisely in mind.

In *Archer v. Warner*[1019] Buyers of a business brought suit in state court against the sellers for fraud connected with the sale. Pursuant to settlement, the sellers executed a $100,000 promissory note, and when they defaulted on their first payment, the buyers brought another suit in state court for payment of the note. The sellers then filed for bankruptcy. After liquidation in a Chapter 7 case was ordered the Buyers filed an adversary complaint seeking judgment for the amount due under the note and a determination that the debt was nondischargeable. The United States Bankruptcy Court for the Middle District of North Carolina found

---

1016 *Id.* at 138, 139.

1017 Blacks Law Dictionary 8th Edition (2004) defines novation as "the act of substituting for an old obligation a new one that either replaces an existing obligation with a new obligation or replaces an original party with a new party. 1. A novation may substitute (1) a new obligation between the same parties, (2) a new debtor, or (3) a new creditor. 2. A contract that (1) immediately discharges either a previous contractual duty or a duty to make compensation, (2) creates a new contractual duty, and (3) includes as a party one who neither owed the previous duty nor was entitled to its performance. — Also termed *substituted agreement.*"

1018 *Brown*, 442 U.S. at 134.

1019 538 U.S. 314 (2003).

the note dischargeable, and the creditors appealed. The District Court affirmed, and the creditors again appealed. The United States Court of Appeals for the Fourth Circuit affirmed. When the case reached the U.S. Supreme Court it held that debt for money promised in the settlement agreement, which settled and released creditors' prior state-law claim against Chapter 7 debtors for fraud in sale of business, could amount to debt for money obtained by fraud, within meaning of Bankruptcy Code's discharge exception for debt for money obtained by false pretenses, false representation, or actual fraud, and reversed the Fourth Circuit.[1020]

In the bankruptcy case of *In re Webb*[1021] lenders obtained a default judgment against their borrower in California state court. Their borrower subsequently filed for bankruptcy. At the time the Bankruptcy Court was about to consider whether the lender's California judgment should be discharged, the lenders asked the court not to discharge it because the debt was incurred by fraud. The debtor asked the court to discharge the debt because of the fact that the California court did not allow punitive damages and pre-judgment interest showed that the debt was not incurred because of malicious injury. The Bankruptcy Judge realized that because of the Full Faith and Credit statute he was required to use California's rules of preclusion. He also observed that because the matter of a discharge in bankruptcy would never be the same as an underlying state court claim, and with a U.S. Supreme Court precedent like *Brown v. Felsen*,[1022] it is California's collateral estoppel (issue) preclusion law, rather than its *res judicata* (claim) preclusion law that must be used.[1023] The court denied both the lenders' and the debtor's requests because it could not be discerned from the record of the California case that either of those issues were considered.[1024]

In *In re C.W. Min. Co.*[1025] Bankruptcy Judge Michael in a Bankruptcy Panel case[1026] opined that "a federal district court judgment is entitled to full faith and

---

[1020] *Id.* at 322.

[1021] 2009 W.L.1139548. (Bankr. N.D. W.Va. 2009).

[1022] *See supra* text accompanying notes 1013-1016, 1018

[1023] *Webb,* 2009 W.L.1139548. at *3. Query: was this the same ruling made by the U.S. Supreme Court in Brown v. Felsen, 442 U.S. 127, 139 n.30? Ed.

[1024] Id. at *10.

[1025] 2009 WL 4798264 (10th Cir. B.A.P. 2009).

credit in a bankruptcy court, [where that federal district court is F-1] absent the most extraordinary of circumstances."[1027]

The significance of a bankruptcy discharge in connection with the full faith and credit motif must be uppermost in the minds of American judges, as the last time it was judicially observed was 1933, when in *Brouwer v. Superior Court in and for Los Angeles County*[1028] Judge Work proclaimed that:

> The effect of an adjudication in bankruptcy upon one having provable claims against the bankrupt, when he attempts to enforce his claims, pending the bankruptcy proceedings, against property honestly acquired after the adjudication by the bankrupt, is too well known to require exposition here. The effect of a discharge in bankruptcy, as to the same matters, is more potent and permanent. [The bankrupt] has been discharged as a bankrupt. Her discharge is in effect a judgment to which the courts of this state must give full faith and credit. She is therefore entitled to be relieved of harassment.[1029]

K. Indian Tribal Court Judgments

A few more than five hundred years ago, when Christopher Columbus, on his intended, and interrupted, but commendable, sale around the world, ran into a land mass, now called North America he mistakenly thought the people he saw were natives of India, a country 7,000 miles away. The colonists, later on, considered those people whom Columbus observed, a necessary nuisance, and the account of how that problem was resolved would fill a sizable library, indeed more than the covers of this lexicon. Suffice it to say that it is thought that the people, apparently wayfarers at the time, migrated 12,000 years ago from regions around what is now known as Siberia, probably seeking a more palatable climate. They trudged not just into what is now known as North America, but around the world. Some of them halted long before their brethren, and are now called Eskimos, most of whom live in the state of Alaska.

1026 Rather to appealing a decision to the Court of Appeals the parties are permitted to appeal a panel of three Bankruptcy Judges.

1027 *C.W. Min. Co., In re* 2009 WL 4798264 *5.

1028 19 P.2d 834 (Cal. App. 2 Dist. 1933).

1029 *Id.* at 835.

Only God knows how many of these people there were at the time Columbus first spied them, but the U.S. Census Bureau estimates that as of 2007 there were 2,570,000 "Indians" living on 55.7 acres (87,000 square miles) of land, called "reservations," held in trust by the U.S. for 561[1030] federally recognized "tribes,"[1031] and administered by the Bureau of Indian Affairs.[1032]

The Indian Reorganization Act of 1934 allowed the "Indians" to establish tribal courts for the enforcement of tribal laws, created by their legislatures. There is not an abundance of information about these tribal courts, though in March, 2000 B.J. Jones, the Chief Judge of the Sisselon-Wahpeton Sioux Tribal court, in Agency, South Dakota wrote a scholarly article about the 150 tribal courts he asserts to exist at the present time.

After more than two hundred years of the existence of the United States of America the relationship between their courts and the Indian courts is still in a state of flux. In the forefront of such uncertainty is the concept of full faith and credit. Judge Jones wrote about efforts to bring some semblance of order into the judicial relationship between what we think of as the greatest country in the world and its original natives, by his saying:

> [I]n many states, tribal-state court forums have been created to allow state and tribal judges to interact about their respective court systems and the dialogue has led to agreements about such issues as full faith and credit.

The U.S. Supreme Court has certainly not ignored Indian tribes.

[1030] It should be remembered that there are also Indian nations, which are affiliations of several tribes, and Indian bands, each of which consists of a group of Indians living in a single community.

[1031] The Bureau of Indian Affairs updates, every two years or so, a list of recognized tribes, which are entitled to services from the Bureau. The list is published in the Federal Register. The judiciary defers to the executive and legislative branches of our government as to the listing of tribes.

[1032] A federal agency under the Department of the Interior, the successor to the first such agency, founded on March 11,1824, under the Department of War.

As early as 1865 in *United States v. Holliday,*[1033] the U.S. Supreme Court said that pursuant to its plenary power rooted in the Indian Commerce Clause,[1034] among other sources,

> Congress has never claimed, and cannot lawfully exercise the power of legislating for Indians, except as *tribes* or *quasi* domestic nations. When they lose this relation and character, and become citizens of a State, or as individuals become separated from their *ordinary* tribal connections, they pass from the jurisdiction of the United States. The limits of the agency are established, as all know, by tribes or geographical boundaries. The general duty of the agent is to manage and superintend the *intercourse with* the Indians. This assumes their separate and social condition.[1035]

In 1883 the Court in *Ex parte Kan-gi-shun-ca,*[1036] opined that our government has always recognized "semi-independent" tribes as being exempt from our laws, and left to their own rules and regulations.[1037] In 1978 the Court observed, by dictum, in *Santa Clara Pueblo v. Martinez*[1038] that tribal courts "have been regarded in some circumstances as entitled to full faith and credit in other courts."[1039] In 1982 the Court said in *Merrion v. Jicarilla Apache Tribe*[1040] that Indian tribes retain all of their sovereignty that has not been "divested by the Federal Government" and that "the proper inference . . . is that the sovereign power . . . remains intact."[1041] In *National Farmers' Union Ins. Companies v. Crow Tribe of Indians,*[1042] a 1985 case, however, the Court cautioned that defendants

---

1033 70 U.S. (3 Wall.) 407, 419 (1865).

1034 U.S. Const. Art I, § 8, Cl. 3 provides, *inter alia*, that "[t]he Congress shall have Power to regulate Commerce with . . . the Indian Tribes."

1035 *Holiday,* 70 U.S. at 411, 412.

1036 109 U..S. 556 (1883).

1037 *Id.* at 572.

1038 436 U.S. 49 (1978).

1039 *Id.* at 65, n.21.

1040 455 U.S. 130 (1982).

1041 *Id.* at 148, 149.

1042 471 U.S. 845 (1985).

have a federal right to be protected against unlawful exercise of Tribal Court Judicial power.[1043] It can be said that while the U.S. Supreme Court has voiced the broad perimeters of the United States' courts, both federal and state, relation with Tribal Courts, it has left to the lower courts, both federal and state, the function of filling the interstices of that important relationship which exists in our country.

Perhaps the area of law which is the busiest in connection with Indian and non-Indian American relations is that of whether P.K.PA. (29 U.S.C. § 1738 A)[1044] applies to Indian Tribal Court-state and federal court relations. Three 19th century 8th Circuit cases, *Mehlin v. Ice,*[1045] *Cornells v. Shannon,*[1046] and *Standley v. Roberts,*[1047] held that Indian tribes were territories under the then existing full faith and credit statute. In *Jim v. CIT Fin Services Corp.*[1048] the New Mexico Supreme Court held that under P.K.P.A. the laws of the Navajo nation are entitled to full faith and credit in its state courts "because the Navajo nation is a territory within the meaning of that statute."[1049] In *Sheppard v. Sheppard*[1050] the Idaho Supreme Court held that P.K.P.A. was meant to include tribes.[1051] *In re Larch,*[1052] a 4th Circuit case, held that the Cherokee tribe is a state for purposes of the P.K.P.A.[1053] In *Martinez v. Superior Court*[1054] *t*he Arizona Supreme Court held that Indian reservations are territories and possessions, hence must be treated as states for purposes of Arizona's U.C.C.J.A.[1055] In *Tracy v. Superior Court*[1056] the Arizona

---

1043 *Id.* at 851.

1044 *See supra* text accompanying note 29.

1045 56 F. 12, 19 (8th Cir.1893).

1046 63 F. 305, 306 (8th Cir.1894).

1047 59 F. 836, 845 (8th Cir.1894).

1048 533 P.2d 751 (N. Mex. 1975).

1049 *Id.* at 752.

1050 655 P.2d 895 (Idaho 1982).

1051 *Id.* at 902.

1052 872 F.2d 66 (4Tth Cir. 1989).

1053 *Id.* at 68.

1054 731 P.2d 1244 (Ariz. 1997).

1055 *Id.* at 1247.

Supreme Court observed that tribal courts in some circumstances have been entitled to full faith and credit in other courts.[1057] In *Halwood v. Cowboy Auto Sales, Inc.*[1058] the New Mexico Supreme Court cited with approval the *Jim* case, which thought that the P.K.P.A. required New Mexico courts to give full faith and credit to the Navajo nation's laws. [1059] *Eberhard v. Eberhard,*[1060] an Indian court case, held that the Cheyanne River Sioux tribe declared that the P.K.P.A. requires tribal courts to afford full faith and credit to judgments of state courts, asserting that Congress intended it to apply to tribes.[1061] On the other hand in *Malaterre v. Malaterre*[1062] the North Dakota Supreme Court refused to attempt a resolution of a child custody dispute between tribal and state courts because North Dakota's U.C.C.J.A. pertains only to disputes between states.[1063] *Desjarlait v. Desjarlait*[1064] ruled that the Minnesota U.C.C.J.A. does not apply to jurisdictional disputes between state and tribal courts since the U.S. Constitution's Full Faith and Credit Clause applies only to states and not to tribes.[1065] In *John v. Baker*[1066] the Alaska Supreme Court held that the P.K.P.A. does not require that full faith and credit be given to Indian trial courts.[1067]

With this conflict of opinions the New Mexico Supreme Court in *Garcia v. Gutierrez,*[1068] a custody dispute, was required to decide whether P.K.P.A. required a tribal court to give full faith and credit to a state court. After a review of the

---

1056 810 P.2d 1030 (Ariz. 1991).

1057 *Id.* at 1038.

1058 946 P.2d 1088, (N. Mex. 1997).

1059 *Id.* at 1090.

1060 24 Indian L. Rptr. 6059 (1997).

1061 *Id.* at 6060, 6065.

1062 293 N.W. 2d 139 (N.D. 1980).

1063 *Id.* at 144.

1064 379 N.W.2d 139 (Minn. Ct. App. 1985).

1065 *Id.* at 144.

1066 982 P.2d 738 (Alaska 1999).

1067 *Id.* at 762.

1068 217 P.3d 591 (N. Mex. 2009).

conflicting judgments it ruled that neither the tribal, nor the state courts were requited to give full faith to each other.[1069] A scholarly Opinion by Justice Bosson, *inter alia,* refused to overrule the *Jim* case,[1070] primarily because that decision referred to 28 U.S.C. § 1738, and not 28 U.S.C. § 1738A (P.K.P.A.), but disparaged the *Jim* decision as being "highly suspect," and influenced by the 19th century 8th Circuit cases,[1071] which the court thought "out of vogue." Justice Bosson indicated that *Merrion*[1072] implied that if Congress intended to extend full faith and credit to Indian tribal courts "it must do so explicitly."[1073] On a very thoughtful note Justice Bosson observed that if we were to interpret "territories" as including states, the inclusion of "territories" in 28 U.S.C. § 1738 B would be superfluous.[1074] The court, however, left the case on a hopeful, yet perhaps confusing note, *vis-a-vis* full faith and credit. It ruled that though the "Full Faith and Credit of P.K.P.A. does not apply to the relationship of state-federal courts with tribal courts, New Mexico's version of the U.C.C.J.A. does. Therefore, even though concurrency runs counter to the U.C.C.J.E.A. (which New Mexico has adopted), and P.K.P.A. the tribal and state courts in this case on remand should treat each other as "concurrent" courts. It was the spirit of 25 U.S.C. § 1902, which provides:

> The Congress hereby declares that it is the policy of this Nation to protect the best interests of Indian children and to promote the stability and security of Indian tribes and families by the establishment of minimum Federal standards for the removal of Indian children from their families and the placement of such children in foster or adoptive homes which will reflect the unique values of Indian culture, and by providing for assistance to Indian tribes in the operation of child and family service programs.

The spirit of 25 U.S.C. § 1901(3) which provides, *inter alia*:

[1069] *Id.* at 606.

[1070] *See supra* text accompanying note 1048, 1049.

[1071] *See* text accompanying notes 1045-1047.

[1072] *See supra* notes 1040, 1041.

[1073] *Garcia,* 217 P. 3d at 605.

[1074] *Id.* at 606.

> Recognizing the special relationship between the United States and the Indian tribes and their members and the Federal responsibility to Indian people, the Congress finds—
>
> > (3) that there is no resource that is more vital to the continued existence and integrity of Indian tribes than their children and that the United States has a direct interest, as trustee, in protecting Indian children who are members of or are eligible for membership in an Indian tribe.

The spirit of the U.S. Supreme Court's message in *Miss. Band of Choctaw Indians v. Holyfield*[1075] which reminded us that the very important aspect of the Indian Welfare Act of 1978[1076] "seeks to protect the rights of the Indian child as an Indian and the rights of the Indian community and tribe in retaining its children."[1077] It was those messages that carried the day for the children, in imposing a spirit of congeniality into this child custody battle. Though the *Garcia* decision was merciful to children, and well-considered, it merely added fuel to the fire of full faith and credit *vel non* in the unsettled question as to whether the Full Faith and Credit Clause applies to Indian tribal courts, or whether the ruling of those courts remain an exception[1078] to full faith and credit. We must remember, however, that the court which decided *Garcia v. Gutierrez*[1079] was a Supreme Court of a state, (New Mexico), not the Supreme Court of the United States, whose wisdom we await

L. Foreign-Country Court Judgments

1. Introductory Remarks

The Full Faith and Credit Clause (Art IV § 1), and its implementing statute (28 U.S.C. § 1738), do not require recognition and enforcement of judgments rendered

[1075] 490 U.S. 30 (1989).

[1076] 25 U.S.C. § 1901 et seq.

[1077] *Holyfield*, 490 U.S. at 37.

[1078] *See supra* text accompanying note 456.

[1079] *See supra* text accompanying notes 1068, 1069.

by foreign countries,[1080] but they do not prohibit such procedures. It has been opined, in fact, that the "prevailing common law view" is that such judgments "are entitled to recognition and enforcement largely to the same extent as sister-state judgments."[1081] As Chief Justice John Marshall once observed: "[i]t is conceded that the legislation of every country is territorial; that beyond its own territory, it can only affect its own subjects or citizens."[1082] In order to familiarize oneself with recognition and enforcement of judgments from foreign countries, therefore, the "common law" must be consulted rather than a Clause of the United States Constitution and its implementing statute. While such inquiry is outside the perimeters of this work, a few words on that subject appear to be in order.

In *Searle v. Searle*[1083] it was opined that a state may extend full faith and credit to judgments of foreign countries only when allowed by treaty or statute.[1084] Requiring a treaty of the national government might be a bit of an overstatement. The recognition of a judgment of a foreign country, however, may be made under the principle of "comity;"[1085] which does not quite have the credentials of a treaty. *Padron v. Lopez*[1086] made it clear that comity differs from constitutional full faith and credit, in that it is not a matter of obligation; it is rendered out of "deference and respect," rather than obligation.[1087]

1080 Home Ins. Co. v. Dick, 281 U.S. 397, 410 (1930); Allstate Ins. Co. v. Hague, 449 U.S. 303, n.4 (1981); Society of Lloyd's v. Reinhart, 402 F. 3d 982, 993 (10th Cir. 2005); Baker & McKenzie Advokatbyra v. Thinkstream Inc. 20 So.3d 1109, 1117, (La. App. 2009); Petkov v. Petkov, 2009 W.L. at *2 (Mich. App. 2009) DRFP, L.L.C. v. The Republica Bolivariana de Venezuela, 2009 WL 948764 at *3 (S.D. Ohio 103701 (Mich. App 2009); Tarikonda v. Pinjari, 2009 W.L. 930007 at *1 (Mich. App. 2009); Osorio v. Dole Food Co., 2010 W.L. 571806 (S.D. Fla. 2010).

1081 Alpine Atlantic Asset Management AG v. Comstock, 552 F. Supp.2d 1268, 1281 (D. Kan. 2008).

1082 Rose v. Himely 8 U.S. (4 Ctanch) 241, 279 (1808).

1083 38 P.3d 307 (Utah App. 2001).

1084 *Id.* at 314.

1085 Milwaukee County v. M.E. White Co., 296 U.S. 268, 271 (1935).

1086 220 P.3d 345 (Kan. 2009). *See supra* notes 347 and 351 in which this case is considered and *infra* text accompanying notes 1086 and 1087 in which this case is considered.

1087 *Id.* at 358.

In *American Banana Co. v. United Fruit Co.*[1088] Judge Noyes announced the conditions of comity in the following words:

> Conditions of comity and of the highest expediency require that the conduct of states, whether in transactions with other states or with individuals, their own citizens, or foreign citizens, should not be called in question by the legal tribunals of any other jurisdiction. The citizens of a state have an adequate redress for any grievance at its hands by an appeal to the courts or the other departments of their own government. Foreign citizens can rely upon the intervention of their respective governments to redress their wrongs even by a resort, if necessary, to the arbitrament of war. It would be not only offensive and unnecessary, but it would imperil the amicable relations between governments and vex the peace of nations, to permit the sovereign acts or political transactions of states to be subjected to the examination of the legal tribunals of other states.[1089]

No doubt it was in recognition of the significance of comity that the American Law Institute proposed the Uniform Foreign Country Money Judgments Recognition Act (UFCMJRA), that appears verbatim in Section B. of this chapter, which, while it does not use the word "comity" specifically, is based upon that principle.[1090]

If one is interested in having a judgment from a foreign country recognized and/or enforced in this country that person should see whether the F-2 state has enacted a statute on point. The state asked to recognize and/or enforce a foreign country judgment (an F-2 court) if it has enacted a statute on point may have been guided by the uniform Act. Of course states may enact their own version of such an Act, and devise their own reasons for denying recognition of a foreign country judgment.[1091]

[1088] 166 F. 261 (2d Cir. 1908).

[1089] *Id.* at 265.

[1090] Sung Hwan Co., Ltd. v. Rite Aid Corp., 841 N.Y.S.2d 828 *1 (N.Y. S. Ct. 2007); Trapp v. Corporation of Lloyd's 2008 W.L. 5758763 at *1 n.3 (S.D. N.Y. 2008).

[1091] *See* Osorio v. Dole Food Co., 2010 W.L. 571806, *4 (S.D. Fla. 2010).

It should be remembered that comity can sometimes be a "two-way street". In *Vorontsova v. Waronzoy*[1092] a trial court refused to recognize a Ukarainian divorce decree, not under full faith and credit, but comity.[1093]

2. The Uniform Foreign County Money Judgment Recognition Act (UFCMJRA)[1094]

§ 1. Short Title
This [act] may be cited as the [Uniform Foreign-Country Money Judgments Recognition Act].

§ 2. Definitions
In this [act]

(1) "Foreign country" means a government other than:

(A) the United States;

(B) a state, district, commonwealth, territory, or insular possession of the United States; or

(C) any other government with regard to which the decision in this state as to whether to recognize a judgment of that government's courts is initially subject to determination under the Full Faith and Credit Clause of the United States Constitution.

(2) "Foreign-country judgment" means a judgment of a court of a foreign country.

Act (Refs & Annos)

§ 3. Applicability.

(a) Except as otherwise provided in subsection (b), this [act] applies to a foreign-country judgment to the extent that the judgment:

(1) grants or denies recovery of a sum of money; and

(2) under the law of the foreign country where rendered, is final, conclusive, and enforceable.

1092 911 N.E.2d 774 (Mass. App. Ct. 2009).

1093 *Id.* at 778.

1094 As of Jan. 15, 2012, the following 12 states have adopted the Uniform Foreign Country Money Judgments Recognition Act (UFCMJRA)t: California, Colorado, Hawai'i, Idaho, Michigan, Montana, Nevada, New Mexico, North Carolina, Oklahoma, Oregon and Washington.

(b) This [act] does not apply to a foreign-country judgment, even if the judgment grants or denies recovery of a sum of money, to the extent that the judgment is:

(1) a judgment for taxes;

(2) a fine or other penalty; or

(3) a judgment for divorce, support, or maintenance, or other judgment rendered in connection with domestic relations.

(c) A party seeking recognition of a foreign-country judgment has the burden of establishing that this [act] applies to the foreign-country judgment.

§ 4. Standards for Recognition of Foreign-Country Judgment.

(a) Except as otherwise provided in subsections (b) and (c), a court of this state shall recognize a foreign-country judgment to which this [act] applies.

(b) A court of this state may not recognize a foreign-country judgment if:

(1) the judgment was rendered under a judicial system that does not provide impartial tribunals or procedures compatible with the requirements of due process of law;

(2) the foreign court did not have personal jurisdiction over the defendant; or

(3) the foreign court did not have jurisdiction over the subject matter.

(c) A court of this state need not recognize a foreign-country judgment if:

(1) the defendant in the proceeding in the foreign court did not receive notice of the proceeding in sufficient time to enable the defendant to defend;

(2) the judgment was obtained by fraud that deprived the losing party of an adequate opportunity to present its case;

(3) the judgment or the [cause of action] [claim for relief] on which the judgment is based is repugnant to the public policy of this state or of the United States;

(4) the judgment conflicts with another final and conclusive judgment;

(5) the proceeding in the foreign court was contrary to an agreement between the parties under which the dispute in question was to be determined otherwise than by proceedings in that foreign court;

(6) in the case of jurisdiction based only on personal service, the foreign court was a seriously inconvenient forum for the trial of the action;

(7) the judgment was rendered in circumstances that raise substantial doubt about the integrity of the rendering court with respect to the judgment; or

(8) the specific proceeding in the foreign court leading to the judgment was not compatible with the requirements of due process of law.

(d) A party resisting recognition of a foreign-country judgment has the burden of establishing that a ground for nonrecognition stated in subsection (b) or (c) exists.

§ 5. Personal Jurisdiction.

(a) A foreign-country judgment may not be refused recognition for lack of personal jurisdiction if:

(1) the defendant was served with process personally in the foreign country;

(2) the defendant voluntarily appeared in the proceeding, other than for the purpose of protecting property seized or threatened with seizure in the proceeding or of contesting the jurisdiction of the court over the defendant;

(3) the defendant, before the commencement of the proceeding, had agreed to submit to the jurisdiction of the foreign court with respect to the subject matter involved;

(4) the defendant was domiciled in the foreign country when the proceeding was instituted or was a corporation or other form of business organization that had its principal place of business in, or was organized under the laws of, the foreign country; (5) the defendant had a business office in the foreign country and the proceeding in the foreign court involved a [cause of action] [claim for relief] arising out of business done by the defendant through that office in the foreign country; or

(6) the defendant operated a motor vehicle or airplane in the foreign country and the proceeding involved a [cause of action] [claim for relief] arising out of that operation.

(b) The list of bases for personal jurisdiction in subsection (a) is not exclusive. The courts of this state may recognize bases of personal jurisdiction other than those listed in subsection (a) as sufficient to support a foreign-country judgment.

§ 6. Procedure for Recognition of Foreign-Country Judgment.

(a) If recognition of a foreign-country judgment is sought as an original matter, the issue of recognition shall be raised by filing an action seeking recognition of the foreign-country judgment.

(b) If recognition of a foreign-country judgment is sought in a pending action, the issue of recognition may be raised by counterclaim, cross-claim, or affirmative defense.

§ 7. Effect of Recognition of Foreign-Country Judgment.
If the court in a proceeding under Section 6 finds that the foreign-country judgment is entitled to recognition under this [act] then, to the extent that the foreign-country judgment grants or denies recovery of a sum of money, the foreign-country judgment is

(1) conclusive between the parties to the same extent as the judgment of a sister state entitled to full faith and credit in this state would be conclusive; and

(2) enforceable in the same manner and to the same extent as a judgment rendered in this state.

§ 8. Stay of Proceedings Pending Appeal of Foreign-Country Judgment.
If a party establishes that an appeal from a foreign-country judgment is pending or will be taken, the court may stay any proceedings with regard to the foreign-country judgment until the appeal is concluded, the time for appeal expires, or the appellant has had sufficient time to prosecute the appeal and has failed to do so.

§ 9. Statute of Limitations.
An action to recognize a foreign-country judgment must be commenced within the earlier of the time during which the foreign-country judgment is effective in the foreign country or 15 years from the date that the foreign-country judgment became effective in the foreign country.

§ 10. Repealed.
[This section of the Act simply instruct the Legislature to insert the identification of the statutes which are repealed].

§ 11. [Time of Taking Effect].
This Act shall take effect _______.

M. Concluding Remarks About Full Faith And Credit

We have observed a considerable extension and application of the Full Faith and Credit Clause, its implementing statutes, and their meaning, but we have not discussed why the framers chose those three words "full," "faith," and "credit." Of course U.S. Supreme Court Justices Butler,[1095] Douglas,[1096] and Reed[1097] have

---

1095 *See supra* text accompanying note 46.

1096 *See supra* text accompanying note 47.

informed us that the faith and credit must be complete, and not half. Why, however did the framers of the Constitution choose the words "faith," and "credit"? In *James v. Allen*[1098] Judge Shippen of the Pennsylvania Court of Common Pleas, in 1786, informed us that "[t]he Articles of Confederation which direct that full faith and credit shall be given in one State to the Records, Acts, and judicial proceedings of the others" was not applicable to the facts of the case before his court.[1099] Reference to the Articles reveals that, indeed, those words appeared in them. James Madison, in No. 42 of The Federalist Papers thought the Constitution's method of enforcement was superior to that of the Articles. He wrote that "[t]he power of prescribing by general laws the manner in which the public acts, records, and judicial proceedings of each State shall be proved, and the effect they shall have in other States, is an evident and valuable improvement on the clause relating to this subject in the Articles of Confederation."[1100] It would appear, therefore, that we must determine, if we can, what meaning the words "faith," and "credit" had when the Articles of Confederation were being drafted in 1777. If judicial writings offer a clue to our quest we can say that the people of that time understood "faith" in the non-religious context, to be the equivalent of honesty, integrity, and a factual representation of fact. *Thompson v. Towson*[1101] defined "bona fide," as being almost identical to "good faith," i.e. "without fraud, or deceit, or collusion."[1102] In *Hawkins v. Hanson*[1103] it was established that if one acts in "good faith and honesty" as to such person "it cannot be presumed that he intended a deception."[1104] The cases of that era when they used the word "credit" were referring to the financial connotation of the term. In *The Resolution,*[1105] a case dealing with a ship, the court said that "no credit or faith is to be given to the papers on the ship because [they are] replete with contradiction and absurdity."[1106] And so even from those few examples[1107] it can be said that the

---

1097 *See supra* text accompanying note 48.

1098 1 U.S. 188, 1786 W.L. 218 (1786).

1099 *Id.* at 191.

1100 The Federalist Papers, No. 42 (Madison).

1101 1 H & McH 504, 1771 W.L. 19 (1772).

1102 *Id.* at *1.

1103 1H & McH 523 , 1774 W.L. 13 (1774).

1104 *Id.* at *4.

1105 2 U.S. 19, 1781 W.L. 45, 1 L.Ed. 271 (1781).

1106 *Id.* at **6.

framers of the unifying clause were attempting to assure that when a state had in its possession a public Act, a Record or a Judicial Proceeding, if for some reason, another state had reason to become privy to it, the object which would be furnished the other state would be an honest, unadulterated, facsimile of it. They did not require that the original be correct, unassailable, in conformity with its counterpart in the other state, or in any manner pleasing to the other state. The thing obtained by the other state must be simply an exact duplicate of the original object as it exists in the state from which it is obtained.

Before we leave the full faith and credit saga we should consider two other element of it. The first is sometimes misleading – what appears to be a full faith and credit problem, but isn't. There is no better example of such situation than *Semtek Int'l Inc. v. Lockheed Martin Corp.*[1108]

In *Semtek,* a federal District Court in California dismissed the plaintiff's diversity jurisdiction lawsuit based on California's two-year statute of limitations. Thereafter, the same plaintiff sued the same defendant on the same cause of action in a Maryland state court.[1109] Had the Maryland state court applied its state's three

---

[1107] The cases decided before the drafting of the Articles of Confederation are not unlike those shortly after. In Miller v. The Resolution. 17 Fed. Cas. 347 (1781), which was affirmed in part and reversed in part by The Resolution, 2 U.S. 19 (1781) the court referred to the "faith" of the alliance of sovereigns. In *In re* Loyal & Greenbrier Cos., 4 Call 21, 1783 W.L. 17 (1783) the court referred to people purchasing land on the "faith" of terms of sale offered by the companies. In Jenkins v. Putnam, 1 Bay 8, 1784 W.L. 36 (1784) the court proclaimed that it was bound by "due faith and credit" of Courts of Admiralty. In Helms' Lessees v. Howard, 2 H. McH. 57, 1784 W.L. 39 (1784) the court mentioned

> "interests or estates acquired under the faith or sanctions of preceding laws." In Izard v. Middleton, 1 Des. 116, 1785 W.L. 38 (1785) the court indicated the similarity of "faith" and reliance. In Dorrow v. Kelly, 1 Dall. 142, 1785 W.L148 (1785) the court said that debts were contracted on the "faith" of a security. In The Ship Emperor, 15 Fed. Cas. 508 (1785) the court opined that: "[t]he money advanced ought to be solely on the faith of the hypothecation and not on any personal credit." In In re Barnet, 1 U.S. 152, (1785) the Court equated "faith" with the honesty of a deponent. In Purviance v. Angus, 1 U.S. 180 (1876) the Court identified "good faith" with integrity.

[1108] 531 U.S. 497 (2001).

[1109] Though the case was filed in state court it was removed to federal court on federal question grounds (as diversity no longer exited), but then it was remanded to state court.

year statute of limitations the claim would have been timely filed. Rather than applying that three-year statute of limitations, however, the Maryland state court dismissed the plaintiff's action based on the preclusive effect of the federal law of *res judicata* as determined by the California federal District Court. When that case got to the U.S. Supreme Court, on Plaintiff's Petition for Certiorari, both parties thought that this was a full faith and credit case. The Supreme Court disagreed. Justice Antonin Scalia writing for the Court, said that neither the Clause nor its implementing statute addressed the issue involved.[1110]

The Court, did not mention *United States v. Kimball Foods, Inc.*,[1111] another case which might appear to be, at first glance, a full faith and credit case, but was not. The Court in *Semtek* did exactly what the Court in *Kimbell Foods* did. It developed a Rule of Decision. Even though Justice Scalia said it would not be a uniform Rule,[1112] it was just that - a uniform rule - to be applied throughout the United States, but one the details of which are made up of the laws of the states, whether the court is a state court, or a federal court, sitting in that state. The Rule does not pertain to preclusive effect, as the Defendant-Respondent thought it should, but of stale claims (statutes of limitations). In other words the Rule of Decision constructed by the Court was that wherever a case is tried in this country, and whether in state or federal court, the same rule applies; the statute of limitations of the state in which the court (state or federal) sits, determines whether the claim has been brought too late.[1113]

[1110] *Semtek,* 531 U.S at 506, 507.

[1111] 440 U.S. 715 (1979) (a case in which the Court developed a Rule of Decision to be applied throughout the United States, to the effect that the terms of federal consensual liens acquired when the United States loaned money, would be structured locally, according to the terms that had been applied successfully in that location.

[1112] *Id.* at 508.

[1113] *Id.* at 509. The Court went so far in tracing Kimbell Foods, without specifically mentioning it, to the extent that that it made certain that federal reference to state law will not obtain where state law is incompatible with federal interests. That is identical to the Court's announcement in Kimbell Foods to the effect that state law regarding such consensual liens would be replaced with other law if needed "to vindicate important national interests." Kimbell Foods, 440 U.S. at 740.

Another subject which should be covered before leaving full faith and credit is choice-of-law. If one reads only *Erie R. Co. v. Tompkins*,[1114] which never mentioned full faith and credit and its follow-on, *Klaxton v. Stentor Electrice Co.*[1115] which distinguished a case that did use the doctrine, one might get the impression that full faith and credit does not figure into the choice-of-law framework. Nothing could be further from the truth.

An excellent example of how full faith and credit applies when courts are confronted with choice-of-law problems is *Phillips Petroleum Co. v. Shutts.*[1116] Phillips Petroleum was a Delaware corporation, headquartered in Oklahoma. Among other things, it purchased natural gas in eleven states. There were royalty owners in 50 states, the District of Columbia and several foreign countries. Twenty-nine thousand of them filed a class action against Phillips Petroleum in Kansas state court, seeking interest on payments Phillips made on their royalties. The Kansas court determined that it was proper for it to use Kansas substantive law in resolving these disputes, and the Kansas Supreme Court affirmed. The U.S. Supreme Court, the then Justice William H. Rehnquist, writing the Opinion of the Court, held that the determination of the Kansas court violated the Full Faith and Credit Clause.

The Kansas Supreme Court had said the there were no "compelling reasons" for the Kansas trial court in this class action to look to "other state laws to determine the rights of the parties involved in this action."[1117] Justice Rehnquist said that the Supreme Court thought that such was a "bootstrape" argument. The Kansas class-action statute, like those of most other jurisdictions, requires that there be "common issues of law or fact." While a State, however, may assume jurisdiction over the claims of plaintiffs whose principal contacts are with other States, it may not use that assumption of jurisdiction as an added weight in the scale when considering the permissible constitutional limits on choice of substantive law. It may not take a transaction with little or no relationship to the forum and apply the law of the forum in order to satisfy the procedural requirement that there be a "common question of law." The issue of personal jurisdiction over plaintiffs in a class action is entirely distinct from the question of the constitutional

---

[1114] 304 U.S. 64 (1938).

[1115] 313 U. S. 487 (1941).

[1116] 472 U.S. 797 (1985).

[1117] *Id.* at 821.

limitations on choice-of-law; the latter calculus is not altered by the fact that it may be more difficult or more burdensome to comply with the constitutional limitations because of the large number of transactions which the State proposes to adjudicate and which have little connection with the forum.

Justice Rehnquist added that Kansas must have a "significant contact or significant aggregation of contacts" to the claims asserted by each member of the plaintiff class. He specified that those contacts must create "state interests," in order to ensure that the choice of Kansas law is not arbitrary or unfair. Given Kansas' lack of "interest" in claims unrelated to that State, and the substantive conflicts with states such as those of Texas, the Court concluded that application of Kansas law to every claim in the case is sufficiently arbitrary and unfair as to exceed constitutional limits. The Court, of course, would not undertake to determine what substantive law must be applied, leaving, an intriguing question to be, perhaps, decided by other Supreme Courts, in the future..

Justice Rehnquist summarized the Court's holding with the following words:

> When considering fairness in this context, an important element is the expectation of the parties. (citation omitted). There is no indication that when the leases involving land and royalty owners outside of Kansas were executed, the parties had any idea that Kansas law would control. Neither the Due Process Clause nor the Full Faith and Credit Clause requires Kansas "to substitute for its own [laws], applicable to persons and events within it, the conflicting statute of another state," *Pacific Employees* [sic] *Ins. Co. v. Industrial Accident Comm'n,* 306 U.S. 493, 502, 59 S.Ct. 629, 633, 83 L.Ed. 940 (1939),[1118] but Kansas 'may not abrogate the rights of parties beyond its borders having no relation to anything done or to be done within them.'[1119]

In the first Chapter of this lexicon we asked, what do the words "full faith and credit" really mean. We reviewed the attempts of the Articles of Confederation's architects to help construct a nation out of a few fledging and separate sovereignties. The framers of the Constitution followed their efforts. The framers'

[1118] *See supra* text accompanying notes 72, 213, 401, 416, and 440.

[1119] *Shutts*, 472 U.S. at 822.

efforts succeeded in establishing a federalism form of government.[1120] As our nation developed, its new members, as well as its original members, all subscribed to the concept of federalism developed by the framers.[1121] Judges and lawyers over the years added new and intriguing meaning to those words. But what do those words really mean? The work of the founders was not without some flaws. Isn't it unfortunate that because of full faith and credit at times a court must accept a legally incorrect decision made by a prior court?[1122] There are at least thirty-two situations, to which full faith and credit does not apply.[1123] But doesn't the overall achievement justify the effort? Do not the words "full faith and credit" fit along these lines: "I don't ask you to do it my way. But if I do it my way, I ask you to respect my doing it my way." Isn't that the American way? Isn't that what federalism and "full faith and credit" really mean?

[1120] *See* RICHARD H.W. MALOY, FEDERALISM AS SEEN BY THE U.S. SUPREME COURT, Vandeplas Publishing (2008).

[1121] As Justice John Paul Stevens gave but one example under Art. I, Clause 1 of the Constitution in Nevada v. Hall, 440 U.S. 410, 425 (1979), "[w]hile sovereign nations are free to levy discriminatory taxes on the goods of other nations or to bar their entry altogether, the States of the Union are not."

[1122] As an example, in Fauntleroy v. Lum. 210 U.S. 230 (1908) a Mississippi court was required to give a Missouri judgment full faith and credit, even though it represented an absurd version of Mississippi law due to a mistake of some Mississippi arbitrators. For further consideration of Fauntleroy *see* the list of citations of that case contained in the Table of Cases.9.

[1123] *See supra* text accompanying notes 258-458 and *see* further Hirschkorn v. Hait 2008 WL 695892, at *7 (N.J. Super A.D 2008: Minnesota, State of v. Northern Securities Co., 194 U.S. 48 (1904) 23, 24: OIAC Cml. Assets, LLC v. Stonegate Village, LP, 2009 W.L.2182601 at * 3 (D. Ariz. 2009): Prashad v. Copeland 685 S.E.2d 199, 204 (Va. App. 2009).

Chapter II
Privileges / Immunities

A. In General

Article IV, § 2 cl. 1 of the U.S. Constitution provides the "[t]he citizens of each state shall be entitled to all Privileges and Immunities of Citizens in the several States."

Chief Justice Fred Vinson once wrote, in *Toomer v. Witsell*[1124] that:

> The primary purpose of this clause, like the clauses between which it is located-those relating to full faith and credit and to interstate extradition of fugitives from justice-was to help fuse into one Nation a collection of independent, sovereign States. It was designed to insure to a citizen of State A who ventures into State B the same privileges which the citizens of State B enjoy. For protection of such equality the citizen of State A was not to be restricted to the uncertain remedies afforded by diplomatic processes and official retaliation.[1125]

What is a "privilege.? What is an "immunity"? The courts have not, in one case, attempted to define either term. Early in the history of the U.S. Supreme Court it explained why it would not do so. In *Conner v. Elliott*[1126] a young lady, native born citizen of Louisiana married, in Mississippi a citizen of Mississippi, where she and her husband resided for their entire married life. During that marriage the husband acquired considerable property in Louisiana, which he titled in his own name, to the exclusion of his wife. Upon his death his widow claimed an interest in that property, though the statutes of Louisiana did not support her

---

[1124] 334 U.S. 385 (1948). *See infra* text accompanying notes 1125, 1160, 1230, 1368, 1369 for additional reference to this case.

[1125] *Id.* at 395.

[1126] 59 U.S. 591 (1855). *See infra* text accompanying notes 1127-1129 concerning additional reference to this case.

application;[1127] and a Louisiana court held against her. The U.S. Supreme Court affirmed. Justice Benjamin R. Curtis, writing the Opinion of the Court, spent considerable time discussing Article IV, § 2 of the U.S. Constitution quoted above. He said that no privileges are secured by the Constitution, except those which are claimed by persons having the citizenship of the place offering the privileges.[1128] The widow's citizenship during the marriage was in Mississippi not in Louisiana. While Justice Curtis did not allege that Mississippi law would apply, he dealt with Mississippi law of contracts at some length. That place, in this case, was Mississippi where the contract of marriage was executed, and apparently performed. Curtis gave, as his explanation why the Court did not attempt a definition of "privileges."

> We do not deem it needful to attempt to define the meaning of the word privileges in this clause of the constitution. It is safer, and more in accordance with the duty of a judicial tribunal, to leave its meaning to be determined, in each case, upon a view of the particular rights asserted and denied therein. And especially is this true, when we are dealing with so broad a provision, involving matters not only of great delicacy and importance, but which are of such a character, that any merely abstract definition could scarcely be correct; and a failure to make it so would certainly produce mischief.[1129]

Though the Court did not define "privileges" in the *Conner* case, in *Strauder v. State of West Virginia*[1130] it defined "immunity" as a right to be immune from "inequality of legal protection, either for life, liberty, or property."[1131] In other cases it has identified the entities which are capable of providing or denying a

---

[1127] One statute provided that unless parties were married in Louisiana community ownership would not apply to property they acquired during their marriage. The other was a bit more lenient. It provided that even if the parties were not married in Louisiana community ownership would apply only if they took up residence in that state, after their marriage in another state.

[1128] *Id.* at 593.

[1129] *Id.*

[1130] 100 U.S. (10 Otto) 303 (1879). *See infra* text accompanying notes 1031, 1194, 1197 for additional reference to this case.

[1131] *Id.* at 310.

privilege or immunity, e.g. a public ship;[1132] a territory; [1133] Indian tribes;[1134] an inn or hotel[1135] purchasers of property;[1136] currency; [1137] treaties;[1138] slaves;[1139] a foreign nation;[1140] lessees of a university;[1141] officers of a bank;[1142] states;[1143] and a theater.[1144]There have been several U.S. Supreme Court decisions, that while not attempting a quotable definition of the term have given it considerable attention. We shall consider those decisions.

The Constitution uses another other word, the meaning of which is important, i.e. "citizen," for that word proclaims who are entitled to privileges and immunities. That same provision, Article. IV, § 2, cl 1, of the Constitution as originally drafted, provided, as it does today, that "[t]he Citizens of each State shall be entitled to all Privileges and Immunities of Citizens in the several States." One of those privileges and immunities is the right to sue in United States courts pursuant to Article III, § 2, cl. 1, of the Constitution. The U.S. Supreme Court in 1839 decided in *Bank of Augusta v. Earle*[1145] that a bank was not a citizen.[1146] It

---

[1132] The Santissima Trinidad, 20 U.S. 283, 337 (1822).

[1133] American Ins. Co. v. 355 Bales of Cotton, 26 U.S. 511, 517 (1828).

[1134] Cherokee Nation v. State of Georgia, 30 U.S. 1, 12 (1831).

[1135] The Civil Rights Cases, 109 U.S. 3, 4 (1883). *See infra* text accompanying notes 1144, 1198-1200, 1356, 1357, 1402-1407 concerning additional reference to this case.

[1136] Hughes v. Trustees of Town of Clarksville, 31 U.S. 369, 606 (1832).

[1137] Briscoe v. Comm'wlth of Kentucky, 36 U.S. 257, 291 (1837).

[1138] Pollard's Heirs v. Kibbe, 39 U.S. 353 (1840).

[1139] Groves v. Slaughter, 40 U.S. 449 , 449, passin (1841).

[1140] The Armistead, 40 U.S. 518, 595 (1841).

[1141] Smith v. Hunter, 48 U.S. 738, 741 (1844).

[1142] Prentice v. Zane' Administrator, 49 U.S. 473, 476 (1850).

[1143] Webster v. Reid, 52 U.S. 437, 452 (1850).

[1144] The Civil Rights Cases, 109 U.S. 3, 4 (1883).

[1145] 38 U.S. (13 Pet.) 519, 606 (1839) (Chief Justice Roger B. Taney writing the Opinion of the unanimous court).

[1146] As an interesting side-light to that decision, is Metropolitan Life Ins. Co v. Ward, 470 U.S. 869, 884 (1985) in which a party based its argument on equal protection (*see infra*

decided, in *Strader v. Graham*[1147] that a slave, who resides in a State authorizing slavery is brought into a State forbidding slavery, and then returned to the original State has not gained freedom, because his status is determined by the State of his residence.[1148] Chief Justice Roger B. Taney wrote the Opinion of a unanimous Court, which has been cited without criticism, 52 times, 8 of which appeared before *Dred Scott v. Sanford* was decided.[1149]

Of course, as it was stated in *Howlett By and Through Howlett v. Rose*[1150] a State may not evade the strictures of the Privileges and Immunities Clause by denying jurisdiction to a court otherwise competent.[1151]

Before beginning our in-depth analysis of "privileges and immunities" we should, even if ever so briefly, refer to another word important to our pursuit – recidivism. Justice O'Connor in *Parke v. Raley*[1152] expressed the thought that: "we have repeatedly upheld recidicism statutes against contentions that they violate constitutional strictures dealing with double jeopardy, *ex post facto* laws, cruel and unusual punishment, due process, equal protection, and privileges and immunities." [1153]

B. Privileges and Immunities Under Article IV. § 2, cl. 1

Article IV, § 2 provides that "[t]he Citizens of each State shall be entitled to all Privileges and Immunities of Citizens in the several States."

---

notes 1377 to 1548) rather than privileges and immunities because it, being a corporation. not authorized to do business in the forum state, was not a "citizen," entitled to privileges and immunities protection. *See also* Hemphill v. Orloff, 277 U.S. 537, 548-550 (1928).

1147 51 U.S. (10 How.) 82 (1850).

1148 *Id.* at 99.

1149 Sixteen years before Strader was decided the Connecticut Supreme Court in Crandall v. State, 10 Conn. Rep.340, 340 (Conn. 1834) had decided that even though slavery was not permitted in Connecticut, slaves could not be citizens of that state.

1150 496 U.S. 356 (1990).

1151 *Id.* at 382.

1152 506 U.S. 20 (1992).

1153 *Id.* at 27.

In *Paul v. Virginia*[1154] Justice Stephen J. Field wrote that the object of the Privileges and Immunities Clause is to "strongly ... constitute the citizens of the United States one people," by "plac[ing] the citizens of each State upon the same footing with citizens of other States, so far as the advantages resulting from citizenship in those States are concerned."[1155]

In *Blake v. McClung*[1156] it was established that the Privileges and Immunities clause entitles persons to use states, other than their places of residence, to ply their trade.[1157]

Perhaps Justice Sandra Day O'Connor, in *Lunding v. New York Tax AppealsTribunal,*[1158] most clearly expressed not only the object of Privileges and Immunities, but the significance of the Clause's term "citizens" in the following words:

> The object of the Privileges and Immunities Clause is to "strongly ... constitute the citizens of the United States one people," by "plac[ing] the citizens of each State upon the same footing with citizens of other States, so far as the advantages resulting from citizenship in those States are concerned."[1159] One right thereby secured is the right of a citizen of any State to "remove to and carry on business in another without being subjected in property or person to taxes more onerous than the citizens of the latter State are subjected to."[1160]

[1154] 75 U.S. (8 Wall.) 168 (1868). *See infra* text accompanying notes 1155, 1159, 1288, 1289, 1386-1388 in which this case is further considered.

[1155] *Id.* at 180.

[1156] 172 U.S. 239 (1898).

[1157] *Id.* at 248-256. (*See also Blake v. McClung,* 172 U.S. 239, 248-256 1898).

[1158] 522 U.S.287 (1998). *See infra* text accompanying notes 1160, 1228-1230 concerning other considerations of this case.

[1159] She referred to *Paul v. Virginia,* (8 Wall.) 168, 180, 19 L.Ed. 357 (1868). as authority for that statement.

[1160] Lunding, 522 U.S. at 296. She referred to Shaffer v. Carter, 252 U.S. 37, 56 (1920), regarding the final quotation, and to *Toomer v. Witsell,* 334 U.S. 385, 396, 68 S.Ct. 1156, 1162, 92 L.Ed. 1460 (1948); *Ward v. Maryland,* 12 Wall. 418, 430, 20 L.Ed. 449 (1871) as further reference.

Dred Scott v. Sanford[1161] was the first and most dramatic of the U.S. Supreme Court's dissertations on the meaning of "citizen" and "citizenship." In that case the plaintiff, Scott and his wife, Harriet, were both persons of African dissent, born into slavery by parents, also slaves. The Scotts, residents of Missouri, attempted to gain their freedom by bringing a legal action in Missouri, which upon appeal to the Missouri Supreme Court resulted in their being denied of the relief they sought, They thereupon filed in the United States Circuit Court, at that time a trial court, seeking the same relief. The Missouri state case which had been remanded to the trial court, was held in abeyance until the U.S. Circuit Court case had been concluded. The Circuit Court, took jurisdiction of the case and entered a judgment in favor of the defendant. The U.S. Supreme Court reversed the Circuit Court on the ground that no judgment could be entered in it because that court did not have jurisdiction of the cause since the Scotts were not citizens of Missouri, the state in which the trial court was situated. Chief Justice Roger B. Taney and seven Justices believed that persons of African descent could not become citizens. Their reasons were not because persons of African descent were unworthy of that privilege and immunity. Their reason was that the framers of the U.S. Constitution held those persons in low esteem, and in the document they constructed (the Constitution) they prevented persons, most of whom were slaves, living on plantations, from ever achieving such privilege and immunity. Taney has been wrongly accused of writing derogatorily of people he honored and befriended. Of course Taney made a mistake in his Opinion of the Court; but it was not of his heart. His mistake was of the law, of the manner in which the Constitution should be interpreted.

He made clear the function of his Court in deciding whether slaves were intended to be included in the Constitution by its framers:

> It is not the province of the court to decide upon the justice or injustice, the policy or impolicy, of these laws. The decision of that question belonged to the political or law-making power; to those who formed the sovereignty and framed the Constitution. The duty of the court is, to interpret the instrument they have framed, with the best lights we can obtain on the subject, and to administer it as we find it, according to its true intent and meaning when it was adopted.[1162]

1161 60 U.S. 393 (1857). *See infra* text accompanying notes 1162-1201, 1335 for further reference to this case.

1162 *Id.* at 405.

The following two paragraphs are, in essence, the Court's analysis of the power of States, concerning citizenship, which existed pursuant to the Constitution, and the Acts of Congress enacted under the Constitution's supremacy:

> [T]hat no State can, by any act or law of its own, passed since the adoption of the Constitution, introduce a new member into the political community created by the Constitution of the United States. It cannot make him a member of this community by making him a member of its own. And for the same reason it cannot introduce any person, or description of persons, who were not intended to be embraced in this new political family, which the Constitution brought into existence, but were intended to be excluded from it.[1163]

> In discussing this question, we must not confound the rights of citizenship which a State may confer within its own limits, and the rights of citizenship as a member of the Union. It does not by any means follow, because he has all the rights and privileges of a citizen of a State, that he must be a citizen of the United States. He may have all of the rights and privileges of the citizen of a State, and yet not be entitled to the rights and privileges of a citizen in any other State. For, previous to the adoption of the Constitution of the United States, every State had the undoubted right to confer on whomsoever it pleased the character of citizen, and to endow him with all its rights. But this character of course was confined to the boundaries of the State, and gave him no rights or privileges in other States beyond those secured to him by the laws of nations and the comity of States. Nor have the several States surrendered the power of conferring these rights and privileges by adopting the Constitution of the United States.[1164]

Taney in the next three paragraphs alludes to the fact that at the time of the decision, 1857, the status of people of African descent, and the respect they then received had considerably improved over that at the time the Declaration of

[1163] *Id.* at 406.

[1164] *Id.*

Independence was written, 1776, the Constitution was drafted, 1787, ratified, 1788, and became effective, 1789.

> It is true, every person, and every class and description of persons, who were at the time of the adoption of the Constitution recognized as citizens in the several States, became also citizens of this new political body; but none other; it was formed by them, and for them and their posterity, but for no one else. And the personal rights and privileges guaranteed to citizens of this new sovereignty were intended to embrace those only who were then members of the several State communities, or who should afterwards by birthright or otherwise become members, according to the provisions of the Constitution and the principles on which it was founded. It was the union of those who were at that time members of distinct and separate political communities into one political family, whose power, for certain specified purposes, was to extend over the whole territory of the United States. And it gave to each citizen rights and privileges outside of his State . . . which he did not before possess, and placed him in every other State upon a perfect equality with its own citizens as to rights of person and rights of property; it made him a citizen of the United States.[1165]
>
> In the opinion of the court, the legislation and histories of the times, and the language used in the Declaration of Independence, show, that neither the class of persons who had been imported as slaves, nor their descendants, whether they had become free or not, were then acknowledged as a part of the people, nor intended to be included in the general words used in that memorable instrument.[1166]
>
> It is difficult at this day to realize the state of public opinion in relation to that unfortunate race, which prevailed in the civilized and enlightened portions of the world at the time of the Declaration of Independence, and when the Constitution of the United States was framed and adopted. But the public history of every European nation displays it in a manner too plain to be mistaken.[1167]

[1165] *Id.* 406, 407.

[1166] *Id.* at 407.

[1167] *Id.*

He referred to statutes enacted by Maryland, a State which approved of slavery, and Massachusetts, a State which did not. Neither of them were complimentary to the status of the people of African descent.

> We give both of these laws in the words used by the respective legislative bodies, because the language in which they are framed, as well as the provisions contained in them, show, too plainly to be misunderstood, the degraded condition of this unhappy race. They were still in force when the Revolution began, and are a faithful index to the state of feeling towards the class of persons of whom they speak, and of the position they occupied throughout the thirteen colonies, in the eyes and thoughts of the men who framed the Declaration of Independence and established the State Constitutions and Governments. They show that a perpetual and impassable barrier was intended to be erected between the white race and the one which they had reduced to slavery, and governed as subjects with absolute and despotic power, and which they then looked upon as so far below them in the scale of created beings, that intermarriages between white persons and negroes or mulattoes were regarded as unnatural and immoral, and punished as crimes, not only in the parties, but in the person who joined them in marriage. And no distinction in this respect was made between the free negro or mulatto and the slave, but this stigma, of the deepest degradation, was fixed upon the whole race.[1168]

Chief Justice Taney then quoted from, and discussed, the Declaration of Independence and how, even though drawn by men of distinction, in the language it used, was clearly understood in its day, though, at the time of the *Dred Scott* decision, completely deceiving, as allowing the supposition that the draftsmen of the Declaration of Independence really thought that all men were created equal.

> We hold these truths to be self-evident: that all men are created equal; that they are endowed by their Creator with certain unalienable rights; that among them is life, liberty, and the pursuit of happiness; that to secure these rights, Governments are instituted, deriving their just powers from the consent of the governed.[1169]

[1168] *Id.* at 409.

[1169] *Id.* at 410.

> The general words above quoted would seem to embrace the whole human family, and if they were used in a similar instrument at this day would be so understood. But it is too clear for dispute, that the enslaved African race were not intended to be included, and formed no part of the people who framed and adopted this declaration; for if the language, as understood in that day, would embrace them, the conduct of the distinguished men who framed the Declaration of Independence would have been utterly and flagrantly inconsistent with the principles they asserted; and instead of the sympathy of mankind, to which they so confidently appealed, they would have deserved and received universal rebuke and reprobation.[1170]

> [T]he men who framed this declaration were great men-high in literary acquirements-high in their sense of honor, and incapable of asserting principles inconsistent with those on which they were acting. They perfectly understood the meaning of the language they used, and how it would be understood by others; and they knew that it would not in any part of the civilized world be supposed to embrace the negro race, which, by common consent, had been excluded from civilized Governments and the family of nations, and doomed to slavery. They spoke and acted according to the then established doctrines and principles, and in the ordinary language of the day, and no one misunderstood them. The unhappy black race were separated from the white by indelible marks, and laws long before established, and were never thought of or spoken of except as property, and when the claims of the owner or the profit of the trader were supposed to need protection.[1171]

Taney then stressed that there was no change in Caucasians' false impression of African inferiority from the time its people were imported into the western hemisphere between the Seventeenth Century and the adoption of the Constitution.

> This state of public opinion had undergone no change when the Constitution was adopted, as is equally evident from its provisions and language.[1172]

[1170] *Id.*

[1171] *Id.*

[1172] *Id.*

The condition in which people of African descent were held by the States leaves no reason to doubt the veracity of his words.

> Indeed, when we look to the condition of this race in the several States at the time, it is impossible to believe that these rights and privileges were intended to be extended to them.[1173]
>
> It is very true, that in that portion of the Union where the labor of the negro race was found to be unsuited to the climate and unprofitable to the master, but few slaves were held at the time of the Declaration of Independence; and when the Constitution was adopted, it had entirely worn out in one of them,[1174] and measures had been taken for its gradual abolition in several others. But this change had not been produced by any change of opinion in relation to this race; but because it was discovered, from experience, that slave labor was unsuited to the climate and productions of these States: for some of the States, where it had ceased or nearly ceased to exist, were actively engaged in the slave trade, procuring cargoes on the coast of Africa, and transporting them for sale to those parts of the Union where their labor was found to be profitable, and suited to the climate and productions. And this traffic was openly carried on, and fortunes accumulated by it, without reproach from the people of the States where they resided. And it can hardly be supposed that, in the States where it was then countenanced in its worst form-that is, in the seizure and transportation-the people could have regarded those who were emancipated as entitled to equal rights with themselves.[1175]
>
> The legislation of the States therefore shows, in a manner not to be mistaken, the inferior and subject condition of that race at the time the Constitution was adopted, and long afterwards, throughout the thirteen States by which that instrument was framed; and it is hardly consistent with the respect due to these States, to suppose that they regarded at that time, as fellow-citizens and members of the sovereignty, a class of beings

---

[1173] *Id.* at 412.

[1174] He probably is referring to Vermont, which though not becoming a state until March 4, 1791, abolished slavery in 1777, when Vermont was still a Territory.

[1175] *Id.*

whom they had thus stigmatized; whom, as we are bound, out of respect to the State sovereignties, to assume they had deemed it just and necessary thus to stigmatize, and upon whom they had impressed such deep and enduring marks of inferiority and degradation; or, that when they met in convention to form the Constitution, they looked upon them as a portion of their constituents,[1176] or designed to include them in the provisions so carefully inserted for the security and protection of the liberties and rights of their citizens.[1177] It cannot be supposed that they intended to secure to them rights, and privileges, and rank, in the new political body throughout the Union, which every one of them denied within the limits of its own dominion. More especially, it cannot be believed that the large slaveholding States[1178] regarded them as included in the word citizens, or would have consented to a Constitution which might compel them to receive them in that character from another State. For if they were so received, and entitled to the privileges and immunities of citizens, it would exempt them from the operation of the special laws and from the police regulations which they considered to be necessary for their own safety.[1179] It would give to persons of the negro race, who were recognized as citizens in any one State of the Union, the right to enter every other State whenever they pleased, singly or in companies, without pass or passport, and without obstruction, to sojourn there as long as they pleased, to go where they pleased at every hour of the day or night without molestation, unless they committed some violation of law for which a white man would be punished; and it would give them the full liberty of speech in public and in private upon all subjects upon which its own citizens might speak; to hold public meetings upon political affairs, and to keep and carry arms wherever they went. And all of this would be done in the face of the subject race of the same color, both free and slaves, and inevitably producing discontent and insubordination among them, and endangering the peace and safety of the State.[1180]

[1176] He is referring to the despicable "three fifths" provision of the Constitution's Art I, § 2, cl.3.

[1177] He is referring to the Constitution's Art. IV, § 2, cl. 3.

[1178] He was probably referring to Virginia, North Carolina and South Carolina.

[1179] He is referring to Art. III, § 2, cl.3.

[1180] *Id.* at 416, 417.

Possibly realizing the non-Slave States' distain of the Court's holding he suggested a sure method of altering that holding – amendment of the Constitution, a rectifying change that did not come about until the year 1865 when the Thirteenth Amendment was adopted, and the year 1868 when the first sentence of § 1 of the Fourteenth Amendment was adopted. The courts are not permitted to amend Constitutions or statutes; only the people may do that.

> If any of its provisions are deemed unjust, there is a mode prescribed in the instrument itself by which it may be amended; but while it remains unaltered, it must be construed now as it was understood at the time of its adoption. It is not only the same in words, but the same in meaning, and delegates the same powers to the Government, and reserves and secures the same rights and privileges to the citizen; and as long as it continues to exist in its present form, it speaks not only in the same words, but with the same meaning and intent with which it spoke when it came from the hands of its framers, and was voted on and adopted by the people of the United States. Any other rule of construction would abrogate the judicial character of this court, and make it the mere reflex of the popular opinion or passion of the day. This court was not created by the Constitution for such purposes. Higher and graver trusts have been confided to it, and it must not falter in the path of duty.[1181]

> [T]he power of Congress over the person or property of a citizen can never be a mere discretionary power under our Constitution and form of Government. The powers of the Government and the rights and privileges of the citizen are regulated and plainly defined by the Constitution itself.[1182]

> [I]n considering the question before us, it must be borne in mind that there is no law of nations standing between the people of the United States and their Government, and interfering with their relation to each other. The powers of the Government, and the rights of the citizen under it, are positive and practical regulations plainly written down. The people of the United States have delegated to it certain enumerated powers, and

---

[1181] *Id.* at 426.

[1182] *Id.* at 449.

> forbidden it to exercise others. It has no power over the person or property of a citizen but what the citizens of the United States have granted. And no laws or usages of other nations, or reasoning of statesmen or jurists upon the relations of master and slave, can enlarge the powers of the Government, or take from the citizens the rights they have reserved. And if the Constitution recognizes the right of property of the master in a slave, and makes no distinction between that description of property and other property owned by a citizen, no tribunal, acting under the authority of the United States, whether it be legislative, executive, or judicial, has a right to draw such a distinction, or deny to it the benefit of the provisions and guarantees which have been provided for the protection of private property against the encroachments of the Government.[1183]
>
> [A]s we have already said in an earlier part of this opinion, upon a different point, the right of property in a slave is distinctly and expressly affirmed in the Constitution. The right to traffic in it, like an ordinary article of merchandise and property, was guarantied to the citizens of the United States, in every State that might desire it, for twenty years.[1184] And the Government in express terms is pledged to protect it in all future time, if the slave escapes from his owner. This is done in plain words-too plain to be misunderstood.[1185] And no word can be found in the Constitution which gives Congress a greater power over slave property, or which entitles property of that kind to less protection that property of any other description. The only power conferred is the power coupled with the duty of guarding and protecting the owner in his rights.[1186]

Chief Justice Taney was saying that the Constitution's reference to citizenship, not having been amended in that regard, must be interpreted in words that came from the drafters, with all that Constitution's deducible nuances. He was not an enemy of the people of African descent. He did not believe in slavery; he was a very religious man[1187] He was not a slaveholder. In fact having inherited slaves

---

[1183] *Id.* at 451.

[1184] He is referring to the Constitution's Art. I, § 9, cl. 1 and cl. 4, and the second part of Art. V.

[1185] He is referring to Art. IV, § 2, cl. 3.

[1186] *Id.* at 451, 452.

[1187] He was a devout Roman Catholic.

from his father,[1188] he soon set them free, with the exception of two who were too old to support themselves. He pensioned those two so that they could live comfortably for the remainder of their lives.[1189] Possibly to set the record straight concerning false assertions circulated about him, he wrote to a friend on August 19, 1857:

> I am not a slaveowner. More than thirty years ago I manumitted every slave I ever owned, except two, who were too old when they became my property, to provide for themselves. Those two I supported in comfort as long as they lived.[1190]

Yes, he did make a mistake – he interpreted the word "citizen" as a large number of the Constitution's framers would have interpreted in at the time of the framing of the Constitution, not at the time the Court interpreted those words. He was of the opinion, apparently, that when all words are used in the Constitution are examined, they must be interpreted as the framers understood them. It was not within his concept of construction of writings, that some words used in the documents under examination, must not be so interpreted, but must be interpreted as they are understood at the time that they are being examined.

That Chief Justice Taney's words did not proclaim his opinion of African descent, but those held by a majority of the framers of the U.S. Constitution is confirmed by Justice William Strong, when in *Strauder v. State of West Virginia*[1191] stated that:

> This is one of a series of constitutional provisions[1192] having a common purpose; namely, securing to a race recently emancipated, a race that through many generations had been held in slavery, all the civil rights that the superior race enjoy. The true spirit and meaning of the amendments, as

---

[1188] The Taneys lived in Maryland, where slavery was permitted.

[1189] CHARLES W. SMITH, JR., ROGER B. TANEY: JACKSONIAN JURIST, 141, 142 (1936).

[1190] Letter to Samuel Nott, Proceedings of the Massachusetts Historical Society, XII, 447.

[1191] 100 U.S. (10 Otto) 303 (1879).

[1192] He was referring to the so-called "Civil War Amendments," to wit: the Thirteenth, Fourteenth and Fifteenth.

> we said in the *Slaughter-House Cases* (16 Wall. 36),[1193] cannot be understood without keeping in view the history of the times when they were adopted, and the general objects they plainly sought to accomplish. At the time when they were incorporated into the Constitution, it required little knowledge of human nature to anticipate that those who had long been regarded as an inferior and subject race would, when suddenly raised to the rank of citizenship, be looked upon with jealousy and positive dislike, and that State laws might be enacted or enforced to perpetuate the distinctions that had before existed. Discriminations against them had been habitual. It was well known that in some States laws making such discriminations then existed, and others might well be expected. The colored race, as a race, was abject and ignorant, and in that condition was unfitted to command the respect of those who had superior intelligence. Their training had left them mere children, and as such they needed the protection which a wise government extends to those who are unable to protect themselves. They especially needed protection against unfriendly action in the States where they were resident. It was in view of these considerations the Fourteenth Amendment was framed and adopted. It was designed to assure to the colored race the enjoyment of all the civil rights that under the law are enjoyed by white persons, and to give to that race the protection of the general government, in that enjoyment, whenever it should be denied by the States. It not only gave citizenship and the privileges of citizenship to persons of color, but it denied to any State the power to withhold from them the equal protection of the laws, and authorized Congress to enforce its provisions by appropriate legislation.[1194]

By his utterances in *The Civil Rights Cases*[1195] U.S. Supreme Court Justice Joseph P. Bradley also gave a lucid description of the persecution inflicted upon people of African descent by Caucasians of that era:

> The long existence of African slavery in this country gave us very distinct notions of what it was, and what were its necessary incidents. Compulsory service of the slave for the benefit of the master, restraint of his

---

[1193] *See infra* text accompanying notes 1290-1347, 1366, 1389, and 1390 for additional consideration of this case.

[1194] *Strauder*, 100 U.S. at 306, 307.

[1195] 109 U.S. 3 (1883).

> movements except by the master's will, disability to hold property, to make contracts, to have a standing in court, to be a witness against a white person, and such like burdens and incapacities were the inseparable incidents of the institution. Severer punishments for crimes were imposed on the slave than on free persons guilty of the same offenses.[1196]
>
> There were thousands of free colored people in this country before the abolition of slavery, enjoying all the essential rights of life, liberty, and property the same as white citizens; yet no one, at that time, thought that it was any invasion of their personal *status* as freemen because they were not admitted to all the privileges enjoyed by white citizens, or because they were subjected to discriminations in the enjoyment of accommodations in inns, public conveyances, and places of amusement. Mere discriminations on account of race or color were not regarded as badges of slavery. If, since that time, the enjoyment of equal rights in all these respects has become established by constitutional enactment, it is not by force of the thirteenth amendment, (which merely abolishes slavery,) but by force of the fourteenth and fifteenth amendments.[1197]

Where the otherwise brilliant jurist, and those six[1198] Justices who agreed with him, made a mistake was in interpreting the word "citizen" as the framers used it. He acknowledged that at least some of the people of the United States, at the time of his constructing the *Dred Scott* Opinion, did not agree with the lowborn opinion of people of African descent held by the framers,[1199] and Taney acknowledged that even by the time that the Articles of Confederation was ratified North Carolina had joined New Hampshire, Massachusetts, New York and New Jersey in granting citizenship to all free, native-born inhabitants, as well as voting rights if they had the necessary qualifications of all other persons, even if descended from African slaves.[1200] He felt compelled, however, to follow the opinions held by a majority of the framers in 1787. U.S. Supreme Court Justice Stephen Breyer refers to jurists

---

[1196] *Id.* at 22.

[1197] *Id.* at 25.

[1198] All six wrote Opinions – James M. Wayne (*id.* 454-457), Samuel Nelson (*id.* 457-469), Robert C. Grier (*id.* 469), Peter V. Daniel (*id.* 469-493), John A. Campbell (*id.* 493-518), John Catron (*id.* 518-529).

[1199] *See* Dred Scott, 60 U.S. at 404, 405, 407.

[1200] *Id.* at 572, 573.

who interpret certain words uttered in the past as being subject to no change, as "originalists."[1201] He wrote:

> The judges who follow this approach look to history to discover what those who wrote the Constitution most likely thought about the content and scope of a constitutional phrase, and they interpret the phrase accordingly.[1202]

Indeed the seven members of the majority in *Dred Scott* were "originalists." The only affirmative possibility that can be said about their ruling was that it might have delayed the Civil War. Talk of the rebellion which commenced just four years later, was prevalent not only in the eleven states which seceded,[1203] but in four others[1204] where slavery was permitted due to commercial reasons. The slaveowners were mollified, as least temporarily.

Neither of the dissenters, Justice John McLean nor Justice Benjamin M. Curtis specifically referred to the principle that the meaning of certain terms used in the Constitution, of which "citizen" and "citizenship" are two, are subject to change as time passes. The closest that McLean got to stating such truism were the following words:

> And when there is a large district of country within the United States, and not within any State Government, if it be necessary to establish a temporary Government to carry out a power expressly vested in Congress-as the disposition of the public lands-may not such Government be

---

1201 *See* STEHEN BREYER, MAKING OUR DEMOCRACY WORK, 76-80.

1202 *Id* at 76. On page 79 he points out that the Eighth Amendment, which forbids "cruel and unusual punishment" would not permit flogging a naval seaman in the twenty-first century, on the ground that flogging was common practice on eighteenth century ships. As logical as Justice Breyer's explanation seems to be, Justice Miller in United States v. Wong Kim Ark, 169 U.S. 649, 679 (1898) appears to give credence to the interpretation of such documents with which their framers were familiar.

1203 Alabama, Arkansas, Florida, Georgia, Louisiana, Mississippi, North Carolina, South Carolina, Tennessee, Texas, and Virginia.

1204 Delaware, Kentucky, Maryland and Missouri.

> instituted by Congress? How do we read the Constitution? Is it not a practical instrument?[1205]

The closest that the most often quoted dissent,[1206] that of Justice Curtis, got to stating such truism, was contained in the following words:

> If power to regulate commerce extends to an indefinite prohibition of the use of all vessels belonging to citizens of the several States, and may operate, without exception, upon every subject of commerce to which the legislative discretion may apply it, upon what grounds can I say that power to make all needful rules and regulations respecting the territory of the United States is subject to an exception of the allowance or prohibition of slavery therein?[1207]

In *Chalker v. Birmingham & Northwestern R. Co*[1208] the U.S. Supreme Court held that a Tennessee tax imposed on a citizen and resident of Alabama for engaging in the business of constructing a railroad in Tennessee violated the Privileges and Immunities Clause. The tax did not on its face draw any distinction based on citizenship or residence. It did, however, impose a higher rate on persons who had their principal offices out of State. Taking judicial notice of the fact that "the chief office of an individual is commonly in the State of which he is a citizen," the Court concluded that the practical effect of the provision was discriminatory.[1209]

In *Shaffer v. Carter*[1210] U.S. Supreme Court Justice Marlon Pitney said that a right secured by the Privileges and Immunities Clause is the right of a citizen of any State to "remove to and carry on business in another without being subjected

---

1205 *Id.* at 544. The entire dissent of Justice McLean appears at 529-564.

1206 *Id.* at 564-633.

1207 *Id.* at 623.

1208 249 U.S. 522 (1919).

1209 *Id.* at 527.

1210 252 U.S. 37 (1920). *See supra* note 1160 in which this case is mentioned, and *see infra* text accompanying notes 1214, and 1228 for further consideration of the case.

in property or person to taxes more onerous than the citizens of the latter State are subjected to."[1211]

In *Doe v. Bolton*[1212] It was established that the right to enter another State for the purpose of seeking abortion services available there is protected by the Privileges and Immunities Clause,. A woman's right to engage in interstate travel for this purpose is either entitled to special respect because she is exercising a constitutional right, or because restrictive rules in her home State may make travel to another State imperative. Federal courts are uniquely situated to protect that right for the same reason they are well suited to protect the privileges and immunities of those who enter other States to ply their trade.[1213]

In *United Bldg. and Const. Trades Council of Camden County and Vicinity v. Mayor and Council of City of Camden* [1214] the Court held that what would be unconstitutional if done directly by the State can no more readily be accomplished by a city deriving its authority from the State.[1215] Thus, even if the ordinance had been adopted solely by a city, and not pursuant to a state program or with state approval, a hiring preference would still have to comport with the Privileges and Immunities Clause.[1216] The Court, in that case, held, furthermore, that the Clause also applies to ordinances that discriminate on the basis of municipal (rather than municipal and state) residency, despite the fact that the Clause fails to specifically refer to municipalities.[1217]

Supreme Court of Virginia v. Friedman [1218] considered a Virginia statute which allowed qualified lawyers admitted to practice in other States may be

---

[1211] *Id.* at 56.

[1212] 410 U.S. 179 (1973).

[1213] *Id.* at 200.

[1214] 465 U.S. 208 (1984).

[1215] The Court cited *Memorial Hospital v. Maricopa County,* 415 U.S. 250, 256 (1974); and *Avery v. Midland County,* 390 U.S. 474, 480, 481 (1968) as authority for that proposition.

[1216] *United Bldg. and Const. Trade,* 465 U.S. at 215.

[1217] *Id.* at 215, 216.

[1218] 487 U.S. 59 (1988).

admitted to the Virginia Bar "on motion," that is, without taking the bar examination which Virginia otherwise requires. The State, however, conditioned such admission on a showing, among other matters, that the applicant is a permanent resident of Virginia. The Court held that such statute violated the Privileges and Immunities Clause of the United States Constitution, Art. IV, § 2, cl. 1.[1219].

Under Article IV, § 2, cl. 1 of the Constitution according to *Barnard v. Thorstenn*[1220] when a challenged restriction deprives nonresidents of a privilege and immunity protected by this Clause, it is invalid unless "(i) there is a substantial reason for the difference in treatment; and (ii) the discrimination practiced against nonresidents bears a substantial relationship to the State's objective."[1221] In deciding whether the discrimination bears a substantial relation to the State's objectives, the Court considers, among other things, whether less restrictive means of regulation are available.[1222]

The Privileges and Immunities Clause of Article IV was said in *Burnham v. Superior Court of California, County of Marin* [1223] to prevent a state government from discriminating against a transient defendant by denying him the protections of its law or the right of access to its courts.[1224]

In *Lunding v. New York Tax Appeals Tribunal*[1225] an action challenging the constitutionality of provisions of a New York statute that effectively denied only nonresident taxpayers an income tax deduction for alimony paid, the Supreme Court held that New York failed to adequately justify discriminatory treatment of nonresidents, and thus, the provision violated Privileges and Immunities Clause.

1219 *Id.* at 61. For a similar holding *see* Supreme Court of New Hampshire v. Piper, 470 U.S. 274, 288 (1985), *infra* text accompanying notes 1230, 1373, and 1374.

1220 489 U.S. 546 (1989).

1221 *Id.* at 559. The Court cited Supreme Court of Virginia v. Friedman, 487 U.S. 59, 65 (1988). as authority for that proposition.

1222 *See Barnard* 489 U.S. at 552, 553.

1223 495 U.S. 604 (1990).

1224 *Id.* at 638.

1225 522 U.S. 287 (1998). *See supra* text accompanying notes 1158 and 1160, and *infra* text accompanying note 1230 for further consideration of this case.

The Court found that Clause affords no assurance of equality in the taxation between residents and non-residents of any particular State.[1226] Justice Sandra Day O'Connor wrote that:

> Because state legislatures must draw some distinctions in light of "local needs," they have considerable discretion in formulating tax policy. *Madden v. Kentucky,* 309 U.S. 83, 88, 60 S.Ct. 406, 408, 84 L.Ed. 590 (1940). Thus, "where the question is whether a state taxing law contravenes rights secured by [the Federal Constitution], the decision must depend not upon any mere question of form, construction, or definition, but upon the practical operation and effect of the tax imposed." *Shaffer, supra,* at 55, 40 S.Ct., at 226; see also *St. Louis Southwestern R. Co. v. Arkansas,* 235 U.S. 350, 362, 35 S.Ct. 99, 102, 59 L.Ed. 265 (1914) ("[W]hen the question is whether a tax imposed by a State deprives a party of rights secured by the Federal Constitution, ... [w]e must regard the substance, rather than the form, and the controlling test is to be found in the operation and effect of the law as applied and enforced by the State"). In short, as this Court has noted in the equal protection context, "inequalities that result not from hostile discrimination, but occasionally and incidentally in the application of a [tax] system that is not arbitrary in its classification, are not sufficient to defeat the law." *Maxwell, supra,* at 543, 40 S.Ct., at 7.
>
> We have described this balance as "a rule of substantial equality of treatment" for resident and nonresident taxpayers.*298 *Austin v. New Hampshire,* 420 U.S. 656, 665, 95 S.Ct. 1191, 1197, 43 L.Ed.2d 530 (1975). Where nonresidents are subject to different treatment, there must be "reasonable ground for ... diversity of treatment." *Travis,* 252 U.S., at 79, 40 S.Ct., at 231; see also *Travellers' Ins. Co. v. Connecticut,* 185 U.S. 364, 371, 22 S.Ct. 673, 676, 46 L.Ed. 949 (1902) ("It is enough that the State has secured a reasonably fair distribution of burdens"). As explained in *Toomer,* the Privileges and Immunities Clause bars "discrimination against citizens of other States where there is no substantial reason for the discrimination beyond the mere fact that they are citizens of other States. But it does not preclude disparity of treatment in the many situations where there are perfectly valid independent reasons for it. Thus the inquiry in each case must be concerned with whether such reasons do exist and

---

[1226] *Id.* at 297.

whether the degree of discrimination bears a close relationship to them. The inquiry must also, of course, be conducted with due regard for the principle that the States should have considerable leeway in analyzing local evils and in prescribing appropriate cures.' 334 U.S., at 396, 68 S. Ct., at 1162.

Thus, when confronted with a challenge under the Privileges and Immunities Clause to a law distinguishing between residents and nonresidents, a State may defend its position by demonstrating that "(i) there is a substantial reason for the difference in treatment; and (ii) the discrimination practiced against nonresidents bears a substantial relationship to the State's objective." Piper, 470 U.S., at 284, 105 S.Ct., at 1278

Our concern for the integrity of the Privileges and Immunities Clause is reflected through a "standard of review substantially more rigorous than that applied to state tax distinctions, among, say, forms of business **775 organizations or different trades and professions." *Austin, supra,* at 663, 95 S.Ct., at 1196. Thus, as both the New York Court of Appeals, 89 N.Y.2d, at 290, 653 N.Y.S.2d at 66, 675 N.E.2d, at 820, and the State, Brief for Respondent *299 Commissioner of Taxation and Finance 10-11, appropriately acknowledge, the State must defend § 631(b)(6) with a substantial justification for its different treatment of nonresidents, including an explanation of how the discrimination relates to the State's justification.[1227]

C. Privileges or Immunities Under Amendment XIV, § 1

The second sentence of § 1 of the Fourteenth Amendment contains wording similar, but not identical to those of Article, IV, § 2, cl.1. That wording is as follows:

> "No State shall make or enforce any law which shall abridge the privileges or immunities of citizens of the United States."

[1227] *Id.* at 297-299.

1. The Civil Rights Act of Feb. 28, 1871

a. General Remarks

Three years after the Fourteenth Amendment was made a part of the Constitution, Congress enacted the Civil Rights Act of 1871.[1228] It is an Act that creates a remedy for violation of federal rights committed by persons acting under color of state law. In relevant part 42 U.S.C. § 1983, its codification, provides as follows:

> Every person[1229] who, under color of any statute, ordinance, regulation, custom, or usage, of any State or Territory or the District of Columbia, subjects, or causes to be subjected, any citizen of the United States or other person within the jurisdiction thereof to the deprivation of any rights, privileges or immunities secured by the Constitution and laws, shall be liable to the party injured in an action at law, suit in equity, or other proper proceeding for redress.

b. The 42 U.S.C.§1983 Civil Rights Act Cases

The cases before the U.S. Supreme Court, in which the "privileges or immunities" phrasing is even mentioned are, for the most part considerations of the Civil Rights Act of 1871, rather than a disquisition of the meaning or the term which varies from its Article IV version. The Civil Rights cases are worth examining, which they are, as follows:

In *Monroe v. Pape*[1230] the Court said that Section 1983 was designed "to give a remedy to parties deprived of constitutionally enumerated rights,, privileges and immunities by an official's abuse of his position;"[1231] in other words, by persons acting "under color of any [state] statute, ordinance, regulation, custom, or usage."[1232]

[1228] Revised Statute § 1979. Presently codified as 42 U.S.C. § 1983.

[1229] A foreign country is not a "person" within the terms of this statute. Bread v. Greene, 523 U.S. 371, 378 (1998).

[1230] 365 U.S. 167 (1961).

[1231] *Id.* at 172.

[1232] *Id.*

In Butz v. Economou[1233] the Court acknowledged that for some "special functions," it is better to leave unredressed the wrongs done by dishonest officers than to subject those who try to do their duty to the constant dread of retaliation.[1234] The court cited additional authority that statement.[1235]

In *Cannon v. University of Chicago*[1236] the U.S. Supreme Court held that a statute is enforceable under implied rights only where Congress "explicitly conferred a right directly on a class of persons that included the plaintiff in the case."[1237] Justice John Paul Stevens wrote that:

> Congress, through § 1 of the Civil Rights Act of 1871, indicated in even more explicit terms that private actions would be available to prevent official interference with the rights guaranteed by § 1 of the 1866 Act. See *Chapman v. Houston Welfare Rights Org.,* 441 U.S., at 627-628, 99 S.Ct., at 1921 (POWELL, J., concurring). Although one might conclude, in light of the 1871 Act, that the 1866 and 1870 Acts did not provide for private actions but merely permitted federal courts to entertain state-law actions affecting the denial of civil rights, an equally plausible reading of those statutes is that Congress created a federal cause of action to enforce § 1 of the 1866 Act.[1238]

In *Maine v. Thiboutot,*[1239] the Court held that § 1983 provides a cause of action for violations of federal statutes as well as the Constitution. There are two exceptions to this rule. A plaintiff alleging a violation of a federal statute will be permitted to sue under § 1983 unless (1) "the statute [does] not create enforceable rights, privileges or immunities within the meaning

---

[1233] 438 U.S. 478 (1978).

[1234] *Id.* at 484.

[1235] *Id.* at 508, 509. the Court cited Wright v. Roanoke Redevelopment and Housing Authority, 479 U.S. 418, 423 (1987), as authority for the final proposition.

[1236] 441 U.S. 677 (1979).

[1237] *Id.* at 690 n.13.

[1238] *Id.* at 737.

[1239] 448 U.S. 1 (1980).

of § 1983," or (2) "Congress has foreclosed such enforcement of the statute in the enactment itself."[1240]

In *Patsy v. Board of Regents of Fla.*[1241] the Court held that when a local actor or agency violates a person's federal right, the aggrieved party may bring an action under 42 U.S.C. § 1983 without first exhausting state remedies.[1242]

The Court in *Memphis Community School Dist. v. Stachura*[1243] said that 42 U.S.C. § 1983 [8] creates " 'a species of tort liability' in favor of persons who are deprived of 'rights, privilegies or immunities secured' to them by the Constitution."[1244]

The Court in *Golden State Transit Corp. v. Los Angeles*[1245] held that in order to seek redress through § 1983 a plaintiff must assert the violation of a federal *right*, not merely a violation of federal *law*.[1246] It also held that: "a claim based on a statutory violation is enforceable under § 1983 only when the statute creates 'rights, privileges or immunities in the particular plaintiff "[1247] In that case Justice John Paul Stevens wrote that:

> Section 1983 provides a federal remedy for "the deprivation of any rights, privileges or immunities secured by the Constitution and laws." As the language of the statute plainly indicates, the remedy encompasses violations of federal statutory as well as constitutional rights. We have repeatedly held that the coverage of the statute must be broadly construed.[1248]

1240 *Id.* at 4.

1241 457 U.S. 496(1982).

1242 *Id.* at 516.

1243 477 U.S. 299 (1986).

1244 *Id.* at 305, 306.

1245 493 U.S. 103 (1989). *See infra* text accompanying notes 1249-1251 for further reference to this case.

1246 *Id.* at 106.

1247 *Id.* at 107, 108, n.4.

1248 *Id.* at 105.

In *Wilder v. Virginia Hosp. Ass'n* [1249] it was said that § 1983 provides a cause of action for "the deprivation of any rights, privileges and immunities secured by the Constitution and laws" of the United States.[1250]

It was opined in *Dennis v. Higgins*[1251] that the Commerce Clause confers "rights, privileges, or immunities" within the meaning of § 1983. In addition to conferring power on the Federal Government, the Clause is a substantive restriction on permissible state regulation of interstate commerce. And individuals injured by state action violating this aspect of the Clause may sue and obtain injunctive and declaratory relief. The three considerations for determining whether a federal statute confers a "right" within the meaning of § 1983 + -that the provision creates obligations binding on the governmental unit, that the plaintiff's interest is not too vague and amorphous to be beyond the judiciary's competence to enforce, and that the provision was intended to benefit the plaintiff-also weigh in favor of recognition of a right under the Clause.[1252]

In *Burns v. Reed*[1253] Justice Byron White said that Title 42 U.S.C. § 1983 is written in broad terms. It purports to subject "[e]very person" acting under color of state law to liability for depriving any other person in the United States of "rights, privileges, or immunities secured by the Constitution and laws." The Court has consistently recognized, however, that § 1983 was not meant "to abolish wholesale all common-law immunities."[1254] The section is to be read "in harmony with general principles of tort immunities and defenses rather than in derogation of them."[1255]

1249 496 U.S. 498 (1990).

1250 *Id.* at 508.

1251 498 U.S. 439 (1991).

1252 *Id.* at 439.

1253 500 U.S. 478 (1991).

1254 He offered *Pierson v. Ray,* 386 U.S. 547, 554, (1967) as authority for that conclusion.

1255 *Burns*, 500 U.S. at 484. Justice White offered *Tenney v. Brandhove,* 341 U.S. 367, 376 (1951) and *Imbler v. Pachtman,* 424 U.S. 409, 418, (1976) as authority for the proposition.

In *Hafer v. Melo*[1256] the requirement of action under color of state law means that an official in an elevated position receives no insulation from suit for improper discharge of an employee in a subordinate position.[1257].

In *Suter v. Artist M*[1258] it was said that § 1983 is not available to enforce a violation of a federal statute where Congress has foreclosed enforcement in the enactment itself and "where the statute did not create enforceable rights, privileges and immunities within the meaning of § 1983"[1259] Congress must confer such rights unambiguously when it intends to impose conditions on the grant of federal moneys.[1260]

Justice Sandra Day O'Connor, in *Wyatt v. Cole*,[1261] has written that "[t]he purpose of § 1983 is to deter state actors from using the badge of their authority to deprive individuals of their federally guaranteed rights and to provide relief to victims if such deterrence fails."[1262]

In *National Private Truck Council, Inc. v. Oklahoma Tax Com'n* [1263] it was said that in *Dennis v. Higgins*[1264] one of the "rights, privileges or immunities" protected by § 1983 was the right to be free from state action which violates the dormant Commerce Clause and affirmed that case. [1265]

[1256] 502 U.S. 21 (1991).

[1257] *Id.* at 27, 28.

[1258] 503 U.S. 347 (1992).

[1259] *Id.* at 348. Roanoke Redevelopment and Housing Authority, 479 U.S. 418, 423 (1987) was cited as authority for the proposition.

[1260] *Id.* at 423. Pennhurst State School and Hospital v. Halderman, 451 U.S. 1, 17 (1991) was also cited as authority for that proposition.

[1261] 504 U.S. 158. (1992).

[1262] *Id.* at 161 (see also Carey v. Piphus, 435 U.S. 247, 254-257 (1978).

[1263] 515 U.S. 582, 585, (1995).

[1264] *See supra* text accompanying notes 1254, 1255.

[1265] *See National Private Truck Council, Inc* 515 U.S. at 585.

In *Morse v. Republican Party of Virginia* [1266] certain registered voters who wished to become delegates to a political party's state convention for the purpose of nominating a candidate for U. S. Senator brought an action which challenged the party's requirement that persons who wanted to become delegates must pay a registration fee. A three-judge United States District Court for the Western District of Virginia, remanded constitutional claims to a single-judge District Court and granted the party's motion to dismiss the claims brought under theVoting Rights Act. The voters appealed. The Supreme Court, held that: (1) the party was "acting under authority explicitly or implicitly granted by a covered jurisdiction," for purposes of the regulation making a political party's change that affects voting subject to the preclearance requirement, when it adopted a filing fee for delegates to the state nominating convention; (2) a filing fee for party delegates operates in precisely the same fashion as other practices covered by the preclearance requirement and, thus, requires preclearance; and (3) a private right of action exists for the purpose of enforcing the Voting Rights Act section that prohibits a poll tax. Justice John Paul Stevens announced the judgment of the Court and wrote an Opinion in which Justice Ruth Bader Ginsburg agreed. In that Opinion Justice Stevens said that:

> It is quite natural, . . that Congress would draw on § 1983 when it sought to draft provisions that established individual liability for persons who violate civil rights such as the right to vote. Section 1983 was designed "to give a remedy to parties deprived of constitutional rights, privileges and immunities by an official's abuse of his position." *Monroe v. Pape,* 365 U.S. 167, 172, 81 S.Ct. 473, 476, 5 L.Ed.2d 492 (1961). Section 11(a) served exactly the same end, and therefore used similar language.[1267]

In *Gonzaga University v. Doe*[1268] the then Chief Justice William H. Rehnquist wrote that :

> [w]e now reject the notion that our cases permit anything short of an unambiguously conferred right to support a cause of action brought under § 1983. Section 1983 provides a remedy only for the deprivation of "rights, privileges or, or immunities secured by the Constitution and laws"

[1266] 517 U.S. 186 (1996).

[1267] Republican Party of Virginia 517 U.S. 186, 221, n. 34 (1996).

[1268] 536 U.S. 273 (2002).

> of the United States. Accordingly, it is *rights,* not the broader or vaguer "benefits" or "interests," that may be enforced under the authority of that section. This being so, we further reject the notion that our implied right of action cases are separate and distinct from our § 1983 cases. To the contrary, our implied right of action cases should guide the determination of whether a statute confers rights enforceable under § 1983.[1269]

The U.S. Supreme Court in *Nelson v. Campbell*[1270] held that § 1983 authorizes a "suit in equity, or other proper proceeding for redress," against any person who, under color of state law, "subjects, or causes to be subjected, any citizen of the United States ... to the deprivation of any rights, privileges or immunities secured by the Constitution.". Despite its literal applicability, however, the Court cited *Preiser v. Rodriguez*[1271] as authority for the proposition that § 1983 must yield to the more specific federal habeas statute, with its attendant procedural and exhaustion requirements, where an inmate seeks injunctive relief challenging the fact of his conviction or the duration of his sentence. Such claims fall within the "core" of habeas corpus and are thus not cognizable when brought pursuant to § 1983.[1272] By contrast, constitutional claims that merely challenge the conditions of a prisoner's confinement, whether the inmate seeks monetary or injunctive relief, fall outside of that core and may be brought pursuant to § 1983 in the first instance.[1273]

The U.S. Supreme Court, in *Mc Donald v. City of Chicago Ill.*[1274] in effect, did away with the Civil Rights Act of 1871 by shifting resolution of the issue of whether a municipality violated the constitution by outlawing private issue of handguns from privileges and immunities to due process.[1275] As Justice Alito wrote

---

[1269] *Id.* at 383.

[1270] 541 U.S.637, 641 (2004).

[1271] 411 U.S. 475 (1973).

[1272] *Id.* at 489.

[1273] *Id.* at 498-49. Muhammad v. Close, 540 U.S. 749, 750 (2004) was offered as authority.

[1274] 130 S. Ct. 3020 (2010). *See infra* text accompanying notes 1278-1280, for further considerations of this case.

[1275] The U.S. Supreme Court held that certain ordinances of certain Illinois municipalities were unconstitutional. Despite the Court's finding that many legal scholars dispute the

in the *Mc Donald* case "[f]or many decades, the question of the rights protected by the Fourteenth Amendment against state infringement has been analyzed under the Due Process Clause of that Amendment and not under the Privileges or Immunities Clause." [1276] The Court made such examination in Part III of its Opinion.[1277]

c. Fourteenth Amendment Non -1781 Civil Rights Act Cases

The second sentence of Section I of the Fourteenth Amendment provides, *inter alia*, that "[n]o State shall make or enforce any law which shall abridge the privileges or immunities of citizens of the United States:" One might wonder whether there is a difference between the Fourteenth Amendment and Article IV, § 2, cl. 1 because the latter refers to "privileges and immunities"[1278] whereas the former refers to "privileges or[1279] immunities." It is submitted that this difference is of no significance, and is simply the result of an oversight of the author of the Fourteen Amendment, U.S. Congressional Representative John A. Bingham, of Ohio. Another oversight of Rep.Binghan, of considerably more importance, was his failure to insert the word "States" in the second sentence of Section I of the Fourteenth Amendment, as will be further pointed out in this work.[1280]

In *Barron v. City of Baltimore*[1281] the U.S. Supreme Court held that as a prelude Fourteenth Amendment, the Bill of Rights applied only to the Federal government. Chief Justice John Marshall wrote in that case:

> Had the framers of these amendments intended them to be limitations on the powers of the state governments, they would have imitated the framers of the original constitution, and have expressed that intention. Had

---

correctness of what they refer to as the "narrow Slaughter-House ruling." it declined to disturb the Slaughter-House ruling because for many decades the question of the protection of the Fourteenth Amendment against state infringement has been analyzed under the Due Process clause and not the "privileges or immunities clause.

1276 *Id.* at 3030-3031.

1277 *Id.* at 3036-3043.

1278 Emphasis supplied.

1279 Emphasis supplied.

1280 *See infra* text accompanying note 1312.

1281 32 U.S. (7 Pet.) 243 (1833).

> congress engaged in the extraordinary occupation of improving the constitutions of the several states, by affording the people additional protection from the exercise of power by their own governments, in matters which concerned themselves alone, they would have declared this purpose in plain and intelligible language.[1282]

In *Crandall v. Nevada*[1283] the Court, further exploring the relationship between state and federal governments, recognized the right of the Federal Government to call "any or all of its citizens to aid in its service, as members of the Congress, of the courts, of the executive departments, and to fill all its other offices," and further recognized that "this right cannot be made to depend upon the pleasure of a State over whose territory they must pass to reach the point where these services must be rendered."[1284]

In the same year that the Fourteenth Amendment was ratified U.S. Supreme Court Stephen J.Field, writing about the amendment, in *Paul v. State of Virgini*a[1285] said:

> It was undoubtedly the object of the clause in question to place the citizens of each State upon the same footing with citizens of other States, so far as the advantages resulting from citizenship in those States are concerned. It relieves them from the disabilities of alienage in other States; it inhibits discriminating legislation against them by other States; it gives them the right of free ingress into other States, and egress from them; it insures to them in other States the same freedom possessed by the citizens of those States in the acquisition and enjoyment of property and in the pursuit of happiness; and it secures to them in other States the equal protection of their laws. It has been justly said that no provision in the Constitution has tended so strongly to constitute the citizens of the United States one people as this.[1286]

1282 *Id.* at 250.

1283 73 U.S. (6 Wall..) 35 (1867).

1284 *Id.* at 43.

1285 75 U.S. 168 (1868).

1286 *Id.* at 180.

Four years after the Fourteenth Amendment became a part of the Constitution the U.S. Supreme Court in *The Slaughter-house Cases*,[1287] had the occasion to review the constitutionality of a Louisiana statute which in the announced quest for cleanliness, created a corporation organized for the purpose of providing the sole opportunity for those butchers who wished to pursue the slaughtering of animals for food, much to the consternation of thousands who wanted to pursue the same livelihood, but on their own terms and conditions - the right of "free labor," as Justice Field called it.[1288] Such state of affairs resulted in litigation at the State level, decrying the authority of the State to make and enforce such legislation. The plaintiffs, however, according to the Louisiana and U.S. courts chose the wrong constitutional provision upon which to rely – the "privileges or immunities section of the Fourteenth Amendment.[1289] The U.S. Supreme Court affirmed the State courts, by a five to four decision. Justice Samuel F. Miller wrote the Opinion of the Court, distributed on April 14 1873, for the majority of Justices - Clifford, Davis, Miller Nelson, and Strong, Chief Justice Chase and Justices Bradley, Field and Swayne, dissented, the latter three writing written Opinions.

Justice Miller, in the Court's Opinion after identifying the Louisiana statute as legislation under the State's police power, which is incapable of exact definition or limitation,[1290] left little time pass before making it plain that the Court thought that the plaintiffs could not complain about Louisiana because the second sentence of § 1 of the Fourteenth Amendment did not apply to state action and applied only to federal action because "States" were not mentioned in that provision, whereas that term was mentioned in § 2 of Article IV, Clause 1. First he wrote:

> [I]t puts at rest both the questions which we stated to have been the subject of differences of opinion. It declares that persons may be citizens of the United States without regard to their citizenship of a particular State.[1291]

1287 83 U.S. (16 Wall.) 36 (1872). *See supra* note 1196 for reference to this case. *See infra* text accompanying notes 1291-1347, 1366, 1389, and 1390 for additional consideration of this case.

1288 *See id.* at 110.

1289 *Id.* at 58, 59.

1290 *Id.* at 62.

1291 *Id.* at 73.

He then identified the first sentence of §1 of the Fourteenth Amendment as mentioning "States" when it provides that "[a]ll persons born or naturalized in the United States, and subject to the jurisdiction thereof are citizens of the United States and of the State wherein they reside." Justice Miller found significant that there was absence of the word "State" in the second sentence of § 1, though present in the first sentence of that section,. and wrote:

> [T]he next paragraph[1292] of this same section, which is the one mainly relied on by the plaintiffs in error, speaks only of privileges and[1293] immunities of citizens of the United States, and does not speak of those as citizens of the several States.[1294]
>
> The language is, 'No State shall make or enforce any law which shall abridge the privileges or immunities of citizens of *the United States*.' It is a little remarkable, if this clause was [sic] intended as a protection to the citizen of a State against the legislative power of his own State, that the word citizen of the State should be left out when it is so carefully used, and used in contradistinction to citizens of the United States, in the very sentence which precedes it.[1295] It is too clear for argument that the change in phraseology was adopted understandingly and with a purpose.[1296]

He concludes that the absence of the word "States" from the pertinent part of the second sentence of the Fourteenth Amendment's § 1.was not only significant, but intentional. perhaps because he had just recognized that eminent jurists had proclaimed that a man may be a citizen of the United States without being a citizen of a State.[1297] As he stated it:

[1292] He is referring to the second sentence (rather than "paragraph"), of section 1 of the Fourteenth Amendment.

[1293] In fact the disjunctive "or." rather than the conjunctive "and" is used.

[1294] *Id.* at 74.

[1295] He was referring to the first sentence of § 1 of Art. IV, which proclaims that: "[a]]l persons born in the United States, and subject to the jurisdiction thereof, are citizen of the United States and of the State wherein they reside."

[1296] *Slaughter-House*, 83 U.S. at 74.

[1297] *Id.* at 74.

> It is quite clear, then, that there is a citizenship of the United States, and a citizenship of a State, which are distinct from each other, and which depend upon different characteristics or circumstances in the individual.[1298]

He then made it clear that the privileges and immunities of the citizens of the States are not protected by the Fourteenth Amendment, though he gave no clue as to where protection of them could be found, as the following words elucidate:

> If, then, there is a difference between the privileges and immunities belonging to a citizen of the United States as such, and those belonging to the citizen of the State as such the latter must rest for their security and protection where they have heretofore rested; for they are not embraced by this paragraph of the amendment.[1299]

Miller resorted to Justice Bushrod Washington in *Corfield v. Coryell* [1300] for a definition of privileges and immunities of States by writing:

> [T]hose privileges and immunities which are *fundamental;* which belong of right to the citizens of all free governments, and which have at all times been enjoyed by citizens of the several States which compose this Union, from the time of their becoming free, independent, and sovereign. What these fundamental principles are, it would be more tedious than difficult to enumerate. They may all, however, be comprehended under the following general heads: protection by the government, with the right to acquire and possess property of every kind, and to pursue and obtain happiness and safety, subject, nevertheless, to such restraints as the government may prescribe for the general good of the whole.[1301]

The Fourteenth Amendment, differed from Art. IV, § 2 not because of its phrasing using "privileges or immunities," rather then "privileges and immunities" but because the Fourteenth Amendment applied to privileges or immunities which

---

1298 *Id.*

1299 *Id.* at 75.

1300 6 Fed. Cas. 546 (C.C. Pa. 1823).

1301 *Slaughter-House*, 83 U.S. at 76.

United States citizens[1302] may have which predated creation of the Federal Government. His words, repeated above, leave no doubt of the Court's intent:

> He further analyzed the rights protected by Art. IV, § 2 by writing that it:
>
> did not create those rights, which it called privileges and immunities of citizens of the States. It threw around them in that clause no security for the citizen of the State in which they were claimed or exercised. Nor did it profess to control the power of the State governments over the rights of its own citizens.[1303]
>
> Its sole purpose was to declare to the several States, that whatever those rights, as you grant or establish them to your own citizens, or as you limit or qualify, or impose restrictions on their exercise, the same, neither more nor less, shall be the measure of the rights of citizens of other States within your jurisdiction.[1304]

He gave a brief recitation of those "fundamental" rights protected by the Fourteenth Amendment clause, e.g. ex post facto laws,[1305] bills of attainder,[1306] laws impairing the obligation of contract.[1307]

Justice Miller asked rhetorically whether the framers of the Fourteenth Amendment, even though they specifically sought to prevent the abridgement of privileges or immunities of "citizens of the United States," by transferring that protection against State action, where it had always existed, to Federal protection. He did so by the following words:

> Was it the purpose of the fourteenth amendment, by the simple declaration that no State should make or enforce any law which shall abridge the privileges and immunities of *citizens of the*

[1302] And not citizens of a State. *Id.* at 77.

[1303] *Id.* at 77.

[1304] *Id.*

[1305] *Id.*

[1306] *Id.*

[1307] *Id.*

> *United States*, to transfer the security and protection of all the civil rights which we have mentioned, from the States to the Federal government? And where it is declared that Congress shall have the power to enforce that article,[1308] was it intended to bring within the power of Congress the entire domain of civil rights heretofore belonging exclusively to the States?[1309]

Justice Miller said that holding in favor of the "free labor" butchers would constitute the U.S. Supreme Court into a "censor" of all legislation of the States on the civil rights of their own citizens.

> [N]ot only are these rights subject to the control of Congress whenever in its discretion any of them are supposed to be abridged by State legislation, but that body may also pass laws in advance, limiting and restricting the exercise of legislative power by the States, in their most ordinary and usual functions, as in its judgment it may think proper on all such subjects. And still further, such a construction followed by the reversal of the judgments of the Supreme Court of Louisiana in these cases, would constitute this court a perpetual censor upon all legislation of the States, on the civil rights of their own citizens, with authority to nullify such as it did not approve as consistent with those rights, as they existed at the time of the adoption of this amendment. The argument we admit is not always the most conclusive which is drawn from the consequences urged against the adoption of a particular construction of an instrument. But when, as in the case before us, these consequences are so serious, so far-reaching and pervading, so great a departure from the structure and spirit of our institutions; when the effect is to fetter and degrade the State governments by subjecting them to the control of Congress, in the exercise of powers heretofore universally conceded to them of the most ordinary and fundamental character; when in fact it radically changes the whole theory of the relations of the State and Federal governments to each other and of both these governments to the people; the argument has a force that is irresistible, in the absence of language which expresses such a purpose too clearly to admit of doubt.[1310]

[1308] He is referring to § 5 of the Fourteenth Amendment.

[1309] *Id.*

[1310] *Id.* at 78.

Justice Miller emphasized the Court's position:

> Having shown that the privileges and immunities relied on in the argument are those which belong to citizens of the States as such, and that they are left to the State governments for security and protection, and not by this article placed under the special care of the Federal government, we may hold ourselves excused from defining the privileges and immunities of citizens of the United States which no State can abridge, until some case involving those privileges may make it necessary to do so.[1311]

Having identified three fundamental rights protected by the "privileges or immunities clause of the Fourteenth Amendment[1312] and choosing not to further identify them,[1313] Miller soon did list the privileges and immunities to which citizens of the States are protected by the Fourteenth Amendment, i.e. those which "own [sic] their existence to the federal government, its National character, Constitution or it laws."[1314] He continued, with his recitation of fundamental rights: the right to come to the seat of government to assert any claim that person may wish to make upon the national government;[1315] free access to seaports; [1316] free access to subtreasuries, land offices, and courts of justice in the several States;[1317] the rights for which the Federal government was established;[1318] the right to demand the care, and protection of the Federal government was established;[1319] the right to demand the care and protection of the Federal government over his life, liberty and property when on the high seas or within the jurisdiction of a foreign country;[1320] the right to peacefully assemble;[1321] to petition for redress of

---

1311 *Id.* at 78, 79.

1312 *See supra* text accompanying notes 1308, 1309 and 1310.

1313 *Id.* at 78, 79.

1314 *Id.* at 79. The word "owe" was intended.

1315 *Id.*

1316 *Id.*

1317 *Id.*

1318 *Id.*

1319 *Id.*

1320 *Id.*

grievances;[1322] the privilege of habeas corpus;[1323] to use the navigable waters of the U.S.;[1324] all rights secured to U.S. citizens by treaties with foreign nations; [1325] to become a citizen of any State of the Union;[1326] rights secured by the Thirteenth and Fifteenth Amends; [1327] Justice Miller thought that further elucidation of such fundamental rights was useless, as the plaintiffs had probably alleged in their Complaints that they, Louisiana citizens rather than U. S. citizens, were being deprived of privileges.[1328] Even had they claimed being denied privileges as United States citizens, moreover, the rights they claimed (the free labor), the Court did not recognize those privileges and immunities as being protected by the Fourteenth Amendment. As Miller stated it "the rights claimed by those plaintiffs in error, if they have any existence, are not privileges and immunities of citizens of the United States within the meaning of the clause of the fourteenth amendment under consideration."[1329]

Justice Stephen J. Field wrote, in dissent, that the Fourteenth Amendment does not to confer new privilege or immunities on citizens. It assumes that there are privileges and immunities already existing in favor of U.S. citizens which Art. IV § 2 prohibits the Federal government from abridging. The Amendment refers to new "privileges or immunities" which the states are specifically prevented from abridging. Hence the Amendment is applicable to this case as apposed to the position taken by the majority. If U.S. citizens had already been protected by Article IV, § 2, the Fourteenth Amendment was meaningless. No new Constitutional Amendment was required to prevent State legislators from interfering with them, for those privileges and immunities were already fully

---

1321 *Id.*

1322 *Id.*

1323 *Id.*

1324 *Id.*

1325 *Id.*

1326 *Id.* at 80.

1327 *Id.*

1328 The Court's Opinion does not clarify under what authority by which the Court declared them solely citizens of Louisiana, rather the citizens of that state and of the United States.

1329 *Id.* at 80.

protected by the supremacy of the United States' Constitution and its laws. Specifically he wrote:

> The amendment does not attempt to confer any new privileges or immunities upon citizens, or to enumerate or define those already existing. It assumes that there are such privileges and immunities which belong of right to citizens as such, and ordains that they shall not be abridged by State legislation. If this inhibition has no reference to privileges and immunities of this character, but only refers, as held by the majority of the court in their opinion, to such privileges and immunities as were before its adoption specially designated in the Constitution or necessarily implied as belonging to citizens of the United States, it was a vain and idle enactment, which accomplished nothing, and most unnecessarily excited Congress and the people on its passage. With privileges and immunities thus designated or implied no State could ever have interfered by its laws, and no new constitutional provision was required to inhibit such interference. The supremacy of the Constitution and the laws of the United States always controlled any State legislation of that character. But if the amendment refers to the natural and inalienable rights which belong to all citizens, the inhibition has a profound significance and consequence.[1330]

In fine, it would seem that Justice Miller and the Court's majority had the better part of the argument. Though the Court failed to address the distinction between "privileges and immunities" and "privileges or immunities" in the two constitutional provisions under consideration, the free interchange of the conjunctive "and" and the disjunctive "or" in both the majority and dissenting Opinions would lead the reader to conclude that, at least the opinion of the Supreme Court Justices, no difference of significance was intended by Ohio Congressman, John A. Bingham, the draftsman of the Fourteenth Amendment, and possibly was an oversight. Most probably another oversight was the omission of the word "State" in the Fourteenth Amendment.[1331] Often cases such as *Dred Scott* and *Slaughter-House* have been described as "awful." Whereas it was the

---

[1330] *Id.* at 96.

[1331] It should be observed, however, that Justice Anthony Kennedy has reported that Representative Bingham said the new draft, acted upon, would give Congress "the power ... to protect by national law the privileges and immunities of all the citizens of the Republic ... whenever the same shall be abridged or denied by the unconstitutional acts of any State." City of Boerne v. Flores 521 U.S. 507, 522 (1997).

provisions they construed which should have been referred to as "awful," rather than the cases that construed the.[1332]

The holding of *Slaughter-House* has been referred to as "narrow."[1333] In fact, it should hardly be considered as "narrow," identifying three examples of fundamental rights which citizens of the United States may claim.[1334] The Court did not render an opinion of what rights State citizens could expect from States. It was not required to do so, and would have been a dictum.. Its sole function was to determine whether the Fourteenth Amendment required Louisiana to safeguard the right of "free labor" as a privilege or immunity. It decided that that question must be answered in the negative, due to the absence of an important word in the Amendment.

What the Court did not say explicitly, left no doubt about its conclusions. Its semble,[1335] is more descriptive of the Fourteenth Amendment than what it did say. As an example:

[1332] Justice William R. Day gave a cogent description of Slaughter-House in Maxwell v. Bugbee, 250 U.S. 525, 538 (1919) when he wrote that:"[w]hat . . . privileges and immunities were was under consideration in Slaughter-House Cases, . . . where it was shown . . . that it was not the purpose of this amendment, by the declaration that no state should make or enforce any law which should abridge the privileges and immunities of citizens of the United States, to transfer from the states to the federal government the security and protection of those civil rights that inhere in state citizenship; and . . . that the privileges and immunities of citizens of the United States thereby placed beyond abridgment by the states were those which owe their existence to the federal government, its national character, its constitution, or its laws. To the same effect is Duncan v. Missouri, 152 U. S. 377, 382, 14 Sup. Ct. 570, 38 L. Ed. 485." He added that "[i]n short, as this Court has noted in the equal protection context, 'inequalities that result not from hostile discrimination, but occasionally and incidentally in the application of a [tax] system that is not arbitrary in its classification, are not sufficient to defeat the law.' *Maxwell, supra,* at 543.

[1333] McDonald v. City of Chicago, Ill., 130 S. Ct. 3020 (2010).. *See* Justice Alito's Opinion *id.* at 27-29; Justice Scalia's, *id.* at 51 and Justice Stevens's, *id.* at 95, 97.

[1334] Those rights are identified *supra*, at text accompanying footnotes 1308, 1309, and 1310.

[1335] A "semble" in legal parlance is something assumed by a court without expressly dealing with it. As an example in Williams v. Vermont, 472 U.S. 14, 27 (1985), Justice Bryon R. White wrote, for the Court, that it was emphasizing more than it was holding – it was actually a very "narrow" holding.

(1) that the "privileges or immunities" of the citizens of the Union are different from those of the citizens of each state.[1336] This unexpressed conclusion complies with Justice Bushrod Washington's following words uttered in *Corfield v. Coryell*:[1337]

> [W]hat are the privileges and immunities of citizens in the several states? We feel no hesitation in confining these expressions to those privileges and immunities which are, in their nature, fundamental; which belong, of right, to the citizens of all free governments; and which have, at all times, been enjoyed by the citizens of the several states which compose this Union, from the time of their becoming free, independent, and sovereign.[1338]

(2) It is unfortunate that the Court was required to leave the eleven states, shortly to secede, to be the sole "censors" of the privilege and immunities" of their slaves. It must be remembered, that the Court had not written the Constitution; it was merely interpreting it.

(3) It is also unfortunate that the Court did not specify what privilege or immunities the States were to protect, but it was neither the right nor the duty of the Court to amend that Constitution, simply because the drafters of the Constitution's amendment failed to include those provisions.

(4) The Court's semble left a strong suggestion that instead of providing that the first portion of the second sentence of the first section of the Fourteenth Amendment which now provides that:

> No State shall make or enforce any law which shall abridge the privileges or immunities of citizens of the United States.

should have provided:

1336 In Zelman v. Simmons-Harris, 536 U.S. 639, 678 (2002) Justice Clarence Thomas said that "the Fourteenth Amendment fundamentally restructured the relationship between individuals and the states."

1337 6 Fed. Cas. 546 (1823).

1338 *Id.* at 551.

> No State shall make or enforce any law which shall abridge the privileges and immunities of citizens of the United States or the States.

What the Chase Court did in *Slaughter-House* was identical to what the Marshall Court did in *Barron v. City of Baltimore*[1339] where it held that the Bill of Rights applied only to the Federal government.[1340] Chief Justice Marshall wrote in that case:

> Had the framers of these amendments intended them to be limitations on the powers of the state governments, they would have imitated the framers of the original constitution, and have expressed that intention. Had congress engaged in the extraordinary occupation of improving the constitutions of the several states, by affording the people additional protection from the exercise of power by their own governments, in matters which concerned themselves alone, they would have declared this purpose in plain and intelligible language.[1341]

The Constitution, though proclaimed by its founders to be the "supreme" law of the land[1342] was not a perfect document. It apparently gave the United States and the States the right to deny or abridge people the right to vote because of race, color or previous condition of servitude until the Fifteenth Amendment corrected that fault in 1870. It apparently gave the United States and the States the right to deny or abridge citizens of the United States the right to vote until the Nineteenth Amendment § 1 corrected that fault in 1920. In 1919 certain people thought that the Constitution contained a flaw in not prohibiting certain disposition of intoxicating liquors; hence the Eighteenth Amendment, doing just that, was ratified that year. Fourteen years later, in 1933, there was a change of opinion; now people thought that the supposed flaw was not a flaw., so the Twenty-First Amendment, repealing the Eighteenth Amendment was ratified. It apparently gave the United States and the States the right to deny or abridge the right of citizens of the United States to vote in certain elections unless they paid a poll tax or other tax, until the Twenty-Fourth Amendment § 1 corrected that fault in 1964 It apparently gave the

---

[1339] 32 U.S. (7 Pet.) 243 (1833).

[1340] *Id.* at 251.

[1341] *Id.* at 250.

[1342] Pursuant to Article VI, § 2.

United States and the States the right to deny citizens of the United States the right to vote until they reached a certain age until the Twenty-Sixth Amendment § 1 corrected that fault in 1971. It was popularly considered that women were not up to the task of sitting on juries, until 1975, when the Supreme Court in *Taylor v. Louisiana*[1343] corrected that flawed perception.[1344]

Perhaps expecting it to not only clearly explicate all of its terms, but to cover mores and inventions that would change the words used, or should have been used, would be expecting an impossible task for the framers to pursue. Though it, and all laws of the United States made in pursuance thereof, are still the supreme law of the land perhaps the framers should be excused for not framing an unchangeable document. Yet, how could they? As this book is being written there exists an unanswered question as to whether children born in the United States to illegal aliens are automatically U.S. citizens. If that question reaches the U.S. Supreme Court five Justices might hold that they are, whereas if a later constituted court considers the same issue five justices might hold that they are not. Diametric opposition in the rulings of our courts, at least our highest court, is the price we pay for the passage of time.

Just three years after the *Slaughter-House* decision the Court in its same complement, except for its Chief Justice[1345] in *United States v. Cruikshank*[1346] affirmed the acquittal of Caucasians accused of murdering a band of unarmed men of African descent in the infamous "Colfax Massacre" on Easter Sunday 1873, in Louisiana.. The ground of the acquittal being that the right of peaceful assembly of the First Amendment applied only to abridgements by the Federal Government, and not those by the States.[1347] The Court did not even mention its prior statement in *Slaughter-House* that it was the responsibility of the States to safeguard United States citizens' right to peacefully assemble,[1348] probably due to the Court's holding in *Dred Scott v. Sanford.*[1349] to the effect that because the framers of the

---

1343 419 U.S. 522 (1975).

1344 *Id* at 537.

1345 Morrison R. Waite had replaced Salmon P. Chase as Chief Justice on March 4, 1874.

1346 92 U.S. 542 (1875). *See infra* text accompanying notes 1350, 1391 and 1392 for further reference to this case.

1347 *Id.* at 551, 552.

1348 *See supra* text accompanying note 1324.

Constitution's wording which prevented former slaves from ever being U.S. Citizens. How could the Supreme Court in the *Slaughter-House* case have re-written the Fourteenth Amendment to correct a mistake of its draftsmen? Only the people may do than by their amendments. Relative to what the Court did in *Slaughter-House* is that the Court in 2010, when it considered *McDonald* it failed to overrule *Slaughter-House* when it had an opportunity to do so.[1350]

Seven years after the *Slaughter-House* decision the Court decided *State of Missouri v. Lewis*[1351] in which one of the *Slaughter-house* dissenters, Justice Joseph P. Bradley, wrote for the Court that the purpose and objective of the Fourteenth Amendment's "privileges or immunities" clause was "to extend United States citizenship to all natives and naturalized persons, and to prohibit the States from abridging their privileges or immunities."[1352]

In *The Civil Rights Cases*[1353] Supreme Court Justice Joseph P. Bradley made a memorable comment about the Privileges and Immunities Clause in the following words:

> Positive rights and privileges are undoubtedly secured by the fourteenth amendment; but they are secured by way of prohibition against state laws and state proceedings affecting those rights and privileges, and by power given to congress to legislate for the purpose of carrying such prohibition into effect; and such legislation must necessarily be predicated upon such supposed state laws or state proceedings and be directed to the correction of their operation and effect.[1354]

In *United States v. Harris*[1355] the United State Supreme Court Justice William B. Woods uttered the following quotable dictum:

1349 *See supra* text accompanying notes 1161 – 1201, 1335

1350 Mc Donald v. City of Chicago Ill., 130 S. Ct. 3020, 3031 (2010) 1.

1351 101 U.S. 22 (1879).

1352 *Id.* at 30.

1353 109 U.S. 3 (1883).

1354 *Id.* at 11, 12.

1355 106 U.S. 629 (1883). *See infra* text accompanying notes 1359, 1400 and 1401 for further reference to this case.

> When the State has been guilty of no violation of [the Fourteenth Amendment's] provisions; when it has not made or enforced any law abridging the privileges or immunities of citizens of the United States; when no one of its departments has deprived any person of life, liberty, or property without due process of law, or denied to any person within its jurisdiction the equal protection of the laws; when, on the contrary, the laws of the State, as enacted by its legislative, and construed by its judicial, and administered by its executive departments, recognize and protect the rights of all persons, the amendment imposes no duty and confers no power upon congress..[1356]

In *St. Louis Southwestern R. Co. v. Arkansas,*[1357] Justice Mahlon Pitney wrote that

> W]hen the question is whether a tax imposed by a State deprives a party of rights secured by the Federal Constitution, ... [w]e must regard the substance, rather than the form, and the controlling test is to be found in the operation and effect of the law as applied and enforced by the State[1358]

In *Colgate v. Harvey*[1359] the U.S. Supreme Court set aside a Vermont statute that excepted from tax income received from intrastate loans, but which taxed income which originated from out of state loans. Justice George Sutherland took the occasion to explain, in the Opinion of the Court, the difference between Article IV, § 2 and the "privileges or immunities clause of the Fourteenth Amendment, in the following words:

> The purpose of the pertinent clause in the Fourth Article was to require each state to accord equality of treatment to the citizens of other states in respect of the privileges and immunities of state citizenship. It has always been so interpreted. One purpose and effect of the privileges and immunities clause of the Fourteenth Amendment, read in the light of this interpretation, was to bridge the gap left by that article so as also to

---

1356 *Id.* 639.

1357 235 U.S. 350 (1914).

1358 *Id.* at 362.

1359 196 U.S. 404 (1935).

> safeguard citizens of the United States against any legislation of their own states having the effect of denying equality of treatment in respect of the exercise of their privileges of national citizenship in other states. A provision which thus extended and completed the shield of national protection between the citizen and hostile and discriminating state legislation cannot be lightly dismissed as a mere duplication, or of subordinate or no value, or as an almost forgotten clause of the constitution.[1360]

In *Madden v. Kentucky*[1361] The U.S. Supreme Court upheld a Kentucky statute which imposed differing taxes on Bank accounts depending whether the fund were deposited in out-of-state banks, or in-state banks, and in the process overruled *Colgate v. Harvey.*[1362] Justice Stanley Reed, in the Opinion of the *Madden* Court opined the effect of the *Slaughter-House* cases. He wrote: that they "extended the benefits of the privileges and immunities clause to other rights which are inherent in national citizenship but denied it to those which spring from state citizenship."[1363] He almost concluded the Court's Opinion with the following words:

> In the states, there reposes the sovereignty to manage their own affairs except only as the requirements of the Constitution otherwise provide. Within these constitutional limits the power of the state over taxation is plenary. An interpretation of the privileges and immunities clause which restricts the power of the states to manage their own fiscal affairs is a matter of gravest concern to them . . . It is only the emphatic requirements of the Constitution which properly may lead the federal courts to such a conclusion.[1364]

1360 *Id.* at 431.

1361 309 U.S.. 83 (1940).

1362 *See supra* text accompanying notes 1364-1367.as an example of the confusion that exists between the two constitutional provisions, Justice Reed, in the opening portion of his Opinion of the Court referred to the provision allegedly claimed to have been violated as "the privileges and immunities clause of the Fourteenth Amendment," rather than the "privileges or immunity clause." *See also id.* at 85, 87, 90, 91, 92, 92 ns. 14 and 21.

1363 Madden, 309 U.S. at 91.

1364 *Id.* at 93.

In *Toomer v. Witsell,*[1365] a case in which the Supreme Court partially affirmed and partially denied the dismissal of an action seeking an injunction against enforcing statutes governing commercial shrimp fishing Chief Justice Fred Vinson said that the Privileges and Immunities Clause bars

> discrimination against citizens of other States where there is no substantial reason for the discrimination beyond the mere fact that they are citizens of other States. But it does not preclude disparity of treatment in the many situations where there are perfectly valid independent reasons for it. Thus the inquiry in each case must be concerned with whether such reasons do exist and whether the degree of discrimination bears a close relationship to them. The inquiry must also, of course, be conducted with due regard for the principle that the States should have considerable leeway in analyzing local evils and in prescribing appropriate cures[1366]

The Court in *Austin v. New Hampshire*[1367] held that the Privileges and Immunities clause was violated where New Hampshire taxed only the incomes of non-residents working in New Hampshire, but not the incomes of workers who were residents of that state.[1368] Our concern for the integrity of the Privileges and Immunities Clause is reflected through a "standard of review substantially more rigorous than that applied to state tax distinctions, among, say, forms of business organizations or different trades and professions."[1369]

In *Supreme Court of New Hampshire v. Piper*[1370] it was held that when confronted with a challenge under the Privileges and Immunities Clause to a law distinguishing between residents and nonresidents, a State may defend its position by demonstrating that: "(i) there is a substantial reason for the difference in treatment; and (ii) the discrimination practiced against nonresidents bears a substantial relationship to the State's objective."[1371]

[1365] 334 U.S. 385 (1943).

[1366] *Id.* at 398

[1367] 420 U.S. 656 (1975).

[1368] *Id.* at 659.

[1369] *Id.* at 663.

[1370] 470 U.S. 274 (1985).

[1371] *Id.* 284.

In *Saenz v. Roe*[1372] It was held that one of the privileges and immunities of Article IV, § 2 of the Constitution is the right to travel.[1373] The "right to travel" embraces at least three different components. It protects the right of a citizen of one State to enter and to leave another State, the right to be treated as a welcome visitor rather than an unfriendly alien when temporarily present in the second State, and, for those travelers who elect to become permanent residents, the right to be treated like other citizens of that State.[1374].

In *Ysursa v. Pocatello Educ. Ass'n* [1375] it was held that "a political subdivision, "created by the state for the better ordering of government, has no privileges or immunitiess under the federal constitution which it may invoke in opposition to the will of its creator."[1376]

1372 526 U.S. 489 (1999).

1373 *Id.* at 503.

1374 *Id.* at 500.

1375 1129 S. Ct. 1093 (2009)

1376 *Id.* at 1101.

Chapter III
The Equal Protection Clause

A. Geneal Statement

The second sentence of Section 1 of the Fourteenth Amendment to the U.S. Constitution provides, *in pari materia*, that "[n]o state shall . . . deny to any person within[1377] its jurisdiction the equal protection of the laws." Section 5 of the Fourteenth Amendment provides that "[t]he Congress shall have power to enforce by appropriate legislation, the provisions of this article,"[1378]

This wording begs an explanation of what constitutes "equal protection,." and what are "the laws"? This lexicon attempts to answer the first question by initially reviewing some of the early, but still authoritative, opinions of those U.S. Supreme Court Justices who commented upon that subject; and then reviewing some of the original, but still authoritative cases concerning varying fact patterns. The Nineteenth Century, in fact, furnished some of the most authoritative opinions and cases extant. This book will refer exclusively to them. A sequel, concerning the Twentieth and Twenty-First century, is in contemplation, and already in preparation. The second question, i.e. what is meant by "the laws," is best addressed by reading Justice Stephen J. Field's dissent in *Baltimore & O.R. Co. v. Baugh*[1379] in which he said:

> When the fourteenth amendment ordains that no state shall deny to any person within its jurisdiction 'the equal protection of the laws,' it means

---

[1377] The U.S. Supreme Court in United States v. Wong Kim Ark, 169 U.S. 649 (1898) opined that the phrase "subject to the jurisdiction thereof.," in the first sentence of § 1, referring to citizens of the United States is identical to the phrase "within its jurisdiction" in the second sentence of that section, which refers to "any persons," while dealing with due process and equal protection of the laws. Blake v. McClung , 172 U.S. 239, 261, 262 (1898) held that a private corporation not created by the laws of Tennessee, nor doing business therein under conditions that subject it to process issuing from the courts of the state, is not "within its jurisdiction."

[1378] "This article," of course refers to the Fourteenth Amendment.

[1379] 149 U.S. 368 (1893)

> equal protection not merely by the statutory enactments of the state, but equal protection by all the rules and regulations which, having the force of law, govern the intercourse of its citizens with each other and their relations to the public, and find expression in the usages and customs of its people and in the decisions of its tribunals. The guaranty of this great amendment, 'as to the equal protection of the laws,' would be shorn of half of its efficacy if it were limited in its application only to written laws of the several states, and afforded no protection against an unequal administration of their unwritten laws. It has never been denied, that I am aware of, that decisions of the regular judicial tribunals of a state, especially when concurring for a succession of years, are, at least, evidence of what the law of the state is on the points adjudged. The law, being thus shown, is as obligatory upon those points in another similar case, arising in the state, as if expressed in the most formal statutory enactments. If this is not so, I may ask, in anticipation of what I may say hereafter, what becomes of the judicial independence of the states?[1380]

B. General Judicial Statements

In *Hunt v. Rousmanier's Administration*[1381] the first case to have mentioned equal protection, Chief Justice John Marshall said that the rights of plaintiff: and defendant

> are the object of equal protection; but to make that protection *equal*, a certain position and condition is assigned to the defendant; he is so placed that he may not be overcome by surprise; the law seeks for actual, not nominal reciprocity; the relative condition of the parties enters into the account; evenhanded justice first corrects the balance, by making the proper allowances before she weighs the merits of the cause.[1382]

[1380] *Id.* at 398. In like effect *see* Justice Horace Gray's comments to Scott v. McNeal, 154 U.S. 34, 45 (1894).

[1381] 21 U.S. (8 Wheat.) 174 (1823).

[1382] *Id* at 196.

It was not until 45 years later before the Equal Protection Clause was considered again. In *Paul v. Virginia,*[1383] the afore-mentioned U.S. Supreme Court Justice Stephen J. Field explained the Equal Protection Clause, albeit dealing primarily with the concept of privileges and immunities.[1384] About "equal protection," Justice Field wrote:

> It was undoubtedly the object of the clause in question to place the citizens of each State upon the same footing with citizens of other States, so far as the advantages resulting from citizenship in those States are concerned. It relieves them from the disabilities of alienage in other States; it inhibits discriminating legislation against them by other States; it gives them the right of free ingress into other States, and egress from them; it insures to them in other States the same freedom possessed by the citizens of those States in the acquisition and enjoyment of property and in the pursuit of happiness; and it secures to them in other States the equal protection of their laws. It has been justly said that no provision in the Constitution has tended so strongly to constitute the citizens of the United States one people as this.[1385]

In *The Slaughter-House Cases*[1386] Justice Noah H. Swayne, in a dissenting Opinion, referred to the clause in the following words:

> [E]qual protection of the laws' is guaranteed to all. Life is the gift of God, and the right to preserve it is the most sacred of the rights of man. Liberty is freedom from all restraints but such as are justly imposed by law. Beyond that line lies the domain of usurpation and tyranny. Property is everything which has an exchangeable value, and the right of property includes the power to dispose of it according to the will of the owner. Labor is property, and as such merits protection. The right to make it available is next in importance to the rights of life and liberty. It lies to a large extent at the foundation of most other forms of property, and of all solid individual and national prosperity. 'Due process of law' is the application of the law as it exists in the fair and regular course of

---

[1383] 75 U.S. (8 Wall.) 168 (1868).

[1384] *See id.* at 177-185..

[1385] *Id* at 180.

[1386] 83 U.S. 36 (1872). *See supra* text accompanying notes 1197, 1290-1347.

administrative procedure. 'The equal protection of the laws' places all upon a footing of legal equality and gives the same protection to all for the preservation of life, liberty, and property, and the pursuit of happiness.[1387]

In *United States. v. Cruikshank* [1388] Chief Justice Morrison R. Waite wrote that

> The fourteenth amendment prohibits a State from denying to any person within its jurisdiction the equal protection of the laws; but this provision does not, . . . add any thing to the rights which one citizen has under the Constitution against another. The equality of the rights of citizens is a principle of republicanism. Every republican government is in duty bound to protect all its citizens in the enjoyment of this principle, if within its power. That duty was originally assumed by the States; and it still remains there. The only obligation resting upon the United States is to see that the States do not deny the right. This the amendment guarantees, but no more. The power of the national government is limited to the enforcement of this guaranty.[1389]

Three years later Chief Justice Waite, in *Munn v. People of State of Illinois*[1390] wrote that:

> After what has already been said, it is unnecessary to refer at length to the effect of the other provision of the Fourteenth Amendment which is relied upon, viz., that no State shall 'deny to any person within its jurisdiction the equal protection of the laws.' Certainly, it cannot be claimed that this prevents the State from regulating the fares of hackmen or the charges of draymen in Chicago, unless it does the same thing in every other place within its jurisdiction. But, as has been seen, the power to regulate the business of warehouses depends upon the same principle as the power to regulate hackmen and draymen, and what cannot be done in the one case in this particular cannot be done in the other.[1391]

[1387] *Id.* at 127.

[1388] 92 U.S. 542 (1875).

[1389] *Id.* at 554-555.

[1390] 94 U.S. 113 (1878).

[1391] *Id.* at 134, 135.

In *Commonweal of Virginia v. Rives*[1392] U.S. Supreme Court Justice William Strong wrote that

> The prohibitions of the Fourteenth Amendment have exclusive reference to State action. It is the State which is prohibited from denying to any person within its jurisdiction the equal protection of the laws, and, consequently, the statutes founded upon the amendment, and partially enumerating what civil rights the colored man shall enjoy equally with the white are intended for protection against State infringement of those rights Sect. 641 was also intended to protect them against State action, and against that alone.[1393]
>
> A State may exert her authority through different agencies, and those prohibitions extend to her action denying equal protection of the laws, whether it be action by one of these agencies or by another. Congress, by virtue of the fifth section of the Fourteenth Amendment, may enforce the prohibitions whenever they are disregarded by either the Legislative, the Executive, or the Judicial Department of the State. The mode of enforcement is left to its discretion. It may secure the right, that is, enforce its recognition, by removing the case from a State court, in which it is denied, into a Federal court, where it will be acknowledged.[1394]

In *Ex Parte Virginia*[1395] U.S. Supreme Court Justice William Strong said

> The constitutional provision . . . must mean that no agency of the State, or of the officers or agents by whom its powers are exerted, shall deny to any person within its jurisdiction the equal protection of the laws. Whoever, by virtue of public position under a State government, deprives another of property, life, or liberty, without due process of law, or denies or takes away the equal protection of the laws, violates the constitutional inhibition; and as he acts in the name and for the State, and is clothed with

---

1392 100 U.S. 313 (1879).

1393 *Id.* at 314.

1394 *Id. See also* Wood v. Brush, 140 U.S. 278 (1891) to the same effect.

1395 100 U.S. 339 (1879).

> the State's power, his act is that of the State. This must be so, or the constitutional prohibition has no meaning.[1396]

In *United States v. Harris*[1397] Supreme Court Justice William B.Woods made the following statement:

> The language of the amendment does not leave this subject in doubt. When the state has been guilty of no violation of its provisions; when it has not made or enforced any law . . . . .and no one of its departments has denied to any person within its jurisdiction the equal protection of the laws; when, on the contrary, the laws of the state, as enacted by its legislative, and construed by its judicial, and administered by its executive departments, recognize and protect the rights of all persons,- the amendment imposes no duty and confers no power upon congress.[1398]

U.S. Supreme Court Justice Joseph P. Bradley, in the *Civil Rights Cases*,[1399] with his five observations gave one of the most cogent descriptions of what the Equal Protection Clause means:

> It is state action of a particular character that is prohibited. Individual invasion of individual rights is not the subject-matter of the amendment. It has a deeper and broader scope. It nullifies and makes void all state legislation, and state action of every kind, which . . . denies to any of them the equal protection of the laws. It not only does this, but, in order that the national will, thus declared, may not be a mere *brutum fulmen*, the last section of the amendment invests congress with power to enforce it by appropriate legislation. To enforce what? To enforce the prohibition. To adopt appropriate legislation for correcting the effects of such prohibited state law and state acts, and thus to render them effectually null, void, and innocuous. This is the legislative power conferred upon congress, and this is the whole of it. It does not invest congress with power to legislate upon subjects which are within the domain of state legislation; but to provide modes of relief against state legislation, or state action, of the kind referred

---

[1396] *Id.* at 347.

[1397] 106 U.S. 629 (1883).

[1398] *Id.* at 639.

[1399] 109 U.S. 3 (1883).

to. It does not authorize congress to create a code of municipal law for the regulation of private rights; but to provide modes of redress against the operation of state laws, and the action of state officers, executive or judicial, when these are subversive of the fundamental rights specified in the amendment.[1400].

[T]he legislation which congress is authorized to adopt in this behalf is not general legislation upon the rights of the citizen, but corrective legislation; that is, such as may be necessary and proper for counteracting such laws as the states may adopt or enforce, and which by the amendment they are prohibited from making or enforcing, or such acts and proceedings as the states may commit or take, and which by the amendment they are prohibited from committing or taking. It is not necessary for us to state, if we could, what legislation would be proper for congress to adopt. It is sufficient for us to examine whether the law in question is of that character.[1401]

[The Fourteenth] amendment prohibits the states from denying to any person the equal protection of the laws, and declares that congress shall have power to enforce, by appropriate legislation, the provisions of the amendment. The law in question, without any reference to adverse state legislation on the subject, declares that all persons shall be entitled to equal accommodation and privileges of inns, public conveyances, and places of public amusement, and imposes a penalty upon any individual who shall deny to any citizen such equal accommodations and privileges. This is not corrective legislation; it is primary and direct; it takes immediate and absolute possession of the subject of the right of admission to inns, public conveyances, and places of amusement. It supersedes and displaces state legislation on the same subject, or only allows it permissive force. It ignores such legislation, and assumes that the matter is one that belongs to the domain of national regulation. Whether it would not have been a more effective protection of the rights of citizens to have clothed congress with plenary power over the whole subject, is not now the question. What we have to decide is, whether such plenary power has been conferred upon congress by the fourteenth amendment, and, in our judgment, it has not.[1402]

[1400] *Id.* at 11, 12.

[1401] *Id.* at 13, 14.

[1402] *Id.* at 18, 19.

> We must not forget that the province and scope of the thirteenth and fourteenth amendments are different: the former simply abolished slavery: the latter prohibited the states from . . . denying to any the equal protection of the laws. The amendments are different, and the powers of congress under them are different. What congress has power to do under one, it may not have power to do under the other. Under the thirteenth amendment, it has only to do with slavery and its incidents. Under the fourteenth amendment, it has power to counteract and render nugatory all state laws and proceedings which have the effect to deny to any of them the equal protection of the laws. Under the thirteenth amendment the legislation, so far as necessary or proper to eradicate all forms and incidents of slavery and involuntary servitude, may be direct and primary, operating upon the acts of individuals, whether sanctioned by state legislation or not; under the fourteenth, as we have already shown, it must necessarily be, and can only be, corrective in its character, addressed to counteract and afford relief against state regulations or proceedings.[1403]
>
> The only question under the present head, therefore, is, whether the refusal to any persons of the accommodations of an inn, or a public conveyance, or a place of public amusement, by an individual, and without any sanction or support from any state law or regulation, does inflict upon such persons any manner of servitude, or form of slavery, as those terms are understood in this country? Many wrongs may be obnoxious to the prohibitions of the fourteenth amendment which are not, in any just sense, incidents or elements of slavery. Such, for example, would be the taking of private property without due process of law; or allowing persons who have committed certain crimes (horse-stealing, for example) to be seized and hung by the *posse comitatus* without regular trial; or denying to any person, or class of persons, the right to pursue any peaceful *24 avocations allowed to others. What is called calss [sic] legislation would belong to this category, and would be obnoxious to the prhibitions [sic] of the fourteenth amendment, but would not to the prohibitions of the fourteenth when not involving the idea of any subjection of one man to another. The thirteenth amendment has respect, not to distinctions of race, or class, or color, but to slavery. The fourteenth amendment extends its protection to races and classes, and prohibits any state legislation which has the effect of

---

[1403] *Id.* at 23.

> denying to any race or class, or to any individual, the equal protection of the laws.[1404]

In *McPherson v. Blacker* [1405] Chief Justice Melville W. Fuller said that:

> The inhibition that no state shall deprive any person within its jurisdiction of the equal protection of the laws was designed to prevent any person or class of persons from being singled out as a special subject for discriminating and hostile legislation.[1406]

In *Hallinger v. Davis* [1407] U.S. Supreme Court Justice George Shiras, Jr. wrote that:

> The fourteenth amendment does not profess to secure to all persons in the United States the benefit of the same laws and the same remedies. Great diversities in these respects may exist in two states separated only by an imaginary line. On one side of this line there may be a right of trial by jury, and on the other side no such right. Each state prescribes its own modes of judicial proceedings. Where part of a state is thickly settled, and another part has but few inhabitants, it may be desirable to have different systems of judicature for the two portions,- trial by jury in one, for example, and not in the other. It would be an unfortunate restriction of the powers of the state government if it could not, in its discretion, provide for these various exigencies.[1408]

In *Yesler v. Board of Harbor Line Com'rs* [1409] Chief Justice Melville W. Fuller opined that:

> The [fourteenth] amendment undoubtedly forbids any arbitrary deprivation of life, liberty, or property, and secures equal protection to all under like

[1404] *Id.* at 23, 24.

[1405] 146 U.S. 1 (1892).

[1406] *Id.* at 39.

[1407] 146 U.S. 314 (1892)

[1408] *Id.* 321, 322.

[1409] 146 U.S. 646 (1892).

> circumstances in the enjoyment of their rights. Assuming our jurisdiction to revise the judgment of a state tribunal upholding a law authorizing the taking of private property without compensation to be unquestionable.[1410]

In *Duncan v. State*[1411] Chief Justice Melville W. Fuller also said that "[T]he equal protection of the laws are secured if the laws operate on all alike, and do not subject the individual to an arbitrary exercise of the powers of government.[1412]

In *Williams v. State of Mississippi*[1413] Justice McKenna, writing about equal protection also opined that:

> Though [a] law itself be fair on its face and impartial in appearance, yet, if it is applied and administered by public authority with an evil eye and an unequal hand, so as practically to make unjust and illegal discriminations between persons in similar circumstances, material to their rights, the denial of equal justice is still within the prohibition of the constitution.[1414]

In *Magoun v. Illinois Trust & Savings Bank*[1415] Justice Joseph McKenna said about the equality required by the equal protection clause that

> What satisfies this equality has not been, and probably never can be, precisely defined. Generally it has been said that it 'only requires the same means and methods to be applied impartially to all the constituents of a class, so that the law shall operate equally and uniformly upon all persons in similar circumstances.' Kentucky Railroad Tax Cases, 115 U. S. 321, 6 Sup. Ct. 57. It does not prohibit legislation which is limited either in the objects to which it is directed, or by the territory within which it is to operate. It merely requires that all persons subjected to such legislation

---

1410 *Id.* at 655, 656.

1411 152 U.S. 377 (1894).

1412 *Id.* at 382.

1413 170 U.S. 213 (1898).

1414 *Id.* at 225.

1415 170 U.S. 283 (1898).

> shall be treated alike under like circumstances and conditions, both in the privilege conferred and the liabilities imposed.[1416]

In *American Refrigerator Transit Co. v. Hall*[1417] Justice George Shiras, Jr. said that

> When the taxpayers of one state perceive that they are subjected to competition by the importation of articles made in another, or that they are contributing continually to the prosperity of foreign corporations, what more natural than that they should demand that some share of the public burdens should be put upon such corporations? The difficult task of the lawmaker is to meet that natural and proper demand without infringing upon the freedom of interstate commerce, or depriving those engaged therein of the equal protection of the laws.[1418]

Mr. Justice David J. Brewer opined in *Atchison, T. & S.F.R. Co. v. Matthews* [1419] that:

> [T]he equal protection guarantied by the constitution forbids the legislature to select a person, natural or artificial, and impose upon him or it burdens and liabilities which are not cast upon others similarly situated. It cannot pick out one individual, or one corporation, and enact that whenever he or it is sued the judgment shall be for double damages, or subject to an attorney's fee in favor of the plaintiff, when no other individual or corporation is subjected to the same rule. Neither can it make a classification of individuals or corporations which is purely arbitrary, and impose upon such class special burdens and liabilities. Even where the selection is not obviously unreasonable and arbitrary, if the discrimination is based upon matters which have no relation to the object sought to be accomplished, the same conclusion of unconstitutionality is affirmed.[1420]

1416 *Id.* at 293.

1417 174 U.S. 70 (1899).

1418 *Id.* at 75.

1419 174 U.S. 96 (1899). *See infra* text accompanying notes 1423, 1485, and 1486 for further reference to this case.

1420 *Id.* at 104, 105.

C. Specific Cases

1. Aliens

In *Chy Lung v. Freeman*,[1421] the Court considered a California law that, with a few exceptions, prohibited any alien who was, or would likely become, "a public charge," from entering the State through any of its ports. The Court held that the statute was pre-empted by federal law. Justice Samuel F. Miller, though not mentioning "equal protection" in his Opinion of the Court clearly wrote about that subject in discussing the relative powers of state and federal government by his following words:

> The passage of laws which concern the admission of citizens and subjects of foreign nations to our shores belongs to Congress, and not to the States. It has the power to regulate commerce with foreign nations: the responsibility for the character of those regulations, and for the manner of their execution, belongs solely to the national government. If it be otherwise, a single State can, at her pleasure, embroil us in disastrous quarrels with other nations.[1422]

In *Yick Wo v. Hopkins*,[1423] it was decided that the fourteenth amendment forbidding any state to deny to any person within its jurisdiction the equal protection of the laws, was violated by a municipal ordinance of San Francisco, which conferred upon the Board of Supervisors Arbitrary Power, without regard to competency of persons or to fitness of places, to grant or refuse licenses to carry on public laundries, and which was executed by the supervisors by refusing licenses to all Chinese residents, and granting them to other persons under like circumstances. The question there was of the power of a state over aliens continuing to reside within its jurisdiction, not of the power of the United States to put an end to their residence in this country.[1424]

[1421] 92 U.S. 275 (1875).

[1422] *Id.* at 280.

[1423] 118 U.S. 356 (1886). This case was confirmed by Wong Wink, v. United States, 163 U.S. 228, 238 (1896).

[1424] *Id.* at 374.

In *Fong Yue Ting v. United States*[1425] however, the U.S. Supreme Court held that Chinese laborers residing in the United States are entitled, like other aliens, so long as they are permitted by the government to remain in the country, to all the safeguards of the Constitution, and to the protection of the laws in regard to their rights of person and of property, and to their civil and criminal responsibility; but, if they have taken no steps to become citizens, and are incapable of becoming such under the naturalization laws of this country, they remain subject to the power of congress to order their expulsion or deportation whenever, in its judgment, such a measure is necessary or expedient for the public interest.[1426]

In *United States v. Wong Kim Ark*[1427] the Court held that Chinese persons, born out of the United States, remaining subjects of the emperor of China, and not having become citizens of the United States, are entitled to the protection of and owe allegiance to the United States, so long as they are permitted by the United States to reside in this country; and are 'subject to the jurisdiction thereof,' in the same sense as all other aliens residing in the United States. Justice Horace Gray expressed the holding of the Court in the following words:

> We are entirely ready to accept the provision proposed in this constitutional amendment, that the children born here of Mongolian parents shall be declared by the constitution of the United States to be entitled to civil rights and to equal protection before the law with others.[1428]

2. Banks

In *Merchants' & Manufacturers' Nat Bank of Pittsburg v. Com. of Pennsylvania* [1429] the U.S. Supreme Court ruled that a Pennsylvania statute which gave banks the right to elect to collect from shareholders and pay into the state treasury a tax of eight mills per dollar on the par value of the shares, in lieu of the

---

[1425] 149 U.S. 698 (1893).

[1426] *Id.* at 762.

[1427] 169 U.S. 649 (1898). *See supra* notes 1205 and 1380 in which this case is mentioned, and *infra* text accompanying note 1431 in which comment is continued.

[1428] *Id.* at 698-699.

[1429] 167 U.S. 461 (1897).

regular tax of four mills on each dollar of the actual value thereof, does not deny "the equal protection of the laws" guarantied by the fourteenth amendment to the federal constitution, though it may result in some banks paying less than others on the actual value of their property.[1430]

3. Corporations

Norfolk & W. R. Co. v. Com. of Pennsylvania[1431] held that the Equal Protection Clause does not prohibit a state from imposing such conditions upon foreign corporations as it may choose, as a condition of their admission within its limits.[1432]

In *Charlotte, C. & A.R. Co. v. Gibbes*[1433] it was held that a South Carolina statute which provided that the entire expenses of that State's railroad commission shall be borne by the several corporations owning or operating railroads within the state, is not in conflict with the Fourteenth Amendment, securing to every person the equal protection of the law.[1434]

People of State of New York v. Roberts[1435] held that a New York statute imposing a franchise tax upon corporations doing business in the state, is not unconstitutional as denying to corporations organized under the laws of other states equal protection because it exempts from the tax corporations wholly engaged in manufacturing or mining within the state, since it makes no discrimination between domestic corporations and those of other states in that regard.[1436]

[1430] *Id.* at 467.

[1431] 136 U.S. 114 (1890).

[1432] *Id.* at 120..

[1433] 142 U.S. 386 (1892).

[1434] *Id.* at 395.

[1435] 171 U.S. 658 (1898).

[1436] *Id.* at 661.

4. Criminal Law

Even though *In re Kemmler* [1437] which held that New York's requirement that the conviction of certain crimes would be by the application of electricity violated neither the Due Process nor the Privileges and Immunities Clauses[1438] Chief Justice Melville W. Fuller referred to the equal protection clause in the following words:

> Undoubtedly the [fourteenth] amendment forbids any arbitrary deprivation of life, liberty, or property, and secures equal protection to all under like circumstances in the enjoyment of their rights; and, in the administration of criminal justice, requires that no different or higher punishment shall be imposed upon one than is imposed upon all for like offenses. But it was not designed to interfere with the power of the state to protect the lives, liberties, and property of its citizens, and to promote their health, peace, morals, education, and good order.[1439]

Ex parte Converse[1440] held that the administration of criminal justice requires equal treatment of all persons accused of the commission of a crime. It does not, however, require that a state abandon its obligation to protect the lives, liberty or property of its citizens.[1441] Chief Justice Melville W. Fuller, more explicitly expressed the holding in the following words:

> [T]the fourteenth amendment undoubtedly forbids any arbitrary deprivation of life, liberty, or property, and, in the administration of criminal justice, requires that no different or higher punishment shall be imposed on one than is imposed on all for like offenses, but it was not designed to interfere with the power of the state to protect the lives, liberty, and property of its citizens, nor with the exercise of that power in

---

[1437] 136 U.S. 436 (1890).

[1438] *Id.* at 449.

[1439] *Id.* at 448, 449.

[1440] 137 U.S. 624 (1891).

[1441] *Id.* at 678.

> the adjudications of the courts of a state in administering the process provided by the law of the state.[1442]

Bergemann v. Backer[1443] held that one New Jersey statute dividing murder into two degrees, and defining them, and another providing that it shall be sufficient in every indictment for murder to charge that defendant did willfully, feloniously, and of his malice aforethought, kill and murder the deceased, a defendant convicted of murder in the first degree under an indictment containing statutory language, and which did not specify the degree of murder charged, was not denied the equal protection of the laws.[1444]

In *Lowe v. State of Kansas*[1445] it was held that where a Kansas statute provided that, when a prosecution was malicious, the prosecutor shall be adjudged to pay the costs, and committed to jail until they are paid, is applicable to all persons under like circumstances, and does not subject the individual to an arbitrary exercise of power, and hence it does not deny him the equal protection of the laws.[1446]

5. Eminent Domain

In *Reagan v. Farmers' Loan & Trust Co.*[1447] the Court held that while it is not the province of the courts to enter upon the merely administrative duty of framing a tariff of rates for carriage, it is within the scope of judicial power, and a part of judicial duty, to restrain anything which, in the form of a regulation of rates, operates to deny to the owners of the property invested in the business of transportation that equal protection which is the constitutional right of all owners of other property. Justice David J. Brewer uttered a dictum, proclaiming that the equal protection clause:

> forbids legislation, in whatever form it may be enacted, by which the property of one individual is, without compensation, wrested from him for

---

[1442] *Id.* at 632.

[1443] 157 U.S. 655 (1895).

[1444] *Id.* at 658.

[1445] 163 U.S. 81 (1896).

[1446] *Id.* at 84.

[1447] 154 U.S. 362 (1894).

the benefit of another, or of the public. This, as has been often observed, is a government of law, and not a government of men; and it must never be forgotten that under such a government, with its constitutional limitations and guaranties, the forms of law and the machinery of government, with all their reach and power, must, in their actual workings, stop on the hither side of the unnecessary and uncompensated taking or destruction of any private property, legally acquired and legally held.[1448].

6. Infrastructure

Covington & L. Turnpike Road Co. v. Sandford[1449] proclaimed that a Kentucky statute reducing the tolls charged by a turnpike company below those prescribed by general statute for other turnpike companies in the state does not necessarily deny to the turnpike company the equal protection of the laws.[1450]

In *Jones v. Brim*[1451] the Supreme Court held that a Utah statute making any one who drives a herd of horses, mules, asses, cattle, sheep, goats, or swine over a public highway constructed on a hillside shall be liable for damages by such animals in destroying the banks, or rolling rocks into the highway, does not deny to such person the equal protection of the laws.[1452]

In *Williams v. Eggleston*[1453] it was held that a state law which places five towns in a class by themselves, organizes them into a municipal corporation, casts upon them the burden of constructing and maintaining highways and bridges, and subjects them to a different control in respect thereto from other towns, is within the province of the state legislature, and not a denial of the equal protection of the laws.[1454]

1448 *Id.* at 399.

1449 164 U.S. 578 (1896).

1450 *Id.* at 595.

1451 165 U.S. 180 (1897).

1452 *Id.* at 181.

1453 170 US. 304 (1898).

1454 *Id.* at 308.

Wilson v. Eureka City [1455] established that a municipal ordinance prohibiting the moving of any building upon or across the streets without the written permission of the mayor or president of the city council, or, in their absence, of a councilor, is not a denial of the equal protection of the law.[1456]

7. Insurance

It was held in *Orient Ins. Co. v. Daggs* [1457] that a "valued policy"[1458] law of a state is not unconstitutional, as denying to persons within its jurisdiction the equal protection of its laws, if it applies only to the business of fire insurance.[1459]

8. Judicial Procedure

In *Louisville & N. R. Co. v. Woodson* [1460] it was held that a Tennessee statute which provided that "not more than two new trials shall be granted to the same party in any action at law, or upon the trial by jury of an issue of fact in equity," referred only to new trials granted because of the insufficiency of the evidence, and it does not apply to situations where there is no evidence to justify the finding, or where there has been error of law. Hence the statute did not violate the prohibition against equal protection of the laws[1461]

In *Fielden v. People of State of Illinois*[1462] the U.S. Supreme Court held that it is bound by the decisions of the supreme court of Illinois that no amendments of its record in derogation of its final judgment can be made after the expiration of the term; and, as this rule is applicable to all persons in the state, its enforcement

---

[1455] 173 U.S. 32 (1899).

[1456] *Id.* at 36.

[1457] 172 U.S. 557 (1899).

[1458] A "valued policy" is an insurance policy that pays a specified sum, not related in any way to the extent of the loss. Barron's Insurance Dictionary.

[1459] *Orient Ins. Co.,* 172 U.S. at 569.

[1460] 134 U.S. 614 (1890).

[1461] *Id.* at 624.

[1462] 143 U.S. 452 (1892).

against a particular person is not a denial by the state of the equal protection of its laws.[1463]

Gibson v. State of Mississippi[1464] held that when the constitution and laws of a state, as interpreted by its highest court, contain no provisions preventing the enforcement of rights secured by any law of the United States for the protection and enforcement of the equal rights of all citizens thereof, the possibility that, during the trial of a particular case, a state court may not respect and enforce the right to the equal protection of the laws, constitutes no ground for removing the prosecution to a federal court, in advance of the trial,[1465]

In *Smith v. State of Mississippi*[1466] it was decided that the omission or refusal of officers to include citizens of African descent in a list from which jurors might be drawn is not, as to a person of such descent subsequently brought to trial, a denial of the equal protection of the laws.[1467]

In *Louisville & N.R. Co. v. City of Louisville*[1468] the U.S. Supreme Court proclaimed that where in an "agreed case" in a state trial court presented no issue as to the validity of a state statute, but simply the question of its construction, and only the question of construction was considered by the highest court of the state on appeal, the Supreme Court cannot take jurisdiction upon the ground that the statute, as construed by that court, . . . denies the equal protection of the laws.[1469]

In *Backus v. Fort St. Union Depot Co*[1470] it was found that even if the courts of a state have uniformly construed a state statute as requiring condemnation proceedings to be had before a jury of inquest, instead of a common-law jury, presided over by a judge, a subsequent determination by those same courts in a

---

1463 *Id.* at 456.

1464 162 U.S. 565 (1896).

1465 *Id.* at 592.

1466 162 U.S. 592 (1896).

1467 *Id.* at 602.

1468 166 U.S. 709 (1897).

1469 *Id.* at 715, 716.

1470 169 U.S. 557 (1898).

given case that the proceedings must be had before a common-law jury is a mere change in mode of procedure, and not a denial of the equal protection of the laws, contrary to the fourteenth amendment.[1471]

It was held in *Wilson v. State*[1472] that the requirement, in the fourteenth amendment, of equal protection of the laws, does not secure a right of jury trial in *quo warranto* proceedings to suspend or remove a state officer in a state court.[1473]

It was said in *Chicago, B. & Q.R. Co. v. State ex rel. City of Omaha*[1474] that where several railroad companies were using tracks passing under a viaduct in a city, some of them being lessees of the others under agreements the terms of which are not disclosed, a court is unable to determine whether a Nebraska statute and municipal ordinance, pursuant thereto, imposing on the lessors the entire burden of keeping the viaduct in repair constitute denials of equal protection of the laws[1475].

In *Tinsley v. Anderson*[1476] it was found that the right to the equal protection of the laws is not denied by a state court where the same course of procedure applied to the person in question would have been applied to any other person in the same state under similar circumstances. Chief Justice Fuller explaining that:

> The right to the equal protection of the laws was certainly not denied, for it is apparent that the same law or course of procedure which was applied to Tinsley would have been applied to any other person in the state of Texas under similar circumstances and conditions; and there is nothing in the record on which to base an inference to the contrary.[1477]

The Supreme Court held in *Chappell Chemical & Fertilizer Co. v. Sulphur Mines Co. of Virginia*[1478] that the provision of the Maryland constitution which

---

1471 *Id.* at 564.

1472 169 U.S. 600 (1898).

1473 *Id.* at 600.

1474 170 U.S. 57 (1898).

1475 *Id.* at 66.

1476 171 U.S. 101 (1898).

1477 *Id.* at 106.

1478 172 U.S. 474 (1899).

authorizes the supreme bench of Baltimore city to provide, by its rules, for requiring causes in the courts of Baltimore city to be tried before the court without a jury unless the litigants, or some one of them, within a reasonable time to be prescribed, shall demand a jury trial. That state constitutional provision does not deny to litigants the equal protection of the laws, within the meaning of the Fourteenth Amendment even, though no such provision is made to respect to the courts of the other counties in the state[1479].

Central Loan & Trust Co. v. Campbell Com'n Co.[1480] established that a statute which requires plaintiff to give a bond as a prerequisite to the issuance of an attachment against a resident, but requires no bond where the attachment is against property of a nonresident, is not a denial of the equal protection of the law.[1481]

In *Atchison, T. & S.F.R. Co. v. Matthews*[1482] it was established that a Kansas statute which, required a reasonable attorney's fee for the plaintiff to be allowed and made a part of the judgment on a recovery against a railroad company for damages from fire caused by the operating of its trains, is not in violation of the fourteenth constitutional amendment as an arbitrary classification of suitors, which deprives those affected of the equal protection of the laws.[1483]

9. Mortgages

In *Savings & Loan Soc. v. Multnomah County*[1484] an Oregon statute which provided for the taxation of the mortgagee's interest in land as real estate regardless of the residence of the mortgagee, was found not deny him the equal protection of the laws.[1485] Justice Horace Gray explained the decision as follows:

[1479] *Id.* at 474.

[1480] 173 U.S. 84 (1899).

[1481] *Id.* at 99.

[1482] 174 U.S. 96 (1899).

[1483] *Id.* at. 104. *See supra* text accompanying note 1420 for further consideration of this case.

[1484] 169 U.S. 421 (1898).

[1485] *Id.* at 431, 432.

> [N]othing is taxed but the real estate mortgaged, the interest of the mortgagee therein being taxed to him and the rest to the mortgagor. There is no double taxation. Nor is any such discrimination made between mortgagors and mortgagees, or between resident and nonresident mortgagees, as to deny to the latter the equal protection of the laws[1486].

10. Peremptory Challenges

In *Neal v. Delaware*[1487] U.S. Supreme Court found that a Missouri statute providing that in capital cases, except in cities having a population of over 100,000 inhabitants, the state shall be allowed eight peremptory challenges to jurors, and in such cities shall be allowed fifteen, does not deprive one indicted for murder in a city of over 100,000 inhabitants of the equal protection of the laws enjoined by the fourteenth amendment to the United States Constitution. Justice John Marshall Harlan, I, wrote that:

> '[W]while a colored citizen, party to a trial involving his life, liberty, or property, cannot claim, as matter of right, that his race shall have a representation on the jury, and while a mixed jury, in a particular case, is not within the meaning of the Constitution, always or absolutely necessary to the equal protection of the laws, it *is* a right to which he is entitled, 'that in the selection of jurors to pass upon his life, liberty, or property, there shall be no exclusion of his race, and no discrimination against them, because of their color.' So that we need only inquire whether, upon the showing made by the accused, the court erred in overruling the motions to quash the indictment and the panels of jurors.[1488]

U.S. Supreme Court Justice Stephen J. Field in *Hayes v. Missouri*[1489]

> Allowing the state 15 peremptory challenges in capital cases, tried in cities containing a population of over 100,000 inhabitants, is simply providing against the difficulty of securing, in such cases, an impartial jury in cities

---

1486 *Id.* at 425.

1487 103 U.S. 370 (1880).

1488 *Id.* at 394. *See* Bush v. Kentucky, 107 U.S. 110, 110 passim (1883) for similar statements.

1489 120 U.S. 68 (1887).

> of that size, which does not exist in other portions of the state. So far from defeating, it may furnish the necessary means of giving, that equal protection of its laws to all persons, which that amendment declares shall not be denied to any one within its jurisdiction.[1490]

In *Brown v. State of New Jersey*[1491] it was decided that a New Jersey statute allowing an accused person only five peremptory challenges in a case where a struck jury has been ordered, while twenty peremptory challenges are allowed in a trial before an ordinary jury, does not constitute a denial of the equal protection of the laws, where the same number of challenges is permitted in all cases in which a struck jury is ordered.[1492]

11. Police Power

Chief Justice Roger B. Taney, in Holmes v. Jennison[1493] gave perhaps the most lucent description of the police powers of the states when he wrote that:

> [T]they may remove from among them any person guilty of, or charged with crimes; and may arrest and imprison them in order to effect this object. This is a part of the ordinary police powers of the states, which is necessary to their very existence, and which they have never surrendered to the general government. They may, if they think proper, in order to deter offenders in other countries from . . . coming among them, make crimes committed elsewhere punishable in their Courts, if the guilty party shall be found within their jurisdiction. In all of these cases the state acts with a view to its own safety; and is in no degree connected with the foreign government in which the crime was committed. The state does not co-operate with a foreign government not [sic] hold any intercourse with it, when she is merely executing her police regulations. . . . The state acts not with a view to protect itself, but to assist another nation which asks its aid.[1494]

1490 *Id.* at 72.

1491 175 U.S. 172 (1899).

1492 *Id.* at 177.

1493 39 U.S. 540 (1840).

1494 *Id.* at 568, 569.

In Barbier v. Connolly[1495] it was objected that a municipal ordinance of San Francisco, prohibiting washing and ironing in public laundries within certain designated limits of the city between the hours of 10 at night and 6 in the morning, was in conflict with the equal protection amendment, in that it discriminated between laborers engaged in the laundry business and those engaged in other kinds of business, and between laborers employed within the designated limits and those without them. But the court held that the provision was merely a police regulation; that it might be a necessary measure of protection in a city composed largely of wooden buildings, like San Francisco, that occupations in which fires are constantly required should cease during certain hours at night, and of the necessity of such a regulation that municipal body was the exclusive judge; that the same authority which directs the cessation of labor must necessarily prescribe the limits within which it shall be enforced, as it does the limits within which wooden buildings must not be constructed; and that restrictions of this kind, though necessarily special in character, do not furnish ground of complaint if they operate alike upon all persons or property under the same circumstances and conditions. 'Class legislation,' said the court, 'discriminating against some and favoring others, is prohibited; but legislation which, in carrying out a public purpose, is limited in its application, if within the sphere of its operation it affects alike all persons similarly situated, is not within the amendment.[1496] Justice Stephen J. Field wrote that:

> The fourteenth amendment, in declaring that no state 'shall . . . deny to any person within its jurisdiction the equal protection of the laws,' undoubtedly intended not only that there should be no arbitrary deprivation of life or liberty, or arbitrary spoliation of property, but that equal protection and security should be given to all under like circumstances in the enjoyment of their personal and civil rights; that all persons should be equally entitled to pursue their happiness, and acquire and enjoy property; that they should have like access to the courts of the country for the protection of their persons and property, the prevention and redress of wrongs, and the enforcement of contracts; that no impediment should be interposed to the pursuits of any one, except as applied to the same

[1495] 113 U.S. 27 (1884). *See supra* text of an Opinion which refers to this case in connection with note 973,and *infra* text accompanying notes 1499-1500, and 1504 for further reference to this case.

[1496] *Id.* at 31. *See also* Wilkerson v. Rohrer, 140 U.S. 545 (1891) to the same effect.

> pursuits by others under like circumstances; that no greater burdens should be laid upon one than are laid upon others in the same calling and condition; and that in the administration of criminal justice no different or higher punishment should be imposed upon one than such as is prescribed to all for like offenses.[1497]

In *Powell v. Com. of Pennsylvania* [1498] a state statute provided "that no person, firm, or corporate body shall manufacture out of any oleaginous substance, or any compound of the same, other than that produced from unadulterated milk, or of cream from the same, any article designed to take the place of butter or cheese produced from pure, unadulterated milk, or cream from the same, * * * nor shall sell, or offer for sale, or have in his, her, or their possession, with intent to sell, the same as an article of food." The statute further provided that all contracts made in violation of the statute were void and subjects the offender to a penalty recoverable in an action of debt, and also to a criminal prosecution. The U.S. Supreme Court held, that the act is a valid exercise of the police power, and does not deprive any one of the equal protection of the laws, as guaranteed by the fourteenth amendment of the federal constitution. In that case Justice John Marshall Harlan, I, wrote that:

> It is scarcely necessary to say that if [the statute under consideration] is a legitimate exercise of the police power of the state for the protection of the health of the people, and for the prevention of fraud, it is not inconsistent with [the Fourteenth] amendment; for it is the settled doctrine of this court that, as government is organized for the purpose, among others, of preserving the public health and the public morals, it cannot divest itself of the power to provide for those objects, and that the fourteenth amendment was not designed to interfere with the exercise of that power by the states.[1499]

In *Minneapolis & St. L. Ry. Co. v. Beckwith*[1500] the U.S. Supreme Court considered a state statute which provided that any railway company that fails to fence its road, where the right to fence exists, shall be liable for the value of stock

---

1497 *Id.*

1498 127 U.S. 678 (1888).

1499 *Id.* at 683.

1500 129 U.S. 26 (1889).

killed or injured by reason of the want of such fence, unless it was caused by the willful act of the owner; and that, if the company neglects to pay within 30 days after notice, the owner may recover double the value. The Court held that the statute is not a denial of the equal protection of the law within the meaning of the Fourteenth Amendment since that clause only requires that legislation shall treat alike all persons brought under subjection to it. Justice Stephen J. Field, writing the Opinion of the Court stated that:

> '[The equal protection\] clause does undoubtedly prohibit discriminating and partial legislation by any state in favor of particular persons as against others in like condition. Equality of protection implies, not merely equal accessibility to the courts for the prevention or redress of wrongs and the engorcement [sic]of rights, but equal exemption with others in like condition from charges and liabilities of every kind. But the clause does not limit, nor was it designed to limit, the subjects upon which the police power of the state may be exerted. The state can now, as before, prescribe regulations for the health, good order, and safety of society, and adopt such measures as will advance its interests and prosperity. And to accomplish this end special legislation must be resorted to in numerous cases, providing against accidents, disease, and danger in the varied forms in which they may come. The nature and extent of such legislation will necessarily depend upon the judgment of the legislature as to the security needed by society. When the calling, profession, or business of parties is unattended with danger to others, little legislation will be necessary respecting it. Thus, in the purchase and sale of most articles of general use, persons may be left to exercise their own good sense and judgment; but when the calling or profession or business is attended with danger, or requires a certain degree of scientific knowledge upon which others must rely, then legislation properly steps in to impose conditions upon its exercise. Thus, if one is engaged in the manufacture or sale of explosive or inflammable articles, or in the preparation or sale of medicinal drugs, legislation for the security of society may prescribe the terms on which he will be permitted to carry on the business, and the liabilities he will incur from neglect of them. The concluding clause of the first section of the fourteenth amendment simply requires that such legislation shall treat alike all persons brought under subjection to it. The equal protection of the law is afforded when this is accomplished. Such has been the ruling of this court in numerous instances where that clause has been invoked against legislation supposed to be in conflict with it. Thus in Barbier v. Connolly,

113 U. S. 27, 5 Sup. Ct. Rep. 357, it was objected that a municipal ordinance of San Francisco, prohibiting washing and ironing *30 in public laundries within certain designated limits of the city between the hours of 10 at night and 6 in the morning, was in conflict with that amendment, in that it discriminated between laborers engaged in the laundry business and those engaged in other kinds of business, and between laborers employed within the designated limits and those without them. But the court held that the provision was merely a police regulation; that it might be a necessary measure of protection in a city composed largely of wooden buildings, like San Francisco, that occupations in which fires are constantly required should cease during certain hours at night, and of the necessity of such a regulation that municipal body was the exclusive judge; that the same authority which directs the cessation of labor must necessarily prescribe the limits within which it shall be enforced, as it does the limits within which wooden buildings must not be constructed; and that restrictions of this kind, though necessarily special in character, do not furnish ground of complaint if they operate alike upon all persons or property under the same circumstances and conditions. 'Class legislation,' said the court, 'discriminating against some and favoring others, is prohibited; but legislation which, in carrying out a public purpose, is limited in its application, if within the sphere of its operation it affects alike all persons similarly situated, is not within the amendment.'[1501]

In *Crowley v. Christensen*[1502] the ordinance of the city and county of San Francisco prohibiting the issuance of a retail liquor dealer's license to any person who has not first obtained the written consent of a majority of the police commissioners, and providing that, in case of refusal in the first instance, such consent shall be given upon the written recommendation of not less than 12 citizens owning real estate in the block or square in which the business is to be carried on, is a valid exercise of the police power of the state and municipality, and not in contravention of the Fourteenth Amendment to the Constitution of the United States, providing that no citizen shall be deprived of the equal protection of the laws.[1503]

[1501] *Id* at 28-30.

[1502] 137 U.S. 86 (1890).

[1503] *Id.* at 94, 95.

In *Minneapolis & St. L. Ry. Co. v. Emmons* [1504] it was determined that a state statute, which, as construed by the courts of the state, gives damages to a landowner for the expense and inconveniences of watching cattle to keep them from going upon a railroad track running through his land, which the company has failed to fence is within the police power of the state, and is not subject to the inhibition of the Fourteenth Amendment against depriving any person of the equal protection of the laws. This ruling was firm, even though, by the general law of the state, penalties and damages are given only for direct injuries sought to be prevented, and do not extend to consequential and possible resulting injuries.[1505]

In *New York & N. E. R. Co. v. Town of Bristol*[1506] it was held that an adjudication of the highest court of a state that a law enacted in the exercise of the police power of the state is not within the constitutional inhibitions . . . of the equal protection of the laws, and will not be reversed by the Supreme Court of the United States upon general ideas of the requirements of natural justice, apart from the provisions of the constitution involved.[1507]

12. Railroads

In *Chicago, M. & St. P. Ry. Co. v. State of Minn. ex rel. R.R. & Warehouse Com'n* [1508] it was held that a Minnesota statute which provided that any railroad company may charge for transportation "such reasonable rate as may be from time to time fixed by said corporation, or prescribed by law," and another statute of that state which provided that no railroad company shall charge an unreasonable price for transportation or other service, do not constitute such a contract with a corporation created thereunder do not deprive the railroad of the equal protection of the laws as the legislature has its power to regulate charges made by the railroad.[1509].

[1504] 151 U.S. 354 (1893).

[1505] *Id.* at 572.

[1506] 151 U.S. 556 (1894).

[1507] *Id.* at 571.

[1508] 134 U.S. 418 (1890).

[1509] *Id.* at 458.

In *Marchant v. Pennsylvania R. Co.*[1510] it was held that the action of a State of Pennsylvania court in allowing compensation to a property owner who is shut off from free access to a street by the building of a railroad along the street, and denying damages to one whose property is depreciated by the operation of a railroad running along the opposite side of the street on the railroad's own property, does not amount to a denial of the equal protection of the laws.[1511].

Pittsburgh, C., C. & St. L. Ry. Co. v. Backus [1512] held that an Indiana statute providing for an assessment of railroad property for taxation by a state board, the fact that but one statutory hearing before the board is given to railroad companies, while the ordinary taxpayer, whose property is assessed by county officials, after hearing before them, has a right of appeal and a hearing before the state board, does not deny the railroad companies the equal protection of the laws.[1513]

In *Plessy v. Ferguson*[1514] it was ruled that a Louisiana statute requiring that all railway companies carrying passengers shall provide equal, but separate, accommodations for the white or "colored" races, by providing two or more passenger coaches for each train, or by dividing passenger coaches, and prohibiting persons from occupying seats in any coaches other than the ones assigned to them on account of the race to which they belong, does not violate the Fourteenth Amendment's equal protection clause.[1515] This ruling was not overruled until 1954 when the U.S. Supreme Court wrote it out of the law. in *Brown v. Board of Education.*[1516]

St. Louis & S.F.R. Co. v. Mathews [1517] held that a Missouri statute making each company owning or operating a railroad within the state liable for property destroyed by fire from its locomotives does not deny to such companies the equal protection of the laws, Justice Horace Gray saying:

1510 153 U.S. 280 (1894).

1511 *Id.* at 286.

1512 154 U.S. 421 (1894).

1513 *Id.* at 436.

1514 163 U.S. 537 (1896).

1515 *Id.* at 551.

1516 347 U.S. 481, 494 (1954).

1517 165 U.S. 1 (1897).

> "[t]he statute is a constitutional and valid exercise of the legislative power of the state, and applies to all railroad corporations alike. Consequently, it neither violates any contract between the state and the railroad company, nor deprives the company of its property without due process of law, nor yet denies to it the equal protection of the laws."[1518]

In *Gulf, C. & S.F. Ry. Co. v. Ellis* [1519] the Supreme Court held that a Texas statute providing that railroad companies failing to pay claims less than $50 for labor, damages, overcharges on freight, or for stock killed, within 30 days after presentation thereof, shall be liable for an attorney's fee not exceeding $10, is void as depriving such companies of the equal protection of the law. In support of the ruling Justice David J. Brewer, in the Opinion of the Court, said the following:

> The act singles out a certain class of debtors, and punishes them when, for like delinquencies, it punishes no others. They are not treated as other debtors, or equally with other debtors. They cannot appeal to the courts, as other litigants, under like conditions, and with like protection. If litigation terminates adversely to them, they are mulcted in the attorney's fees of the successful plaintiff; if it terminates in their favor, they recover no attorney's fees. It is no sufficient answer to say that they are punished only when adjudged to be in the wrong. They do not enter the courts upon equal terms. They must pay attorney's fees if wrong. They do not recover any if right; while their adversaries recover if right, and pay nothing if wrong. In the suits, therefore, to which they are parties, they are discriminated against, and are not treated as others. They do not stand equal before the law. They do not receive its equal protection. All this is obvious from a mere inspection of the statute.[1520]

In *New York, N.H. & H.R. Co. v. People of the State of New York* [1521] it was decided that a New York statute forbidding the heating of passenger cars by stoves, on railroads of over 50 miles in length. Laws N.Y.1887, c. 616, is not such

---

[1518] *Id.* at 27.

[1519] 165 U.S. 150 (1897).

[1520] *Id.* at 153.

[1521] 165 U.S. 628 (1897).

a discrimination against roads of greater length as to amount to a denial of the equal protection of the laws.[1522] Justice John Marshall Harlan, I, explained why:

> [A] road only 50 miles in length would seldom have a sleeping car attached to its trains; and passengers traveling on roads of that kind do not have the apprehension ordinarily felt by passengers on trains regularly carrying sleeping cars, or having many passenger coaches, on account of the burning of cars in case of their derailment or in case of collision. In any event, there is no such discrimination against companies having more than 50 miles of road as to justify the contention that there has been a denial to the companies named in the act of the equal protection of the laws. The statute is uniform in its operation upon all railroad companies doing business in the state of the class to which it is made applicable.[1523]

The Supreme Court in *Smyth v. Ames*[1524] found that a railroad corporation is a person, within the meaning of the fourteenth amendment, declaring that no state shall deny to any person within its jurisdiction the equal protection of the laws. Consequently a Nebraska law attempting to regulate railroads and fix maximum freight rates, is void in that the fixing of particular rates prescribed, denied the companies the equal protection of the laws.[1525]

13. Real property

In *Eldridge v. Trezevant*[1526] it was held that a citizen of a state other than Louisiana, whose land is subject to the law of Louisiana allowing the public to impose servitude on such land, without compensation, for the purpose of making and repairing levees, cannot complain that he was denied the equal protection of the laws, if the Louisiana law was impartially administered.[1527]

[1522] *Id.* at 634.

[1523] *Id.* at 634.

[1524] 169 U.S. 466 (1898).

[1525] *Id.* at 549.

[1526] 160 U.S. 452 (1896).

[1527] *Id.* at 468.

14. Safety Regulations

In *Holden v. Hardy*[1528] the Supreme Court held that a Utah statute forbidding the employment of workingmen for more than eight hours a day in mines, and in the smelting, reduction, or refining of ores or metals, is not a denial of . . . the equal protection of the laws.[1529]

15. Schools

In *Cumming v. Board of Ed. of Richmond County*[1530] it was held that a decision by a state court, denying an injunction against the maintenance by a board of education of a high school for "white" children, while failing to maintain one for "colored" children also, for the reason that the funds were not sufficient to maintain it in addition to needed primary schools for "colored" children, does not constitute a denial to "colored" persons of the equal protection of the law . . . of citizens of the United States. Justice John Marshall Harlan, I, wrote, almost apologetically, for the Court:

> It is difficult, ... for us to determine whether [the fourteenth] amendment had been violated. If any authority had been cited, we could from that have determined which paragraph or clause counsel relied upon, but as he has left us in the dark we can only say that in our opinion none of the clauses of any of the paragraphs of the amendment, under the facts disclosed by the record, is violated by the board. There is no complaint in the petition that there is any discrimination made in regard to the free common schools of the county. So far as the record discloses, both races have the same facilities and privileges of attending them. The only complaint is that these plaintiffs, being taxpayers, are debarred the privilege of sending their children to a high school which is not a free school, but one where tuition is charged, and that a portion of the school fund, raised by taxation, is appropriated to sustain white high schools to which negroes are not admitted. We think we have shown that it was in the discretion of the board to establish high schools. It being in their discretion, they could, without a violation of the law or of any constitution, devote a portion of

---

1528 169 U.S. 366 (1798).

1529 *Id.* at 396.

1530 175 U.S. 528 (1899).

> the taxes collected for school purposes to the support of this high school for white girls and to assist a county denominational high school for boys. In our opinion, it is impracticable to distribute taxes equally. The appropriation of a portion of the taxes for a white girls' high school is not more discrimination against these colored plaintiffs than it is against many white people in the county. A taxpayer who has boys and no girls of a school age has as much right to complain of the unequal distribution of the taxes to a girls' high school as have these plaintiffs. The action of the board appears to us to be more a discrimination as to sex than it does as to race. While the board appropriates some money to assist a denominational school for white boys and girls, it has never established a high school for white boys, and, if the contention of these plaintiffs is correct, white parents who have boys old enough to attend a high school have as much right to complain as these plaintiffs, if they have not more. Without, therefore, going into an analysis of the different clauses of the Fourteenth Amendment of the Constitution of the United States, we content ourselves by saying that, in our opinion, the action of the board did not violate any of the provisions of that amendment. It does not . . . deny to any person within the state the equal protection of its laws.[1531]

16. Taxation

In *Bell's Gap R. Co. v. Com. of Pennsylvania*[1532] the U.S. Supreme Court held that the laws of Pennsylvania, taxing bonds and other securities issued by corporations on their nominal, instead of their actual, value are not an unjust discrimination, and do not violate the Fourteenth Amendment, forbidding a state to withhold from any person the equal protection of its laws. Justice Joseph P.Bradley wrote that

> The provision in the fourteenth amendment, that no state shall deny to any person within its jurisdiction the equal protection of the laws, was not intended to prevent a state from adjusting its system of taxation in all proper and reasonable ways. It may, if it chooses, exempt certain classes of property from any taxation at all, such as churches, libraries, and the property of charitable institutions. It may impose different specific taxes

[1531] *Id.* at 542, 543.

[1532] 134 U.S. 232 (1890).

> upon different trades and professions, and may vary the rates of excise upon various products; it may tax real estate and personal property in a different manner; it may tax visible property only, and not tax securities for payment of money; it may allow deductions for indebtedness, or not allow them. All such regulations, and those of like character, so long as they proceed within reasonable limits and general usage, are within the discretion of the state legislature, or the people of the state in framing their constitution. But clear and hostile discriminations against particular persons and classes, especially such as are of an unusual character, unknown to the practice of our governments, might be obnoxious to the constitutional prohibition. It would, however, be impracticable and unwise to attempt to lay down any general rule or definition on the subject that would include all cases. They must be decided as they arise. We think that we are safe in saying that the fourteenth amendment was not intended to compel the states to adopt an iron rule of equal taxation. If that were its proper construction, it would not only supersede all those constitutional provisions and laws of some of the states, whose object is to secure equality of taxation, and which are usually accompanied with qualifications deemed material, but it would render nugatory those discriminations which the best interests of society require; which are necessary for the encouragement of needed and useful industries, and the discouragement of intemperance and vice, and which every state, in one form or another, deems it expedient to-adopt.[1533]

In *Home Ins. Co. v. State of New York* [1534] it was held that a New York statute which provided that every corporation, with certain exceptions, doing business in the state, shall be subject to a tax upon its "corporate franchise or business," to the amount of one-quarter of a mill upon its capital stock for each 1 per cent. of its dividends, when they amount to 6 per cent.on its capital, a less rate to be paid where the dividends are less than 6 per cent was not unconstitutional as depriving any person, natural, or artificial, of the equal protection of the laws; for, under its provisions, all corporations of the same kind are subject to the same tax.[1535]

[1533] *Id.* at 237. *See* First Nat. Bank v. Chahalls County, 166 U.S. 440 (1897) to the same effect.

[1534] 134 U.S. 594 (1890).

[1535] *Id.* at 606.

In *Giozza v. Tiernan*[1536] a Texas statute requiring an applicant for a liquor license to execute in advance a bond payable to the state, conditioned that he will not sell liquor to any person after having been notified by an officer or by certain relatives of such person not to do so, any of whom are authorized to sue on the bond in case of a breach, and further imposing a state and county occupation tax, and requiring payment of all taxes a year in advance, is not in conflict with the fourteenth amendment of the constitution of the United States, providing that no state shall deny any person the equal protection of the law.[1537]

In *Columbus Southern Ry. Co. v. Wright* [1538] a Georgia statute distributing for purposes of taxation, the rolling stock and personal property of railroad companies among the several counties traversed by the road, and subjecting it to the varying rates of taxation prevailing therein, instead of taxing it in the county of its principle office, as is done in the case of individuals and other corporations, is not a discrimination against the railroad, in violation of the Fourteenth Amendment to the constitution of the United States. Justice Howell F. Jackson stated the Court's rationale for its decision in the following words:

> [[T]he fact that the rate of taxation varied in the different counties, according to their respective wants and necessities, . . .involved no discrimination against the railroad company. The state having the undoubted authority to fix the situs of such property, and having lawfully distributed it proportionately between the several counties traversed by the road, it thereby became subject to the same rate of taxation as other property in the respective counties. This involved no inequality, and violated no provision of either the state or federal constitution. It certainly did not involve a failure to extend to the plaintiff in error the equal protection of the laws.[1539]

In *Sanford v. Poe (U.S. Reports Title: Adams Express Company v. Ohio State Auditor)* [1540] the U.S. Supreme Court held that an Ohio statute providing that the

---

[1536] 148 U.S.657 (1893).

[1537] *Id.* at 660.

[1538] 151 U.S. 470 (1894).

[1539] *Id.* at 482, 493.

[1540] 165 U.S. 184 (1897).

taxable value of the property of telegraph, telephone, and express companies shall be determined with reference to the value of the entire capital stock, does not deny to such companies the equal protection of the laws[1541] Chief Justice Fuller explained the holding in the following words:

> [T]he equal protection of the laws . . . in the fourteenth amendment 'was not intended to prevent a state from adjusting its system of taxation in all proper and reasonable ways,' nor was that amendment 'intended to compel a state to adopt an iron rule of equal taxation.[1542]

In *Western Union Telegraph Co. v. State of Indiana*[1543] the Supreme Court held that an Indiana stature imposing on express, telegraph, telephone, and sleeping-car companies a penalty of 5 per cent. for nonpayment of taxes, does not deny such companies the equal protection of the laws. In explanation of the ruling Chief Justice Fuller wrote the following:

> It has been repeatedly laid down, . . . 'that a system which imposes the same tax upon every species of property, irrespective of its nature or condition or class, will be destructive of the principle of uniformity and equality in taxation, and of a just adaptation of property to its burdens'; and it is equally true as to the particular means taken to enforce the collection of taxes,- one rule may be adopted in respect of the admitted use of one kind of property, and another rule in respect of the admitted use of another, in order that all may be compelled to contribute their proper share to the burdens of government.[1544]

In King v. Mullins[1545] the West Virginia Constitution which exempted tracts of land of less than 1,000 acres from certain forfeitures under the tax laws to which larger tracts are made liable, is not a denial to the owners of larger tracts of the equal protection of the laws guarantied by the federal Constitution. Justice John Marshall Harlon, II gave the following reasons for the Court's position:

1541 *Id.* at 263.

1542 *Id.* at 228.

1543 165 U.S. 304 (1897).

1544 *Id.* at 309.

1545 171 U.S. 404 (1898).

> The evil intended to be remedied by the constitution and laws of West Virginia was the persistent failure of those who owned or claimed to own large tracts of lands, patented in the last century, or early in the present century, to put them on the land books, so that the extent and boundaries of such tracts could be easily ascertained by the officers charged with the duty of assessing and collecting taxes. Where the tract was a small one, the probability was that it was actually occupied by some one, and its extent or boundary could be readily ascertained for purposes of assessment and taxation. We can well understand why one policy could be properly adopted as to large tracts, which the necessities of the public revenue did not require to be prescribed . . . as to small tracts. The judiciary should be very reluctant to interfere with the taxing systems of a state, and should never do so unless that which the state attempts to do is in palpable violation of the constitutional rights of the owners of property. Under this view of our duty, we are unwilling to hold that the provision referred to is repugnant to the clause of the fourteenth amendment forbidding a denial of the equal protection of the laws.[1546]

17. Warehouses

In *Brass v. North Dakota ex rel. Stoeser*[1547] it was held that a North Dakota statute regulating public warehouses, prescribing maximum rates of charges for storing and handling grain therein, and requiring the grain stored to be insured at the expense of the warehouseman, is not a denial of the equal protection of the laws, even though it was applied to an elevator owner whose principal business is storing his own grain, the storage of grain for others being a mere incident in his business.[1548].

1546 *Id.* at 435, 536.

1547 153 U.S. 391 (1894).

1548 *Id.* at 404, 405.

Concluding Remarks

This book was written because it was thought that the three provisions of the U.S. Constitution analyzed herein, e.g. the giving of full faith and credit, the entitlement to privileges and immunities, and the prohibition of the denial of equal protection of the laws, were interesting. Indeed they are interesting; but they are far more than that. They are vital to the preservation of that form of federalism we hold so dear, and they are becoming increasingly necessary to this nation's survival, it would seem, with each succeeding day.

TABLE OF CASES

References Are To Footnotes

INDEX

References Are To Pages

www.ingramcontent.com/pod-product-compliance
Lightning Source LLC
LaVergne TN
LVHW052223200926
848481LV00001B/192

* 9 7 8 1 6 0 0 4 2 1 5 1 8 *